I0868397

AI and New Forms of Exclusion

Tania Elena González Alvarado
University of Guadalajara, Mexico

Jesús F. Lampón
University of Vigo, Spain

IGI Global
Scientific Publishing
Publishing Tomorrow's Research Today

Vice President of Editorial	Melissa Wagner
Director of Acquisitions	Mikaela Felty
Director of Book Development	Jocelynn Hessler
Production Manager	Mike Brehm
Cover Design	Jose Rosado

Published in the United States of America by
IGI Global Scientific Publishing
701 East Chocolate Avenue
Hershey, PA, 17033, USA
Tel: 717-533-8845
Fax: 717-533-7115
Website: https://www.igi-global.com E-mail: cust@igi-global.com

Copyright © 2026 by IGI Global Scientific Publishing. All rights reserved. No part of this publication may be reproduced, stored or distributed in any form or by any means, electronic or mechanical, including photocopying, without written permission from the publisher.

Product or company names used in this set are for identification purposes only. Inclusion of the names of the products or companies does not indicate a claim of ownership by IGI Global Scientific Publishing of the trademark or registered trademark.

Library of Congress Cataloging-in-Publication Data

Names: González Alvarado, Tania, 1973- editor | Lampón, Jesús F., 1971- editor
Title: AI and new forms of exclusion / [edited by] Tania González Alvarado, Jesús F. Lampón.
Description: Hershey, PA : IGI Global Scientific Publishing, [2026] | Includes bibliographical references and index. | Summary: "This book aims to analyze the contradictions of inclusion in the face of a more sensitive society accustomed to virtual life with artificial intelligence"-- Provided by publisher.
Identifiers: LCCN 2025022511 (print) | LCCN 2025022512 (ebook) | ISBN 9798337326856 hardcover | ISBN 9798337326863 paperback | ISBN 9798337326870 ebook
Subjects: LCSH: Technological innovations--Management | Technological innovations--Social aspects | Artificial intelligence--Social aspects
Classification: LCC HD45 .A4779 2025 (print) | LCC HD45 (ebook) | DDC 658.5/14--dc23/eng/20250912
LC record available at https://lccn.loc.gov/2025022511
LC ebook record available at https://lccn.loc.gov/2025022512

British Cataloguing in Publication Data
A Cataloguing in Publication record for this book is available from the British Library.

All work contributed to this book is new, previously-unpublished material.
The views expressed in this book are those of the authors, but not necessarily of the publisher.
This book contains information sourced from authentic and highly regarded references, with reasonable efforts made to ensure the reliability of the data and information presented. The authors, editors, and publisher believe the information in this book to be accurate and true as of the date of publication. Every effort has been made to trace and credit the copyright holders of all materials included. However, the authors, editors, and publisher cannot assume responsibility for the validity of all materials or the consequences of their use. Should any copyright material be found unacknowledged, please inform the publisher so that corrections may be made in future reprints.

Table of Contents

Detailed Table of Contents

This chapter explores workplace inclusion and exclusion, their impact on value creation, and their role within sustainability frameworks. It examines leadership's role in fostering inclusivity, the relationship between inclusion, exclusion, and stakeholder value, and the processes that drive long-term success. The discussion integrates ESG and SDG principles, highlighting challenges in defining inclusion and exclusion within organizations. The chapter argues for a transformative leadership approach that rethinks strategy, structure, and workforce dynamics. It calls for a two-dimensional perspective on inclusion/exclusion and urges further research into balancing these dynamics for sustainable value creation.

As artificial intelligence becomes woven into the fabric of decision-making, it quietly inherits the very inequalities it was meant to neutralize. Algorithmic discrimination—rooted in biased data, opaque models, and uncritical deployment—represents a new, insidious form of inequality. This chapter examines how AI systems reproduce and sometimes intensify historical injustices, often in ways that are hidden behind the technical sheen of objectivity. By exploring the sociotechnical roots of bias, the chapter highlights the moral imperative to rethink how algorithms are trained, evaluated, and governed. Rather than treating AI as a neutral tool, it calls for a paradigm shift—one that centers ethics, equity, and the lived experiences of marginalized communities. Only by acknowledging the silent exclusions encoded in code can we hope to build AI systems that reflect, rather than distort, our collective ideals of justice.

As artificial intelligence becomes deeply embedded in higher education—from admissions algorithms to adaptive learning systems—questions of equity take center stage. While AI promises personalization and efficiency, it also risks entrenching structural inequalities, often in ways that go unnoticed. For learners already on the margins—those from low-income backgrounds, with disabilities, or limited digital access—AI systems can inadvertently become gatekeepers rather than enablers. This chapter interrogates how algorithmic design choices, data gaps, and institutional priorities can exclude vulnerable students under the guise of innovation. It advocates for an ethical and inclusive approach to educational AI—one grounded in transparency, human oversight, and genuine stakeholder inclusion. In doing so, it reframes technological advancement not as an inevitable march forward, but as a set of choices with profound implications for who gets to learn, succeed, and belong in the digital university.

This study examines the interplay between knowledge management, educational quality, and institutional competitiveness in higher education. Using structural equation modeling (SEM), we analyzed survey data from 210 professors at the University of Guadalajara to assess how knowledge creation, dissemination, and application influence academic excellence and competitive positioning. The model confirms knowledge management as a critical driver of both quality enhancement ($p = 0.852$) and institutional competitiveness ($p = 0.962$), highlighting gaps in measuring intangible factors. The findings advocate for integrated knowledge strategies aligned with academic missions and suggest exploring emerging technologies, such as artificial intelligence (AI), to optimize these processes. This research provides actionable insights for universities seeking to leverage knowledge assets for sustainable innovation in increasingly interconnected academic landscapes.

Food industry and globalization has changed how we consume food, being food security a central issue on the international agenda. Food safety and trade regulations create barriers for specific groups, although are supposed to reduce social exclusion and improve global food chain´s transparency and sustainability among others. However, international collaborations and global standards addressed these problems collaboratively, displaying the power of collective intelligence. This chapter addresses economic, social, and governance dynamics linked to international food trade and quality and safety standards and how these elements affect consumers, producers, and governments. These dynamics involve aspects of social exclusion and corrective strategies through collective Intelligence.

As machine learning systems become increasingly embedded in our daily lives, the biases they inherit and perpetuate carry real-world consequences—often exacerbating the very inequities they claim to neutralize. This chapter examines the multifaceted nature of bias in machine learning, not as a technical glitch, but as a reflection of societal structures encoded into data, design, and deployment processes. It explores how exclusion happens invisibly—through underrepresentation, flawed assumptions, and biased benchmarks—and challenges dominant notions of "objectivity" in AI. By reframing fairness through the lens of inclusivity and social justice, the chapter outlines tangible steps toward building equitable systems. It calls for a reimagining of machine learning not simply as a tool for efficiency, but as a moral and social force shaped by choices—human ones. The path to truly inclusive AI lies in questioning who gets to decide what intelligence is, and for whom it works.

The ongoing globalization of markets has sparked a tremendous interest in emerging economies, particularly in the 'bottom of the pyramid' (BoP), prompting national corporations (MNCs) to address the unique marketing considerations for serving people experiencing poverty. Effective marketing for people experiencing poverty requires bridging the gaps in the conception of market offerings, information, physical access, price affordability, and distribution and service channels. These gaps are more pronounced in India, with its vast middle and lower-class population, and differing economic, cultural, and regulatory contexts, albeit with a rich pool of problems and opportunities. Using global value chain (GVC) analysis, marketing theory is expanded by increasing understanding of how gaps can be bridged and how these efforts facilitate development in emerging economies

This chapter examines how dynamic capabilities can be used to address technological exclusion in SDVs, where algorithm-driven features and data-centric business models increasingly reshape human-car relations. Drawing on the theoretical framework established by Teece and Eisenhardt, the chapter explores how sensing, seizing, and reconfiguring capabilities can be strategically utilized to mitigate algorithmic bias, enhance data transparency, and foster inclusive innovation. It analyzes how firms can shift from reactive adaptation to proactive governance by integrating ethical foresight and inclusive design into their dynamic capabilities framework. The chapter also discusses global regulatory discrepancies and cross-industry collaborations as key elements in establishing equitable algorithmic governance in the SDV era. Ultimately, the chapter argues that firms strategically aligning dynamic capabilities with ethical governance can transform algorithmic control into a mechanism for inclusive mobility, positioning themselves as leaders in a rapidly evolving automotive landscape.

A new industrial revolution is transforming nearly all sectors. One of the most strategic is mobility, where AI plays a key role by enabling connected and autonomous vehicles. AI is now widely adopted—75% of employees already use it—but firms may misinterpret its outputs or overlook opportunities due to its limitations. This chapter explores bias in generative AI applied to mobility, focusing on economic-

Preface

In an era marked by unprecedented technological advancement, the promise of inclusion is more visible than ever, and yet, so are the forces of exclusion. The growing integration of artificial intelligence into the fabric of our institutions, economies, and everyday lives has created new opportunities for participation and innovation. At the same time, it has surfaced complex contradictions that challenge long-standing efforts to build equitable societies. As we continue to develop mechanisms that promote inclusion through citizen science, social innovation, and public awareness, AI systems have, in some cases, begun to reproduce and even intensify the very inequalities we have sought to eliminate.

AI and New Forms of Exclusion is born from this tension. This edited volume critically examines how AI can both enable and obstruct inclusion across social, economic, and environmental dimensions. It invites readers to reflect on the responsibilities of developers, institutions, and societies in guiding AI toward equitable outcomes. With contributions from scholars and practitioners across diverse fields, the chapters offer deep and multifaceted perspectives on the interplay between innovation and injustice.

CHAPTER OVERVIEW

The volume opens with a discussion on the role of leadership and governance in shaping inclusive workplace cultures. The first chapter argues for a transformative approach to organizational inclusion, integrating ESG and SDG frameworks to foster long-term value. Rather than treating inclusion as a static goal, the authors position it as a dynamic process tied to strategy, workforce structures, and stakeholder relationships.

Chapter 2 introduces algorithmic discrimination as one of the most pressing challenges of our time. Despite AI's image as an objective tool, the systems it powers often carry forward biases embedded in the data and decisions that shape them. This chapter calls for a paradigm shift in how we understand and govern algorithms, centering ethics and the lived experiences of those most affected by automated decisions.

The third chapter turns to AI's growing presence in higher education. While technologies promise personalization and efficiency, they may inadvertently marginalize vulnerable learners. This chapter interrogates how admissions tools, adaptive learning platforms, and institutional priorities may exclude students with limited access or differing needs, and it proposes strategies for ethical, inclusive educational technology.

Knowledge itself becomes the focus of Chapter 4, which explores how universities can strategically manage knowledge creation, dissemination, and application to enhance both academic quality and institutional competitiveness. Using empirical data from professors in Mexico, the chapter shows how integrated knowledge strategies, potentially supported by AI, can drive sustainable innovation.

Chapter 5 addresses exclusion in the global food trade, particularly how regulations and standards meant to improve safety and equity may still generate unintended barriers. By highlighting the role of collective intelligence and international collaboration, this chapter explores ways in which governance and information-sharing can help counteract exclusionary dynamics in global supply chains.

Machine learning bias is examined more deeply in Chapter 6, where the authors argue that exclusion in AI is not a glitch but a systemic reflection of society. This chapter urges developers and institutions to reimagine fairness through the lens of justice, proposing tangible approaches for inclusive AI system design that prioritizes representation and accountability.

Chapter 7 takes us into the realm of marketing and global value chains. With a focus on emerging economies like India, it explores how multinational corporations can adapt marketing strategies to reach underserved populations. The chapter highlights the importance of addressing gaps in access, pricing, and information in order to serve communities at the bottom of the pyramid more effectively.

Technological exclusion in the automotive industry is the focus of Chapter 8. As software-defined vehicles become more prevalent, firms must adapt their capabilities to address algorithmic bias and data governance. Drawing on dynamic capabilities theory, the chapter proposes ethical foresight and inclusive design as essential tools for equitable innovation in mobility systems.

In Chapter 9, the implications of AI bias in the mobility sector are further explored through a cross-cultural study involving ChatGPT, DeepSeek, and Gemini. The chapter uncovers how representation and geographical bias can skew innovation, often privileging efficiency over inclusivity. It argues that AI ethics must become part of a firm's strategic capabilities to ensure equitable transformation in mobility ecosystems.

Citizen engagement becomes the subject of Chapter 10, which examines how participation contributes to a culture of peace and social innovation in urban communities. Drawing on survey data from Guadalajara, the authors demonstrate the powerful impact of civic action on social cohesion and sustainability, highlighting the intersection between local engagement and systemic change.

The volume concludes with a bibliometric analysis of research in Sustainable Supply Chain Management. Chapter 11 reveals how supply chains are becoming critical arenas for sustainability, with AI playing a growing but double-edged role. While it can enhance competitiveness and transparency, AI also introduces new risks that demand careful oversight and inclusive strategies.

Together, these chapters underscore a shared truth: inclusion is not an inevitable outcome of technological advancement. It is a deliberate and continuous choice. As AI becomes further embedded in our institutions and lives, we must ask difficult questions about who is being served, who is being left behind, and how we can design systems that reflect the values of equity, transparency, and shared responsibility. This volume does not offer simple solutions, but it provides critical tools and insights for those who seek to navigate this complex terrain with purpose and integrity.

We hope that the ideas presented here will inspire entrepreneurs, academics, policymakers, investors, and engaged citizens to rethink the role of AI not just as an innovation tool, but as a force that shapes and must be shaped by our collective commitment to inclusion.

Chapter 1
The Dynamics of Inclusion and Exclusion:
Governance, Leadership, and Transformative Value in Organizations

Michael Steggemann
https://orcid.org/0009-0008-2693-4289
Universidad la Salle, Mexico

ABSTRACT

This chapter explores workplace inclusion and exclusion, their impact on value creation, and their role within sustainability frameworks. It examines leadership's role in fostering inclusivity, the relationship between inclusion, exclusion, and stakeholder value, and the processes that drive long-term success. The discussion integrates ESG and SDG principles, highlighting challenges in defining inclusion and exclusion within organizations. The chapter argues for a transformative leadership approach that rethinks strategy, structure, and workforce dynamics. It calls for a two-dimensional perspective on inclusion/exclusion and urges further research into balancing these dynamics for sustainable value creation.

INSPIRING WORKPLACE INCLUSION: A TRANSFORMATIVE VALUE INITIATIVE

> *May our reality be that we live in a world where we are not asked to be inclusive but simply to be inclusive by nature!*
> *Sofía Salafranca Pérez*

DOI: 10.4018/979-8-3373-2685-6.ch001

Copyright © 2026, IGI Global Scientific Publishing. Copying or distributing in print or electronic forms without written permission of IGI Global Scientific Publishing is prohibited.

INTRODUCTION

There has been a growing recognition of the need for transformation within companies and organizations. Transformation means rethinking the operating model, strategy, organizational structure, workforce, and processes to address emerging challenges and opportunities. (BCG, 2014)

Digitalization across industries, especially artificial intelligence, is shifting how work is done, how individuals interact, and what customers expect.

In this context, inclusivity is a topic of significant importance for organizations worldwide. Companies, politicians, and policymakers actively address inclusivity in their platforms and legislation to promote sustainable development, equality, and diversity, thereby engaging people from diverse backgrounds, perspectives, and experiences.

The Cambridge Dictionary (2024) defines inclusion as "the idea that everyone should be able to use the same facilities, take part in the same activities, and enjoy the same experiences, including people who have a disability or disadvantage". According to Talmage and Knopf (2017), inclusion is a process that involves the **entire** community, and inclusiveness is the desired[1] outcome of this process, which utilizes diversity as a valuable resource; diversity is used to improve inclusiveness, and inclusiveness refers to a community's ability to include all its members and implies their integration into systems, decision-making processes, and actions.

They use Sustainable Development Goals (SDGs) to guide environmental, social, and governance (ESG) factors.

Companies often address the issue of diversity, inclusion/exclusion, and inclusivity in one of two ways: firstly, when it is mandatory to do so, either by investors or stakeholders following an ESG investment strategy. Secondly, when they recognize the potential benefits of doing so, particularly in terms of profitability. (Investopedia, 2024; McKinsey & Company, 2020)

Conversely, organizations often overlook diversity and inclusion/exclusion when developing strategies. The question is why.

To answer this question in this context would go beyond the scope of this chapter. This chapter focuses on inspiring inclusion and exclusion in the workplace and their potential impact on value creation for individuals, groups, and businesses. As some might assume, the focal point is not workplace integration for individuals and groups. This chapter deals with personal and team-experienced inclusion /exclusion, diversity, and the corresponding (outcome) benefits for individuals, groups, businesses, and society.

The following central research question guides this chapter:

How can workplace inclusion and exclusion be rethought and transformed to unlock stakeholder value?

Supporting sub-questions include:

- How can leadership foster an inclusive workplace while respecting individual authenticity?
- What are the key relationships between workplace inclusion, exclusion, and value creation?
- How can processes and structures encouraging inclusivity and managing exclusion drive long-term organizational success?

The premise is that independently rethinking processes and structures with meaningful and mindful actions can transform experiences of inclusion and exclusion, positively impacting integrity, collective intelligence, and resilience, and unlocking value for individuals, groups, businesses, and society.

The methodology for answering the question involves a conceptual approach to the problem, enriched by the author's experience.

Establishing conceptual boundaries and their relationships is crucial for understanding the main ideas discussed in this paper, encompassing ESG, SDG, inclusion/exclusion, diversity, and value creation.

This chapter offers guidance for individuals and those in leadership positions, encouraging inclusion and exclusion within the framework of sustainability initiatives. In a workplace setting, it is crucial to implement processes and structures that can generate value for individuals, groups, businesses, and society to foster integrity. By ensuring that everyone feels respected and valued, the full potential of a diverse workforce can be unlocked and transformed to positively impact society.

This chapter is organized into seven sections. Part 1 introduces the overall topic. Part 2 discusses the importance of the UN's 2030 Agenda for Sustainable Development and its relationship with ESG principles. Part 3 examines differing interpretations of materiality in ESG sustainability evaluation, those central to financial accounting auditors, those relevant to investors, and a third, often neglected view focused on personal integrity and how individuals and teams reconcile expectations with actual performance. Part 4 reviews the concepts of inclusion and exclusion as understood in the literature. Part 5 explores whether inclusion and exclusion can function as mechanisms within the sustainability framework. Part 6 outlines the managerial implications of inclusion and exclusion in workplace environments. Finally, Part 7 presents conclusions and suggests directions for future research.

ESG AND THE UN'S 2030 AGENDA FOR SUSTAINABLE DEVELOPMENT AT A GLANCE

This section explores the relationship between Environmental, Social, and Governance (ESG) principles and the UN's 2030 Agenda for Sustainable Development. With companies increasingly promoting sustainability initiatives and embracing the UN's Sustainable Development Goals (SDGs), the section discusses how ESG factors serve as a crucial framework for addressing environmental, social, and governance challenges. It also delves into the origins and applications of ESG, highlighting its role in guiding corporate behavior, investment decisions, and fostering long-term sustainable value.

Environmental, Social, and Governance - ESG

The increasing number of sustainability awards and recognitions has led organizations to promote themselves as "sustainable companies" by highlighting their inclusion initiatives and successes. This has given rise to an entire industry of consultants and firms that help companies with sustainability processes. Sustainability is presented as a positive force that drives a shift away from the exploitative practices that have traditionally characterized organizations. (Adamson et al., 2020)

Many companies reference the UN's 2030 Agenda and the Sustainable Development Goals (SDGs) as a quality guide for environmental, social, and governance (ESG) factors. Environmental criteria (E) scale how a company safeguards the environment. Social criteria (S) examine how it manages relationships with employees, suppliers, customers, and communities. Governance (G) measures a company's leadership, executive pay, audits, internal controls, and shareholder rights. (Investopedia, 2024; GRI & UN, 2018)

"ESG" is a "Financial Sector Initiative," and the term was first introduced in 2004 by UN Secretary-General Kofi Annan and CEOs of major financial institutions aimed at incorporating ESG factors into capital markets in a report called "Who Cares Wins" (WB, 2017). ESG was structured collaboratively by various stakeholders, including governments, corporations, investors, NGOs, and international organizations.

Figure 1. ESG key recommendations

Source: WB (2017).

The fundamental idea behind ESG is to incorporate environmental, social, and governance factors to build trust and achieve long-term sustainable value for stakeholders. The UN's 2030 Agenda for Sustainable Development is a guiding framework that provides context for the ESG criteria.

UN's 2030 Agenda for Sustainable Development

Two thousand and fifteen world leaders adopted the 2030 Agenda for Sustainable Development and its 17 Sustainable Development Goals (SDGs). The 17 goals correspond to 1: Poverty, 2: Hunger and food security, 3: Health, 4: Education, 5: Gender equality and women's empowerment, 6: Water and Sanitation, 7: Energy, 8: Economic Growth, 9: Infrastructure, industrialization, 10: Inequality, 11: Cities, 12: Sustainable consumption and production, 13: Climate Change, 14: Oceans, 15:

Biodiversity, forests, desertification, 16: Peace, justice and strong institutions, 17: Partnerships. The SDGs offer a practical and effective pathway to achieve sustainable development by integrating economic growth, social well-being, and environmental protection. There are 169 quantitative targets underlying the 17 SDGs, outlining the responses needed from governments, businesses, civil society organizations, and individuals to align their efforts towards common objectives. (Cruz & Matos, 2023; UN, 2015)

The ESG criteria and the UN's 2030 Agenda for Sustainable Development and its 17 SDGs are intricately linked and provide a comprehensive framework to guide corporate behavior, investment decisions, and global initiatives aimed at addressing the quality of environmental, social, and governance issues.

For example, environmental criteria (E) relate to goals such as clean water and sanitation (Goal 6), affordable and clean energy (Goal 7), and climate action (Goal 13). Social criteria (S) are linked to goals such as no poverty (Goal 1), good health and well-being (Goal 3), and gender equality (Goal 5). Governance criteria (G) are associated with goals such as peace, justice, and strong institutions (Goal 16).

It is essential to understand the link between ESG and SDGs. The term ESG/SDG will emphasize this connection in the following discussion. However, when discussing these concepts individually, it is best to refer to them as ESG or SDG separately.

By incorporating ESG/SDG principles into decision-making processes, companies can create sustainable value and promote positive social and environmental change. This can lead to a more equitable and prosperous future for all.

The UN recognizes that achieving these goals is challenging and requires collaboration and partnership at local, national, and global levels. It also necessitates innovative solutions, investment in research and development, and a commitment to leaving no one behind (UN, 2015).

As Nansai et al. (2019) illustrated, "society's current approach to [for example] sustainable material appears broken, as rising populations and deepening industrialization lead to modern society's ever-growing appetite for raw materials" as shown in Figure 1, reflected in the notable rise in elements used in the energy industry in the last centuries.

Figure 2. Elements widely used in the energy industry.

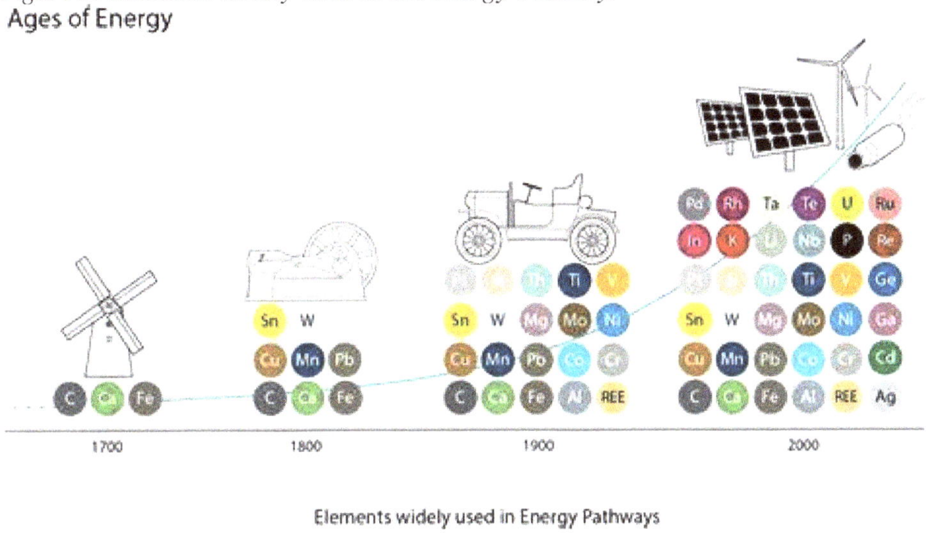

Source: Zepf et al. (2014)

Fig.1 shows the increase in the elements widely used in the ages of energy.

This growing material demand is driven by three factors, worsening SDG indicators (Berlenbach, 2024):

- Global population growth and the transformation of parts of the population into the growing middle class
- The digitalization of all areas of life
- The energy transition requires significantly more metallic raw materials than energy generation from fossil fuels.

Figure 3. SDG indicators that have worsened[2].

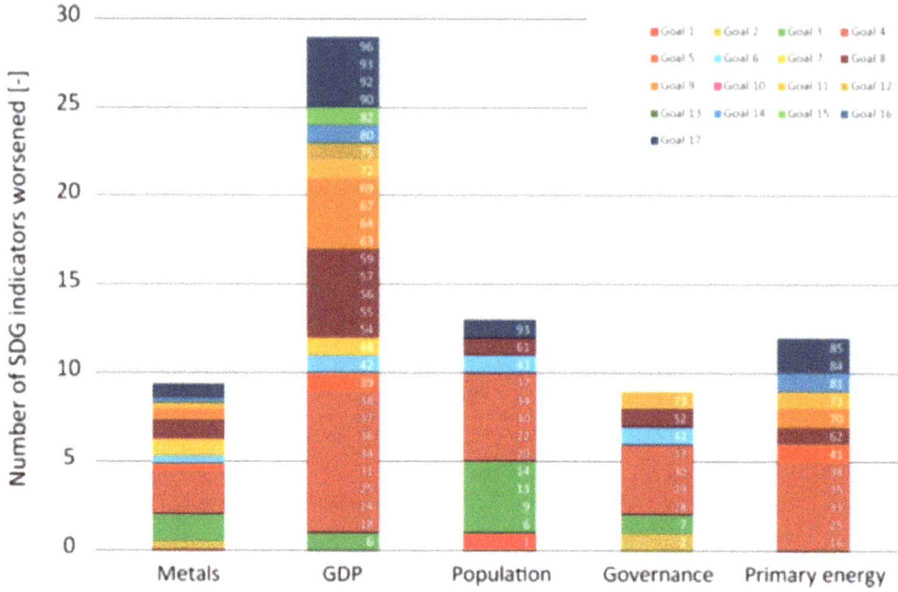

Source: Nansai et al. (2019)

Figure 2 demonstrates the impact of various socio-economic factors and metal inputs on the Sustainable Development Goals (SDGs). The graph shows the number of SDG indicators negatively affected by increased GDP, population, governance level, primary energy consumption, and metal input. (Nansai et al. 2019)

Therefore, the issue of sustainability is complex, and it can be difficult to determine where it begins and ends. Take copper, for example. While the raw material mining industry that produces copper has typically been viewed as environmentally damaging and unsustainable, impact-focused investments in this industry could have a higher ESG contribution than investments in the "clean" end-product. This is because copper mining is essential for the energy transition (Berlenbach, 2024).

Another example is ASML (2023), the Dutch semiconductor machinery producer. In their 2023 annual report, page 70, they admit: "The benefits our industry brings come at a cost, including energy and resource use. We are committed to innovating and investing to enable our company and the industry [...] to reduce these and other negative impacts."

Similarly, factors that directly impact the customer, such as fair treatment of employees and locally sourced products, can create a higher social value than ESG/SDG benefits related to the broader social good, as Tesla[3] shows (He et al., 2024).

It is essential to consider all these factors when evaluating the sustainability of a business or investment.

Many companies disclose their ESG/SDG performance in annual reports, including how they contribute to sustainable development and support specific SDGs.

However, the reality is different. While there is no agreed-upon list or reporting framework for ESG/SDG information (Lau, 2024), businesses or organizations often employ a variety of approaches and indicators when disclosing their performance on ESG/SDG criteria.

Swain (2018) criticizes ESG/SDGs as inconsistent and difficult to quantify, implement, and monitor. Others raise questions about the measurability and monitoring of the broadly framed SDGs, as the goals are non-binding, with each country being expected to create national or regional plans (Swain, 2018). Moreover, the source(s) and the extent of the financial resources and investments for the SDG are ambiguous.

The biggest challenge concerns the authority of the ESG/SDGs, as they do not have unconditional validity that takes precedence over corporate and local standards. This lack of standardization and transparency increases the complexity and opens the door for presenting a company's activities as more environmentally friendly or socially responsible than they are. (Liu, 2024). This diversity can create challenges for investors and other stakeholders trying to assess and measure the ESG/SDG endeavors and materiality, what matters for the business, and its value creation.

The reason is that the ESG frameworks were designed to disclose evidence of bad corporate behavior, such as damaging the environment, inhumane employee treatment, mishandling personal data, etc. ESG frameworks and data collection were never designed to help investors and equity analysts improve financial returns or evaluate societal impact. (Saul & Kurlander, 2022)

ESG measures and data collection often prioritize easily quantifiable inputs over complex and nuanced outcomes and impacts. Companies must move beyond simple measurement to thoroughly comprehend these outcomes and impacts, requiring a more comprehensive and in-depth approach (Howard-Grenville, 2021). The author provided the following description to illustrate this point:

> *"Many ESG measures already very effectively capture inputs, but they presume causality that adding women to top management teams, say, will produce better outcomes. But measures that capture inputs (such as the numbers of women on those teams) don't capture outcomes (such as decision-making that reflects diverse perspectives) and impacts (such as the social value created by such decisions)." (Howard-Grenville, 2021) 4*

Saul & Kurlander (2022) suggest separating the benefits of ESG measures into extrinsic and intrinsic. He described extrinsic ESG benefits as "related to broader social good but not related to the customer's direct exchange with the firm (such as environmental friendliness or community support) and intrinsic ESG benefits as those that "pertain to the customer's direct exchange with the firm (such as fair treatment of employees and locally sourced products)." (Saul & Kurlander, 2022)

Khan et al. (2016) indicated that firms with strong ratings on material (i.e., intrinsic) sustainability topics outperform firms with poor ratings. “In contrast, firms with strong ratings on immaterial sustainability topics do not outperform firms with poor ratings on the same topics.” (Khan et al., 2016)

Consequently, reasonable investors would expect corporate ESG activities with strong intrinsic value to benefit the company financially. In contrast, companies that score high on extrinsic ESG ratings may not perform as well (Saul & Kurlander, 2022).

In conclusion, incorporating ESG principles alongside the UN's 2030 Agenda for Sustainable Development is essential for creating sustainable value and promoting positive social and environmental change. However, challenges remain in standardizing ESG and SDG reporting, as well as ensuring that these measures lead to meaningful outcomes. While ESG frameworks help identify corporate behaviors that affect sustainability, they must evolve to capture the more profound impacts on business performance and societal value. Companies must integrate extrinsic and intrinsic ESG benefits to achieve real progress, focusing on what truly matters for long-term value creation and sustainability.

Let's explore the concept of value and its significance, focusing on what truly matters most.

VALUE AND ITS MATERIALITY

This section aims to explore the concept of value in both a business and societal context, focusing on the distinction between economic value and personal values. Exploring the subjective and objective dimensions delves into how materiality shapes business decisions, profitability, and sustainability. Additionally, the discussion highlights how companies integrate environmental, social, and governance (ESG) factors into their strategies, aligning them with broader ethical and economic frameworks.

Values represent the inherent qualities of things or people, regardless of personal preferences. Something's worth, both in monetary terms and in terms of its importance to individuals within an organization, influences a company's performance, profitability, and competitiveness, contributing to its economic value.

There are diverse types of value. Value is different from values. Silva (1998) describes this in his short essay “Lo que vale.” The author says that there are no values; there are only people and valuable things. Today, the price of things is confused with their value.

However, the human being and what things are worth (their price) go together: things are worth what they are. Value depends on what things are and what they know they are; therefore, it is subjective. On the other hand, values belong to society, and regardless of our tastes or desires, they represent how things or people are (Silva, 1998).

What a thing is worth, measured quantitatively in money and qualitatively by the personality system of the members of the organization, customers, and stakeholders, among others, influences the performance of the company system, reflected in its profitability and competitiveness, and condensed in the creation of economic value for the company. (Steggemann, 2015)

Saul and Kulander (2022) propose that corporations prioritize inherent (intrinsic) impacts on their business and form an integral part of their company strategy. This includes a business's direction and approach to achieve sustainable competitive advantage and long-term success. The concepts of materiality and strategy of a business are interdependent, with materiality providing information for strategic decision-making and strategy determining how materiality is assessed within the broader context of a business's mission and vision.

Materiality is the line of demarcation between what matters (is material) and what does not matter (is immaterial). The concept of materiality is essential for organizations to go beyond sheer regulatory compliance and start prioritizing factual issues that can positively impact their operations. In the context of ESG research, as a "Financial Sector Initiative," materiality refers to the level of importance attributed to specific environmental or social factors by an organization. By considering materiality, organizations can identify the most relevant issues for their operations and take action to address them, leading to enhanced sustainability and overall performance. (ESG, 2024)

Materiality is essential for collecting data and developing ESG ratings, but its definition has led to tension. There are two interpretations: one relevant to financial accounting auditors and the other to investors.

In financial accounting, materiality determines whether a particular item needs to be reported or disclosed in financial statements based on its relevance and impact on decision-making (strategy) by users of those statements. (ESG, 2024)

Materiality extends beyond financial reporting to include various aspects such as environmental impacts, social responsibility, and operational risks. **"Materiality in investment** analysis means that certain key factors drive an organization's value, which also means that certain key factors could significantly affect an organization's value." (ESG, 2024) These factors are often called critical success factors, which must be measured to understand their importance for business success.

What is this disconnection about? Like the research of Howard-Grenville (2021), Saul and Kurlander (2022) conclude that "t*he controversy around ESG stems not from a flawed investment thesis but rather from flawed data. What ESG investors want is data that measures the impact of ESG factors on corporate financial performance.*

Instead, what investors have today is a list of perfunctory ESG statistics regarding management policies, operating principles, and adherence to codes of conduct."

Hence, there is another disconnect that is often overlooked. What is materiality, the value for **the individual's integrity,** when comparing expectations and experienced performance at individual and team levels? Remember, ESG/SDG is a "Financial Sector Initiative.

As ESG/SDG is an inextricable part of doing business, its elements are interlinked. For example, social criteria overlap with environmental criteria and governance when companies seek to comply with environmental laws and broader concerns about sustainability. The focus is mostly on environmental and social criteria, but governance can never be hermetically separate.

Creating an inclusive business environment involves designing processes[5] and structures that ensure active participation and representation of all stakeholders, regardless of their backgrounds or differences. The goal is to provide equal opportunities, access to resources, information, and decision-making for everyone. This approach fosters diversity and aims to create a sustainable environment where everyone feels valued, respected, and empowered to contribute.

Companies are made up of individuals, and the intelligence of each person influences the resilience and sustainability of both the company and society as a whole. When individuals act with integrity, they create a sense of unity and purpose within the company and the wider community.

Steggemann (2023) notes that when people act with integrity, they uphold their principles and values, respecting the dignity of others by treating them honestly, fairly, and compassionately. Conversely, compromising one's integrity through unethical behavior diminishes not only one's dignity but also the dignity of everyone affected by those actions. Dignity is tied to freedom, which Boehm (2022) describes as the ability not to be determined solely by strict facts.

This is quite conflicting when companies address the issues of diversity, inclusion, and inclusivity. Kant described it centuries ago.

> *"Everything has either a price or a dignity. Those things that have a price can be replaced by something else of the same value. However, certain things are priceless and cannot be replaced by any equivalent. These things have a value that is not relative or comparative but absolute. Such things possess a dignity that is above all price.*
>
> *Morality is the state in which a rational being can only be considered an end in itself. This is because it allows for freedom. Therefore, morality and humanity, if they can achieve it, are the only things that have true dignity."* [6]

Only humans have dignity, not companies. The company is not a thinking entity but rather an abstraction (Steggemann, 2025) that displays its "values in action", the quality through teams and work groups.

In summary, value is a multifaceted concept, encompassing subjective perceptions and objective measurements. For businesses, understanding and integrating material aspects—both financial and non-financial—into their strategies is essential for long-term sustainability. Companies can enhance their competitive edge and ethical standing by aligning their operations with values that reflect their commitment to people and the environment, beyond mere compliance with financial metrics.

INCLUSION/EXCLUSION, A LITERATURE REVIEW

The purpose of this section is to explore the interrelated concepts of inclusion and exclusion and their significance in organizational contexts. By reviewing key literature, it investigates how inclusion, as a desired outcome in many organizations, affects employees' sense of belonging and uniqueness. The section also contrasts Western and non-Western perspectives on inclusion/exclusion, revealing diverse cultural understandings and implications for organizational practice. It aims to provide a comprehensive understanding of how inclusion can both empower and restrict individuals based on how boundaries and norms are applied within groups.

It is important to understand the link between inclusion and exclusion. They are complementary. In general terms, descriptions are complementary if they are incompatible, yet together, they are necessary to generate a complete picture of the described situation (Steggemann, 2015). Complementarity does not only mean the opposite but maximum incompatibility, as Walach (2003) points out. Examples of complementarity in everyday language include subject-object, inclusion-exclusion, universalism-particularism, individual-society, beginning-end, freedom-responsibility, and others, to name just a few.

In the following discussion, the term inclusion/exclusion will be used to emphasize this complementarity. However, when debating these concepts individually, it is best to refer to them as inclusion and exclusion.

The inclusion-exclusion binary is a conceptual instrument used to understand and analyze the dynamics of acceptance and rejection within various contexts. The binary explores how boundaries are drawn within societies, groups, or systems and how these boundaries affect individuals and entities.

As reviewed by Adamson et al. (2021), previous research has extensively discussed what inclusive organizations may look like (CIPD, 2019; Ferdman, 2017; Ferdman & Deane, 2014; Mor Barak, 2011; Podsiadlowski & Hofbauer, 2014) and what practices hinder or facilitate inclusion (Córdoba, 2007; Janssens & Zanoni, 2014; Pless & Maak, 2004; Roberson, 2006). Inclusion is considered a positive and desirable outcome in Western developed economies, according to Nishii (2013) and Roberson (2006). Adamson et al. (2021) are focused on the context of inclusion in

Western developed economies, while the research of Vu & Burton (2024) is focused more on the non-Western perception of inclusion/exclusion.

Vu & Burton (2024) contribute to the critical scholarship on inclusion/exclusion by presenting a non-Western perspective on inclusion/exclusion in response to the problematic inclusion-exclusion binary in the literature (Adamson et al., 2021; Rennstam & Sullivan, 2018). Within their context, individuals saw neither senses of inclusion nor exclusion as permanent. They had no expectations to be included and no fear of being excluded, realizing the impracticability of fulfilling everyone's expectations. This is remarkable as inclusive organizations are valued positively and, therefore, desired by ESG/SDG principles to create sustainable value and promote positive social and environmental change.

Subsequently, I will review the concepts of inclusion/exclusion in the literature as reviewed by Adamson et al. (2021) and Vu & Burton (2024).

Inclusion is a crucial principle that should be incorporated into an organization's practices, norms, and functions, as defined by Nishii and Rich (2014). Meanwhile, Shore et al. (2018) describe inclusion as the development of an organizational environment that every employee perceives as inclusive.

Shore et al. (2018) identified various themes of inclusion mentioned in the literature, including feeling safe, respected, and valued, being involved, having influence, self-authenticity, and recognizing and honoring diversity. Inclusive practices have been defined in multiple ways, exploring organizational and individual practices (Nishii, 2013; Roberson, 2006; Solebello et al., 2016). These practices encompass inclusive leadership (Cottrill et al., 2014) and the lived experience of inclusion by individuals (Cho, 2008; Sahin et al., 2019).

Inclusion is a term that has different meanings in different contexts, whether at the organizational or individual level. Studies that focus on inclusion in the organizational context usually examine how individuals experience inclusion within a workgroup (Combs et al., 2019; Roberson, 2006). However, lived experiences of inclusion can be shaped by several factors, such as national, cultural, and institutional norms, organizational culture, and the subjective experience of individuals (Ferdman & Deane, 2014). A sense of belonging and uniqueness is essential for individuals to perceive a sense of inclusion (Shore et al., 2018). The psychological experience of inclusion plays a crucial role in shaping the perceived experience of inclusion (Ferdman & Deane, 2014), as individuals have a fundamental emotional need for both personal uniqueness and collective belongingness (Lirio et al., 2008; Shore et al., 2011).

On the other hand, workplace exclusion, especially in the Western developed economies, is a form of social sanction against those who do not follow commonly held norms and expectations, which poses a threat to social stability (Scott et al., 2014, p. 1236). While often viewed negatively, exclusion can also be necessary in certain contexts, as interpreted by Vu & Burton (2024). Drawing from Kant's idea of "Have the courage to use your own understanding," it involves setting boundaries and making choices about inclusion, exclusion, and participation based on specific criteria or values.

Shore and his colleagues have suggested that both uniqueness and belonging are key factors for inclusive experiences. If an individual experiences high levels of both, they feel included. However, if they experience low levels of both, they feel excluded. When individuals are assimilated into an organization, only when they conform to the organizational culture and its norms do they experience belonging without uniqueness. On the other hand, if they are valued for their uniqueness but do not feel a sense of belonging, they are not considered part of the relevant group. Therefore, a sense of inclusion is experienced only when there is a balance between a sense of uniqueness and a sense of belonging. (Shore et al., 2011)

According to Mor Barak (2015), individuals can experience social exclusion in the workplace when they are forced to give up their unique identities. She stresses that the ability to express uniqueness is crucial to the existing ideas of inclusion.

Inclusion is a process that organizations and groups follow to benefit from their diversity management initiatives. Inclusion is understood as maximizing the advantages of diversity (Combs et al., 2019), and it is important to examine its negative side, the power dynamics and norms that underpin organizational inclusion (Adamson et al., 2021). For example, being included may require hiding or downplaying unique characteristics of one's self-identity that are not considered relevant, valuable, or appropriate (Vu & Burton, 2024). This is referred to as 'normative violence' used by organizations to achieve their goals (Bryer, 2020; Tyler, 2019, p. 53), enacted through managerial control over the narratives of inclusion (Noon & Ogbonna, 2021). These insights suggest that uniqueness is continually shaped and instrumentalized by the conforming pressures of inclusion, especially for minority groups.

Overall, perceptions of inclusion/exclusion are complex, multifaceted, and paradoxical, as noted by Ferdman (2017) and Solebello et al. (2016). Perception involves the initial intake and interpretation of information from the environment, as described by the different authors.

In conclusion, the literature demonstrates that inclusion and exclusion are deeply interconnected, with inclusion often requiring individuals to balance personal uniqueness and collective belonging. The analysis of Western and non-Western perspectives reveals that inclusion is not a one-size-fits-all concept and may involve trade-offs, such as conformity to organizational norms. Understanding these dynamics is crucial for organizations seeking to foster inclusive environments while managing the complexities of diversity and social expectations.

Can inclusion/exclusion be regarded as mechanisms?

The aim of this section is to explore whether inclusion and exclusion can be understood as mechanisms or whether they are better characterized as complex processes involving human thought and interaction. By comparing the structured, outcome-driven nature of mechanisms with the organic, evolving nature of human decision-making and inclusivity, the section aims to highlight the limitations of mechanistic approaches, such as Artificial Intelligence, in fostering true inclusiveness. This examination is critical for understanding how inclusion and exclusion function within organizations, particularly in terms of governance and collective responsibility.

Inclusion and exclusion are processes—not mechanisms—that involve the entire community. The desired outcome of these processes is inclusiveness or exclusiveness.

A mechanism is a technique or system to achieve a predetermined result. Mechanisms are entities and activities to produce regular changes from start or set-up to finish or termination conditions (Machamer et al., 2000). Artificial Intelligence is an example: defined as the capacity of an information processing system to adapt to its environment while operating with insufficient knowledge and resources based on an algorithm that will only do things for which it was designed. Human thought surpasses the capabilities of mechanisms.

Brain-to-brain communication involves certain things that a mechanism or an algorithm, such as AI, cannot offer. When you are upset and get an idea, it is like biological development. We progress by making mistakes and sometimes taking the wrong path. Then suddenly, a spark of inspiration emerges. That is something that a mechanism or AI is not doing. AI never makes mistakes. Humans get bored. We are not designed to live with perfection. We need an "AI stupidity engine" (Falk, 2021) to have something that needs to be solved. We must maintain a problem-solving mindset, talk, and interact with each other.

Trying to understand why another person thinks differently does not necessarily convince you to think the same way. However, the effort to understand can lead to the development of ideas and perspectives. It is like your brain shifts to a different point of focus, unrelated to what you were initially hearing.

The scientific reduction of thought to blind mechanistic processes undermines the authority of science itself, reducing knowledge to a mere myth. The authority of enlightened science can only be maintained if its necessary limits are critically examined, demonstrating that human thought remains beyond its sphere of competence. This is especially important because the authority of science relies on the authority of thought (Boehm, 2022, page 47). Kant (1870) stressed the unrestricted nature of thoughts, emphasizing their independence from external authority.

To get a better understanding, it is helpful to focus on Kant´s understanding of immaturity in "What is Enlightenment?"

Enlightenment is the exit of man from his self-inflicted immaturity. Immaturity is the inability to use one's mind without the guidance of another. This is self-inflicted immaturity if the cause of it is not the lack of intellect but the determination and courage to make use of it without the guidance of another. *Sapere aude!* Having the courage to use your intellect is therefore the maxim of Enlightenment.

The importance of something for the individual will lead the individual to take responsibility for it. Meaning is to be found in responsibility.

Maturity is inseparable from taking responsibility, an achievement that depends on the ability to think independently and is anything but a matter of course. Developing one's human sense of uniqueness and a sense of belonging (Shore et al., 2011), key factors for inclusive/exclusive experiences, is not a natural consequence of human existence, but a task for individuals and groups in organizations and the workplace (Boehm, 2022).

To refine the Inclusion-Exclusion complementarity, it is recommended to understand the quality of Inclusion-Exclusion, whether a company's governance tends to be more inclusionary or exclusionary, supporting a sense of uniqueness and a sense of belonging. The instruments used should aim to measure inclusive quality independently of exclusive quality, in analogy with studies (Fincham et al., 1997). The differentiation between inclusion and exclusion as independent dimensions of quality allows for two additional categories, typically rated in the middle of a bipolar scale: those who score high on both inclusion and exclusion are ambivalent. In contrast, those who achieve a low score on both can be described as indifferent, as shown in Table 1.

The quality of governance depends on its inclusivity or exclusivity. Effective governance balances these two aspects. To measure and know the quality of governance well, you must know how inclusive and exclusive it is and balance the two. By measuring the balance, it is possible to see what type of governance the companies analyzed have. They could be inclusive, exclusive, ambivalent—an ambivalent perception of the quality of governance—or indifferent, as the table shows.

Table 1. Experienced Quality Typology

Experienced Quality Typology	**Type of Company**
High level of inclusion and exclusion	ambivalent
Low level of inclusion, high level of exclusion	exclusive
High level of inclusion, low level of exclusion	inclusive
Low level of inclusion and exclusion	indifferent

Source. Own elaboration.

Understanding the aforementioned information is crucial for individuals and those in leadership positions. It is the foundation for critical thinking processes, which significantly transform and impact social identity, rationality, collaboration, problem-solving strategies, integrity, collective intelligence, and collective resilience, resulting in value generation for individuals, groups, businesses, and society (Figure 1).

In conclusion, inclusion and exclusion should not be viewed merely as mechanisms but as processes shaped by human thought, responsibility, and interaction. While mechanisms can produce predetermined outcomes, true inclusiveness requires adaptability, critical thinking, and a balance between uniqueness and belonging. Understanding these dynamics helps leaders and organizations improve governance by balancing inclusion and exclusion in a way that fosters collective intelligence, collaboration, and resilience, ultimately benefiting individuals, businesses, and society.

INSPIRING WORKPLACE INCLUSION AND UNLOCKING TRANSFORMATIVE VALUE.

This section aims to explore how organizations can inspire workplace inclusion and unlock transformative value through strategic initiatives and leadership approaches. It emphasizes the role of transformative leadership in creating systemic, positive change by fostering an inclusive environment where diversity is recognized and valued. By focusing on sustainable practices, organizations can achieve deeper levels of engagement and innovation, generating value for the business, individuals, and society. This section highlights the importance of moving beyond surface-level inclusivity and critically examining how inclusion and exclusion are experienced and managed in the workplace.

A "transformative value initiative" refers to a strategic approach, program, or project designed to create significant, positive, and systemic change within an organization, community, or society. The focus is on delivering strong, sustainable, and lasting value beyond incremental improvements, aiming instead to alter practices, behaviors, or outcomes. A focus on value generation can start an organizational and business transformation. This initiative involves innovation, leadership, and a clear vision for a better future. (BCG, 2014)

This requires a leadership approach where "the leader identifies the needed change, creates a vision to guide the change through inspiration, and executes the change with the commitment of the group members," a transformational leadership approach (Business Dictionary, 2024).

As Odumeru & Ogbonna (2013) describe, a transformational leader is a person who inspires and transforms followers to achieve extraordinary outcomes (Robbins & Coulter, 2007) by paying attention to the concerns and developmental needs of individual followers; they change followers' awareness of issues by helping them to look at old problems in a new way. It is all about leadership that creates positive change in the followers, who care for each other's interests and act in the group´s interests, raising followers' maturity, ideals, and concerns for achievement (Warrilow, 2012).

A leader is a role model, someone who exemplifies the highest standards of behavior and performance, inspires others, and positively transforms and influences the culture and success of the organization. To be a transformative leader, governance and management must work toward a sustainable society by promoting equality, diversity, and inclusion by engaging people from diverse backgrounds, perspectives, and experiences.

Being a role model is not enough. Maturity, inseparable from taking responsibility, is needed. An achievement that depends on the ability to think independently. What are we modeling? Developing an individual's sense of uniqueness and belonging is a task for individuals and groups in organizations and the workplace. The world of business leads us to think and feel in diverse ways. Sometimes, there is a disconnect between when we become aware of our positive or negative emotions and our desire to see those emotions reflected in others. Remember, we do not demand or desire something because we think it is good; on the contrary, we consider something good because we desire it (Baruch Spinoza, cited in Boehm, 2022). However, we do not often look into ourselves and consider how we perceive others. We always assume, "Of course, I have value and compassion. I do not mind if others have those qualities, but do not expect me to demonstrate them. I love it when others are kind to me. I recognize the value of compassion in others, but do not expect me to reciprocate." This becomes a significant issue when discussing inclusion/exclusion in team building. Even though we have defined goals and expect every team member to embody these values, we are not internalizing them ourselves.

Humans have a multilayer dynamic relationship with the world, consciously organized and, more frequently, unconsciously organized by interest and desires, influenced by reflection of the past, present-day feelings, and future expectations. It manifests meaning as sense (Steggemann, 2025), likewise an explication of implicit meaning (Atmanspacher & Rickles, 2022). At its core, inclusion is about recognizing and respecting the diversity of individuals and ensuring that everyone feels valued and included. It implies the integration of all members into various systems, decision-making processes, and actions. It is a mindset and a set of behaviors that can be applied in various contexts, whether within a family, a company, a community, or a broader society. While human beings' instincts might incline towards forming close groups or communities, it does not mean that individuals are incapable of extending inclusivity beyond those boundaries. Furthermore, the capacity for inclusivity is part of our social and moral development as humans. We can consciously cultivate and practice it in all aspects of our lives, regardless of the specific environment we find ourselves in.

The human brain looks for patterns to simplify and create habits. Addressing issues of inclusion or exclusion as meaning based on categories of moral tradition, for example, influences perceptions of inclusion and exclusion.

This is recognized as common sense. Common sense is often the inability of conformists to have the courage to think for themselves. This results in a culture that focuses on strict regulatory compliance, such as ESD/SDG, as determined by the majority. In Western developed economies, for example, inclusion is often infused with a positive tone and exclusion with a negative tone (Adamson et al., 2021). This two-dimensional logic is the thinking behind the controversy around ESG criteria, the UN's 2030 Agenda for Sustainable Development, and its 17 SDGs. They are intricately linked and provide concepts and a comprehensive framework to guide personal and corporate behavior, investment decisions, and global initiatives aimed at addressing environmental, social, and governance issues.

Individuals and those in positions of governance should have and promote "the courage to use their own understanding. " They should reflect on their core values and consider whether they are in line with the values of the company or governing body. Are these values compromising personal integrity and the feeling of uniqueness and belonging of individuals and teams? Do they make individuals feel like they are just part of a crowd? As a result, being excluded from the crowd could bring back a desired sense of freedom.

According to the research of Vu and Burton (2024), individuals do not necessarily perceive a sense of inclusion or exclusion as permanent. They do not expect to be included, nor fear being excluded, as it is impractical to fulfill everyone's expectations. This perspective emphasizes that organizational concepts such as inclusion and exclusion are means for interpretative purposes, as people can only interpret a small amount of the information they perceive (Kudesia, 2019).

In developed Western economies, "inclusion" has become widely used in business rhetoric (CIPD, 2019; O'riordan, 2014; Sherbin & Rashid, 2017). Relying solely on fixed concepts and "buzzwords" [7] to interpret situations and contexts can result in overlooking aspects of lived experience and perception (Ashforth & Fried, 1988).

Practicing mindfulness[8] and meaningfulness[9] helps to reframe experiences of inclusion and exclusion by recognizing that any categories or labels are temporary. By letting go, we can more easily bring our experiences and perceptions to bear upon organizational life. (Vu & Burton, 2024)

Categories and labels, often buzzwords, are criticized for lacking substance, as they may be used more for their rhetorical impact than for conveying meaningful information. They can also serve as shorthand for complex concepts to initiate a shift in thinking within a particular domain. For example, until recently, every European politician who wanted to be at the forefront of the debate was talking about "sustainability," "climate neutrality," or "strategic sovereignty," but the current buzzwords are "competitiveness" or "technology gap" (Sauga, 2024)

As stated, what is vital for an operation extends beyond financial reporting to include various aspects such as environmental impacts, social responsibility, governance, and operational risks. From the managerial point of view, inclusion and exclusion are significant challenges for all companies in the context of ESG sustainability because they are "people business." We need a critical inclusion policy that questions what we are doing. Who defines and classifies inclusivity? How inclusive is the inclusive, and how exclusive is the exclusive? Is inclusivity always desired? By the individual, by the society?

Whether in our personal or professional lives, we are becoming increasingly conscious of how our actions can impact the world beyond our immediate surroundings. Everything we do has the potential to affect the environment or society. The framework of rules, practices, and processes by which an organization is directed and controlled can never be isolated. Excelling in governance calls for mastering not just the letter of laws but also their spirit, such as getting in front of violations before they occur (values in action) or ensuring transparency and dialogue with employees, authorities, regulators, etc., instead of formalistically submitting a report and letting the results speak for themselves.

In conclusion, inspiring workplace inclusion and unlocking transformative value require a strategic focus on leadership, responsibility, and critical reflection on values and practices. True inclusion goes beyond regulatory compliance and buzzwords, demanding thoughtful engagement with diverse perspectives and lived experiences. Organizations can drive innovation, resilience, and sustainable value by cultivating an environment where individuals feel both unique and a sense of belonging. The commitment to inclusion must be intentional, ensuring that governance and leadership practices align with organizational behavior's broader social and environmental impacts.

CONCLUSION

As the chapter explains, the issue of sustainability and the perceptions of inclusion/exclusion as an important part of it are complex, multifaceted, and paradoxical, and it can be difficult to determine where they begin and end.

The premise holds that independently rethinking processes and structures with meaningful and mindful actions can transform experiences of inclusion and exclusion, positively impacting integrity, collective intelligence, and resilience, and unlocking value for individuals, groups, businesses, and society.

Developing an individual's sense of uniqueness and belonging, crucial for inclusion or exclusion, is not inherent but a deliberate effort for individuals and groups in organizations and the workplace. The maturity of individuals and those in leadership positions, inseparable from taking responsibility, is needed. Maturity is an achievement that depends on the ability to think independently.

The "transformative value initiative" requires a transformative leadership approach that inspires comprehensive rethinking of the operating model, strategy, organizational structure, workforce, and processes. This involves addressing concerns, developmental needs, and opportunities for effective organizational and business transformation. By focusing on these areas, leaders can drive significant and sustainable change.

Many organizations promote themselves as "sustainable companies" by emphasizing their inclusion initiatives and successes. They portray sustainability as a positive force that drives a shift away from the exploitative practices traditionally associated with organizations. Due to the lack of a universal reporting framework, they often use various approaches to disclose their performance on ESG/SDG criteria, particularly regarding inclusion and exclusion issues. Inclusion and exclusion have different meanings across contexts, leading to tensions over what is considered material or immaterial, often ignoring individual integrity and dignity.

The human brain forms habits through patterns, with inclusion or exclusion often seen as common sense shaped by moral traditions. This can limit independent thinking, leading to a compliance-focused culture when evaluating sustainability. Challenging these patterns, labels, and categories is essential for true inclusion and innovation.

Companies are made up of individuals whose actions and contributions drive resilience and sustainability. When individuals act with integrity, they uphold their principles and values, showing respect for others' dignity, which is above any price.

Companies, being abstractions, cannot possess dignity; only humans can. A company's values are expressed through its teams and work groups, recognizing inclusion and exclusion and respecting diversity, ensuring everyone feels valued and free from rigid norms. Unlike mechanisms, inclusion and exclusion are community processes aiming for inclusiveness or exclusiveness as outcomes.

Vu and Burton (2024) highlight that inclusion and exclusion are seen as transient in non-Western contexts, with no expectations or fears, acknowledging the impracticality of meeting everyone's expectations. This perspective is significant, as ESG/SDG principles aim for inclusivity to create sustainable value and promote positive change.

Understanding the inclusion/exclusion complementarity is crucial for individuals and those in leadership positions, as it underpins critical thinking processes that significantly transform and impact social identity, rationality, collaboration, problem-solving, integrity, collective intelligence, and resilience. This understanding generates value for individuals, groups, businesses, and society.

The notion that inclusion is inherently positive and exclusion negative is not conclusive. True inclusion is when individuals feel free without needing to seek inclusion (Vu & Burton, 2024).

Implications For Further Research

The team's diversity and inclusivity are vital when representing a clear governance strategy. People's attitudes are assessed frequently by placing them on a bipolar evaluative continuum, which perceives positive and negative elements as stored along a single dimension. For example: "inclusion is often infused with a positive tone and exclusion with a negative tone" (Adamson, 2021). This is an oversimplified perspective, as it is commonly believed that positive emotions, beliefs, and behaviors can counteract negative ones. More importantly, this bipolar logic is a precondition for conflicts (Steggemann, 2015)

The possibility of studying inclusion/exclusion quality from a two-dimensional perspective, as Fincham and Linfield (1997) proposed for marital quality, has received little attention in this context. This perspective perceives separate positive and negative dimensions and proposes that people can possess any combination of positivity or negativity in their attitudes.

Therefore, further research on inclusion and exclusion could focus on understanding the inclusion/ exclusion complementarity well in the organizations using a two-dimensional approach. This would involve identifying how inclusive the inclusive is and how exclusive the exclusive is and making a balance between the two. By measuring the balance, it is possible to see what type of administration the stakeholders of the companies analyzed perceive. They could be inclusive, exclusive, ambivalent—an ambivalent perception of the administration, or indifferent.

The information from an inclusion/exclusion analysis and a business strategy are interdependent. The inclusion/ exclusion analysis provides the information for strategic decision-making, and revealing the strategy determines how inclusion/ exclusion is assessed within the broader context of a business's mission and vision.

Furthermore, it is important to explore why organizations often overlook diversity and inclusion when developing their strategies. One explanation could be that organizations operate with restrictions on what is deemed reasonable practice. These boundaries are defined by what corporations are willing to accept, which is influenced by their commercial and political interests.

REFERENCES

Adamson, M., Kelan, E., Lewis, P., Śliwa, M., & Rumens, N. (2021). Introduction: Critically interrogating inclusion in organizations. *Organization*, *28*(2), 211–227. DOI: 10.1177/1350508420973307

Ashforth, B. E., & Fried, Y. (1988). The mindlessness of organizational behaviors. *Human Relations*, *41*(4), 305–329. DOI: 10.1177/001872678804100403

ASML. (2023). *2023 Annual Report*. ASML.

Atmanspacher, H., & Rickles, D. (2022). *Dual-Aspect Monism and the Deep Structure of Meaning*. Routledge., DOI: 10.4324/9781003270584

BCG. (2014). *Transformation, the imperative to change*. BCG. Link: https://www.bcg.com/publications/2014/people-organization-transformation-imperative-change

Berlenbach (2024). *Die Jagd auf Kupfer: Bergbau-Aktien vs. Rohstoff-ETC*. Podcast. Link. https://www.wiwo.de/podcast/lebenmitaktien/podcast-leben-mit-aktien-die-jagd-auf-kupfer-bergbau-aktien-vs-rohstoff-etc/29777844.html

Boehm, O. (2022). *Radikaler Universalismus: Jenseits von Identität| Ausgezeichnet mit dem Leipziger Buchpreis zur Europäischen Verständigung 2024*. Ullstein Buchverlage.

Bryer, A. (2020). Making Organizations More Inclusive: The Work of Belonging. *Organization Studies*, *41*(5), 641–660. DOI: 10.1177/0170840618814576

Business Dictionary. (2024). *Transformational Leadership*. Business Dictionary. Link. http://www.businessdictionary.com/definition/transformational-leadership.html

Cambridge Dictionary. (2024). *Inclusion*. Cambridge Dictionary.

Cho, S. (2008). Post-racialism. *Iowa Law Review*, *94*, 1589.

CIPD. (2019). *Building Inclusive Workplaces: Assessing the Evidence. Research report*, September. CIPD. Link: https://www.cipd.co.uk/Images/building-inclusive-workplaces-report-sept-2019_tcm18-64154.pdf accessed 18-05-2024.

Claborn, K. (2024). *Exploring the Spread, Use, and Impact of Buzzwords on Decision Making in Conservation: A Mixed Methods Approach*. Arizona State University.

Combs, G. M., Milosevic, I., & Bilimoria, D. (2019). Introduction to the Special Topic Forum: Critical Discourse: Envisioning the Place and Future of Diversity and Inclusion in Organizations. *Journal of Leadership & Organizational Studies*, *26*(3), 277–286. DOI: 10.1177/1548051819857739

Córdoba, J. (2007). Developing Inclusion and Critical Reflection in Information Systems Planning. *Organization*, *14*(6), 909–927. DOI: 10.1177/1350508407082266

Cottrill, K., Lopez, P. D., & Hoffman, C. C. (2014). How authentic leadership and inclusion benefit organizations. *Equality, Diversity and Inclusion*. Advance online publication. DOI: 10.1108/EDI-05-2012-0041

Cruz, C. A., & Matos, F. (2023). ESG Maturity: A software framework for the challenges of ESG data in investment. *Sustainability (Basel)*, *15*(3), 2610. DOI: 10.3390/su15032610

ESG (2024). *What is Materiality in ESG? - ESG | The Report*. Link: esgthereport.com

Falk, M. (2021). Artificial stupidity. *Interdisciplinary Science Reviews*, *46*(1-2), 36–52. DOI: 10.1080/03080188.2020.1840219

Ferdman, B. M. (2017). Paradoxes of Inclusion: Understanding and Managing the Tensions of Diversity and Multiculturalism. *The Journal of Applied Behavioral Science*, *53*(2), 235–263. DOI: 10.1177/0021886317702608

Ferdman, F. M., & Deane, B. R. (2014). *Diversity at Work: The Practice of Inclusion*. Jossey-Bass., DOI: 10.1002/9781118764282.ch1

Fincham, F. D., & Linfield, K. J. (1997). A new look at marital quality: Can spouses feel positive and negative about their marriage? *Austin. Journal of Family Psychology*, *11*(4), 489–502. DOI: 10.1037/0893-3200.11.4.489-502

GRI & UN. (2018). *Integrating the SDGs into Corporate Reporting: A Practical Guide*. GRI & UNGC. Link: https://sdgs.un.org/sites/default/files/2021-07/GRI%20-%20Integrating%20SDGs%20in%20Global%20Reporting.pdf

He, Y., Liu, Y., & Pu, Q. (2024). Is ESG a 'Scam'? Correlation Between ESG and Corporate Performance. *Highlights in Business. Economics and Management*, *24*, 1485–1493.

Howard-Grenville, J. (2021). ESG impact is hard to measure-but it is not impossible. *Harvard Business Review*. https://doi.org/DOI: 10.17863/CAM.64207

Investopedia (2024). (ESG) Investing. What Is ESG Investing? *Investopedia*.

Janssens, M., & Zanoni, P. (2014). Alternative Diversity Management: Organizational practices fostering Ethnic Equality at Work. *Scandinavian Journal of Management*, *30*(3), 317–331. DOI: 10.1016/j.scaman.2013.12.006

Kant, I. (1870). *Grundlegung zur metaphysik der sitten*. L. Heimann.

Khan, M., Serafeim, G., & Yoon, A. (2016). Corporate sustainability: First evidence on materiality. *The Accounting Review*, *91*(6), 1697–1724. DOI: 10.2308/accr-51383

Kudesia, R. S. (2019). Mindfulness as metacognitive practice. *Academy of Management Review*, *44*(2), 405–423. DOI: 10.5465/amr.2015.0333

Lau, J. (2024). *Partner, HLB Australia, Melbourne, The Importance of being an ESG-Centric business for long-term success.* HLB.

Lirio, P., Lee, M. D., Williams, M. L., Haugen, L. K., & Kossek, E. E. (2008). The Inclusion Challenge with Reduced Load Professionals: The Role of The Manager. *Human Resource Management*, *47*(3), 443–461. DOI: 10.1002/hrm.20226

Liu, J. (2024). Dilemma of ESG Development: Investors' Perspectives. Advances in Economics. *Management and Political Sciences*, *74*(1), 209–215. DOI: 10.54254/2754-1169/74/20241546

Machamer, P., Darden, L., & Craver, C. F. (2000). Thinking about mechanisms. *Philosophy of Science*, *67*(1), 1–25. DOI: 10.1086/392759

McKinsey & Company. (2020). *Diversity wins: How inclusion matters.* McKinsey & Company. Link. https://www.mckinsey.com/business-functions/people-and-organizational-performance/our-insights/diversity-wins-how-inclusion-matters

Mor Barak, M. E. (2011). *Managing Diversity: Toward a Globally Inclusive Workplace.* SAGE.

Mor Barak, M. E. (2015). Inclusion is the key to diversity management, but what is inclusion? *Human Service Organizations, Management, Leadership & Governance*, *39*(2), 83–88. DOI: 10.1080/23303131.2015.1035599

Nansai, K., Kondo, Y., Giurco, D., Sussman, D., Nakajima, K., Kagawa, S., Takayanagi, W., Shigetomi, Y., & Tohno, S. (2019). Nexus between economy-wide metal inputs and the deterioration of sustainable development goals. *Resources, Conservation and Recycling*, *149*, 12–19. DOI: 10.1016/j.resconrec.2019.05.017

Nishii, L. H. (2013). The benefits of climate for inclusion for gender-diverse groups. *Academy of Management Journal*, *56*(6), 1754–1774. DOI: 10.5465/amj.2009.0823

Noon, M., & Ogbonna, E. (2021). Controlling management to deliver diversity and inclusion: Prospects and limits. *Human Resource Management Journal*, *31*(3), 619–638. DOI: 10.1111/1748-8583.12332

O'riordan, T. (2014). *Environmental science for environmental management.* Routledge. DOI: 10.4324/9781315839592

Odumeru, J. A., & Ogbonna, I. G. (2013). Transformational vs. transactional leadership theories: Evidence in literature. *International Review of Management and Business Research*, *2*(2), 355.

Pless, N. M., & Maak, T. (2004). Building an Inclusive Diversity Culture: Principles, Processes and Practice. *Journal of Business Ethics*, *4*(2), 129–147. DOI: 10.1007/s10551-004-9465-8

Podsiadlowski, A., & Hofbauer, A. (2014). Envisioning 'inclusive organization'. *Equality, Diversity and Inclusion*, *33*(3), 214–219. DOI: 10.1108/EDI-01-2014-0008

Rennstam, J., & Sullivan, K. R. (2018). Peripheral inclusion through informal silencing and voice—A study of LGB officers in the Swedish police. *Gender, Work and Organization*, *25*(2), 177–194. DOI: 10.1111/gwao.12194

Robbins, S. P., & Coulter, M. (2007). *Principles of management. Translated by Seyyed Mohammad Arabi and Mohammed Ali Hamid Rafiee and Behrouz Asrari Ershad* (4th ed.). Office of Cultural Studies.

Roberson, Q. M. (2006). Disentangling the Meanings of Diversity and Inclusion in Organizations. *Group & Organization Management*, *31*(2), 212–236. DOI: 10.1177/1059601104273064

Şahin, O., Van der Toorn, J., Jansen, W. S., Boezeman, E. J., & Ellemers, N. (2019). Looking beyond our similarities: How perceived (in) visible dissimilarity relates to feelings of inclusion at work. *Frontiers in Psychology*, *10*, 575. DOI: 10.3389/fpsyg.2019.00575 PMID: 30971969

Sauga, M. (2024). *Europa muss mehr Kapitalismus wagen. Kolumne - DER SPIEGEL*. Spiegel Magazin.

Saul, J., & Kurlander, C. P. (2022). ESG: Right Thesis, Wrong Data. *J. Financ. Transform*, 56, 79-84.

Scott, K. L., Zagenczyk, T. J., Schippers, M., Purvis, R. L., & Cruz, K. S. (2014). Co-worker exclusion and employee outcomes: An investigation of the moderating roles of perceived organizational and social support. *Journal of Management Studies*, *51*(8), 1235–1256. DOI: 10.1111/joms.12099

Sherbin, L., & Rashid, R. (2017). Diversity doesn't stick without inclusion. *Harvard Business Review*, *1*, 1–5.

Shore, L. M., Cleveland, J. N., & Sanchez, D. (2018). Inclusive Workplaces: A Review and Model. *Human Resource Management Review*, *28*(2), 176–189. DOI: 10.1016/j.hrmr.2017.07.003

Shore, L. M., Randel, A. E., Chung, B. G., Dean, M. A., Holcombe Ehrhart, K., & Singh, G. (2011). Inclusion and Diversity in Work Groups: A Review and Model for Future Research. *Journal of Management, 37*(4), 1262–1289. DOI: 10.1177/0149206310385943

Silva, J. (1998). Valores / Lo que vale: ¿Dónde están los Valores, *Periódico Reforma*. 17-May-1998.

Solebello, N., Tschirhart, M., & Leiter, J. (2016). The paradox of inclusion and exclusion in membership associations. *Human Relations, 69*(2), 439–460. DOI: 10.1177/0018726715590166

Steggemann, M. (2015) *Complementariedad entre universalismo y particularismo en la empresa filial de la trasnacional alemana ubicada en México.* Universidad La Salle, https://doi.org/DOI: 10.13140/RG.2.1.3687.8564

Steggemann, M. (2023). Collective Intelligence synergizing into Collective Resilience. *Mercados y Negocios, 24*(49), 65–82. DOI: 10.32870/myn.vi49.7700

Steggemann, M. (2025). Managing AI in the Workplace to Enhance Collective Intelligence and Resilience. In *Navigating Collective Intelligence for Sustainable Futures* (pp. 33–64). IGI Global Scientific Publishing.

Swain, R. B. (2018). A Critical Analysis of the Sustainable Development Goals. In Leal Filho, W. (Ed.), *Handbook of Sustainability Science and Research.* World Sustainability Series. Springer., DOI: 10.1007/978-3-319-63007-6_20

Talmage, C., & Knopf, R. C. (2017). Rethinking Diversity, Inclusion, and Inclusiveness: The Quest to Better Understand Indicators of Community Enrichment and Well-Being. In Kraeger, P., Cloutier, S., & Talmage, C. (Eds.), *New Dimensions in Community Well-Being. Community Quality-of-Life and Well-Being.* Springer., DOI: 10.1007/978-3-319-55408-2_2

Tyler, M. (2019). Reassembling difference? Rethinking inclusion through/as embodied ethics. *Human Relations, 72*(1), 48–68. DOI: 10.1177/0018726718764264

UN. (2015). *Sustainable development goals: 17 goals to transform our world.* United Nations.

Vu, M. C., & Burton, N. (2024). Beyond the Inclusion-Exclusion Binary: Right Mindfulness and Its Implications for Perceived Inclusion and Exclusion in the Workplace. *Journal of Business Ethics, 191*(1), 147–165. DOI: 10.1007/s10551-023-05457-2

Walach, H. (2003). *Generalisierte Quantentheorie (Weak Quantum Theory): Eine theoretische Basis zum Verständnis transpersonaler Phänomene. Auf dem Weg zu einer Psychologie des Bewusstseins.* Bibliotheks-und Informationssystem der Universität Oldenburg, 13-46.

Warrilow, S. (2012). Transformational leadership theory- The 4 key components in leading change & managing change. *Harvard Business Review*, *2*(3), 101–104.

WB. (2017). *Who cares wins: connecting financial markets to a changing world.* World Bank Group.

Zepf, V., Reller, A., Rennie, C., Ashfield, M., & Simmons, J. (2014). *Materials critical to the energy industry. An introduction.* 2nd edition. BP.

ENDNOTES

1 We demand nor desire something because we think it is good, on the contrary, we consider something good because we desire it. Free translation of: Wir velangen weder nach etwas noch begehren es weil wir es für gut halten, im Gegenteil, wir halten es für gut weil wir es begehren, Baruch de Spinoza, cited in Boehm (2022).

2 The higher the value on the vertical axis, the more significant the role of the given factor in influencing the SDGs. The colors in the bar graph correspond to the affected SDG, while the numbers represent the specific SDG-related indicators. However, it is worth noting that the "metals" category represents an average value for all the metals studied, and thus there are no specific numbers for it.

3 He et al. (2024): Tesla is a company where new energy vehicles replace fuel vehicles and clean energy replaces fossil. ESG scores range from 0-100, with a score below 50 deemed poor and a score above 70 deemed good, and Tesla only scored 37. Tesla scored 9.1 out of 10 on environmental grounds, against an industry average of 6.5. This made up 30% of its total ESG score. On social issues, however, it ranked 1.4 compared with an average of 3.5, while on governance it scored 5.1 against an average of 3.2 [5]. Tesla's supercharger uses renewable energy by 2021, and Tesla at public charging facilities produces no net emissions. Tesla's battery recycling program is also an area of excellence in sustainability, as Tesla can recycle 100% of the waste batteries generated during the manufacturing process, allowing it to reuse most of its end-of-life batteries to make new ones. Tesla's 2021 Impact Report shows that Tesla's

2021 cumulative savings of 8.4 million tons of carbon dioxide equivalent from the use of its cars and solar panels globally is equivalent to the emissions reductions of more than 3,400 acres of forest for one year. However, the discrepancy between Tesla's operations and the comprehensiveness of the ESG rating creates a conflict, leading to a low overall ranking. Its environmental factor meets the criterion, but social and governance do not.

4 ESG measurement is an increasingly popular way of holding companies accountable when it comes to sustainability efforts, and of giving companies an incentive to improve them. But measurement, no matter how sophisticated, is much better at capturing easily quantifiable inputs than complex and messy outcomes and impacts. Companies need to do everything they can to understand those outcomes and impacts — and that requires doing more than just measurement. Companies need to do three things: (1) zoom in to develop insights on processes, (2) zoom out to see broader systems, and (3) value curiosity and learning. (Howard-Grenville, 2021)

5 It is important to note, that internalized processes, not the structure of the area of performance are the value-adding features.

6 Free translation of: Alles hat entweder einen Preis oder eine Würde. Was einen Preis hat, an dessen Stelle kann auch etwas anderes als Äquivalent gesetztwerden; was dagegen über allen Preis erhaben ist, mithin kein Äquivalent verstattet, [...] hat nicht bloss einen relativen Werth, d.i. einen Preis sondern eien inneren Werth, d.i. Würde. Nun ist moralität die bedingung, unter der allein ein vernünftiges Wesen Zweck an sich selbst sein kann, weil nur durch sie es möglich ist, [frei] zu sein. Also ist Sittlichkeit und die Menschheit, so sie derselben fähig ist, dasjenige, was allein Würde hat. (Kant, 1870; Boehm, 2022).

7 Often, if something is at the forefront of the debate, the reality is more complicated. Inclusivity is a buzzword. Buzzwords are a unique type of communicative device that have typically been characterized by their high degree of imprecision/ambiguity, normative qualities, and widespread use. Buzzwords deflect critical inquiry and limit useful action because they present a readymade view of the world (Claborn, 2024).

8 It involves being fully aware and engaged in the current experience without judgment or distraction. ... I [...] practice mindfulness more freely now, without being attached to an outcome, which has helped me to experience impermanence and emptiness more effectively (Vu & Burton, 2024).

9 What is meaningful depends on what is essential for the observer, what has significance, and what is valued by the observer at a specific time and a specific place.

Chapter 2
Algorithmic Discrimination:
The New Face of Inequality in AI Systems

Mustafa Kayyali
https://orcid.org/0000-0003-3300-262X
Maaref University of Applied Sciences, Syria

ABSTRACT

As artificial intelligence becomes woven into the fabric of decision-making, it quietly inherits the very inequalities it was meant to neutralize. Algorithmic discrimination—rooted in biased data, opaque models, and uncritical deployment—represents a new, insidious form of inequality. This chapter examines how AI systems reproduce and sometimes intensify historical injustices, often in ways that are hidden behind the technical sheen of objectivity. By exploring the sociotechnical roots of bias, the chapter highlights the moral imperative to rethink how algorithms are trained, evaluated, and governed. Rather than treating AI as a neutral tool, it calls for a paradigm shift—one that centers ethics, equity, and the lived experiences of marginalized communities. Only by acknowledging the silent exclusions encoded in code can we hope to build AI systems that reflect, rather than distort, our collective ideals of justice.

INTRODUCTION

It begins with a promise. Artificial intelligence was heralded as the great equalizer—capable of removing human error, eliminating prejudice, and making decisions with clinical objectivity. Courts would be fairer. Hiring would be mer-

DOI: 10.4018/979-8-3373-2685-6.ch002

Copyright © 2026, IGI Global Scientific Publishing. Copying or distributing in print or electronic forms without written permission of IGI Global Scientific Publishing is prohibited.

itocratic. Lending would be blind to race, gender, or background. This was the vision sold to the world: a future where machines could correct the moral failings of humankind. But in practice, this utopian dream has been quietly unraveling. AI, it turns out, does not merely replicate society's values—it often cements its worst inequalities into systems we can no longer see or question.

Algorithmic discrimination is not science fiction. It is present in predictive policing tools that disproportionately target minority neighborhoods (Egbert, S., & Mann, 2021). It lurks in facial recognition systems that misidentify Black faces at significantly higher rates. It influences hiring algorithms that "learn" to prefer male candidates because the historical data was drawn from industries dominated by men. These aren't anomalies; they are symptoms of a much deeper structural problem. As AI systems increasingly mediate access to housing, employment, education, healthcare, and even freedom, the consequences of algorithmic bias are no longer abstract—they are systemic, measurable, and painfully real.

Yet what makes algorithmic discrimination so uniquely dangerous is its invisibility. Bias used to have a face. A hiring manager. A judge. A police officer. Now, it is cloaked in code and buried in layers of neural networks that even their creators struggle to interpret. It is precisely this veneer of technical neutrality that allows discrimination to flourish unchecked. The algorithm becomes the perfect bureaucrat: unaccountable, inscrutable, and allegedly objective.

This chapter explores how algorithmic systems come to encode and reproduce societal inequalities. But more than that, it asks us to confront a difficult truth—one that lies at the intersection of data, design, and power. AI systems are not born biased; they are made biased, often inadvertently, through the data we feed them and the goals we set for them (Rejmaniak, 2021). These decisions are not purely technical. They are political, historical, and ethical. They reflect choices—about whose voices count, whose histories matter, and whose futures are prioritized.

Through a multidisciplinary lens, this chapter examines the mechanics of algorithmic discrimination and how it intersects with longstanding systems of exclusion—racial, economic, gendered, and more (Kyriakidou, 2025). It reflects on the myth of neutrality in machine learning and scrutinizes the narratives that often absolve technologists from responsibility. It also engages with emerging frameworks for ethical AI and the global movement demanding transparency, accountability, and justice in the development and deployment of algorithmic systems.

In short, this is not merely a technical discussion—it is a human one. It concerns not just what our machines are doing, but who we are allowing them to become. As we stand at the threshold of a future shaped by artificial intelligence, we must ask: Are we designing tools to dismantle inequality—or to disguise it more elegantly?

FROM BIAS TO CODE: TRACING THE ORIGINS OF ALGORITHMIC DISCRIMINATION

It never starts with the code. Before the algorithm. Before the training data. Before the weight matrices and probability scores and ranked outputs. It begins somewhere quieter, older, harder to pin down (Bhasin, 2023). It begins in assumptions—in what is seen, what is ignored, what is remembered, and what is deliberately forgotten. It begins in history, in pain passed down and normalized, in hierarchies that have outlived empires and slipped quietly into spreadsheets. Bias, in this sense, isn't a technical flaw. It's a sociological echo. And algorithms, for all their mathematical precision, are often just the next vessel.

We like to think of machines as impartial. That's their mythos. Steel nerves. No gut instinct. Just logic. They don't carry grudges, they don't sweat under pressure, they don't judge people by how they look or where they're from. And that illusion—because it is an illusion—is exactly what makes algorithmic discrimination so dangerous. It hides in the folds of so-called objectivity. It dresses up inherited prejudice in clean, clinical code. It makes systemic bias feel like statistical truth. But how does bias find its way into machines built by smart people with good intentions? How do centuries of inequality filter down into models trained over months? Let's start with data.

Data is messy. It's never neutral. Every dataset is a frozen slice of reality, often shaped by the context in which it was collected. Think about predictive policing systems (Brayne, 2021). They rely on crime statistics—numbers generated by human reporting, law enforcement patterns, neighborhood surveillance, court outcomes. But these numbers are soaked in history. They reflect decades of over-policing in communities of color, under-reporting of white-collar crime, and deeply unequal access to legal representation. The algorithm doesn't know this. It just learns from the patterns it sees. It doesn't ask *why* a certain zip code generates more arrests. It just starts recommending more patrols there. Bias in, bias out. No malice, no conspiracy—just a blind loop that mimics the past. And therein lies the first trap: mistaking data for truth.

Data is not the world—it is a lens on the world, often a cracked one. It's shaped by who collects it, what gets measured, and what gets left out. If a healthcare algorithm is trained mostly on white patients, it will struggle to diagnose conditions that present differently in Black patients. If an employment model is built on resumes from past hires at a male-dominated company, it will quietly learn to downrank women (Geffner, 2023). If a loan approval model draws on financial histories skewed by redlining and generational poverty, it will replicate those exclusions with astonishing precision. But it's not just the data. The design of the model matters too.

The moment someone decides what counts as success—what outcome the model should optimize for—they're making a judgment call. Do we prioritize efficiency or equity? Do we care about false positives more than false negatives? Who bears the brunt of mistakes, and who gets the benefit of the doubt? These aren't just technical questions. They're ethical ones. They reveal the values embedded in the system, often implicitly. And when these questions go unasked—as they often do—the default becomes whatever aligns most comfortably with the status quo.

There's also the question of *representation*. Not just in the data, but in the room. Who is building these systems? Whose voices shape the product requirements, the benchmarks, the evaluation criteria? Too often, it's a narrow slice of the world—technically skilled, yes, but demographically and ideologically homogeneous. When development teams lack diversity—of race, gender, socioeconomic background, life experience—they're more likely to miss the cracks where bias seeps in. Not because they're malicious, but because their worldviews are limited. They build for themselves, not out of arrogance, but out of habit. And when the tools of the future are designed in echo chambers, the risk of exclusion becomes systemic.

Let's be blunt: technology does not exist in a vacuum. Every system reflects the social, economic, and political forces of its time (Volti & Croissant, 2024). Algorithms are no exception. They're shaped by funding pressures, market incentives, deadlines, and organizational blind spots. An AI built to optimize ad clicks will likely favor provocative content, even if it reinforces stereotypes. A tool designed to reduce costs may quietly learn to avoid "high-risk" demographics, even if that risk is itself a reflection of unequal opportunity. When profit drives design more than fairness, the algorithm simply mirrors the inequalities that capitalism has long normalized. And yet, even as these systems discriminate—sometimes subtly, sometimes blatantly—they are often wrapped in the language of progress. "Innovation." "Efficiency." "Scalability." But innovation for whom? Efficiency at what cost? Scalable to whose experience? These aren't rhetorical questions. They're the cracks in the foundation. The uncomfortable truths that tech culture has spent years glossing over in favor of sleek interfaces and investor pitches.

The myth of neutrality runs deep. It's what lets companies say, "The algorithm made the decision," as if the algorithm were some disembodied intelligence, free of human influence. But that's a cop-out. Algorithms don't emerge from the ether. They are designed, trained, tuned, deployed. Every step involves human decisions. And every decision carries assumptions—about what matters, who matters, and what fairness even means.

Fairness, by the way, is not a universal concept. It's cultural, contextual, contested. What's fair in one society may be exclusionary in another. And yet many AI systems are exported across borders, imposed on populations with wildly different norms and histories. A facial recognition tool developed in a predominantly white context may perform poorly on darker skin tones—but still get adopted globally (Yucer et al, 2025). A predictive model trained on U.S. criminal justice data may be used in jurisdictions with entirely different legal frameworks. This kind of technological imperialism—unintentional or not—risks amplifying inequalities at a global scale. So, what do we do with all of this?

- First, we stop pretending that bias is an exception. It's the norm—unless we actively intervene. We need to acknowledge that discrimination can be encoded not just in bad data, but in the very structure of our algorithms, the goals we set, the incentives we reward, and the silences we tolerate.
- Second, we need new languages of accountability. It's not enough to publish fairness metrics or conduct internal audits. We need systems that allow those affected by algorithmic decisions to understand, challenge, and influence those decisions. We need governance structures that don't just check for harm after the fact, but actively involve communities in the design process. Inclusion isn't a checkbox. It's a practice. A messy, ongoing negotiation of power.
- Finally, we need to embrace discomfort. Talking about algorithmic discrimination means confronting history, privilege, complicity. It means asking hard questions about whose lives are being shaped by our code—and whether we're okay with that. It means recognizing that technical brilliance doesn't excuse moral blindness. That "we didn't mean to" is not a defense. That building better systems means building a better understanding of justice, one that transcends metrics and gets back to something more fundamental: dignity.

Because at the end of the day, this isn't just about code. It's about people. The job applicant who keeps getting mysteriously rejected. The teenager flagged as a threat by a school surveillance system. The patient misdiagnosed because their symptoms weren't in the training data. These aren't edge cases. They're the human cost of pretending that math is apolitical. So, let's trace it back—this arc from bias to code. Let's unearth the decisions, the blind spots, the assumptions that silently shape our machines. Let's stop asking whether AI can be fair, and start asking whether we're willing to do the work to make it so. Because the algorithm doesn't decide. We do.

INVISIBLE BARRIERS: HOW ALGORITHMS PERPETUATE AND AMPLIFY SOCIAL INEQUITIES

You don't always see the wall until you walk straight into it. That's the thing about algorithmic systems. They don't scream discrimination. They don't wear hoods or badges. They don't scrawl slurs on bathroom walls. Their harm is quieter, more bureaucratic, wrapped in probabilities, embedded in pipelines, distributed across servers and decision trees (Sinnreich & Gilbert, 2024). And yet, for those on the receiving end—those flagged as "high risk," as "less qualified," as "not a cultural fit"—the exclusion is real. Tactile. Denied opportunities. Fewer resources. Less dignity. Invisible, yes, but absolutely material.

To understand how algorithms perpetuate and amplify social inequities, we have to begin with a hard admission: most of these systems were never designed with equity in mind. Efficiency? Sure. Scale? Of course. Profit? Always. But equity—real equity—requires something these systems rarely accommodate: historical context. Lived experience. Power dynamics. And that's the problem. When AI models operate as if everyone starts at the same line, they end up rewarding the privileged and penalizing the rest. Not because they're malicious. Because they're blind. Take the job market, for instance.

Hiring platforms that automate resume screening don't discriminate out of hatred. They do it out of pattern recognition (Andrews & Bucher, 2022). They look for matches with past hires, with "successful candidates," with profiles that statistically align with retention and performance. But here's the catch: if those past hires were overwhelmingly white, male, and educated at elite institutions, the system quietly learns to see that as the norm. It's not taught to question why those patterns exist—it's trained to replicate them. And so a woman who took time off to care for a child is flagged as having "gaps." A Black applicant with a non-Western name is ranked lower (Thijssen et al, 2022). A self-taught coder from a rural background gets lost in the shuffle because they didn't go to Stanford. No one said, "Reject these people." The system just did what it was built to do—optimize. But optimize for what? That question rarely gets asked. And when it does, it's often too late.

Then there's education. Predictive analytics now determine everything from college admissions to student drop-out risks (Gonzalez-Nucamendi et al, 2023). On the surface, it seems helpful—identify students who might need support early on. But these models often pull from data points like attendance, standardized test scores, neighborhood demographics—each one a proxy for deeper social and economic realities. A student from an underfunded school district might be flagged as "at-risk" before they even step foot on campus (McDaniel, 2023). Not because they lack potential, but because the system interprets their zip code as a liability. These predictions—often sealed in code—can shape how teachers treat them, how resources are distributed, even how much those students believe in their own success. The irony is bitter: the very tools built to help end up reinforcing the circumstances they were meant to mitigate. And what about healthcare? It's one of the clearest examples of algorithmic disparity. In 2019, a major study found that an algorithm used to allocate health services in the United States was systematically underestimating the needs of Black patients (Coots et al, 2025). Why? Because it used healthcare spending as a proxy for health needs—and historically, Black patients have received less medical care, not because they are healthier, but because of long-standing inequalities in access, trust, and diagnosis. The algorithm wasn't explicitly racist. It simply encoded racism through its choice of metric. And no one caught it—until lives had already been affected.

The damage, of course, doesn't stop at individual outcomes. Algorithms scale. They replicate decisions across millions of cases, across time zones, across borders. A single flawed model can shape mortgage approvals, prison sentencing, welfare eligibility. The impact isn't one mistake—it's thousands. Tens of thousands. And because these systems often lack transparency, the people harmed by them rarely even know what hit them.

What makes it worse is the myth of fairness baked into the narrative. People are told the algorithm is impartial, that the machine sees things humans cannot. There's a certain techno-authority that makes it hard to argue with a score or a ranking, especially when you're already marginalized (Bigman et al, 2023). "It's not personal," they're told. But what's more personal than being evaluated by a system that doesn't know your story, yet still decides your worth? Let's be clear: this isn't just about technical flaws. It's about social reproduction. These systems inherit the inequalities of the societies they emerge from. They operationalize injustice and wrap it in optimization. And because they do it quietly, often without fanfare or visibility, they avoid scrutiny. They slide under the radar, regulating lives in ways that evade protest.

Think about facial recognition. For years, studies have shown that these systems are significantly less accurate when identifying people with darker skin tones—especially Black women (Yucer et al, 2024). In some cases, error rates have been as high as 34% compared to less than 1% for white men. Yet these systems are being adopted by law enforcement agencies, airports, even schools. What happens when an innocent person is misidentified? What happens when that error leads to arrest, detention, a criminal record? These are not hypothetical questions. These are documented realities. The kicker? In many of these cases, consent is either coerced or entirely absent. People are scanned, scored, surveilled—without knowing, without opting in, without recourse. It's the perfect storm: technological opacity meets structural inequality, and the ones most affected are often the least equipped to fight back. But let's not just focus on the big, headline-grabbing examples. Algorithmic exclusion happens in subtler ways too. Like the gig worker who gets deactivated by a ride-sharing algorithm for "low ratings"—a system that can be influenced by customer bias, language barriers, even the driver's accent (Zhu, 2024). Or the tenant denied an apartment because an automated background check flagged a decades-old misdemeanor. Or the family seeking social services, only to find their application routed through a risk assessment system that sees poverty not as misfortune, but as risk. And every time these systems are challenged, the same defense gets trotted out: "It's just math." But math isn't apolitical. Statistics aren't neutral. Every model is a product of design choices, trade-offs, simplifications (Nickel, 2021). They're built by humans, with all our flaws and worldviews and blind spots. The algorithm isn't the villain. It's just the tool. The deeper issue is how that tool is wielded—and by whom.

So how do we begin to dismantle these invisible barriers?

- First, we have to see them. Truly see them. That means interrogating the systems we've come to trust, demanding explanations, refusing to accept "black box" excuses. It means empowering communities to audit these technologies, not just after deployment, but during design. It means shifting the burden of proof—not on the harmed to prove they were harmed, but on the system creators to prove their models are just.
- Second, we must center the voices of those most affected. Not just as subjects of research or footnotes in case studies—but as co-creators, co-designers, decision-makers. Equity cannot be engineered from afar. It requires proximity, humility, and genuine collaboration. It requires technologists to get uncomfortable, to listen more than they talk, to let go of the fantasy that expertise equals authority.
- Third, we need policy. Not the kind that gets watered down by lobbying or delayed by endless studies. Real, enforceable regulation that demands transparency, prohibits discriminatory outcomes, mandates audits, and holds institutions accountable. Technology moves fast. That's no excuse for ethics to lag behind.
- Finally, we need to reimagine what it means to design AI systems. Not just smarter systems. Kinder ones. More just ones. Tools that don't just process data, but understand context. That don't just predict outcomes, but reckon with causes. That don't just amplify what is, but imagine what could be.

Because here's the truth: invisible barriers don't stay invisible forever. Eventually, people notice. They talk. They organize. They push back. And when they do, the systems that seemed so invincible start to crack. The question is, will we wait until then? Or will we build something better now—before another life is rerouted, another future denied, another story erased in the name of efficiency? It's easy to blame the algorithm. But the real work begins with us.

THE DATA DILEMMA: HISTORICAL INJUSTICE EMBEDDED IN TRAINING SETS

The problem isn't that the data lies. It's that it remembers too well. Every dataset is a fossil. A fragment of some larger, messier, and often darker history—compressed, anonymized, and formatted into neat columns for machine consumption. We treat it as fact, as evidence, as the raw material of truth. But truth, when extracted from unjust systems, comes laced with distortion. The algorithm doesn't forget what the world taught it. And when the world has been cruel, biased, and unjust, the data becomes an echo chamber for old hierarchies, sharpening them into digital edges (Gigerenzer, 2022).

This is the quiet scandal of modern artificial intelligence: that its intelligence is often trained on human injustice (Hull, 2023). We don't talk about it enough. Or we talk about it in the wrong way. "Garbage in, garbage out," the engineers say, as if it's just a quality control issue. As if fairness could be debugged like faulty code. But the problem is deeper. It's not just about dirty data or flawed inputs—it's about power, legacy, and the kind of forgetting that lets inequity sneak into the future disguised as innovation.

Let's be blunt: most training datasets are not designed with justice in mind. They're scraped, harvested, stitched together—often without consent, rarely with context. ImageNet, a foundational dataset in computer vision, was built from photos pulled from the internet, many of them labeled in ways that now raise deep ethical questions (Tahir, 2024). Sentiment analysis datasets have been known to assign negative emotions to words associated with African American Vernacular English. Crime prediction tools learn from arrest records riddled with racial profiling. These datasets aren't neutral—they're cultural artifacts. And like any artifact, they carry the fingerprints of the systems that created them.

Take COMPAS, the infamous recidivism prediction tool used in the U.S. justice system (Bejarano Carbo, 2021). It was trained on data from previous arrests and convictions. But arrest data is not an objective record of crime—it's a record of policing. And policing has never been evenly distributed. Communities of color have long been over-surveilled, over-arrested, over-penalized. So when the model learns from this history, it doesn't just reflect bias—it cements it. A young Black man flagged as high risk may be no more likely to reoffend than his white counterpart, but the model sees him through the lens of precedent. And that precedent is soaked in racial injustice. Now scale that up.

Think of facial recognition algorithms trained disproportionately on light-skinned faces (Buolamwini, 2024). Think of healthcare models built on datasets that under-represent women, or misdiagnose Indigenous communities, or treat chronic pain in Black patients as psychological rather than physiological (Gartner et al, 2023). Think of resume screening tools that learn to down-rank women because, historically, men were more likely to get hired and promoted in STEM fields. None of these systems *intend* to discriminate. But they do. Because the data taught them to. And because we never stopped to ask whether the data should be trusted in the first place.

The issue isn't that the past is in the data. The issue is that the past was unjust—and we never corrected for it before feeding it to a machine.

What makes this dilemma so treacherous is the illusion of objectivity. Numbers seem clean. Datasets feel distant from the politics that produced them. But the reality is far messier (Poirier, 2021). A mortgage approval model might seem objective until you realize it's trained on lending decisions shaped by decades of redlining. A university admissions algorithm might seem meritocratic until you learn it gives preference to standardized test scores that correlate strongly with income and parental education. The model doesn't ask *why* these patterns exist. It just learns them. Embeds them. Deploys them. And in doing so, it becomes a vessel for historical injustice—automated, accelerated, and scaled.

There's a phrase that gets thrown around a lot in machine learning circles: "Let the data speak." But data doesn't speak. It whispers, it mutters, it hints. And if you're not listening carefully—if you lack the historical and sociological literacy to understand its language—you'll mistake its murmurs for truth. That's how bias becomes embedded: not just through bad intentions, but through silence. Through the absence of questions that should've been asked before the model was ever trained. You see it most starkly in the global South.

Many datasets used in AI are heavily Western-centric. English-dominated. White-coded. Trained on cultural assumptions that simply don't hold elsewhere (Jones, 2021). So when those models are exported—under the banner of technological development—they often fail catastrophically. Voice assistants that don't recognize regional accents. Medical diagnostic tools that misinterpret symptoms common in tropical climates. Language models that erase Indigenous terms or treat them as noise. These aren't just technical failures. They're cultural erasures. The data didn't include these people, so the model acts as if they don't exist. And what about the people who *are* included in the data, but never gave consent?

Scraping forums, transcriptions, social media posts—this is standard practice in building large language models. But it raises ethical red flags. Whose words are being harvested? Whose images? Whose pain is being commodified in the name of progress? When datasets include deeply personal or traumatic content without consent—domestic violence forums, mental health support threads, images of protestors—the harm isn't hypothetical. It's real. And yet, it happens quietly, in the shadows of code and copyright loopholes.

There's an uncomfortable irony here. The same communities that have historically been surveilled, exploited, and marginalized are now being used to train the very systems that may continue to exclude them. Their data—collected under unequal conditions—is turned into capital. Their experiences—filtered, flattened—become inputs. And yet they remain largely absent from the rooms where these technologies are built, discussed, deployed. The systems extract their stories, but not their voices. And once the model is trained, the damage is hard to reverse.

Bias in training data creates what's known as "baked-in" bias. You can try to tune the model. You can apply fairness corrections. You can adjust weights. But if the foundation is compromised—if the data reflects a broken world—you're building a machine that will break people in eerily familiar ways. This isn't pessimism. It's caution. It's the recognition that you can't fix injustice by optimizing around it. You have to confront it directly. Even if that means scrapping the dataset and starting over. Even if that means slowing down development. Even if that means admitting that the data we've been treating as gospel is, in many ways, a record of failure. So, what do we do?

- First, we have to reimagine what responsible data collection looks like. That means context, not just content. That means documenting datasets—who collected them, when, how, and why. It means understanding the social dynamics behind the numbers. Was this dataset built from surveillance? Was it drawn from communities without consent? Does it reinforce existing hierarchies? If so, do we really want to model the future on it?
- Second, we need to diversify our datasets—not just by including more demographics, but by shifting who decides what data is worth collecting. Community-based data collection. Participatory annotation. Ethical frameworks that prioritize dignity over convenience. Imagine datasets where the subjects are collaborators, not just sources. Where the design reflects their needs, not just the developers' assumptions.
- Third, we need to challenge the fetishization of "big data." Bigger isn't always better. More data doesn't mean more truth. In fact, scale often obscures bias—it buries it under the illusion of statistical significance. Sometimes, smaller, carefully curated datasets—designed with care, context, and consent—can lead to more just outcomes. It's not about quantity. It's about integrity.

And finally, we have to tell the truth about our data. We have to stop pretending that datasets are neutral or universal. We must stop handing them off to algorithms like sacred texts and start treating them like what they are—historical records, full of mess and meaning (Wiggins & Jones, 2023). We must build a new culture of transparency, where data provenance is treated with the same seriousness as model performance. Where harm isn't something we apologize for after the fact but something we actively design against from the start. Because if we don't, we're not just building biased systems. We're hard-coding injustice into the future. And the future deserves better.

ACCOUNTABILITY IN THE AGE OF AUTOMATION: WHO IS RESPONSIBLE FOR BIAS?

Responsibility is a slippery thing when machines are involved. It used to be easier—or at least more straightforward. If a bank clerk denied you a loan based on your race, you knew where to point your anger. If a hiring manager passed over your résumé because of your name, you could hold them accountable (Aydın & Turan, 2023). But what do you do when the rejection comes from an algorithm? When the voice on the other end of the system says nothing at all? When the decision arrives stripped of intention, concealed in code, and no one—not even the developers—can quite explain how it was made?

The age of automation has brought with it a kind of moral fog. A quiet, pervasive unaccountability. Bias exists, yes. Harm happens (Keles, 2023). But when you try to locate the culprit, it dissolves into the machine. The system is the new scapegoat. "The algorithm did it," they say. As if that ends the conversation. As if the algorithm weren't designed, trained, deployed, and continually tweaked by human hands. So, let's ask the question plainly: Who is responsible for bias in automated systems? It's not a comfortable question. It disrupts the fantasy that technology is neutral, that engineers are just builders, that companies are just platforms, that governments are just adopters. But discomfort is where accountability begins.

Let's start with the developers—the engineers, the data scientists, the coders who build these systems line by line, model by model. Some will say their job is purely technical. That they're optimizing parameters, tuning models, cleaning datasets—not writing policy or reshaping society. But that's a false dichotomy. The moment you design a system that impacts real people—decides who gets hired, who gets parole, who gets housing—you're no longer just an engineer. You're an architect of consequence. And pretending otherwise is not humility. It's abdication.

The decisions made at the design level—what data to include, what labels to assign, what thresholds to set, what metrics to optimize—are ethical decisions, even when they're framed in code (Gogoll et al, 2021). A model trained to maximize click-through rates without considering misinformation is not failing—it's succeeding at the wrong goal. A classifier that predicts creditworthiness without interrogating the colonial logic of wealth accumulation is functioning exactly as designed. Bias is not a bug here. It's a blueprint. But let's not stop at the developers. What about the companies that fund, market, and deploy these systems?

Tech firms have long hidden behind the language of disruption (Roblek et al, 2021). They frame themselves as innovators, not institutions. Agile, not accountable. But when their products shape elections, filter job applicants, or determine access to public services, they're no longer startups—they're power brokers. And with power comes responsibility.

Still, these companies often outsource the blame. "It's the client's fault for how they used the tool." Or "We just provide the platform—it's up to users to apply it ethically." Or worse, "The model is proprietary—we can't explain how it works." This is corporate theater—sleight of hand dressed up as policy. Transparency becomes a trade secret. Responsibility becomes a press release. Meanwhile, people are denied services, flagged as threats, dehumanized by systems they never agreed to and can't appeal. Let's talk about governments too.

Public agencies increasingly rely on automated systems to distribute resources, enforce law, manage populations (Rahmani et al, 2024). Predictive policing, risk assessments in child welfare, welfare eligibility algorithms—they're all dressed up in the language of efficiency. But when these systems discriminate—as they often do—the state rarely takes the fall. Officials blame the software. Contractors blame the agency. Everyone blames the data. And round and round we go. This bureaucratic loop is deeply dangerous (Davies, 2025). It turns the very notion of accountability into a ghost. And it leaves those harmed by these systems—often the poorest, the least resourced, the least visible—without anyone to turn to. Try asking a machine for justice. See what it says. But the truth is, responsibility doesn't belong to a single party. It's shared. Distributed. Which makes it harder, but no less essential.

Data annotators—those often-overlooked workers who label images, transcribe voices, tag text—play a role too. Their cultural assumptions, their context, their working conditions shape how data is framed. An annotator who labels a young Black man's face as "aggressive" is encoding their perception into a dataset that might later inform policing systems. That's not a small thing. And yet these workers are often underpaid, untrained, and invisible in the AI supply chain. Ethics, it seems, stops at the border of convenience.

Researchers and academics carry weight as well. Those who build new architectures, publish benchmark datasets, write glowing reviews of AI's potential without examining its sociopolitical context—they help define what progress means (Thiyagalingam et al, 2022). They shape the discourse. And when they treat fairness as an afterthought, or dismiss social critique as "non-technical," they legitimize a culture of tunnel vision. One where performance metrics matter more than people.

Let's not forget the users—the organizations and institutions that implement these systems in the wild. Schools, hospitals, HR departments, police departments. They decide whether to buy the tool, how to integrate it, whether to question its outputs. Yet far too often, they treat the algorithm like an oracle. A neutral third party. A shield from liability. The machine said this student was likely to drop out. The model said this person was a fraud risk. As if delegation erases moral responsibility. It doesn't. Delegating a decision to a machine does not absolve you from the outcome. If anything, it demands more scrutiny, not less. And then there's us.

The broader society. The consumers, the citizens, the ones who benefit—often unknowingly—from biased systems. It's easy to think, "Well, I don't build algorithms. I'm not complicit." But complicity isn't just about action. It's about inaction. It's about where we place our outrage. Whose stories we listen to. Whether we demand transparency. Whether we care only when harm reaches our doorstep.

We live in a time where algorithms curate our news, recommend our jobs, shape our credit scores. The world is being quietly refactored around automated logic. If we do nothing—if we let that happen unchecked—we are not just bystanders. We are collaborators in a future we did not consciously choose. So, what would real accountability look like?

It would start with traceability. We'd be able to track how a model was trained, who designed it, what data it used, how it's updated, who audits it. Every decision point would be documented—not buried in white papers, but publicly available, in plain language. Not just for engineers, but for everyone affected by the system (Driscoll et al, 2022). It would mean legal frameworks with teeth. Not polite guidelines or voluntary pledges, but enforceable regulation. Laws that hold companies liable for discriminatory outcomes. Standards that mandate human oversight in high-stakes decisions. Mechanisms for redress when harm occurs. Because accountability without consequences is just theater. It would mean empowering the people most likely to be harmed. Letting them opt out. Letting them challenge decisions. Letting them co-design systems that impact their lives. It would mean listening to activists, not just academics. Listening to the undocumented worker, the tenant on a blacklist, the child flagged by a risk model. Their lived experience is not anecdotal. It's evidence. It would also mean shifting incentives.

Right now, the incentive is speed. Launch fast, iterate later. But when lives are at stake, "move fast and break things" becomes a violent motto. We need a culture where ethical design is rewarded. Where taking time to do it right isn't seen as a weakness but a sign of maturity (Lloyd, 2022). Where success is measured not just by market share, but by moral imagination.

That kind of shift won't happen overnight. And it won't happen without resistance. People will say it's too complicated, too costly, too idealistic. But isn't it more costly to build systems that harm? Isn't it more naive to believe we can ignore injustice and somehow arrive at a just future? Let's stop pretending we don't know how bias happens. We know. It starts with who builds the systems. Who funds them. Who gets excluded. Who's considered "normal." Who's never in the room. Who benefits. Who doesn't. Who can appeal. Who can't. Who lives in the margins of the dataset. Who disappears in the code. Accountability in the age of automation means refusing to let these patterns go unchallenged. It means pulling the curtain back—on the model, the process, the power. The algorithm didn't choose this. We did. Now the question is: What will we choose next?

TOWARD INCLUSIVE AI: ETHICAL DESIGN, REGULATION, AND SOCIAL JUSTICE

The future doesn't arrive fully formed. It's built—line by line, law by law, assumption by assumption. And when it comes to artificial intelligence, we are still, despite the velocity and volume of its proliferation, in the middle of building it. This, paradoxically, is both the danger and the gift (Bremmer & Suleyman, 2023). Because it means we still have a choice. Not just over what AI will do, but over who it will serve, who it will silence, and who will be allowed to shape it.

We've spent years talking about innovation—faster models, more parameters, higher performance. But very little of that noise has concerned itself with equity. With inclusivity. With justice. Ethical design has too often been reduced to a checklist, a footnote in grant applications, a marketing veneer thin enough to see through. And yet, ethics—when taken seriously—isn't a layer you slap on after the fact. It's the architecture. The frame. The bones. Without it, what we're building isn't intelligence. It's automation masquerading as progress. So, what does it really mean to build inclusive AI?

It begins, as all things do, with listening. Not just to the loudest voices in the room, not just to the well-published or well-funded, but to those at the margins. The ones who've been historically ignored, misrepresented, or actively harmed by systems of power. The single mother denied benefits because a risk algorithm flagged her household as unstable. The transgender teenager misgendered by a content filter. The Indigenous elder whose language was omitted from a speech recognition dataset, as though their culture didn't belong in the digital future. If your AI doesn't account for these voices, then it isn't inclusive—it's extractive.

Ethical design, then, must start with a radically different question. Not *what can the model do?* but *who might it harm?* Not *how accurate is the output?* but *how fair is the process?* This reframing changes everything. It means abandoning the notion of neutrality—not just acknowledging bias, but accepting that every system reflects a set of values. If those values are not deliberate, they will default to the dominant ones. And history has shown us what that leads to: exclusion, erasure, silence dressed up as efficiency.

To build systems that do better, we have to break the binary between "technical" and "social." Ethics is not some distant philosophical add-on (Poszler & Lange, 2024). It's embedded in every choice—what data you include, who annotates it, how labels are defined, what the model is optimized for. Take, for instance, predictive policing tools. The decision to treat historical arrest data as an objective input—rather than a record of over-surveillance and racial targeting—is not a technical oversight. It's a moral failure. An inclusive approach would start by questioning whether that model should exist at all. And yet, design alone isn't enough. Intentionality is important—but so is accountability.

This is where regulation must step in. Not as an enemy of innovation, but as its necessary companion. We've allowed the tech sector to operate under the mythology of meritocracy for far too long. The idea that the "best" product will win. That the market will sort it out. But when the product is a facial recognition system that misidentifies Black faces, or an algorithm that flags poverty as risk, the stakes are too high to leave to market logic.

We need regulation with teeth. Real legal frameworks that go beyond soft ethical principles and actually mandate protections (Marchant & Gutierrez, 2022). That means enforceable standards around data transparency, consent, auditability, and harm mitigation. It means requiring companies to conduct algorithmic impact assessments—not just for PR, but as a precondition for deployment. It means giving individuals the right to know when they're being scored by an algorithm, the right to contest that score, the right to opt out. But regulation must also be imaginative. Not just reactive. It must ask: What kind of digital society do we want to build? One where efficiency trumps empathy? Where automation replaces deliberation? Or one where technology expands the horizon of human dignity?

An inclusive AI future also requires rethinking power—who holds it, who shapes the narrative, who profits (Sartori & Theodorou, 2022). Today, a handful of corporations control the infrastructure of AI. They decide what datasets are collected, what languages are prioritized, what problems are "worth solving." This centralization of power leads to a monoculture of thought—homogeneous teams building systems for a heterogeneous world. To counter that, we need to democratize AI development. That means funding community-led AI initiatives, supporting open-source alternatives, ensuring that public interest research isn't drowned out by corporate agendas. It means empowering local voices, especially in the Global South, to define their own technological needs instead of having tools imposed upon them from Silicon Valley.

Social justice isn't a buzzword. It's a design principle. It asks us to stop building for scale and start building for solidarity. Not "how many users?" but "which users?" Not "how fast can we deploy?" but "who gets left behind when we do?" It urges us to slow down. To reflect. To recognize that not every problem needs an algorithm, and not every form of intelligence is digital.

Take language models, for example. The race to build bigger and better ones has led to breathtaking advances—but also breathtaking erasures (Wang et al, 2025). Languages with fewer speakers are often ignored. Dialects are flattened. Cultural nuance is lost. And yet, the same communities whose languages are excluded are often the most vulnerable to misinformation, surveillance, and digital marginalization. Inclusive AI would prioritize these voices—not because they make the model "better," but because they matter.

Sometimes inclusion means stepping back. It means choosing not to automate certain decisions because doing so would strip away human nuance, empathy, or agency. It means acknowledging that some questions—Who deserves asylum? What is justice?—cannot be reduced to probabilities. But sometimes inclusion means stepping up. It means designing systems that actively redress inequality. Think of AI that helps translate endangered languages. Or tools that amplify the work of underrepresented artists. Or models trained to detect discrimination in hiring practices. This is the kind of AI we could build—not as saviors, but as accomplices in the work of equity. And let's not pretend this will be easy. Inclusion is messy. It slows things down. It demands uncomfortable conversations, conflicting viewpoints, structural overhaul. But that discomfort is necessary. Because the alternative—the path of least resistance—leads to a future that's efficient, profitable, and profoundly unjust.

We must also interrogate the myth of "user-centered design" as it currently exists (Strantz, 2025). Too often, it centers the imagined average user—a statistical composite who is usually white, male, affluent, able-bodied, and English-speaking. Inclusive AI shifts the focus. It centers those who have the most to lose. Those for whom bias is not theoretical but daily reality. Those who are seen as edge cases in datasets but are, in truth, the moral center of any ethical system. Real inclusivity is proactive. It's not about fixing harm after it happens. It's about designing in a way that anticipates harm and actively works to prevent it. It's about asking: Who are we forgetting? Who doesn't have a seat at this table? Who will bear the brunt of our "solution"? And let's be clear: the work doesn't end when the system is built. It requires maintenance. Evaluation. Accountability loops. Because context changes. Societies shift. What's ethical today might be inadequate tomorrow. Inclusive AI is not a destination. It's a practice. A commitment. A form of ongoing attention.

This is why we need interdisciplinary teams—not just coders, but ethicists, historians, sociologists, artists, community organizers. People who understand power, narrative, harm. People who will ask the questions that machines cannot. So, where do we begin? We begin by refusing to believe that the future is fixed. That it must look the way Silicon Valley imagines it. That bigger models, faster chips, and deeper learning are the only markers of progress.

We begin by insisting that fairness is not a feature—it's a foundation. We begin by listening. Deeply. Uncomfortably. Especially to those who've been ignored. We begin by asking better questions. And by admitting that sometimes, we won't have the answers. But we keep asking. Because the moment we stop asking—the moment we let the system run on autopilot—is the moment we surrender our future to logics we never fully chose. Inclusive AI is not a guarantee. It's a wager. A wager on empathy over efficiency. On complexity over convenience. On humanity over hype. It is slower. Messier. Harder. And it is the only kind of AI worth building.

CONCLUSION

There is a temptation—especially in conversations about technology—to see the problem as mechanical and the solution as more code. If the algorithm is flawed, improve the model. If the data is biased, diversify the dataset. But algorithmic discrimination is not a mere bug in the system. It is a mirror held up to our society, reflecting the very hierarchies we have failed to dismantle. Any attempt to confront it requires more than technical patchwork; it demands a moral reckoning.

Throughout this chapter, we have examined how machine learning systems can absorb and amplify existing inequalities, often under the illusion of objectivity. We have seen how predictive policing, hiring algorithms, credit scoring models, and facial recognition technologies—all powered by AI—can marginalize those who are already vulnerable. Not because the machines hate them, but because the systems were never designed with them in mind. When historical injustices become datasets, the past is quietly baked into the future. When marginalized communities are underrepresented in training data, their realities are erased. When developers fail to question who benefits from an algorithm's decisions, discrimination becomes destiny.

What is perhaps most insidious is the way algorithmic systems can make inequality feel like fate—calculated, justified, unchangeable. An algorithm doesn't raise its voice. It doesn't wear a uniform. It simply computes, and in doing so, shifts blame away from human actors and onto impersonal processes. This dehumanization is part of what makes algorithmic discrimination so hard to confront. It is harder to protest a neural network than a police officer. It is harder to hold an algorithm accountable when its decision-making process is obscured behind proprietary walls and mathematical abstractions. And yet, if AI is indeed a reflection of human values, then it is also a site of possibility. We can choose to encode empathy. We can prioritize fairness. We can build models that account for historical injustice, that include marginalized voices in their design, that are interpretable and contestable. But doing so requires a cultural shift—not just within tech companies, but across academia, government, and civil society. It demands that we stop treating ethics as an afterthought and start seeing it as foundational to innovation.

Crucially, we must abandon the myth that AI development exists in a vacuum. Every dataset has a context. Every model has assumptions. Every algorithm has consequences. And behind each of these elements are people—developers, decision-makers, policy architects—who shape the trajectory of AI in ways that will define our collective future. So, what do we do now?

We start by listening—to those who have been harmed by these systems. We design with the most vulnerable in mind. We legislate with clarity and courage, ensuring transparency, auditability, and recourse. We invest in interdisciplinary approaches that combine technical excellence with critical social understanding. And above all, we remain vigilant—recognizing that exclusion wears many faces, and in this new era, the algorithm is simply its latest mask.

The future of AI is still being written. Whether it will be a tool of liberation or a mechanism of control depends on the choices we make today. To confront algorithmic discrimination is not merely to fix broken systems—it is to ask, with clarity and conviction, what kind of world we are willing to build. And who we are willing to include in it.

REFERENCES

Andrews, L., & Bucher, H. (2022). Automating discrimination: AI hiring practices and gender inequality. *Cardozo Law Review*, *44*, 145.

Aydın, E., & Turan, M. (2023). An AI-based shortlisting model for sustainability of human resource management. *Sustainability (Basel)*, *15*(3), 2737. DOI: 10.3390/su15032737

Bejarano Carbo, M. P. (2021). Machine learning applications in the United States criminal justice system: A critical content analysis of the COMPAS recidivism risk assessment.

Bhasin, H. (2023). *Machine Learning for Beginners: Build and deploy Machine Learning systems using Python*. BPB Publications.

Bigman, Y. E., Wilson, D., Arnestad, M. N., Waytz, A., & Gray, K. (2023). Algorithmic discrimination causes less moral outrage than human discrimination. *Journal of Experimental Psychology. General*, *152*(1), 4–27. DOI: 10.1037/xge0001250 PMID: 35758989

Brayne, S. (2021). *Predict and surveil: Data, discretion, and the future of policing*. Oxford University Press.

Bremmer, I., & Suleyman, M. (2023). The AI power paradox: Can states learn to govern artificial intelligence-before it's too late? *Foreign Affairs*, *102*, 26.

Buolamwini, J. (2024). *Unmasking AI: My mission to protect what is human in a world of machines*. Random House.

Coots, M., Linn, K. A., Goel, S., Navathe, A. S., & Parikh, R. B. (2025). Racial bias in clinical and population health algorithms: A critical review of current debates. *Annual Review of Public Health*, *46*(1), 46. DOI: 10.1146/annurev-publhealth-071823-112058 PMID: 39626231

Davies, D. (2025). *The Unaccountability Machine: Why Big Systems Make Terrible Decisions—and How the World Lost Its Mind*. University of Chicago Press.

Driscoll, P. J., Parnell, G. S., & Henderson, D. L. (Eds.). (2022). *Decision making in systems engineering and management*. John Wiley & Sons.

Egbert, S., & Mann, M. (2021). Discrimination in predictive policing: The (dangerous) myth of impartiality and the need for STS analysis. In *Automating crime prevention, surveillance, and military operations* (pp. 25–46). Springer International Publishing. DOI: 10.1007/978-3-030-73276-9_2

Gartner, D. R., Maples, C., Nash, M., & Howard-Bobiwash, H. (2023). Misracialization of Indigenous people in population health and mortality studies: A scoping review to establish promising practices. *Epidemiologic Reviews*, *45*(1), 63–81. DOI: 10.1093/epirev/mxad001 PMID: 37022309

Geffner, C. J. (2023). *Building a new leadership ladder: Transforming male-dominated organizations to support women on the rise*. Mit Press. DOI: 10.7551/mitpress/14386.001.0001

Gigerenzer, G. (2022). *How to stay smart in a smart world: Why human intelligence still beats algorithms*. MIT Press.

Gogoll, J., Zuber, N., Kacianka, S., Greger, T., Pretschner, A., & Nida-Rümelin, J. (2021). Ethics in the software development process: From codes of conduct to ethical deliberation. *Philosophy & Technology*, *34*(4), 1085–1108. DOI: 10.1007/s13347-021-00451-w

Gonzalez-Nucamendi, A., Noguez, J., Neri, L., Robledo-Rella, V., & García-Castelán, R. M. G. (2023, October). Predictive analytics study to determine undergraduate students at risk of dropout. []). Frontiers Media SA.]. *Frontiers in Education*, *8*, 1244686. DOI: 10.3389/feduc.2023.1244686

Hull, G. (2023). Dirty data labeled dirt cheap: Epistemic injustice in machine learning systems. *Ethics and Information Technology*, *25*(3), 38. DOI: 10.1007/s10676-023-09712-y

Jones, C. (2021). Western centric research methods?: Exposing international practices. *Journal of ASEAN Studies*, *9*(1), 87–100. DOI: 10.21512/jas.v9i1.7380

Keles, S. (2023). Navigating in the moral landscape: Analysing bias and discrimination in AI through philosophical inquiry. *AI and Ethics*, •••, 1–11.

Kyriakidou, O. (2025). Algorithms and global diversity management. In *Research Handbook on Global Diversity Management* (pp. 148–163). Edward Elgar Publishing. DOI: 10.4337/9781035311170.00018

Lloyd, P. (2022). Ethical imagination and design. In *About Designing* (pp. 85–99). CRC Press.

Marchant, G. E., & Gutierrez, C. I. (2022). Soft law 2.0: An agile and effective governance approach for artificial intelligence. *Minnesota Journal of Law, Science & Technology*, *24*, 375.

McDaniel, A. (2023). *How Do At-Risk and Non-At-Risk School District Business Leaders Approach and Perceive Planning for Capital Projects?* Hofstra University.

Nickel, J. (2021). Trade-offs in Design: A Theory Building Qualitative Study on the Role of Problem Formulation and Framing in Resolving Trade-offs in Design (Master's thesis, University of Waterloo).

Poirier, L. (2021). Reading datasets: Strategies for interpreting the politics of data signification. *Big Data & Society*, *8*(2), 20539517211029322. DOI: 10.1177/20539517211029322

Poszler, F., & Lange, B. (2024). The impact of intelligent decision-support systems on humans' ethical decision-making: A systematic literature review and an integrated framework. *Technological Forecasting and Social Change*, *204*, 123403. DOI: 10.1016/j.techfore.2024.123403

Rahmani, E., Zandi, S., & Kiani, F. (2024). AI in Public Administration: Legal Implications for Automated Government Decision-Making. *Legal Studies in Digital Age*, *3*(1), 35–43.

Rejmaniak, R. (2021). Bias in artificial intelligence systems. *Białostockie Studia Prawnicze*, *3*(26), 25–42. DOI: 10.15290/bsp.2021.26.03.02

Roblek, V., Meško, M., Pušavec, F., & Likar, B. (2021). The role and meaning of the digital transformation as a disruptive innovation on small and medium manufacturing enterprises. *Frontiers in Psychology*, *12*, 592528. DOI: 10.3389/fpsyg.2021.592528 PMID: 34177680

Sartori, L., & Theodorou, A. (2022). A sociotechnical perspective for the future of AI: Narratives, inequalities, and human control. *Ethics and Information Technology*, *24*(1), 4. DOI: 10.1007/s10676-022-09624-3

Sinnreich, A., & Gilbert, J. (2024). *The secret life of data: Navigating hype and uncertainty in the age of algorithmic surveillance*. MIT Press. DOI: 10.7551/mitpress/14040.001.0001

Strantz, A. (2025). Coding Ethically as a Writer and Designer. In *The Routledge Handbook of Ethics in Technical and Professional Communication* (pp. 221–229). Routledge. DOI: 10.4324/9781003434375-26

Tahir, G. A. (2024). Ethical Challenges in Computer Vision: Ensuring Privacy and Mitigating Bias in Publicly Available Datasets. arXiv preprint arXiv:2409.10533.

Thijssen, L., Van Tubergen, F., Coenders, M., Hellpap, R., & Jak, S. (2022). Discrimination of black and muslim minority groups in western societies: Evidence from a meta-analysis of field experiments. *The International Migration Review*, *56*(3), 843–880. DOI: 10.1177/01979183211045044

Thiyagalingam, J., Shankar, M., Fox, G., & Hey, T. (2022). Scientific machine learning benchmarks. *Nature Reviews. Physics*, *4*(6), 413–420. DOI: 10.1038/s42254-022-00441-7

Volti, R., & Croissant, J. (2024). *Society and technological change*. Waveland Press.

Wang, A., Morgenstern, J., & Dickerson, J. P. (2025). Large language models that replace human participants can harmfully misportray and flatten identity groups. *Nature Machine Intelligence*, *7*(3), 1–12. DOI: 10.1038/s42256-025-00986-z

Wiggins, C., & Jones, M. L. (2023). *How data happened: A history from the age of reason to the age of algorithms*. WW Norton & Company.

Yucer, S., Tektas, F., Al Moubayed, N., & Breckon, T. (2024). Racial bias within face recognition: A survey. *ACM Computing Surveys*, *57*(4), 1–39. DOI: 10.1145/3705295

Zhu, Y. (2024). The Impact of Algorithmic Control and Algorithmic Management in Online Labor Platforms (Doctoral dissertation, University of Arkansas).

Chapter 3
AI in Higher Education: The Risk of Excluding Vulnerable Learners

Mustafa Kayyali
https://orcid.org/0000-0003-3300-262X
Maaref University of Applied Sciences, Syria

ABSTRACT

As artificial intelligence becomes deeply embedded in higher education—from admissions algorithms to adaptive learning systems—questions of equity take center stage. While AI promises personalization and efficiency, it also risks entrenching structural inequalities, often in ways that go unnoticed. For learners already on the margins—those from low-income backgrounds, with disabilities, or limited digital access—AI systems can inadvertently become gatekeepers rather than enablers. This chapter interrogates how algorithmic design choices, data gaps, and institutional priorities can exclude vulnerable students under the guise of innovation. It advocates for an ethical and inclusive approach to educational AI—one grounded in transparency, human oversight, and genuine stakeholder inclusion. In doing so, it reframes technological advancement not as an inevitable march forward, but as a set of choices with profound implications for who gets to learn, succeed, and belong in the digital university.

INTRODUCTION

The rapid integration of artificial intelligence into higher education is often framed in the language of progress. Universities are increasingly adopting AI-powered tools to automate admissions, personalize learning, identify at-risk students, manage administrative loads, and streamline decision-making processes. This momentum

DOI: 10.4018/979-8-3373-2685-6.ch003

Copyright © 2026, IGI Global Scientific Publishing. Copying or distributing in print or electronic forms without written permission of IGI Global Scientific Publishing is prohibited.

is not without reason. The sheer scale and complexity of today's educational systems demand efficiencies that human-led operations alone struggle to meet. With the growing pressure to do more with less, AI offers a seductive promise: faster evaluations, deeper insights, and greater personalization at a fraction of the cost (Vallabhaneni et al, 2024).

Yet, behind this optimism lies a quieter, more unsettling reality—one that speaks to who benefits from AI in education, and who risks being left behind. When technologies are deployed without careful scrutiny of the social systems in which they operate, they risk amplifying the very inequalities they purport to solve. Nowhere is this tension more visible than in how AI tools interact with students on the margins—those whose lives, learning needs, and lived realities fall outside the dominant data narratives. First-generation college students, learners with disabilities, students from impoverished or rural backgrounds, and those facing linguistic, racial, or gender-based discrimination often find themselves misunderstood or misclassified by systems trained on normative datasets.

Artificial intelligence is only as fair as the data it's built upon and the assumptions it encodes (McCarthy, 2022). When educational AI systems are trained on datasets that reflect historical bias, socioeconomic imbalance, and cultural exclusion, the risk is not merely technical—it is profoundly ethical. These systems become mechanisms of silent gatekeeping, reinforcing systemic disadvantages under the guise of neutrality. A recommendation algorithm may steer certain students toward less rigorous courses. An automated essay scorer may penalize non-native writing patterns. A facial recognition system may fail to identify students of color during online proctoring (Labayen et al, 2021). These are not edge cases; they are lived realities for many vulnerable learners navigating an already unequal educational landscape.

This chapter does not argue against AI in higher education. Rather, it makes a plea for a deeper reckoning—one that centers ethical inclusion, human oversight, and social justice in every stage of AI's educational lifecycle. It invites educators, policymakers, developers, and students to ask harder questions: Who is shaping these tools? Whose voices are missing? Whose data is deemed valid? What assumptions are encoded into the models? What trade-offs are being made—and by whom? The risks of exclusion are not theoretical; they are unfolding in real time, often invisibly, beneath the surface of well-meaning innovation. Unless these challenges are brought into the open, the digital university of tomorrow may reproduce the same barriers that have long existed—only now, with greater scale, speed, and opacity. As we stand at this critical juncture, the choices we make today will determine not only the future of educational technology, but the kind of society we are shaping through it.

UNEQUAL FOUNDATIONS: HOW AI MIRRORS EDUCATIONAL INEQUITIES

There's a common misconception about technology—particularly artificial intelligence—that it emerges from some sterile vacuum, a realm where logic is pure, data is truth, and decisions are made free of the messy constraints of human bias (Williams, 2022). This belief, seductive in its simplicity, is especially persistent in education, a field that has long struggled with subjectivity, inequality, and the aching burden of overburdened systems. Many want to believe that AI can be a great leveler, finally offering a meritocratic framework where performance—not privilege—guides outcomes. But when we look closely, when we really pay attention, the picture gets murkier. AI doesn't cleanse us of our biases. It codifies them. It sharpens them. And often, it hides them so deep within its architecture that by the time they surface, the harm is already done.

Let's begin with something basic—data. The cornerstone of any AI system. But data, contrary to the popular notion of it being "objective," is anything but. It's historical, contextual, and deeply human. It reflects decisions made over decades—sometimes centuries—of policy, pedagogy, and privilege. In the realm of higher education, data means grades, attendance, test scores, application histories, behavioral flags, digital interaction patterns (Weinberg, 2024). All of these are shaped by prior experiences and unequal starting lines. A low GPA isn't just a number; it might be a marker of attending underfunded schools, juggling part-time jobs to support family, or navigating undiagnosed learning challenges without support. A gap in digital engagement may have less to do with student motivation and more to do with unreliable broadband or shared household devices (Kayyali, 2025 d).

Yet AI systems don't typically ask "why" when processing these signals. They recognize patterns. They reward consistency. And in doing so, they begin to replicate the exact disparities that have long haunted educational systems. When an algorithm is trained on past admissions data that privileged applicants from elite schools, it learns to value those credentials more heavily. When a predictive model is built on student success rates skewed by race, geography, or disability, it learns that success looks a certain way—and flags deviations as risk (Brooks et al, 2023). It's not that the algorithm "wants" to discriminate. It simply reflects the world we gave it, and in doing so, gives that world back to us with the cold authority of math.

Here's the quiet tragedy: most of these systems operate behind the scenes. Their decisions are rarely visible to the students they affect. A learner may never know that their application was downgraded by an algorithm that saw their zip code as a red flag. A student flagged as "at risk" by a retention tool might receive extra support—or be subject to increased surveillance—without understanding the why behind it. Transparency, already scarce in bureaucratic education systems, becomes even more elusive in the age of machine learning. And then there's the myth of personalization. AI in education is often sold on the promise of tailored learning—platforms that adapt to student pace, interest, and ability (Rane et al, 2023). But what happens when the adaptation is based on flawed assumptions? A system might lower the difficulty of reading materials for a student flagged as struggling, limiting exposure to challenging content. An early classification as a "slow learner" might shape all subsequent learning trajectories, creating a self-fulfilling prophecy masked as customized instruction. Under the guise of help, the system narrows possibilities.

In vulnerable student populations—those historically underserved by education—this is particularly dangerous. Students with learning disabilities may find that AI-based assessments penalize their atypical responses (Hu, 2024). Those with non-standard English patterns, shaped by bilingual households or regional dialects, may be rated lower by automated grading systems. Students from minority groups might find that facial recognition tools used for remote proctoring struggle to identify them, leading to flagging or even disciplinary actions. These aren't hypotheticals. These are documented realities. And let's not forget the infrastructure gap—the chasm between students who have reliable access to devices, quiet study spaces, and high-speed internet, and those who don't. The assumption that AI-enhanced learning can be equitably accessed across the board is a fantasy. A machine-learning model might recommend additional resources, but what if the student doesn't have the bandwidth to download them? What if their home environment is too chaotic for sustained concentration? What if they're working a night shift and the system marks their asynchronous participation as disengagement?

AI doesn't see context. It sees data. And data, absent of human nuance, is a dangerous thing to build decisions upon. But perhaps the most insidious danger of all is subtlety (Comşa et al, 2021). AI rarely excludes in overt, headline-grabbing ways. It doesn't slam doors. It quietly nudges them closed. A student's recommendations may shift slightly. Their visibility within the system may decline. Opportunities may gradually bypass them. These are exclusions by a thousand cuts—hard to detect, harder to contest, and nearly impossible to trace back to a single decision point. The student may internalize these signals: *Maybe I'm just not smart enough. Maybe I don't belong here.* And the system, humming along invisibly, reinforces the cycle.

There's also the matter of who gets to build these systems in the first place. Educational AI tools are often developed by private companies—tech firms far removed from the day-to-day realities of classrooms and campus life (Qutieshat, 2025). Their design teams may lack diversity. Their product goals may prioritize scalability over sensitivity, market fit over moral fit. When vulnerable learners are not at the table in the development of these tools, their needs are not reflected in the outcome. Inclusion must start not just with users, but with creators.

This isn't to paint all of AI as villainous. There are genuinely powerful examples of AI helping bridge educational gaps—tools that transcribe lectures for hearing-impaired students, platforms that help dyslexic learners engage with text more fluently, or systems that flag early warning signs for mental health risks. But the line between help and harm is razor-thin, and often the difference lies not in the algorithm itself, but in the awareness, intention, and ethics of those who deploy it. So, what can be done?

- First, we must stop treating AI as a magic fix. It's not a replacement for human judgment, but a supplement—one that requires critical oversight, contextual understanding, and ongoing interrogation. Educational institutions must demand transparency from vendors, ask hard questions about data provenance, and involve educators and students—especially those from vulnerable groups—in the design and review of these tools.
- Second, we need to build richer, more representative datasets. This means not just collecting more data, but better data—data that accounts for socio-economic variables, access gaps, learning differences, and cultural nuance. It means acknowledging that standardized measures of success are deeply flawed and expanding the ways we define learning, engagement, and growth.
- Third, we must center ethics—not as an afterthought, but as the foundation. Bias audits, impact assessments, and inclusive design protocols must be baked into every phase of AI development and deployment. Accountability must be built in—not only technically, but institutionally and socially. If a tool causes harm, there must be mechanisms for redress, for human appeal, for reconsideration.
- Finally, we need a culture shift. We need to resist the seduction of efficiency when it comes at the expense of empathy. We must remember that education is not just about knowledge transmission. It is about dignity, about possibility, about shaping futures. If our tools don't uplift the most vulnerable, they're not innovative—they're just new iterations of the same old injustice.

There's a haunting irony at the heart of this discussion. Many of the students most at risk of exclusion are those for whom higher education represents the greatest hope (Berry et al, 2024). They come seeking transformation, opportunity, a way out of generational cycles of struggle. They come trusting that the system will see them, support them, and help them rise. If AI blinds us to their realities—if it encodes their disadvantage into the system—it doesn't just fail them. It betrays them.

This chapter doesn't pretend to have all the answers. But it insists on better questions. It demands that we pay attention to the hidden seams, the unseen forces, and the silent signals embedded in our educational technologies. It urges us to interrogate not just what AI *does*, but what it *means*—for access, for equity, and for the very purpose of education itself. We are standing on unequal foundations. And unless we reckon with them honestly, the structures we build—no matter how advanced—will always be tilted. Not by malice, but by neglect. Not by design, but by default. And that, perhaps, is the most urgent truth of all.

ALGORITHMIC GATEKEEPERS: BIAS, DATA, AND THE MARGINALIZED STUDENT

It's easy to miss the gatekeepers when they don't wear uniforms or sit behind glass. They don't raise eyebrows or ask for paperwork. They don't speak, really. Not in the way we expect. Instead, they live in code—in tangled lines of algorithms hidden behind institutional dashboards and polished ed-tech interfaces. They score, predict, recommend, approve, deny. Quietly. Invisibly. And without ever asking the student how they got here, what they're carrying, or what they've already had to overcome just to sit in a virtual classroom and be counted. These are the algorithmic gatekeepers of modern higher education. And they are changing everything. Not always in the ways we think.

It starts with data. Not the abstract kind we talk about in conferences or policy briefs, but real data—raw, messy, intimately human data: grades, attendance, login times, IP addresses, facial expressions, eye movement, keystroke dynamics. It piles up in the background of every click, every module completed, every multiple-choice question attempted at midnight on a borrowed device. Universities, once mostly analog in their systems of evaluation, now traffic in torrents of digital traces. And somewhere, deep in the back end of these systems, algorithms hum away—processing, analyzing, comparing.

The idea, in theory, is sound: to use data to enhance decisions, personalize learning, detect problems early (Chen, 2023). But here's the thing about algorithms: they don't understand context. They don't pause to ask why a student submitted five assignments at 3 a.m., or why their webcam feed was blurry during an exam. They don't consider that someone might be learning in a car, parked outside a fast food restaurant, just to get Wi-Fi. They aren't wired for empathy. They're wired for output. And the outputs? They matter. Sometimes, they matter *too* much. An admissions algorithm might flag an applicant's profile as "low probability of success" based on patterns from previous cohorts—patterns that disproportionately favor students from better-funded schools, those with AP credits, extracurriculars, stable housing. A retention tool might assign a risk score based on GPA dips and decreased LMS (Learning Management System) activity, overlooking that the student in question is dealing with a death in the family or a job loss (Ortakand, 2024). A facial recognition system used for online proctoring might fail to detect darker skin tones, prompting alerts or accusations of cheating.

Each of these instances, taken in isolation, might seem like technical bugs, anomalies to be patched. But when they accumulate—when they become part of the architecture of academic systems—they cease to be glitches. They become structural. Predictable. Systemic. And students who already exist at the periphery—students of color, disabled students, international students, first-generation college-goers—start to experience technology not as a bridge, but as a barrier.

Table 1. Common AI Biases and Their Impact

AI Function	Type of Bias	Impact on Learners
Essay Scoring	Linguistic Bias	Penalizes non-native English patterns
Facial Recognition	Racial Bias	Fails to recognize darker skin tones during proctoring
Admissions Algorithms	Socioeconomic Bias	Flags low-income ZIP codes as risk
Learning Analytics	Behavioral Bias	Interprets irregular study patterns as disengagement

There's an eerie kind of automation bias at play here—the belief that decisions made by machines are somehow more objective, more trustworthy, than those made by people (Jones-Jang & Park, 2023). It's understandable. Human decision-makers are fallible. They carry conscious and unconscious bias. But so do machines. The difference is: machines don't *know* they're doing it. They can't unlearn it. Not without our intervention. And that's the catch—most institutions don't really know how these algorithms work. Many of the tools used in higher education today are proprietary, black-box systems developed by private vendors. Universities buy them, plug them in, and trust them to function. Rarely is there meaningful transparency about how these models were trained, what data was used, or what biases might be embedded within them. Faculty and staff may not be trained to interpret algorithmic outputs. Students are almost never consulted. And so a strange dynamic emerges: decisions are made, often with significant impact, by systems no one fully understands.

There's something haunting about that. Because when an algorithm decides a student is likely to fail, that student might be steered away from more challenging coursework. Or they might be offered remedial content that bores them, further disengaging them. Or they might not be offered anything at all—just quietly deprioritized in the backend of some intervention queue. The system, seeking to optimize outcomes, has already placed its bets. The student? They're just data now. But students aren't data. They're complex, contradictory, evolving human beings. They grow. They regress. They surprise. They don't always fit neatly into predictive models—and that's exactly why education exists in the first place: to help people become more than their pasts. More than their metrics.

The algorithm doesn't always see that. Especially not when it's trained on past performance indicators that already reflect historical inequities (Coglianese & Lai, 2021). Because let's be honest: data doesn't just fall from the sky. It's harvested from systems built on uneven ground. If marginalized students have historically had lower graduation rates, higher dropout rates, or inconsistent attendance, that's not a reflection of who they are—it's a reflection of what they've faced. When an algorithm treats these outcomes as neutral inputs, it absorbs the bias and magnifies it. Not out of malice. Out of math. So where does that leave the marginalized student?

In many cases, it leaves them behind. They are less likely to have access to the kinds of digital devices and broadband connections that AI-powered platforms assume. Less likely to be represented in the datasets used to train these systems. Less likely to have advocates within institutions who understand the ways AI may disadvantage them. And more likely to be misunderstood, miscategorized, or simply missed.

Some might argue that the answer is more data—better data. And yes, richer, more inclusive datasets are part of the solution. But they are not the whole answer. Because the deeper issue is not just data, but power. Who designs the algorithms? Who owns them? Who audits them? Who gets to define what "success" looks like? These are not technical questions. They are moral ones. Political ones.

If we want to challenge algorithmic bias in education, we have to start there—with the politics of prediction (Baker & Hawn, 2022). With the uncomfortable recognition that not all students start from the same place, and that using their past to predict their future can be a form of quiet violence. We have to build systems that account for complexity, that ask more than just "What is likely?" but "What is fair?" "What is humane?" "What is possible?"

Figure 1. Algorithmic bias

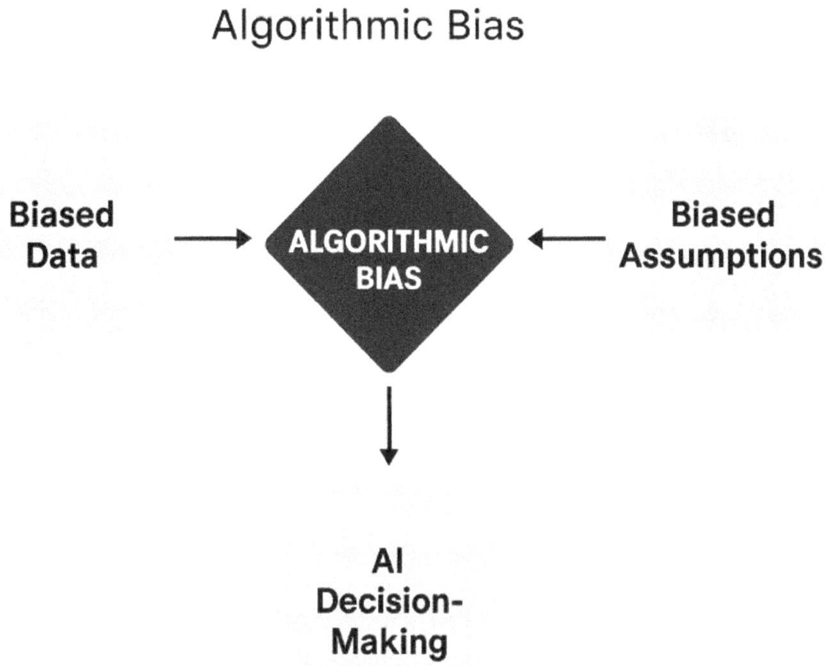

That means designing with the marginalized student in mind—not as an afterthought, but as the standard. It means involving those students in conversations about how these systems are built and used. It means creating mechanisms for appeal, for oversight, for redress. It means opening the black box. And it means, perhaps most radically, slowing down. In a culture that worships efficiency, that values automation and scale, slowing down feels counterintuitive. But it's necessary. Because inclusion takes time. Justice takes care. And if we move too fast—if we rely too heavily on machines to make decisions we haven't fully thought through—we risk building systems that are efficient, scalable, and utterly inhumane.

There's a line from a student interview I can't stop thinking about. She said, "It feels like the system already decided I wasn't going to make it. Before I even got a chance to prove I could." That's what an algorithm can do, when it's fed a narrow view of the world and unleashed without accountability. It can make the decision before the student ever opens their mouth. We have to be better than that. We have to remember that education, at its core, is not about predicting outcomes. It's about expanding them (Maghsudi et al, 2021). It's about believing that people can change, can grow, can overcome. And that belief cannot be coded into an algorithm. It lives in the space between people—in the pause before a decision, in the choice to ask another question, in the willingness to hold possibility open just a little longer. Algorithms may be part of the future of education. But they must never become its soul.

THE SILENT DIVIDE: DIGITAL LITERACY AND ACCESS DISPARITIES

You don't always see the divide. It's not marked by fences or gates, not etched into the pavement or coded into policy in any explicit way. No sign tells you who can cross and who can't. It exists in silences, in absences, in subtle lags and dropped connections. In the nervous glance of a student unsure which button to click, or the hesitation in their voice when asked to share a screen. It exists in the awkward confessions—*"My camera doesn't work,"* or *"Sorry, I missed the deadline; the internet went out again."* And sometimes, it doesn't exist in words at all. It exists in the students who simply disappear.

The digital divide is rarely loud. It doesn't usually erupt in protest or policy scandal (Taylor, 2023). It's not photogenic. It doesn't make headlines—at least not often. But it is everywhere, pulsing just beneath the surface of classrooms that have gone virtual, learning that's gone algorithmic, systems that are now built with AI, connectivity, and 24/7 access assumed as default. But here's the thing: access isn't default. It never has been.

Figure 2. Digital Divide

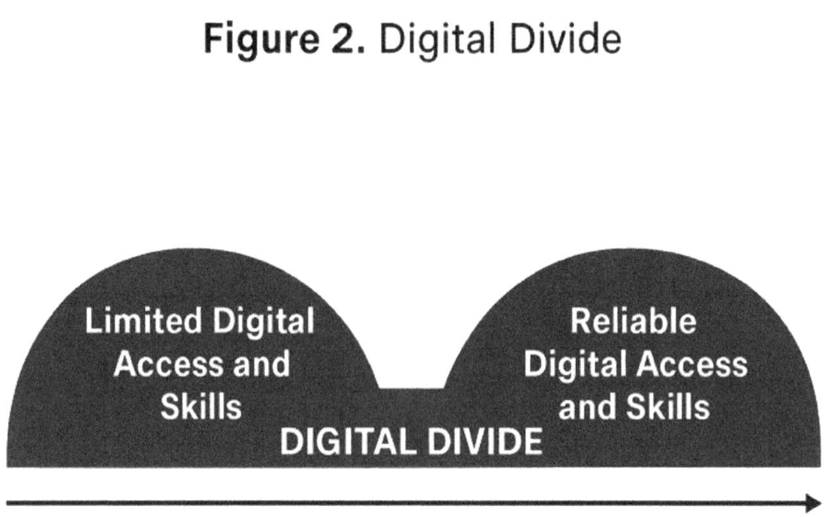

There's this dangerous assumption floating around the edtech space—that because students are "digital natives," they must be digitally fluent. As if growing up with smartphones magically equips one to navigate complex digital ecosystems, to interpret algorithmic feedback, to troubleshoot system crashes during high-stakes assessments. It doesn't. Not automatically. Not evenly. Not fairly. Watching videos on TikTok is not the same as understanding how to manipulate a digital dashboard, submit multimedia coursework, or recognize when your learning analytics profile is steering your academic path in a certain direction (Elkadi, 2021). There's a literacy gap, and it's not about age—it's about opportunity.

Digital literacy is not just about knowing how to use technology. It's about knowing *what* the technology is doing (Nikou et al, 2022). It's about understanding that a score generated by a machine can carry weight, that clicking "agree" on a pop-up may have consequences, that data trails are being left behind and may be used to shape—or limit—your experience. It's about being critically aware. And in a higher education landscape increasingly reliant on AI-powered tools, that awareness isn't just useful—it's essential. But many students never get that awareness. Not because they're incapable. Because no one teaches it. Because we assume they already have it. Because we think access to the internet is the same as access to understanding. It's not.

Let's talk about infrastructure. Let's talk about the students whose homes double as classrooms, whose younger siblings fight for bandwidth, whose quietest study space is a parked car or a public library that closes too early. Let's talk about the cracked phone screens, the outdated operating systems, the laptops that take 15 minutes just to boot up. These aren't fringe cases. They're reality for millions of learners across the world, even in so-called "developed" countries. And yet, our systems move forward as if everyone's on the same page, on the same device, with the same stability.

We build AI learning systems that require consistent engagement—daily logins, timed assessments, real-time feedback loops (Godwin Olaoye et al, 2024). We automate support services and academic counseling, assuming students can navigate a maze of drop-down menus and chatbot interactions. We create dashboards full of data visualizations, assuming students know how to interpret the arcs and dots and trend lines that supposedly represent their learning journey. But what happens when they don't? What happens when digital literacy lags behind the sophistication of the tools?

What happens is that students start falling behind—not because they're not intelligent, not because they lack ambition—but because they're navigating a system built on assumptions that do not include them. And the worst part? Many of them blame themselves. They don't say, "This tool wasn't designed with me in mind." They say, "Maybe I'm just not cut out for this." They internalize the friction, the struggle, the confusion. They think the problem is them. But the problem is us. It's institutional. It's architectural. It's the silent divide baked into our digital transformation plans and AI rollouts. Let's look at something as simple—and as revealing—as email.

In some universities, students are expected to monitor multiple inboxes: institutional accounts, learning platform messages, automated reminders from scheduling bots (Mithun et al, 2024). A missed message can mean a missed deadline, a missed opportunity, a dropped course. But digital communication assumes fluency—understanding the tone of academic emails, recognizing legitimate sources, responding appropriately. For students from under-resourced educational backgrounds, or for first-generation students unfamiliar with higher ed's linguistic norms, this can be a minefield. A simple misstep can lead to misunderstanding, embarrassment, or worse. And then there's AI.

AI-driven platforms often don't explain themselves. They make recommendations or decisions—course suggestions, warnings, performance nudges—without clarifying how those conclusions were reached (Luo et al, 2024). For students with high digital confidence, this might not be a problem. They'll click around, explore, decode. But for students with limited digital literacy, it creates confusion and anxiety. Some won't ask for help because they're embarrassed. Others will ask and be met with blank stares from instructors equally unsure of how the system works. The opacity compounds. The silence grows. And the divide deepens. Here's something else we don't talk about enough: cultural literacy in digital environments.

Imagine a student from a rural area, or a refugee background, or an indigenous community, logging into a platform built by and for urban, Western, middle-class learners (Mangion, 2024). The language might be English, but it's coded in ways that alienate. The examples are foreign. The icons don't make sense. The humor feels off. Even the help center articles feel like they're written for someone else.

This isn't just about hardware. It's about identity. About belonging. About whether students see themselves reflected in the systems designed to "help" them. And when they don't, they disconnect—not just technically, but emotionally. They disengage. They fade. You'll hear educators say, "They stopped coming to class." But often, it starts earlier: *They stopped feeling seen.* And let's not forget disabled students—learners with visual, auditory, cognitive, or motor impairments who often face multiple layers of exclusion in digital learning environments. Many AI-powered tools aren't designed with accessibility in mind. Automated captioning systems mangle speech. Screen readers get lost in poorly coded content. Keyboard navigation is inconsistent. Even something as simple as a timed quiz can become an insurmountable barrier. These students don't lack digital literacy. The systems lack them.

We talk so much about "closing the gap," but rarely do we ask who created the gap to begin with. Technology didn't invent inequity. But it often exacerbates it. Quietly. Efficiently. At scale. So, what do we do?

- First, we have to name it. We have to acknowledge that digital access is not binary—it's not just about having or not having a device. It's about stability, reliability, usability, and cultural legibility. It's about whether students can use the tools *effectively*, *comfortably*, *confidently*. That's digital inclusion.
- Second, we have to embed digital literacy into the curriculum—not as a side note, but as a core component of education (Kayyali, 2025 c). Students need to understand how their data is used, how AI makes decisions, how to advocate for themselves in algorithmic systems. They need to learn the soft skills of tech navigation: how to communicate digitally, how to recognize bias, how to stay safe online. These are not "extras." They are survival skills in a digitized world.
- Third, we have to demand that edtech companies and AI developers work in partnership with educators and learners—especially marginalized learners. We need co-design, not top-down deployment. We need systems built with multilingualism, accessibility, and cultural context baked in from the start—not tacked on as afterthoughts.
- Fourth, institutions need to provide real infrastructure support. Loaner devices are not enough. There must be funding for Wi-Fi access, for tech troubleshooting, for quiet study spaces. There must be respect for students who learn in non-traditional ways, who juggle caregiving responsibilities, who live in digital deserts.
- Finally, we have to humanize our systems. Not everything should be automated. Not every message should come from a bot. Sometimes what students need most is not a recommendation, but a conversation. Not a dashboard, but a door that's open.

Because the digital divide isn't just about technology. It's about humanity (Voss, 2024). It's about who feels welcome, who feels supported, who feels like they matter in a system increasingly driven by code. There's no algorithm for that. But there's you. And me. And the choices we make—about design, about policy, about where we put our attention. The silent divide doesn't have to stay silent. If we listen closely, it's already speaking. And we still have time to answer.

INCLUSIVE BY DESIGN? RETHINKING AI FOR EDUCATIONAL JUSTICE

There's a buzz around the word *"inclusive."* Everyone's using it. University mission statements, edtech startups, corporate press releases, even the fine print of AI-powered learning platforms. *Inclusive by design* (Chopra et al, 2024). It sounds good. Progressive. Ethical. But if we lean in—if we really examine what's behind that phrase—we find that inclusion is too often assumed, not interrogated. Claimed, not earned. Declared, not lived. In the architecture of AI systems used in higher education, the promise of inclusion has become a veneer—something that coats the surface but rarely reaches the core. What would it mean to truly design for inclusion? Not as a branding strategy, but as a moral imperative?

The answer isn't easy. It's not a checklist or a plug-in or a last-minute accessibility patch. Designing AI that genuinely serves educational justice requires us to sit with discomfort, to challenge assumptions, to unearth the quiet violences baked into our data and decisions (Macgilchrist, 2023). It demands that we slow down—radically slow down—in a system obsessed with optimization. It calls for a reckoning: not just with our tools, but with ourselves. Because the truth is, AI does not exist apart from the world. It reflects it. Distorts it. Sometimes crystallizes it. And if that world is unjust—which it is—then so too are the systems we build with it, unless we intervene deliberately, boldly, and continually. Let's talk design.

Most AI systems in higher education today are not built by educators (Doğan et al, 2025). They're built by engineers, designers, data scientists—often with limited understanding of the classroom, of pedagogy, of the chaotic, messy, beautiful variability of human learning. And even when these teams include educational consultants or instructional designers, how often are students—especially those from marginalized groups—brought into the process? Rarely. And that matters. Because inclusion isn't something you can retroactively add. You can't build a structure for the average user and then hope it accommodates those at the edges. You have to start at the margins. You have to build *with* the most excluded students in mind—from the beginning. That's what inclusive design really means. But to do that, you have to ask hard questions.

Who gets to define what counts as "success" in an AI model? Is it GPA? Course completion? Retention? These are institutional goals, not necessarily learner goals. And they're shaped by histories of exclusion. If your model defines a "successful student" using data from the past, and that data skews white, affluent, neurotypical, able-bodied—you're going to design a system that performs well for those students and fails others in silence. You'll get polished dashboards and predictive insights. But you won't get justice. And justice, in education, is not a technical achievement.

It's a relational one. It's about who gets seen, who gets supported, who gets space to grow in ways that may not be legible to algorithms.

There's a myth in AI that fairness is something you can bake into the code (Blackwell, 2024). Add a fairness constraint here, balance the dataset there, and voila! An equitable system. But fairness isn't just about symmetry. It's about context. Two students might receive the same "personalized" learning path, but one had to work two jobs to get there, the other had private tutoring. One has dyslexia, the other doesn't. One has trauma that shapes their cognition, the other walks into class with a clear head. Equity demands we respond to these differences, not flatten them. AI, at its worst, flattens.

It's built on averages, on standard deviations, on norms. But education should be anything but normative. It should celebrate deviance—from expected paths, from standardized benchmarks, from rigid outcomes. Inclusive AI design must resist the pull toward uniformity. It must build for plurality, for outliers, for the students who've never fit into neat categories. And that's hard. Technically hard. Politically hard. Institutionally hard.

It means designing systems that don't just *scale*, but *listen*. That adapt not just based on performance metrics, but based on dialogue, on human feedback, on lived experience. It means integrating qualitative data, narrative data, emotional data. It means building systems that are accountable—not just in the legal sense, but in the ethical sense (Kayyali, 2025 b). Systems that can be questioned, challenged, revised.

Take explainability, for example. Most AI systems in education offer little to no insight into *how* decisions are made. A student is flagged as at-risk. A course recommendation is made (Wang, 2021). A writing score is generated. But on what basis? What signals were prioritized? What trade-offs were made? Inclusive design demands transparency—not just for auditors or developers, but for students themselves. Especially marginalized students, who have every reason to be wary of systems that classify them. They should be able to ask: *Why was I flagged? What data informed this suggestion? Can I opt out? Can I appeal?* And the system should respond—not with static FAQ pages or boilerplate blurbs, but with clarity, with humility, with mechanisms for redress. Because inclusion without agency is not inclusion. It's control.

Inclusive AI must give power back to learners. It must recognize that students are not just subjects of analysis, but agents of their own learning (Bulathwela et al, 2024). They should have access to their data, the ability to contest it, the opportunity to shape it. And that includes shaping the very systems that govern them. This means bringing students—especially those at the margins—into the design process. Not in tokenistic ways. Not as a focus group to validate a finished product. But as co-creators, co-deciders. Ask them: *What do you need from this system? What are your fears, your hopes, your frustrations?* Then listen. Deeply. Uncomfortably. Because when you design with exclusion in mind—when you assume that bias will creep in unless you actively fight it—you build differently. You ask different questions. You make different choices. And you learn that inclusion isn't a static state. It's a practice. Ongoing. Messy. Iterative. Let's talk failure.

An inclusive system must be able to fail gracefully. That is, it must be designed with the expectation that it will make mistakes—and that those mistakes will disproportionately affect those already at risk. If your system flags a student incorrectly, how easy is it for that student to contest it? Is there a human they can talk to? Will they be believed? If not, then you haven't built for justice. You've built for efficiency. And efficiency, while seductive, is rarely equitable.

Table 2. Strategies for Inclusive AI Design

Design Principle	Description
Participatory Design	Involve diverse students in AI system development
Bias Audits	Regularly evaluate datasets for embedded biases
Explainability	Ensure students understand how decisions are made
Infrastructure Support	Provide reliable devices and internet access

The deeper challenge here is epistemological. Inclusive AI requires us to rethink what we value in education. Do we prioritize speed, scale, prediction? Or do we prioritize care, complexity, and growth? The former lends itself to automation (Younas & Zeng, 2024). The latter resists it. But perhaps resistance is what we need. Not resistance to AI, but resistance to uncritical adoption. To techno-solutionism. To the belief that inclusion is a feature, not a philosophy. Because justice isn't found in an API. It's found in the pause before deployment. In the conversation after an alert is triggered. In the decision to prioritize human judgment over algorithmic inference—when it really matters.

Designing for inclusion means embracing the fact that the neatest solution may not be the most ethical one (Zallio, M., & Clarkson, 2021). That sometimes, the most powerful thing an AI system can do is *ask the human to decide.* And when it does act, it must act with care. That's not a word you often hear in AI circles. But it should be. Care means slowing down when a student falters. It means building systems that can say, *"We see you. We're not sure what's going on, but we're here."* Care means recognizing that data tells part of the story, and that part may be wildly misleading. Care means building systems that don't just respond to metrics, but to meaning. And meaning comes from relationship—from the bond between teacher and student, mentor and learner, peer and peer.

AI can support that. It can scaffold it. But it cannot replace it. So where do we go from here? We reimagine. We stop asking how AI can make education more efficient, and start asking how it can make education more humane. We stop asking how to scale learning, and start asking how to deepen it. We stop building systems *for* students, and start building systems *with* them. We embrace the fact that inclusion is not a destination. It's a direction. A way of walking. A way of seeing. And if we walk that path—if we design with intention, with humility, with care—we just might build systems that not only include, but transform. Not just education. But us.

BUILDING AN EQUITABLE FUTURE: POLICIES, PEDAGOGIES, AND HUMAN OVERSIGHT

Equity is not an app you can download. It's not a checkbox on an audit form or a line item buried in a university's strategic vision statement. It's not the latest buzzword woven into edtech marketing. No, it's messier. Slower. More human. Equity is built—brick by brick—through daily decisions, institutional will, cultural shifts, and above all, through deliberate care (Todic et al, 2022). And when artificial intelligence enters the picture, equity doesn't automatically scale. It either fractures further or forces us to finally face the cracks we've ignored for too long.

Let's begin with a simple, unavoidable tension: AI is here. It's embedded in the rhythms of higher education now—in course design, administrative workflows, admissions filtering, plagiarism detection, early-alert systems, adaptive testing, even student mental health triage (Weinberg, 2024). The promise? Faster. Smarter. Fairer. But as we've seen, especially through the quiet testimonies of students most likely to be overlooked, AI is not inherently equitable. It mirrors power. It reflects its makers. It amplifies whatever values and assumptions are smuggled into its architecture—silently, persistently, and at scale. So how do we interrupt this trajectory? How do we pivot from systems that automate exclusion to ones that anticipate injustice and actively resist it?

Let's not pretend this is a purely technical problem. It's a political one. A cultural one. A pedagogical one. To build an equitable future in the age of AI, we need to recalibrate the entire ecosystem of higher education—from how policies are written to how pedagogy is practiced to how oversight is embedded not as an afterthought, but as a living ethical force. Start with policy.

But not the kind of policy that lives in dusty PDFs or floats above the heads of students and educators in some bureaucratic ether. We need grounded policy—flexible, alive, embedded into practice. Policies that don't just talk about diversity in abstract terms but specify mechanisms for equity in data collection, algorithm deployment, and platform accountability (Yu, 2021). We need language that insists on participatory design and continuous bias audits. Language that mandates accessibility as a non-negotiable baseline, not a feature for later. Language that protects students' rights to understand how their data is used, to challenge automated decisions, to opt out without penalty. And these policies must be crafted with students—especially those from historically excluded groups—not just included but empowered. Co-authorship is not symbolic. It's strategic. Because those closest to harm often hold the clearest insights into what safety, dignity, and justice would actually look like. But policies alone don't transform culture. They can guide, but they can't inspire. That's where pedagogy enters.

Pedagogy is more than method. It's worldview. It's the daily choreography of how we teach, how we learn, how we treat each other in the sacred (and now digital) spaces of inquiry and growth. If AI is changing the tools, pedagogy must change the questions. It must ask: *What does it mean to teach with machines that learn? What does it mean to assess a student through layers of algorithmic inference? How do we ensure that personalization doesn't become prediction, and prediction doesn't become prescription?*

An equitable pedagogy in the AI era begins with humility. It acknowledges that no system, no matter how sophisticated, can replace the relational depth of education (Lettieri, 2025). That feedback loops and recommendation engines may assist, but they cannot interpret the silences in a student's eyes, the hesitation in their voice, the weight of the world they carry into a classroom. Technology may signal, but it is pedagogy that interprets. That translates. That responds. And so educators must be trained—not just in how to use AI tools, but in how to critique them, how to contextualize them, how to question their recommendations. Critical digital pedagogy should be standard, not optional. Students, too, must be invited into these conversations. They must learn not just how to navigate platforms, but how to recognize algorithmic bias, how to advocate for themselves, how to co-author their learning paths.

Imagine a classroom where the learning management system makes a suggestion, but it's treated not as a directive, but a prompt for dialogue. Imagine students asking: *Why was this recommended? What were the underlying signals? Does this path align with my goals, or does it reflect assumptions about who I'm supposed to be?* That's pedagogical justice. That's digital agency. Now, none of this is possible without oversight. But oversight, too, needs reimagining. It can't just be reactive. It must be anticipatory, iterative, collaborative. We need ethical review boards for educational AI systems—ones that include not just technologists and administrators, but educators, students, accessibility experts, cultural anthropologists (Nguyen et al, 2023). People who understand that fairness is contextual. That equity can't be abstracted from lived experience. And this oversight must be continuous. AI systems learn. They evolve. They drift. A model that performs fairly today may be wildly off-target tomorrow as usage patterns shift, new cohorts arrive, or external contexts change. Equity can't be one audit and done. It has to live in the system—through regular impact assessments, feedback loops, student reporting mechanisms, and institutional transparency dashboards that show, in real time, where inequities may be emerging.

Oversight also means consequences. If a system is found to disadvantage a certain group—intentionally or not—there must be pathways for redress. For accountability. For reparation. Too often, the burden of proof falls on students to demonstrate harm, to navigate appeals, to beg for reconsideration. An equitable future flips that burden (Kayyali, 2025 a). It asks institutions to prove that their systems are safe, just, inclusive. That may require uncomfortable introspection. Disbanding tools that seemed promising. Canceling contracts. Publicly acknowledging harm. But this is the price of justice. Not just money, but humility. And then—there's the bigger picture. The cultural one. What kind of academic culture do we want in the age of AI?

Do we want one where students are numbers in dashboards, risk scores in spreadsheets, targets in marketing funnels? Or one where they are treated as whole people—messy, unpredictable, brilliant in ways no machine can anticipate? Do we want institutions to chase automation for the sake of budget cuts? Or to pause, reflect, and ask what role humans should continue to play—must continue to play—in learning, mentorship, and care? Do we want AI to make decisions *about* students? Or to support decisions *with* them? These aren't just design questions (Feroz et al, 2024). They're moral questions. And they demand moral courage. Because equity in the AI age isn't just about inclusion. It's about transformation. It's about rebuilding systems that were never neutral. Rewriting rules that were never fair. Redistributing power in spaces where some voices have always been louder, more legible, more welcome. And that kind of rebuilding—it's slow. It's not flashy. It doesn't lend itself to press releases or KPI charts. But it's necessary. Urgent. Non-negotiable.

Maybe that's the paradox we have to embrace: using technology to slow down. To deepen. To listen more, automate less. To invite reflection before reaction. To center care over calculation. Because equity, in the end, is not about getting everyone to the same place using the same path. It's about recognizing that people start in different places, carry different burdens, move at different speeds—and building systems that adapt with integrity. AI can help us do that. But only if we let it be a tool, not a truth. A partner, not a prophet. A mirror, not a master. And only if we stay involved. Fully. Humanly. Relentlessly. Because building an equitable future isn't just the job of policymakers or engineers or ethicists (Kayyali, 2024). It's all of us. Every syllabus we write. Every tool we deploy. Every policy we revise. Every student we see. Especially the ones the system doesn't.

CONCLUSION

As we reflect on the expanding role of artificial intelligence in higher education, it becomes painfully clear that technological advancement is not a neutral process. It is deeply political, laden with values, assumptions, and worldviews that shape who is seen, who is supported, and who is rendered invisible. AI holds the potential to personalize learning journeys, reduce dropout rates, and improve educational outcomes—but it also holds the potential to exacerbate structural inequities if not governed wisely.

This duality presents both a challenge and a responsibility. If the design and deployment of AI systems are left solely to technocrats or market-driven imperatives, they will inevitably serve the most visible, measurable, and already-advantaged groups. Vulnerable learners—those who navigate education with fewer resources, less support, and greater systemic barriers—will continue to fall through algorithmic cracks. Their absence in training data, their divergence from normative benchmarks, and their limited access to digital infrastructure all contribute to a self-reinforcing cycle of exclusion.

What is urgently needed now is a shift in how we conceptualize "intelligence"—both human and artificial—in the educational sphere. Intelligence cannot be reduced to test scores, behavioral patterns, or predicted learning paths. Nor should we treat it as something that AI alone can map or manage. True educational intelligence is empathetic, relational, contextual, and responsive to complexity. It involves listening to the margins, valuing human judgment, and building systems that are not just efficient, but equitable.

This means embracing a new paradigm: inclusion by design. From the earliest stages of algorithm development, we must ask who stands to benefit and who stands to lose. Inclusion must not be an afterthought or a set of patches applied post-hoc. It must be embedded in the data we collect, the questions we ask, and the metrics we use to define success. Educational institutions must work alongside communities of learners—especially those who are marginalized—to co-create technologies that reflect their realities, respect their autonomy, and support their aspirations.

Moreover, we must move beyond the idea that AI can, or should, replace human insight in matters of judgment and care. There is a profound difference between optimizing student performance and nurturing student potential. The former can be programmed; the latter requires presence, intuition, and moral imagination. If we are to build truly just educational futures, we must ensure that AI supports—not supplants—the human relationships at the heart of learning.

In the end, the question is not whether AI belongs in higher education. It already does. The real question is: Whose education will it enhance—and at what cost? This chapter calls for a future in which innovation is not measured solely by speed or scale, but by the extent to which it uplifts the most vulnerable, restores human dignity, and cultivates a culture of care in digital spaces. Only then can we say that AI in education is truly serving its purpose—not just to inform, but to include.

REFERENCES

Baker, R. S., & Hawn, A. (2022). Algorithmic bias in education. *International Journal of Artificial Intelligence in Education*, •••, 1–41.

Berry, C., Acharya, N., & Crowter, L. (2024). The light at the end of the tunnel? A systematic review of higher education student experiences of hope. *PLoS One*, *19*(6), e0304596. DOI: 10.1371/journal.pone.0304596 PMID: 38885226

Blackwell, A. F. (2024). *Moral Codes: Designing Alternatives to AI*. MIT Press. DOI: 10.7551/mitpress/14872.001.0001

Brooks, C., Kovanović, V., & Nguyen, Q. (2023). Predictive modeling of student success. In *Handbook of artificial intelligence in education* (pp. 350–369). Edward Elgar Publishing. DOI: 10.4337/9781800375413.00027

Bulathwela, S., Pérez-Ortiz, M., Holloway, C., Cukurova, M., & Shawe-Taylor, J. (2024). Artificial intelligence alone will not democratise education: On educational inequality, techno-solutionism and inclusive tools. *Sustainability (Basel)*, *16*(2), 781. DOI: 10.3390/su16020781

Chen, Z. (2023). Artificial intelligence-virtual trainer: Innovative didactics aimed at personalized training needs. *Journal of the Knowledge Economy*, *14*(2), 2007–2025. DOI: 10.1007/s13132-022-00985-0 PMID: 40479149

Chopra, A., Patel, H., Rajput, D. S., & Bansal, N. (2024). Empowering Inclusive Education: Leveraging AI-ML and Innovative Tech Stacks to Support Students with Learning Disabilities in Higher Education. In *Applied Assistive Technologies and Informatics for Students with Disabilities* (pp. 255–275). Springer Nature Singapore. DOI: 10.1007/978-981-97-0914-4_15

Coglianese, C., & Lai, A. (2021). Algorithm vs. algorithm. *Duke Law Journal*, *71*, 1281.

Comşa, I. S., Molnar, A., Tal, I., Bergamin, P., Muntean, G. M., Muntean, C. H., & Trestian, R. (2021). A machine learning resource allocation solution to improve video quality in remote education. *IEEE Transactions on Broadcasting*, *67*(3), 664–684. DOI: 10.1109/TBC.2021.3068872

Doğan, M., Celik, A., & Arslan, H. (2025). AI In Higher Education: Risks and Opportunities From the Academician Perspective. *European Journal of Education*, *60*(1), e12863. DOI: 10.1111/ejed.12863

Elkadi, L. (2021). Student Engagement with Specialised Videos in Higher Education (Doctoral dissertation, University of East Anglia).

Feroz, A. K., Khan, G. F., & Sponder, M. (2024). *Digital analytics for marketing*. Routledge.

Godwin Olaoye, J. O., Flypaper, D., Oluwaseyi, J., & Brightwood, S. (2024). Ai-driven adaptive learning systems: enhancing student engagement.

Hu, A. (2024). Developing an ai-based psychometric system for assessing learning difficulties and adaptive system to overcome: A qualitative and conceptual framework. arXiv preprint arXiv:2403.06284.

Jones-Jang, S. M., & Park, Y. J. (2023). How do people react to AI failure? Automation bias, algorithmic aversion, and perceived controllability. *Journal of Computer-Mediated Communication*, *28*(1), zmac029. DOI: 10.1093/jcmc/zmac029

Kayyali, M. (2024). Future possibilities and challenges of AI in education. In *Transforming education with generative AI: Prompt engineering and synthetic content creation* (pp. 118–137). IGI Global Scientific Publishing. DOI: 10.4018/979-8-3693-1351-0.ch006

Kayyali, M. (2025a). The Future of AI in Education: Predictions and Emerging Trends. Next-Generation AI Methodologies in Education, 367-406.

Kayyali, M. (2025b). Ethical Implications of Generative AI in Education: Privacy, Bias, and Integrity. In Transformative AI Practices for Personalized Learning Strategies (pp. 185-218). IGI Global Scientific Publishing.

Kayyali, M. (2025c). AI in Higher Education: Revolutionizing Curriculum and Administration. In AI Adoption and Diffusion in Education (pp. 31-62). IGI Global Scientific Publishing.

Kayyali, M. (2025d). Harnessing AI for Digital Entrepreneurship: Strategies and Best Practices. In Improving Entrepreneurial Processes Through Advanced AI (pp. 1-20). IGI Global.

Labayen, M., Vea, R., Flórez, J., Aginako, N., & Sierra, B. (2021). Online student authentication and proctoring system based on multimodal biometrics technology. *IEEE Access : Practical Innovations, Open Solutions*, *9*, 72398–72411. DOI: 10.1109/ACCESS.2021.3079375

Lettieri, M. (2025). Embracing Empathy: How AI Technologies Enhance the Pedagogy of Kindness in Education. In Redefining Education With Pandemic Pedagogies (pp. 167-186). IGI Global.

Luo, Y., Kumar, N., & Yazdanmehr, A. (2024). Ai Nudging and Decision Quality: Evidence from Randomized Experiments in Online Recommendation Setting. Available at *SSRN* 4967812. DOI: 10.2139/ssrn.4967812

Macgilchrist, F. (2023). Design justice and educational technology: Designing in the fissures. In *World Yearbook of Education 2024* (pp. 294–310). Routledge.

Maghsudi, S., Lan, A., Xu, J., & van Der Schaar, M. (2021). Personalized education in the artificial intelligence era: What to expect next. *IEEE Signal Processing Magazine*, *38*(3), 37–50. DOI: 10.1109/MSP.2021.3055032

Mangion, A. (2024). Making good on migration: Exploring narratives of aspiration and imagined futures with students from migrant backgrounds (Doctoral dissertation, Australian Catholic University).

McCarthy, J. (2022). Artificial intelligence, logic, and formalising common sense. Machine Learning and the City: Applications in Architecture and Urban Design, 69-90.

Mithun, P., Kumar, R. D., & Dikshit, S. (2024, April). IntelliCampus: AI-Powered College Portal with Auto-Scheduler and News Sharing. In *2024 International Conference on Knowledge Engineering and Communication Systems (ICKECS)* (Vol. 1, pp. 1-11). IEEE. DOI: 10.1109/ICKECS61492.2024.10616672

Nguyen, A., Ngo, H. N., Hong, Y., Dang, B., & Nguyen, B. P. T. (2023). Ethical principles for artificial intelligence in education. *Education and Information Technologies*, *28*(4), 4221–4241. DOI: 10.1007/s10639-022-11316-w PMID: 36254344

Nikou, S., De Reuver, M., & Mahboob Kanafi, M. (2022). Workplace literacy skills—How information and digital literacy affect adoption of digital technology. *The Journal of Documentation*, *78*(7), 371–391. DOI: 10.1108/JD-12-2021-0241

Ortakand, B. R. (2024). Monitor and Predict Student Engagement and Retention Using Learning Management System (LMS). In Teaching and Learning in the Digital Era: Issues and Studies (pp. 259-277).

Qutieshat, A. (2025). *Artificial Intelligence in Higher Education: A Contemporary Examination of Illich's Theories*. Springer Nature. DOI: 10.1007/978-981-97-9989-3

Rane, N., Choudhary, S., & Rane, J. (2023). Education 4.0 and 5.0: Integrating artificial intelligence (AI) for personalized and adaptive learning.

Taylor, J. (2023). *Digital tools, rhetoric, and meaning-making: A critical exploration of addressing the digital divide and accessibility to improve our digital landscape*. Iowa State University.

Todic, J., Cook, S. C., Spitzer-Shohat, S., Williams, J. S.Jr, Battle, B. A., Jackson, J., & Chin, M. H. (2022). Critical theory, culture change, and achieving health equity in health care settings. *Academic Medicine*, *97*(7), 977–988. DOI: 10.1097/ACM.0000000000004680 PMID: 35353723

Vallabhaneni, A. S., Perla, A., Regalla, R. R., & Kumari, N. (2024). The Power of Personalization: AI-Driven Recommendations. In Minds Unveiled (pp. 111-127). Productivity Press.

Voss, A. (2024). The Future We're Building: How Today's Innovations Will Shape Tomorrow's World. eBookIt. com.

Wang, Y. (2021). When artificial intelligence meets educational leaders' data-informed decision-making: A cautionary tale. *Studies in Educational Evaluation*, *69*, 100872. DOI: 10.1016/j.stueduc.2020.100872

Weinberg, L. (2024). *Smart University: Student Surveillance in the Digital Age*. JHU Press. DOI: 10.56021/9781421450018

Williams, D. P. (2022). Belief, Values, Bias, and Agency: Development of and Entanglement with "Artificial Intelligence" (Doctoral dissertation, Virginia Polytechnic Institute and State University).

Younas, A., & Zeng, Y. (2024). A Philosophical Inquiry into AI-Inclusive Epistemology. Available at *SSRN* 4902415.

Yu, P. K. (2021). Beyond transparency and accountability: Three additional features algorithm designers should build into intelligent platforms. *NEULR*, *13*, 263.

Zallio, M., & Clarkson, P. J. (2021). Inclusion, diversity, equity and accessibility in the built environment: A study of architectural design practice. *Building and Environment*, *206*, 108352. DOI: 10.1016/j.buildenv.2021.108352

KEY TERMS AND DEFINITIONS

Algorithmic Bias: Systemic distortions in AI decision-making caused by biased data or assumptions embedded in algorithms.

Automation Bias: The tendency to over-rely on machine-generated decisions, often at the expense of human judgment or fairness.

Digital Divide: The gap between individuals with reliable digital access and skills and those without, affecting educational equity.

Educational Inequity: Structural disparities in learning opportunities and outcomes, often reinforced by uncritical adoption of AI technologies.

Ethical Oversight: Continuous human evaluation of AI systems to ensure transparency, fairness, and accountability in education.

Inclusion by Design: An intentional approach to building AI systems that prioritize the needs of marginalized learners from the outset.

Predictive Modeling: The use of AI algorithms to forecast student performance or risk based on historical and behavioral data.

Chapter 4

Knowledge Management as a Strategic Driver of Educational Quality and Institutional Competitiveness in Higher Education

Manuel Alfredo Ortiz-Barrera
https://orcid.org/0000-0001-6738-8941
University of Guadalajara, Mexico

Luis Alberto Bellon-Alvarez
https://orcid.org/0000-0001-5630-4263
University of Guadalajara, Mexico

Jorge Pelayo-Maciel
https://orcid.org/0000-0003-4011-0178
University of Guadalajara, Mexico

ABSTRACT

This study examines the interplay between knowledge management, educational quality, and institutional competitiveness in higher education. Using structural equation modeling (SEM), we analyzed survey data from 210 professors at the University of Guadalajara to assess how knowledge creation, dissemination, and application influence academic excellence and competitive positioning. The model confirms knowledge management as a critical driver of both quality enhancement

DOI: 10.4018/979-8-3373-2685-6.ch004

Copyright © 2026, IGI Global Scientific Publishing. Copying or distributing in print or electronic forms without written permission of IGI Global Scientific Publishing is prohibited.

($p = 0.852$) and institutional competitiveness ($p = 0.962$), highlighting gaps in measuring intangible factors. The findings advocate for integrated knowledge strategies aligned with academic missions and suggest exploring emerging technologies, such as artificial intelligence (AI), to optimize these processes. This research provides actionable insights for universities seeking to leverage knowledge assets for sustainable innovation in increasingly interconnected academic landscapes.

INTRODUCTION

The university stands as one of the oldest and most esteemed institutions in the entire span of human history, holding a significant place in the legacy of higher education. Its importance is deeply rooted in its unique structure, which, despite being rooted in tradition and history, has consistently served a vital role in nurturing and training professionals across a wide array of fields and disciplines, making it a cornerstone in the development of knowledge and expertise worldwide.

For each graduate leaving the classroom, their education has played a significant role in shaping their respective societies, especially from economic, social, scientific, and cultural viewpoints, thereby positioning them as agents of change (Chankseliani & McCowan, 2020).

The educational mission of the university goes far beyond simply transmitting knowledge to students. It also encompasses the vital task of shaping and fostering critical thinking, responsibility, and a strong sense of social commitment among its students. These qualities are essential for cultivating citizens who are not only well-educated but also actively engaged and instrumental in bringing about positive societal transformation.

On the other hand, integrating Artificial Intelligence (AI) into academic institutions is rapidly transforming the teaching process.

It presents a multitude of advantages, including the facilitation of individualized learning experiences, which enables learners to progress at their rhythm following their specific requirements (Fui-Hoon Nah et al., 2023); enhanced instructional methodologies, as it fosters critical thinking and aligns pedagogical frameworks such as constructivism and self-directed learning; and it cultivates efficiency and innovation through the automation of administrative functions, complemented by curriculum development, thereby liberating educators to concentrate on strategic and creative endeavors (Maphalala & Ajani, 2025).

Notwithstanding the benefits, AI engenders various ethical dilemmas, including concerns regarding academic integrity, as it has the potential to produce plagiarism and diminish creativity and originality in both teaching and research.

An additional concern pertains to data privacy and security, given that AI systems often aggregate personal information, as well as the phenomenon of human displacement arising from the growing reliance on AI in educational decision-making processes (Khatri & Karki, 2023; Mauti & Ayieko, 2025).

To address these challenges, it is crucial to establish robust ethical guidelines and frameworks that prioritize transparency and accountability in AI applications within the education sector.

Within this framework, the richness and diversity of academic thought that emanate from universities constitute an inexhaustible source of proposals, ideas, and solutions to address the multiple challenges posed by an increasingly complex, dynamic, and interconnected world (Fialho et al., 2023).

This plurality of voices and perspectives enhances the academic environment, positioning the university as a privileged space for critical reflection, knowledge creation, and the formulation of responses to global issues.

This continuous process of transformation and adaptation primarily depends on considering educational elements as a crucial link. However, it is also essential to understand that the issues confronting higher education institutions (HEIs) extend beyond just pedagogical concerns.

Contemporary demands also necessitate a thorough reassessment of the administrative and managerial models that govern university operations. In this regard, the growing need for more efficient and innovative approaches to university management has become increasingly evident.

Knowledge management emerges as a crucial and highly valuable tool for effectively addressing and overcoming various complex challenges faced by organizations. It accomplishes this by facilitating the comprehensive consolidation of organizational learning, enabling the organization to systematically gather, organize, and retain its collective knowledge. Additionally, it promotes the effective capitalization and utilization of existing knowledge, encouraging continuous innovation and adaptation within the organization. Furthermore, by leveraging these capabilities, knowledge management helps in constructing and maintaining sustainable competitive advantages that can endure over time, ensuring long-term success and resilience.

This concept, understood as a strategic administrative instrument, has gained growing relevance across various types of organizations, particularly in those where knowledge is considered the most valuable and abundant asset (Laal, 2011).

Nevertheless, its growing popularity should not be perceived as a fleeting trend or a short-term tendency; rather, it reflects a new productive and economic paradigm in which knowledge, in its multiple forms, becomes the central axis for generating value, efficiency, and differentiation (Stankosky, 2005).

Within this new framework, effective knowledge management requires the development of organizational capabilities to identify, structure, share, and utilize accumulated information and experience, thereby fostering continuous learning at both the individual and institutional levels.

The transformations shaping today's global landscape require universities to establish adaptive processes that respond quickly and effectively. These processes depend on environments with strong personal and digital connections, allowing knowledge to be shared, reused, and turned into innovative solutions.

Such dynamics enable the creation of unique and differentiating elements that directly contribute to the continuous improvement of academic, pedagogical, and administrative processes within higher education institutions.

Against this backdrop, the primary objective of the present study is to analyze how the effective implementation of knowledge management can act as a catalyst for the development of competitive advantages in the university setting.

Through this approach, it becomes possible to enhance the quality of educational programs, optimize academic and teaching activities, and foster an institutional culture that is oriented toward innovation, excellence, and sustainability.

Ultimately, understanding and applying the principles of knowledge management in higher education institutions not only constitutes a strategy for addressing current challenges but also offers an opportunity to redefine the university's role as a driver of social and scientific development in the twenty-first century.

ARTIFICIAL INTELLIGENCE: DIGITAL GAPS AND BIASES IN HIGHER EDUCATION

Education in the 21st Century is undergoing a rapid transformation, primarily driven by Technological advancements, globalization, and demographic shifts (Rahiman & Kodikal, 2023).

Among these technological advances, artificial intelligence (AI) represents significant progress in understanding interdisciplinary roles within the educational environment, serving as a sophisticated tool that can be applied across diverse domains of human knowledge.

Contemporary challenges in information processing within higher education institutions are often hindered when proper technical tools are not integrated into institutional operations (Ryzheva et al., 2024).

AI-based systems typically operate within clear, rule-based frameworks. These systems utilize machine learning and deep learning algorithms to drive generative AI technologies (Sabbaghan & Eaton, 2025).

Such generative interfaces currently represent the height of computational progress, as they can convert written data into audio, images, reconfigurable text, and problem-solving outputs through ongoing machine learning (Dogru et al., 2023).

This suggests that integrating AI as an educational tool in higher education institutions could provide significant benefits in teaching, research, and learning, if its use is properly guided and strategically managed to maximize its positive effects (Bozkurt, 2024).

From a pedagogical perspective, it is therefore crucial to establish specific criteria for its implementation—criteria that support not only technical skills but also academic reflexivity and integrity, while encouraging critical values such as honesty, courage, fairness, and responsibility (Moya et al., 2023).

This necessity is further emphasized by the ambivalent perceptions associated with the integration of artificial intelligence in educational environments—marked by students' enthusiasm for the technology and educators' concerns about possible violations of academic integrity (Chan & Hu, 2023).

Particular attention has been paid to generative AI applications, which, as previously noted, are highly versatile in educational settings. However, these technologies also pose ethical challenges related to authorship, originality of academic work, and potential algorithmic biases (Cordero et al., 2024).

Such concerns are not surprising, given that the integration of advanced technology into teaching and learning processes is still a relatively new development (Voss et al., 2023; Watermeyer et al., 2023).

Nevertheless, given the current state of universities worldwide, the rise of AI represents a paradigm shift—one that can align with traditional education principles but requires an evaluative perspective that considers the interaction between human cognition and the effects of machine language development (Sabbaghan & Eaton, 2025).

Within this framework, AI algorithms can play a key role in the academic process, offering flexible adjustments to the curriculum, automating mundane tasks, and—most importantly—reducing disparities in student understanding (Jereb & Urh, 2024).

These disparities, often inherent in traditional learning environments, may be seen as a variable within human cognition (Baker & Hawn, 2022). However, in virtualized learning settings, the focus should be on reducing such biases through uniform instructional design that accommodates diverse learning styles within the classroom (Holstein & Doroudi, 2021).

Therefore, the goal of integrating AI into education must extend beyond simply generating prompts; it should focus on enhancing the effective use of technology in the classroom and supporting the development of a more comprehensive educational model for both instructors and students (Baker & Hawn, 2022).

Although such implementations might seem seamless in the daily operations of universities, several challenges still exist, especially from a Latin American perspective.

First, structural constraints persist, as many campuses still lack the necessary physical infrastructure to support widespread adoption of AI technology.

Second, economic inequality among technological stakeholders, namely, instructors and students, continues to restrict access to digital tools, becoming a significant barrier to equitable participation (Subramaniam et al., 2023).

Nonetheless, this should not be perceived as an insurmountable barrier, but rather as an opportunity to formulate integrated mixed-method strategies that synergize technological implementation with pedagogical innovation (Marinovic, 2025). Over time, such methodologies have the potential to significantly mitigate existing digital disparities and facilitate profound educational transformation by enhancing intangible academic and cognitive competencies.

KNOWLEDGE IN HIGHER EDUCATION INSTITUTIONS

At the higher education level, the educational sector is currently in a critical phase that challenges existing administrative and pedagogical paradigms (Khoa & Huynh, 2023).

While knowledge remains a vital asset in the daily operations of educational institutions, the global perspective increasingly supports greater interconnectedness and the strategic use of internally generated knowledge.

Effective knowledge management recognizes the intangible nature of cognitive resources while also understanding their invaluable worth. It has become a core element for universities that aim not only to deliver education but also to promote scientific progress actively (Galdames, 2024).

Knowledge is the most abundant resource within what are called "learning organizations," and its use and management promote stakeholder collaboration under three key conditions (Santos et al., 2024): creation, dissemination, and application.

These three foundational elements strengthen the roles of researchers, students, faculty, and, more broadly, knowledge producers (Antunes & Pinheiro, 2019)—even when they work with tacit knowledge, which is difficult to codify and recognize due to its inherent nature.

Based on this academic perspective, higher education institutions must examine and promote strategies that strengthen internal relationships between knowledge producers and consumers, as well as to develop organizational capabilities to effectively adapt to changes in the surrounding environment (Donate & Canales, 2012).

According to Nonaka (1994), the original knowledge management model emphasizes the dynamic interaction between human capital and environmental factors.

This interaction, coupled with an ongoing pursuit of innovation, contributes to the development of resilient organizational structures that can capture ideas, convert them into knowledge, and, in certain instances, cultivate organizational wisdom.

Such processes strike a balance between experiential knowledge and systematic understanding, thereby enhancing the organization's intellectual robustness (Allal-Chérif & Makhlouf, 2015).

However, valuing knowledge availability and quality requires solid foundations that support proper and sustainable use through three key factors (Chen & Wang, 2012):

- Engagement with stakeholders, especially external ones.
- Advancement in technology and the search for new, research-driven knowledge.
- Organizing existing tacit knowledge.

The main challenge involves separating epistemological foundations within cognitive theory and developing them to support empirical contributions, thus encouraging real changes in Higher Education Institutions (HEIs).

Learning, knowledge creation, and proper storage are essential pillars in building sustainable competitive advantages within organizations (Zutshi et al., 2023). However, simply accumulating knowledge is not enough; its actual value becomes apparent when effective dissemination strategies are employed, transforming this intangible asset into concrete innovation (Chen et al., 2024).

Therefore, disseminating research-based knowledge is a strategic necessity (Siegel et al., 2004), serving not only as the final step in academia but also as a bridge linking theory and practice.

Its proper implementation bridges the traditional gap between conceptual frameworks and the practical demands of industry, creating a two-way knowledge exchange that benefits both academia and the productive sector.

EDUCATIONAL QUALITY AND KNOWLEDGE MANAGEMENT

Following the 2020 pandemic, educational institutions gleaned critical insights, particularly regarding the integration of information technologies to augment pedagogical effectiveness (Ban et al., 2024).

While many schools worldwide had already adopted this process earlier, the post-pandemic period saw a surge in efforts to enhance remote connectivity (Muca et al., 2022).

However, beyond technological updates, a radical shift occurred in understanding educational quality standards. Although these frameworks were already in use, they needed significant adjustments to meet modern demands (Krooi et al., 2024).

Higher education institutions (HEIs) have increasingly shifted toward operational models that resemble global industries more than traditional academic structures. This shift has created a demand for more highly qualified professionals across diverse - often interdisciplinary - fields of knowledge (Naidoo, 2006).

Within this context, educational quality has become a strategic factor that allows HEIs to concentrate on meeting environmental needs while establishing clear, measurable standards.

From a utilitarian perspective, control systems generally operate as feedback loops that provide outputs and ongoing assessments of teaching staff, curricula, and learning objectives (Aoudia et al., 2015).

From the students' perspective, educational quality mainly relates to personal fulfillment, practical features, and the dependability of their interactions with educational services. Essentially, it covers their everyday experiences and the expectations they have from their service providers (Hammound, 2015).

For the productive sector, educational quality ensures that university graduates are adequately prepared to meet the demands of the labor market, thereby contributing to economic development and the competitiveness of businesses and nations.

To achieve this, the educational system must be flexible, practical, and focused on developing valuable skills while maintaining a strong connection with the productive sector (Demchig, 2015).

From the government's perspective, educational quality encompasses equity, accessibility, continuous improvement, relevance, and the holistic development of students.

The government aims to ensure that the educational system equips students to be productive and engaged members of society, thereby contributing to national socioeconomic progress.

These elements are interconnected to form a dynamic and multifaceted framework that supports the proper development of human capital while adapting knowledge to the realities of its environment.

Various mechanisms enable HEIs to enhance both internal and external quality indicators, ensuring that expected outcomes directly impact student learning and development.

These mechanisms also provide pathways for cognitive development, both tacit and explicit, strengthening teaching and administrative functions, while fostering institutional empowerment and commitment (Bendermacher et al., 2017).

In this way, knowledge management becomes a key element for improving educational quality.

This is not only due to its capacity to compile and systematize knowledge within an environment of cognitive creation, but also because genuine knowledge exchange within HEIs can strengthen their institutional potential, adapting to both internal and external societal needs, and increasing innovation in educational processes (Gebreyohans et al., 2022).

Therefore, active members of the institution are encouraged to cultivate a collaborative environment where knowledge flows freely among faculty, students, and administrative staff, fostering spaces of ongoing exchange.

Such an environment not only strengthens individual capacities but also builds an institutional culture that values continuous learning and innovation, while also facilitating the identification of best practices.

COGNITIVE COMPETITIVENESS IN HIGHER EDUCATION INSTITUTIONS

The role that information and knowledge currently play in the "education industry" is essential for the actions and activities it naturally produces (Kettinger et al., 2021).

Knowledge and the assets derived from managing it serve as key elements in the ongoing improvement of educational organizations, boosting their potential through proper scientific development. This is why knowledge management should be viewed as a source of competitive advantage, innovation, and enhanced organizational performance (Kusa et al., 2024; Wales et al., 2023; Shekhar & Valeri, 2023).

In the context of higher education institutions (HEIs), the strategic utilization of intangible resources—particularly those conferring competitive advantages—is essential for effectively responding to the dynamic and evolving competitive environment (Barney, 1995; Santati et al., 2024). Nevertheless, each university encounters distinct operational conditions influenced by environmental parameters and organizational factors (Sum & Jessop, 2012).

In this regard, HEIs must consider substantial changes to address these challenges, grounded in their organizational knowledge, knowledge management practices, and human capital (Hart & Rogers, 2023). By embracing organizational learning, institutions can enhance their competitive performance, fostering capabilities for continuous innovation and adaptability to changing environments (Jiménez-Jiménez & Sanz-Valle, 2010).

When examining competitive factors, the role of HEIs is closely tied to the concept of quality. While institutional processes, services, and intangible assets can be measured, the most emphasized dimensions include:

- Academic performance

- Academic reputation
- Faculty engagement
- Student satisfaction (Tarasenko et al., 2024)

Through these indicators, competitiveness can be assessed based on the quality of education. This approach also promotes the development of initiatives that support the local context and strategic partnerships with productive organizations (Davies et al., 2024).

HEIs are increasingly seeking to improve not only their standing in the academic landscape but also their sustainable development within broader societal systems (Mars, 2011).

Thus, competitive development is essential for enhancing relationships among HEIs, their human resources, and the intangibility of intellectual thought (Guzman et al., 2023).

It provides critical components for optimizing the use of knowledge and for strengthening educational quality through institutional wisdom and the effective utilization of internal resources.

METHODOLOGY

From a research-oriented perspective, the development of administrative elements aims to accurately describe existing patterns within organizations, which are conceived as living entities (Mogalakwe, 2006).

This process is typically supported by auxiliary methods, primarily the collection of secondary data, to clarify actions and elements that have emerged from similar situations.

Accordingly, the present study adopts a documentary research methodology (Baileys, 1969), drawing on previous investigations to analyze existing phenomena, as well as the various pathways associated with artificial intelligence, knowledge management, and competitiveness in higher education institutions.

Based on its technical and methodological characteristics, this document provides a foundation for specifically examining the factors related to each of these topics from a cross-sectional perspective.

This cross-sectional approach offers a snapshot of the research at a particular moment in time (Rodríguez & Mendivelso, 2018). Furthermore, the study is enriched by the active involvement of the research group in identifying theoretical elements and applying them throughout the research process.

As a complementary element, a confirmatory quantitative approach was chosen, grounded in the optimistic assumption that there is a single, objective reality (Claydon, 2015). This approach employs quantitative methods, with results interpreted in a balanced and objective manner (Higgins & Green, 2008).

Field implementation required the design of a closed-ended questionnaire, consisting of three main sections. The items are structured as Likert-type scale elements with five response options, which facilitates both rapid data collection and efficient processing.

Additionally, the sample was composed of 210 faculty members from the University of Guadalajara. The sampling strategy was determined using an infinite population formula, with a 95% confidence level and a 7% margin of error. The final sample size was then selected based on convenience.

To ensure the appropriate treatment of data, the initial step involved validating the instrument by calculating Cronbach's alpha coefficient. This statistic provides an indication of internal consistency and reliability, measuring the internal correlations of variables across different groups and offering a confidence index that supports the credibility of the collected data (Quero, 2010).

A correlational analysis using a structural equation modeling (SEM) approach is also proposed. SEM is a multivariate statistical technique that estimates parameters across multiple equations, allowing for the inclusion of multiple latent variables (factors).

This model aims to determine the existence of causal relationships, such as confirmatory hypothesis testing based on unidirectional elements (Stein et al., 2011). Through graphical representations, it is possible to observe the influence of a set of independent variables on a dependent variable.

This allows for the identification of whether the proposed factors are functionally appropriate for addressing the constructions under investigation and for assessing the pursuit of generally accepted truths.

Through this structural modeling process, it becomes possible to identify, first, which factors are functionally aligned with each section of the questionnaire, and second, to analyze the interrelationships among those factors.

In doing so, the model exhibits a high degree of replicability, enhancing the explanatory power of the research and validating the use of this methodological framework.

FINDINGS AND INTERPRETATION

An instrument designed based on the collection of secondary literature was applied. The resulting work generated a closed questionnaire with three sections: the first focused on knowledge management, assessing the tacit and explicit knowledge of organizations; the second on elements that constitute desirable educational quality; and the third on elements that measure organizational competitiveness.

This document obtained firsthand responses, which were used to perform correlational measurements between the dimensions proposed in the title of this document.

The sample cohort was based on stratified convenience sampling, where 210 professors from the University of Guadalajara were selected. They were active, had groups that collectively worked at least 8 hours per week, and were willing to provide their opinions on educational quality.

Regarding the sample, the results were determined with a 95% confidence level and a 7% margin of error. The numbers were analyzed based on the available sample, the requested characteristics, and, above all, the existing response capacity. This data was calculated using the infinite sampling formula.

Reliability of the Sample

The sample's reliability level was estimated based on Cronbach's alpha. An instrument's reliability values reflect the internal properties generated by the scalar consistency with which it was administered (Kılıç, 2016).

Although the measure is not perfect, it adequately approximates the internal consistency of the items, that is, the extent to which the items measure the same thing as the construct proposed ex ante (Tavakol & Dennick, 2011). Mathematically, reliability can be interpreted as the ratio of the actual variance score to the total variance score (McDonald, 1985; Carmines & Zeller, 1979).

Table 1. Nivel de Consistencia Interna con Alfa de Cronbach

Reliability Coefficient	Number of Items
Cronbach's $\alpha = 0.968$	50

Source: Self-produced from survey results

The data in Table 1 show that the internal consistency, measured by Cronbach's alpha, is very good. This agrees with researchers who suggest that a value of 0.8 or higher indicates reliable internal consistency (Kerlinger & Lee, 2002; Carmines & Zeller, 1979; Nunally, 1978).

Based on this result, it is assumed that the questionnaire includes the essential basic elements needed to be effectively processed and, therefore, to obtain projections or other relevant statistical data for creating an explanatory model using the available items and responses.

Measurement Model Fit Analysis

Confirmatory factor analysis (CFA) is a type of modeling using structural equations that allows for observing a priori the existing relationships between observed measures, or observed indicators, in terms of real variables and latent variables (Emmert-Aronson et al., 2014).

Figure 1. Internal Reliability Indices for the Education Quality Measurement Model

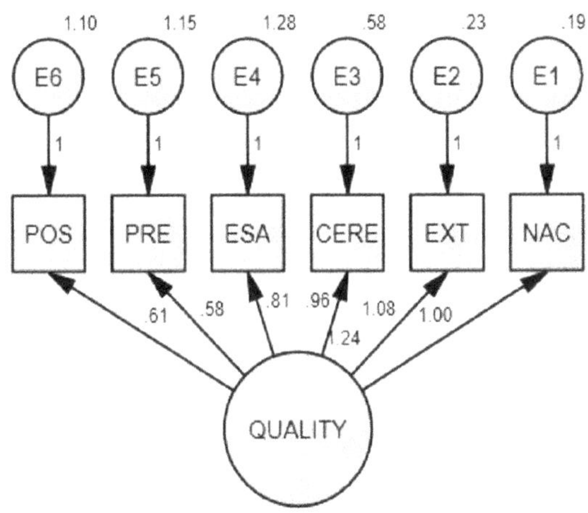

Source: Self-produced from survey results

Figure 1 shows a model that evaluates how well the variables used directly measure quality as a broad concept.

The results from the model, based on an analysis using structural equations, show that the elements of Postgraduate Certification (POS), Undergraduate Certification (PRE), and Standardized Tests (ESA) have significant values (1.10, 1.15, and 1.28, respectively), indicating that, overall, these key variables are significantly related. In other words, they can be considered essential components for measuring the quality in higher education institutions.

In cases of collaboration with external entities (EXT) and national entities (NAC), the values are very low, indicating a lack of sufficient evidence to include them in the model; that is, the quality of these relationships does not necessarily depend on their inclusion.

Table 2. Variable Ordering According to Structural Equation Estimates

Key	Variable	Initial Result	Std. Error
POS	Grad. Certification	0.61	1.10
PRE	Undergrad. Certification	0.58	1.15
ESA	Standardized Tests	0.81	1.28
CERE	External Bodies	1.2	0.58
EXT	External Collaboration	1.08	0.23
NAC	National Collaboration	1.00	0.29

Source: Self-produced from survey results

According to Mayer et al. (2019), the observed error metrics, exemplified by the data in the fourth column of Table 2, are affected by the correlation among these direct elements. This suggests that the assessment of the elements within the Quality dimension lacks consistency, implying that each item functions independently without synergistic interaction in the process of evaluating educational quality.

That is, based on the sample population, professors at the University of Guadalajara collaborate with national and international university entities, in addition to overseeing postgraduate and undergraduate certifications, and developing internal and external standardized tests.

However, none of these activities are truly associated with an educational quality process, demonstrating that this work, as such, must be developed broadly and with the capacity for honest work, benefiting both professors and higher education institutions. Furthermore, the fit values of the models were examined, particularly in their correlation with the variables considered latent in the structural equations, competitiveness, and knowledge management.

In both cases, the aim was to measure the relationship between covariances, specifically the relationship between educational quality and competitiveness, as well as educational quality and knowledge management.

Although both latent variables have their items, it was decided to perform a unitary dimension analysis. To achieve this, the average of the factors was calculated, and the dimensional impact was determined.

Table 3. Chi Square Minimum – Quality Competitiveness

Model Type	Parameters (NPAR)	Chi-Square (CMIN)	Degrees of Freedom (DF)	p-value
Default Model	12	12.63	9	0.962
Saturated Model	21	15.26	0	0.982
Independence Model	6	15.30	15	0.936

Source: Self-produced from survey results

The "P" value, related to significance levels, shows there are few meaningful differences between the observed and estimated covariance matrices, which is a positive aspect in structural equation analysis. This suggests that the proposed model effectively represents the data.

More specifically, even when educational quality is examined in isolation, on an individual level, it positively influences the competitiveness of higher education institutions, which in turn tangibly affects the overall model's performance.

This is because the actions taken to improve the relationship between knowledge creation and its implementation in organizational quality are of interest to improve the real competitive advantage of higher education institutions.

According to the CMIN values, the Default Model presents a value of 12.63, indicating a low discrepancy between the observed and estimated covariance matrices, suggesting that the model adequately fits the data. In contrast, the Saturated Model has a CMIN value of 15.26; however, this result is not relevant, as the saturated model consistently achieves a perfect fit due to its unrestricted nature.

Finally, the Independence Model shows a CMIN of 15.3, indicating a significant discrepancy. This reflects the fact that this model, by assuming complete independence between variables, fails to describe the data accurately. Overall, the Default Model is the most appropriate due to its low CMIN value and good fit.

Table 4. Chi Square Minimum – Knowledge Management

Model Type	Free Parameters	χ^2 Statistic	df	p-value
Default Model	12	11.25	12	0.852
Saturated Model	21	9.36	17	0.862
Independence Model	6	12.20	22	0.847

Source: Self-produced from survey results

Based on the CMIN values, the Default Model scores 11.25 with 12 degrees of freedom and a p-value of 0.852, showing a minimal difference between the observed and estimated covariance matrices, which indicates a good fit of the model to the data.

This finding indicates a connection between knowledge management and educational quality. However, their impact appears less significant compared to competitiveness, which remains an important factor to consider when interpreting the results.

Similarly, the Saturated Model has a CMIN of 9.36, indicating an excellent fit; this is expected since it is an unrestricted model with all parameters estimated.

Finally, the Independence Model, with a chi-square statistic (CMIN) of 12.2 and 22 degrees of freedom (df), indicates a poor model fit under the assumption of complete independence between variables, as suggested by the high chi-square value. Nevertheless, the associated p-value of 0.847 exceeds the typical significance threshold of 0.05, implying that the null hypothesis of perfect independence cannot be rejected at the 5% significance level.

Overall, the Default Model demonstrates acceptable goodness-of-fit indices, evidenced by its low CMIN value, relatively high degrees of freedom, and p-value > 0.05, indicating an adequate model fit.

This establishes a direct correlation between knowledge management and educational quality, which can be leveraged to achieve tangible improvements in these areas and thereby foster cohesion within the organization.

CONCLUSION

This study examines the application of knowledge management strategies as a means of augmenting the competitive advantage of higher education institutions through the enhancement of educational quality.

A systematic understanding of this tool demands actively implementing information technologies, not only to stay ahead in innovation but also to enhance the creative capacity of academic communities.

Implementing artificial intelligence (AI) processes and virtual tools in the classroom can greatly enhance organizational performance. At the same time, they have the potential to tailor learning to each student's individual needs.

It is crucial to recognize that the main role of universities is to produce knowledge. However, their duty also involves transforming and sharing that knowledge through widely accessible platforms that encourage the growth of this intangible asset.

As a result, this shift produces widespread benefits for both the university community and society at large, enhancing cognitive relationships among all participants within the academic ecosystem.

Nonetheless, it must be acknowledged that, like any administrative management model, the knowledge management process is not immune to challenges, obstacles, and resistance, whether internal or external.

As identified in this study, the primary issues arise not from limitations within existing artificial intelligence models but rather from the difficulty of capturing generalizable elements that remain embedded in the collective intelligence of thc university.

From a quantitative standpoint, the analysis of the proposed structural model highlights two key criteria of notable statistical and conceptual significance.

First, the accreditation of both undergraduate and graduate programs emerges as a factor with high potential to directly influence the continuous improvement of educational quality, which in turn is recognized as a strategic element in strengthening institutional competitiveness. These accreditations, linked to international standards and systematic evaluation processes, serve as tangible mechanisms for quality assurance. For this, it is necessary to collect and process relevant data through big data techniques to identify concrete administrative actions, placing data at the core of decision-making.

Second, it was observed that factors related to institutional communication and partnerships with national or international entities do not show a statistically significant impact on organizational quality, at least as operationalized in the present model.

However, this does not mean that such factors should be disregarded or underestimated. If the absence of measurable impact equates to a lack of competitiveness, it would be a methodological and conceptual error.

In other words, intangible values do have a proper place within institutional evaluation frameworks if they can be translated into observable, active, and quantifiable variables. This would enable their full inclusion in the construction of more comprehensive analytical models, thereby enriching our understanding of the underlying processes that shape organizational performance in the university context.

In conclusion, the results derived from the proposed structural model indicate a significant relationship between the components of knowledge management, educational quality, and institutional competitiveness. This relationship, far from being merely correlational, reflects a strategic alignment among these three elements, which higher education institutions can leverage to design pathways toward institutional improvement and consolidation.

In this context, a new line of research is emerging focused on exploring the role of advanced technologies, such as artificial intelligence (AI), in knowledge management processes.

AI stands out as a powerful tool for addressing many of the previously mentioned challenges, enabling the automation of repetitive tasks, predictive data analysis, knowledge generation from hidden patterns, and the enhancement of strategic decision-making.

Its integration would not only modernize existing models but also introduce more agile, adaptive, and efficient dynamics, thus contributing to the improvement of the quality, relevance, and social impact of higher education institutions.

REFERENCES

Allal-Chérif, O., & Makhlouf, M. (2015). Using serious games to manage knowledge: The SECI model perspective. *Journal of Business Research*, *69*(5), 1539–1543. DOI: 10.1016/j.jbusres.2015.10.013

Antunes, H., & Pinheiro, P. G. (2019). Linking knowledge management, organizational learning, and memory. *Journal Of Innovation & Knowledge*, *5*(2), 140–149. DOI: 10.1016/j.jik.2019.04.002

Aoudia, M., Marji, K., & AlQahsi, D. A. (2015). Assessment of Higher Education Quality by Using Cohort of First-year in University. *Procedia: Social and Behavioral Sciences*, *191*, 330–335. DOI: 10.1016/j.sbspro.2015.04.310

Baker, R. S., & Hawn, A. (2022). Algorithmic bias in education. *International Journal of Artificial Intelligence in Education*, •••, 1–41.

Ban, O. I., Hatos, R., Bugnar, N., Sasu, D., Popa, A. L., & Fora, A. (2024). Evaluation of the Quality of Higher Education Services by Revised IPA in the Perspective of Digitization. *Sustainability (Basel)*, *16*(7), 3017. DOI: 10.3390/su16073017

Barney, J. B. (1995). Looking inside for a competitive advantage. *The Academy of Management Perspectives*, *9*(4), 49–61. DOI: 10.5465/ame.1995.9512032192

Bendermacher, G. W. G., Egbrink, M. G. A. O., Wolfhagen, H. A. P., Leppink, J., & Dolmans, D. H. J. M. (2017). Reinforcing pillars for quality culture development: A path analytic model. *Studies in Higher Education*, *44*(4), 643–662. DOI: 10.1080/03075079.2017.1393060

Bozkurt, A. (2024). Cocreation, authorship, ownership, academic ethics and integrity in a time of generative AI. *Open Praxis, 16*(1), GenAI. https://doi-org.wdg.biblio.udg.mx:8443/10.55982/openpraxis.16.1.654

Carmines, E., & Zeller, R. (1979). *Reliability and Validity Assessment*. DOI: 10.4135/9781412985642

Chan, C. K. Y., & Hu, W. (2023). Students' voices on generative AI: Perceptions, benefits, and challenges in higher education. *International Journal of Educational Technology in Higher Education*, *20*(1), 43. https://doi-org.wdg.biblio.udg.mx:8443/10.1186/s41239-023-00411-8. DOI: 10.1186/s41239-023-00411-8

Chankseliani, M., & McCowan, T. (2020). Higher education and the Sustainable Development Goals. *Higher Education*, *81*(1), 1–8. DOI: 10.1007/s10734-020-00652-w PMID: 33173242

Chen, J., Weng, G. K., Cho, R. L., & Wei, H. (2024). Knowledge dissemination trajectory of bim in construction engineering applications. *Journal of Civil Engineering and Management, 30*(4), 343–353. DOI: 10.3846/jcem.2024.21353

Chen, W. L., & Wang, C.-J. (2012). Study of the Construction of Assessment System on Regional Innovation Capacity in Knowledge Management. *Procedia Engineering, 29*, 1830–1834. DOI: 10.1016/j.proeng.2012.01.221

Chen, Y., Pan, X., Liu, P., & Vanhaverbeke, W. (2024). How does digital transformation empower knowledge creation? Evidence from Chinese manufacturing enterprises. *Journal Of Innovation & Knowledge, 9*(2), 100481. DOI: 10.1016/j.jik.2024.100481

Claydon, L. S. (2015). Rigour in quantitative research. *Nursing Standard, 29*(47), 43–48. DOI: 10.7748/ns.29.47.43.e8820 PMID: 26198528

Cordero, J., Torres-Zambrano, J., & Cordero-Castillo, A. (2024). Integration of Generative Artificial Intelligence in Higher Education: Best Practices. *Education Sciences, 15*(1), 32. DOI: 10.3390/educsci15010032

Davies, S., Seitamaa-Hakkarainen, P., & Hakkarainen, K. (2024). Knowledge creation through maker practices and the role of teacher and peer support in collaborative invention projects. *International Journal of Computer-Supported Collaborative Learning, 19*(3), 283–310. DOI: 10.1007/s11412-024-09427-2

Demchig, B. (2015). Knowledge Management Capability Level Assessment of the Higher Education Institutions: Case Study from Mongolia. *Procedia: Social and Behavioral Sciences, 174*, 3633–3640. DOI: 10.1016/j.sbspro.2015.01.1082

Dogru, T., Line, N., Hanks, L., Acikgoz, F., Abbott, J., Bakir, S., Berbekova, A., Bilgihan, A., Iskender, A., Kizildag, M., Lee, M., Lee, W., McGinley, S., Mody, M., Onder, I., Ozdemir, O., & Suess, C. (2023). The implications of generative artificial intelligence in academic research and higher education in tourism and hospitality. *Tourism Economics, 0*(0), 13548166231204065. https://doi-org.wdg.biblio.udg.mx:8443/10.1177/13548166231204065

Donate, M. J., & Canales, J. I. (2012). A new approach to the concept of knowledge strategy. *Journal of Knowledge Management, 16*(1), 22–44. DOI: 10.1108/13673271211198927

Emmert-Aronson, B. O., Moore, M. T., & Brown, T. A. (2014). Differential Item Functioning of the Symptoms of Major Depression by Race and Ethnicity: An Item Response Theory Analysis. *Journal of Psychopathology and Behavioral Assessment, 36*(3), 424–431. DOI: 10.1007/s10862-014-9407-4

Fialho, I., Cid, M., & Coppi, M. (2023). Pedagogical Assessment in Higher Education: The Importance of Training. *Education Sciences*, *13*(12), 1248. DOI: 10.3390/educsci13121248

Fui-Hoon Nah, F., Zheng, R., Cai, J., Siau, K., & Chen, L. (2023). Generative AI and ChatGPT: Applications, challenges, and AI-human collaboration. *Journal of Information Technology Case and Application Research*, *25*(3), 277–304. https://doi-org.wdg.biblio.udg.mx:8443/10.1080/15228053.2023.2233814. DOI: 10.1080/15228053.2023.2233814

Galdames, I. S. (2024). Modelos de gestión del conocimiento en educación superior. *European Journal of Education and Psychology*, •••, 1–23. DOI: 10.32457/ejep.v16i2.2437

Gebreyohans, G., Croasdell, D., & Meshesha, M. (2022). A Systematic Literature Review on Digital Knowledge Sharing in Higher Education. *Proceedings Of The . . . Annual Hawaii International Conference On System Sciences/Proceedings Of The Annual Hawaii International Conference On System Sciences.* https://doi.org/ DOI: 10.24251/HICSS.2022.668

Guzman, J. H. E., Zuluaga-Ortiz, R. A., Garizabal-Donado, L. E., Mora-Garcia, Y. A., Sandoval-Karam, M., Molina-Guerrero, C. J., & Delahoz-Dominguez, E. J. (2023). Determining elements used to measure knowledge management in higher education institutions' research divisions. *Procedia Computer Science*, *224*, 538–543. DOI: 10.1016/j.procs.2023.09.078

Hart, P. F., & Rodgers, W. (2023). Competition, competitiveness, and competitive advantage in higher education institutions: A systematic literature review. *Studies in Higher Education*, *49*(11), 2153–2177. DOI: 10.1080/03075079.2023.2293926

Higgins, J., & Green, S. (2008). *Definition of qualitative research.* Cochrane Handbook for Systematic Review of Interventions. handbook.cochrane.org/v5.0.0

Holstein, K., & Doroudi, S. (2021). Equity and artificial intelligence in education: will" aied" amplify or alleviate inequities in education? *arXiv preprint arXiv:2104.12920.*

Jereb, E., & Urh, M. (2024). The Use of Artificial Intelligence among Students in Higher Education. *Organizacija*, *57*(4), 333–345. DOI: 10.2478/orga-2024-0024

Jiménez-Jiménez, D., & Sanz-Valle, R. (2010). Innovation, organizational learning, and performance. *Journal of Business Research*, *64*(4), 408–417. DOI: 10.1016/j.jbusres.2010.09.010

Kerlinger, F., & Lee, H. (2002). *Investigación del comportamiento, métodos de investigación en ciencias sociales.*

Kettinger, W. J., Ryoo, S. Y., & Marchand, D. A. (2021). We're engaged! Following the path to a successful information management capability. *The Journal of Strategic Information Systems*, *30*(3), 101681. DOI: 10.1016/j.jsis.2021.101681

Khatri, B. B., & Karki, P. D. (2023). Artificial Intelligence (AI) in Higher Education: Growing Academic Integrity and Ethical Concerns. *Nepalese Journal Of Development and Rural Studies*, *20*(01), 1–7. DOI: 10.3126/njdrs.v20i01.64134

Khoa, B. T., & Huynh, T. T. (2023). The effectiveness of knowledge management systems in motivation and satisfaction in higher education Institutions: Data from Vietnam. *Data in Brief*, *49*, 109454. DOI: 10.1016/j.dib.2023.109454 PMID: 37577732

Kılıç, S. (2016). Cronbach's alpha reliability coefficient. *Journal of Mood Disorders*, *6*(1), 47–48. DOI: 10.5455/jmood.20160307122823

Krooi, M., Whittingham, J., & Beausaert, S. (2024). Introducing the 3P conceptual model of internal quality assurance in higher education: A systematic literature review. *Studies in Educational Evaluation*, *82*, 101360. DOI: 10.1016/j.stueduc.2024.101360

Kusa, R., Suder, M., & Duda, J. (2024). Role of entrepreneurial orientation, information management, and knowledge management in improving firm performance. *International Journal of Information Management*, *78*, 102802. DOI: 10.1016/j.ijinfomgt.2024.102802

Laal, M. (2011). Knowledge management in higher education. *Procedia Computer Science*, *3*, 544–549. DOI: 10.1016/j.procs.2010.12.090

Maphalala, M. C., & Ajani, O. A. (2025). Leveraging artificial intelligence as a learning tool in higher education. *Interdisciplinary Journal Of Education Research*, *7*(1), a01. DOI: 10.38140/ijer-2025.vol7.1.01

Marinovic, A. (2025). Universities and the digital divide: The capabilities approach from a Latin American perspective. In Torres Jarrín, M. (Ed.), *The University in the Digital Age* (pp. 201–220). Peter Lang.

Mars, M. M. (2011). Chapter 9: An Innovative Vision for Economic Development in Higher Education: An Essay on Balancing Community Growth and Global Competitiveness. In *Advances in the study of entrepreneurship, innovation, and economic growth* (pp. 219–233). https://doi.org/DOI: 10.1108/S1048-4736(2011)0000022012

Mauti, J. M., & Ayieko, D. S. (2025). Ethical Implications of Artificial Intelligence in University Education. *East African Journal of Education Studies*, *8*(1), 159–167. DOI: 10.37284/eajes.8.1.2583

Mayer, A., Zimmermann, J., Hoyer, J., Salzer, S., Wiltink, J., Leibing, E., & Leichsenring, F. (2019). Interindividual Differences in Treatment Effects Based on Structural Equation Models with Latent Variables: An EffectLiteR Tutorial. *Structural Equation Modeling*, *27*(5), 798–816. DOI: 10.1080/10705511.2019.1671196

McDonald, R. P. (1985). *Factor Analysis and Related Methods*. Erlbaum.

Mogalakwe, M. (2006). The use of documentary research methods in social research. *African Sociological Review, 10(*1), 221–230. https://www.jstor.org/stable/afrisocirevi.10.1.221

Moya, B. A., Eaton, S. E., Pethrick, H., Hayden, K. A., Brennan, R., Wiens, J., McDermott, B., & Lesage, J. (2023). Academic integrity and artificial intelligence in higher education contexts: A rapid scoping review protocol. *Canadian Perspectives on Academic Integrity, 5*(2), 59–75. https://doi-org.wdg.biblio.udg.mx:8443/10.11575/cpai.75990

Muca, E., Cavallini, D., Odore, R., Baratta, M., Bergero, D., & Valle, E. (2022). Are Veterinary Students Using Technologies and Online Learning Resources for Didactic Training? A Mini-Meta Analysis. *Education Sciences*, *12*(8), 573. DOI: 10.3390/educsci12080573

Naidoo, V. (2006). International education. *Journal of Research in International Education*, *5*(3), 323–345. DOI: 10.1177/1475240906069455

Nonaka, I. (1994). A Dynamic Theory of Organizational Knowledge Creation. *Organization Science*, *5*(1), 14–37. DOI: 10.1287/orsc.5.1.14

Quero, M. (2010). Confiabilidad y coeficiente de Alfa de Cronbach. *Telos*, *12*(2), 248–252.

Rahiman, H. U., & Kodikal, R. (2023). Revolutionizing education: Artificial intelligence empowered learning in higher education. *Cogent Education*, *11*(1), 2293431. Advance online publication. DOI: 10.1080/2331186X.2023.2293431

Rodríguez, M., & Mendivelso, F. (2018). Diseño de investigación de Corte Transversal. *Revista Médica Sanitas*, *21*(3), 141–146. DOI: 10.26852/01234250.20

Ryzheva, N., Nefodov, D., Romanyuk, S., Marynchenko, H., & Kudla, M. (2024). Artificial Intelligence in higher education: Opportunities and challenges. *Revista Amazonia Investiga*, *13*(73), 284–296. DOI: 10.34069/AI/2024.73.01.24

Sabbaghan, S., & Eaton, S. E. (2025). Navigating the Ethical Frontier: Graduate Students' Experiences with Generative AI-Mediated Scholarship. *International Journal of Artificial Intelligence in Education.* Advance online publication. DOI: 10.1007/s40593-024-00454-6

Santati, P., Sulastri, Perizade, B., & Widiyanti, M. (2024). Intellectual capital for higher Education competitiveness. *KnE Social Sciences.* https://doi.org/DOI: 10.18502/kss.v9i14.16120

Santos, E., Carvalho, M., & Martins, S. (2024). Sustainable Enablers of Knowledge Management Strategies in a Higher Education Institution. *Sustainability (Basel), 16*(12), 5078. DOI: 10.3390/su16125078

Shekhar, N., & Valeri, M. (2023). Trends in knowledge management research in small businesses. *European Business Review, 35*(5), 573–599. DOI: 10.1108/EBR-10-2022-0200

Stankosky, M. A. (2005). Advances in Knowledge Management: University Research Toward an Academic Discipline. In *Elsevier eBooks* (pp. 1-14). https://doi.org/DOI: 10.1016/B978-0-7506-7878-0.50005-3

Stein, C. M., Morris, N. J., & Nock, N. L. (2011). Structural equation modeling. In *Methods in molecular biology* (pp. 495-512). https://doi.org/DOI: 10.1007/978-1-61779-555-8_27

Subramaniam, L., Jalaludin, F. W., Hen, K. W., & Yap, C. S. (2023). The second and third levels of digital divide among Malaysian university students during the Covid-19 pandemic. *Telkomnika, 21*(6), 1326. DOI: 10.12928/telkomnika.v21i6.25258

Sum, N., & Jessop, B. (2012). Competitiveness, the Knowledge-Based Economy and Higher Education. *Journal of the Knowledge Economy, 4*(1), 24–44. DOI: 10.1007/s13132-012-0121-8

Tarasenko, O., Lysenko, S., Tarlopov, I., Pidkaminnyi, I., & Verhun, M. (2024). Analysis of the competitiveness of higher education institutions in Ukraine in the context of recovery and development after the war. *Multidisciplinary Science Journal, 6,* 2024ss0210. https://doi.org/DOI: 10.31893/multiscience.2024ss0210

Tavakol, M., & Dennick, R. (2011). Making sense of Cronbach's alpha. *International Journal of Medical Education, 2,* 53–55. DOI: 10.5116/ijme.4dfb.8dfd PMID: 28029643

Voss, E., Cushing, S. T., Ockey, G. J., & Yan, X. (2023). The use of assistive technologies including generative AI by test takers in language assessment: A debate of theory and practice. *Language Assessment Quarterly*, *20*(4–5), 520–532. https://doi-org.wdg.biblio.udg.mx:8443/10.1080/15434303.2023.2288256. DOI: 10.1080/15434303.2023.2288256

Wales, W. J., Covin, J. G., Schüler, J., & Baum, M. (2023). Entrepreneurial orientation as a theory of new value creation. *The Journal of Technology Transfer*, *48*(5), 1752–1772. DOI: 10.1007/s10961-023-10021-1

Watermeyer, R., Phipps, L., Lanclos, D., & Knight, C. (2023). Generative AI and the Automating of Academia. *Postdigital Science And Education*, *6*(2), 446–466. DOI: 10.1007/s42438-023-00440-6

Zutshi, A., Creed, A., Bhattacharya, A., Sohal, A., & Bavik, A. (2023). Mandated media innovation impacts on knowledge dissemination in workplace training. *Knowledge Management Research and Practice*, •••, 1–17. DOI: 10.1080/14778238.2023.2209745

Chapter 5
Social Exclusion and Collective Intelligence in Global Supply Chains

Almeirim Isabel Acosta Bahena
https://orcid.org/0000-0002-4233-5226
Universidad de Guadalajara, Mexico

Tania Elena González Alvarado
https://orcid.org/0000-0002-3062-9665
Universidad de Guadalajara, Mexico

Mariana Toussaint
Food and Agriculture Organization, Italy

ABSTRACT

Food industry and globalization has changed how we consume food, being food security a central issue on the international agenda. Food safety and trade regulations create barriers for specific groups, although are supposed to reduce social exclusion and improve global food chain´s transparency and sustainability among others. However, international collaborations and global standards addressed these problems collaboratively, displaying the power of collective intelligence. This chapter addresses economic, social, and governance dynamics linked to international food trade and quality and safety standards and how these elements affect consumers, producers, and governments. These dynamics involve aspects of social exclusion and corrective strategies through collective Intelligence.

DOI: 10.4018/979-8-3373-2685-6.ch005

Copyright © 2026, IGI Global Scientific Publishing. Copying or distributing in print or electronic forms without written permission of IGI Global Scientific Publishing is prohibited.

INTRODUCTION

Food is indispensable for life. Humans can do without leisure, transportation, technology, and many other things, but we cannot do without food. However, the way we feed ourselves has undergone a transformation. The food industry has changed how we view and consume food (Pilcher, 2023). Food consumption exceeds local production; much of it comes from other parts of the world (Stein & Santini, 2022). Food security is a central issue on the international agenda and a challenge for governments (Clapp et al., 2022).

At the same time, artificial intelligence (AI) has emerged as a solution in food supply chains, promising enhanced efficiency, logistics, and improved sustainability outcomes (Yalamati, 2024). However, it is not overlooked that, as with any innovation, the risk of the benefits not being evenly distributed is present. Social exclusion[1] remains a critical issue in global food systems that evolve constantly and acquire complex particularities, even within the same culture.

The increasing diversity and complexity of food supply chains (Davis et al., 2021) perpetuate social exclusion on one hand, while fostering collective Intelligence to decrease exclusion on the other (Bracic, 2020). Food safety and trade regulation challenges create barriers for specific groups (Alvarado, 2003). However, at the same time, international collaboration and the creation of global standards reflect the power of collective Intelligence to address complex problems collaboratively. Ideally, global food trade reduces social exclusion by providing equitable access to information, resources, and markets while harnessing collective intelligence to enhance the transparency, safety, and sustainability of the global food chain (Gerardi, 2023).

This chapter examines the economic, social, and governance dynamics associated with international food trade, quality, and safety standards, and how these factors impact consumers, producers, and governments. These dynamics involve aspects of social exclusion and corrective strategies through collective Intelligence.

THE CHALLENGES OF SOCIAL EXCLUSION

Most research focuses on social inclusion, which positively addresses social and economic problems. However, addressing social exclusion with greater emphasis can facilitate a deeper understanding and correction. Social exclusion refers to the processes by which certain groups of people are denied access to fundamental resources, such as education, healthcare, employment, and full social and economic participation (Brockie et al., 2023). This phenomenon also manifests in various ways within food supply chains.

One such form is unequal access to safe, quality food. International food safety standards, such as those regulated by the Agreement on the Application of Sanitary and Phytosanitary Measures (SPS) (Casey, 2007), create barriers for producers in certain countries or communities that lack the resources to meet stringent international standards. These standards exclude producers in developing countries from global markets, limiting their ability to compete and access trade opportunities and affecting food availability in certain regions (Alvarado, 2003).

Another form is misinformation about food quality and safety (Diekman et al., 2023). The difficulty of verifying the quality and safety of food products leads to invisible social exclusion, as specific consumers require access to sufficient information to make informed decisions about the products they purchase (Machin et al., 2024). Additionally, low-income consumers are more likely to consume lower-quality food due to their limited economic capacity, which exacerbates health and well-being inequalities (Martínez et al., 2023).

A third way is the inaccessibility of international certification and standards. Small businesses or local producers often lack the resources to obtain the necessary certifications to market their products internationally. This structural exclusion leaves certain vulnerable groups outside the global supply chain, limiting their economic opportunities and perpetuating poverty in certain regions.

And the most recent addition to social exclusion in the food supply chain is the implementation of AI. The benefits of AI are clear; it enables precision farming, automates sorting and packaging, improves demand forecasting, and optimizes supply routes. The most significant benefits stem from AI-based platforms that can reduce food waste and enhance traceability throughout the food supply chain (Taneja et al., 2023). However, the applications benefit actors with sufficient capital to access and leverage AI systems. For example, AI-driven yield forecasting using satellite data is hardly accessible to smallholder farmers (Dhal & Kar, 2024). A similar situation is presented in logistics and processing, a sector that may be threatened by automation, primarily affecting workers with low digital literacy.

These situations, which create a scenario marked by social exclusion, can and are being corrected. Collective Intelligence is considered a long-term corrective factor that can transcend local actions to establish international or global initiatives aimed at reducing social exclusion in food.

COLLECTIVE INTELLIGENCE DECREASES SOCIAL EXCLUSION.

Collective Intelligence refers to the capacity of a group or community to solve problems more efficiently than an individual, leveraging cooperation, information exchange, and knowledge diversity (Galesic et al., 2023). Collective Intelligence involves a collective's decisions and actions to further its interests (Kao et al., 2024). In food supply chains, collective Intelligence is applied at different levels (global, sectoral, and company).

Global Level. It is about global collaboration for common standards. Creating international standards for food safety and quality (such as SPS agreements and technical trade barriers) is an example of applied collective intelligence global governance. Different countries and market players collaborate to establish standards, ensuring food quality worldwide, which benefits consumers by reducing the risk of illnesses associated with the consumption of unsafe products. Multi-stakeholder participation enables the development of more robust standards and facilitates the effective resolution of trade disputes. However, numerous stakeholders participate only occasionally in creating international standards.

Sector level. It consists of certification and transparency in the supply chain. Food certification improves openness and confidence in the global food market. Collective Intelligence between producers, governments, and international organizations significantly verifies food quality and safety, reducing misinformation and consumer exclusion. Technology, such as digital traceability systems and electronic certifications, also plays a crucial role in improving confidence and efficiency in the food chain.

Company level. It involves innovation in food production and distribution. Technological advances, such as real-time quality monitoring systems and new e-commerce platforms, enable producers to collaborate more efficiently, share information, and improve their practices.

This collaboration generates a collective intelligence that favors more efficient, sustainable, and accessible food production for all, reducing social exclusion in supply chains and providing access to better products and markets for more people. From a global, sectoral, or business perspective, it is possible to focus efforts on improving food quality and reducing social exclusion. By understanding the stages of the food supply chain and recognizing how different economic actors can potentially be excluded, practical strategies and actions can be developed to mitigate this exclusion.

IN THE FOOD SUPPLY CHAIN, WHAT IS EXCLUDED?

The food supply chain encompasses all stages from food production to the final consumer. It involves various actors and activities, including production, processing, distribution, marketing, and consumption. Each link in the chain adds value to the food product, and each stage generates challenges related to quality, safety, logistics, and costs, among others. (Xiao et al., 2024)

The key stages of the food supply chain are five: 1) primary production, 2) food processing, 3) distribution, 4) commercialization, and 5) consumption. In each of these, we will address elements of exclusion.

Primary production (agriculture, livestock, fishing, and others) is the chain's first link. Food is grown, raised, or harvested. It includes activities such as agriculture (the cultivation of cereals, fruits, and vegetables), livestock (the production of meat, milk, and eggs), fishing (the harvesting of seafood or fish), and the harvesting of forest products (such as timber and fruits). Lack of access to resources perpetuates the economic exclusion of small producers, who are trapped in a cycle of poverty due to the impossibility of improving their production conditions and increasing their competitiveness. (Alvarado, 2012)

Collective Intelligence facilitates the creation of crowdfunding or micro-financing platforms that connect small producers with investors interested in supporting sustainable, low-impact businesses (Nurse, 2016). In terms of AI^2, Collective Intelligence is a path to democratize and engage farmers, laborers, consumers, cooperatives, and other stakeholders in decisions about which problems AI should solve and how success is defined (Manning et al., 2022; Steggemann, 2023). These mechanisms enable economic and technical support networks among local producers. Producer associations harness the power of collective Intelligence to share resources, access group purchases of inputs at lower costs, and negotiate better prices in local and international markets. Additionally, cooperatives provide training and support in business management, marketing, and compliance with quality standards (Alvarado, 2012).

The second link is food processing. Once the primary products are harvested, they are processed before being marketed. Processing includes cleaning, packaging, transformation (for example, making wheat flour or turning tomatoes into sauce), and preservation (such as refrigeration, canning, drying, or pasteurization).

Small producers, especially in developing countries, often need help to meet stringent international food safety and quality standards, such as those established by agreements like the Agreement on the Application of Sanitary and Phytosanitary Measures (SPS). It prevents them from accessing global markets and obtaining higher product prices. Additionally, processing can be costly and result in financial losses. Lack of access to international markets perpetuates poverty in rural areas, where farmers cannot compete with larger producers with access to the resources, technology, and financing needed to meet global standards (Alvarado, 2012). Furthermore, the data used to train modern AI systems often fails to account for informal economies or small-scale processors, resulting in their marginalization in procurement decisions and market access (Kaplinsky & Kraemer, 2022).

Collective Intelligence helps to meet this challenge through international cooperation networks. This includes data collection, validation, and audit processes that AI models employ to ensure diverse economic realities are considered and reduce informational asymmetries among producers (Mattsson, 2022). Through these networks, producer organizations, governments, and global entities share knowledge and resources to help small producers improve their capabilities (González & Martin, 2018). Access to training on quality standards and international certifications is included.

The third link is distribution. Once processed, food is transported from factories or processing centers to retailers, supermarkets, wholesalers, and other points of sale. This link includes the logistics of transportation, storage, and handling. Much of the food could be recovered or used. This waste is particularly severe in regions with limited infrastructure and resources, negatively impacting food security and the economy of rural and vulnerable communities (Alvarado, 2012).

Food waste in high-poverty areas limits vulnerable populations' access to essential commodities and increases food inequalities (Warshawsky, 2024). Collective Intelligence facilitates the creation of food redistribution platforms (Kenney et al., 2020). Food waste is significantly reduced through collaborative networks, such as apps and digital platforms that connect retailers, restaurants, and producers with aid organizations or consumers in need of food. These platforms also improve marginalized communities' access to fresh, quality food (Rampa et al., 2020).

Collective Intelligence promotes responsible consumption, reduces food waste through awareness campaigns, and educates consumers and producers about food handling and conservation practices (Stanciu et al., 2022).

The fourth link is marketing. It involves selling food to consumers through supermarkets, local stores, online marketplaces, and others. Products are sold directly to consumers or through intermediaries such as retailers and distributors. Trade policies and tariff barriers (such as taxes on exports and imports) disproportionately affect poorer countries, hindering their ability to access international markets. National and international regulations that favor large companies exclude small producers from critical markets (Alvarado, 2003). It leaves small or developing country producers out of the global economy, affecting their ability to generate income, build their businesses, and improve their livelihoods.

Collective Intelligence helps through fair trade movements and inclusive policies. Collective Intelligence drives global fair-trade movements, advocating for more inclusive trade policies that prioritize small and local producers. It also advocates for reducing tariff barriers and regulations that limit developing countries' access to global markets. International organizations and NGOs utilize their collective knowledge to advocate for reforms in trade policies and establish support platforms that help small producers overcome trade barriers, thereby enabling them to access larger markets (Alvarado, 2012).

The fifth and final link is consumption. At this stage, the consumer evaluates the quality and safety of the food based on their experience and the guarantees provided (labels, certifications). At the consumption level, AI is increasingly used to guide food choices. However, AI can embed cultural biases by ignoring local dietary patterns or being inaccessible to digitally marginalized populations (Lugo-Morín, 2024).

In many parts of the world, consumers need help accessing reliable information on the quality and safety of food products. It includes the product's origin, production process, and labor practices. Lack of information also generates distrust of local products, which affects producers in vulnerable areas. Consumers with fewer resources or limited education are often victims of misinformation or low-quality products, which exacerbates health inequalities and limits access to safer and higher-quality products.

Collective Intelligence helps through traceability and transparency technologies. Technology platforms based on blockchain and other traceability technologies enable consumers to easily access information about a product's origin, production process, and characteristics. Some examples of this include living labs, public forums, and participatory platforms that enable diverse consumers to co-develop AI tools that are context-sensitive, linguistically inclusive, and culturally appropriate (Raman, 2022). This fosters trust in products from small producers, enabling consumers to make informed purchasing decisions. Utilizing collective intelligence systems, such as mobile applications or online platforms managed by consumer communities, fosters transparency throughout the food supply chain, ultimately benefiting both consumers and local producers (Gligor et al., 2022).

The growing diversity and complexity of food supply chains, in terms of variety and international trade, have become an increasingly important and controversial issue in the global economy.

These developments are reflected in increased discussions and conflicts over market access, national and international food safety standards, and other regulatory issues. In recent years, quality and safety standards have improved, marking a significant shift in global trade in food and agricultural products. The Agreement on the Application of Sanitary and Phytosanitary Measures (SPS) and the Agreement on Technical Barriers to Trade provide the framework for dispute settlement about these standards (Overbosch & Blanchard, 2023). Food safety remains a crucial issue for consumers, food producers and processors, as well as governments, which must ensure the health of their citizens and resolve trade disputes.

Information about quality, safety, or the process through which food is manufactured is often difficult to observe. This situation is especially concerning for credibility attributes, for which consumers' evaluations, even after consumption, usually lead to incorrect perceptions (Kovacs & Keresztes, 2022). The producer may then decide not to supply the credibility attribute or not to supply the desired level of the attribute because the consumer is not willing to pay for it. Consequently, the loss of information can lead to inefficiency and ultimately result in reduced consumption of certain products. This is especially true in the case of food.

FOOD CERTIFICATIONS: QUALITY INSTRUMENTS

Food certification is becoming an important tool used by governments and food producers to assure consumers of the quality and safety of their products. A food certificate is a written or electronic document that attests to the fact that a specific aspect of a food product or its manufacturing process meets particular standards. It can be used to ensure the quality and integrity of food products for domestic and international markets. Food manufacturers, retailers, and food service operators often require food certificates as evidence of compliance with various quality, safety, or other attribute standards (Hu et al., 2023).

Definition and Purpose of Food Certifications

Food certification is a third-party verification (assessment) that ensures that products, processes, or services in the food supply chain comply with standards (rules) or other normative documents (certification criteria), such as food quality and safety requirements. Food certifications aim to restore consumer confidence (Hu et al., 2023). In the era of globalization, when food is produced worldwide, consumers cannot personally inspect production processes and, therefore, rely on signaling mechanisms to indicate whether a product is safe or sound. Certifications, labels, brands, and other signaling mechanisms are relatively robust instruments that can compensate for consumers' limited knowledge about product characteristics.

The credibility of certifications depends on their perceived credibility and the certification body's ability to apply the certification criteria (Starobin, 2021). Therefore, food certifications require a degree of uniformity and comparability of product attributes between products from different origins. Certification aims to make certified products nearly homogeneous and more easily recognizable by consumers. The uniformity of attributes and the credibility of certification systems help to maintain and even increase the effect of certifications in reallocating food product consumption (Sorbo et al., 2022).

This chapter provides an overview of current traditional and specialty food certification systems worldwide. Food certification is crucial for ensuring food safety and quality, enhancing consumer confidence, and facilitating international trade. While the research may shed light on various food certification systems, this paper will also highlight the challenges that food producers face in obtaining certification.

These certifications also enable more effective control over product demand. They are a response to dismantling the protectionist agricultural policies of the European Union and the United States, which were considered highly restrictive at the time. In other words, these policies excluded food exporters from third countries not based on food security but because of the quantity of products available on the market and the final price. These measures sought to guarantee high wages for domestic producers by excluding foreign competitors. Although this mechanism seemed beneficial, it was not, since the European Union and the United States remained free to export to these third countries with almost no obstacles. Exported products could be sold at prices considerably lower than those on the local market, thanks to the subsidies and protectionist measures offered by their governments to farmers. (Alvarado, 2003)

Global Certification Systems

The growth in the number of food certification schemes is a relatively recent phenomenon, but has captured the attention of food producers worldwide. An increasing number of consumers are seeking "assurances" regarding the quality and safety of the food they purchase and consume, and many of these consumers are seeking those "assurances" in the form of certification labels (Hu et al., 2023; Lang & Conroy, 2022). In addition to the traditional focus on certification systems such as organic, halal, and kosher, there has been a proliferation of new food certification systems, including ISO 9000 (quality), Hazard Analysis Critical Control Point (HACCP), British Retail Consortium (BRC), Safe Quality Food (SQF), to name a few. In addition, the increased emphasis on the environment has led to the development of environmental management standards, such as the ISO 14000 series, and assurance schemes incorporating environmental standards (Holah, 2023). It is not only growing private sector food certification systems, but many countries now require certification of food products to ensure food safety.

In the U.S., certification is primarily used to ensure food safety, and the most well-known certified foods are organic foods and those certified under the Hazard Analysis and Critical Control Point (HACCP) system (Radu et al., 2023). In the European Union, certification is primarily used to ensure food quality and production methods, with several certification systems in place for various food and food production methods.

The most recognized certified foods in the European Union are organic, foods certified by the International Organization for Standardization (ISO) system, foods approved by the HACCP system, and foods certified by some food associations (Sorbo et al., 2022; Prylipko et al., 2021). In Japan, certification is primarily used for food quality assurance. The most well-known certified foods in Japan are those certified by the Japan Agricultural Standard (JAS) system and those bearing the so-called Tennen (Natural) mark (Rupprecht et al., 2020). Almost all types of food carry some certification or eco-label. The market share of certified foods is highest in Japan, followed by the European Union.

Several food certification schemes operate globally. Most schemes operate in developed and developing countries, although they vary in coverage, rigor, and administration. They are commercially based in that they charge producers for certification and charge buyers or their agents for access to a database detailing certified producers and their products. The primary costs for certified producers include third-party inspections, internal record-keeping, and process adjustments (Dos Santos et al., 2021). Producers often apply for certification to access niche markets or high-value supermarket chains, especially in developed countries.

Types of Food Certifications

There are three types of food certifications. The first group is process-based certifications, which verify and ensure that a particular production process has been carried out. This group includes Halal and Kosher certifications, providing food products that adhere to specific religious rules and regulations. The second type is input-based certifications, which focus on the attributes and characteristics of the materials used in food production. An example is organic certification, which verifies that products have been produced in accordance with a uniform set of standards. The third and broadest type is outcome-based certifications, which focus on the final product and evaluate the presence of specific characteristics or attributes. This type includes certifications for non-GMO products, gluten-free products, or quality labels such as the Blue Flag for fish (Lang & Conroy, 2022).

In addition to these three types of certifications, several voluntary certifications do not fall into the above categories but can have a significant impact on food consumption. These include local certifications, which ensure that products have been manufactured or originated in a regional area, and animal welfare certifications, which ensure that products have been produced using methods that protect farm animals from mistreatment or abuse (Boatey & Minegishi, 2022).

KOSHER certification is required for food products that Jews consume worldwide (Shuhaimi et al., 2022). BRC certification is explicitly needed for retailers offering branded food products produced by manufacturers (Lambert & Frenz, 2021). Private industries require IFS certification for those companies producing food products under private labels (Bomba & Susol, 2020). GLOBALGAP certification is required for agricultural products throughout the production process. It is essential for workers' safety, health, and welfare and for protecting the environment (Bomba & Susol, 2020)

ISO 22000 certification allows food manufacturers to implement an in-house food safety management system (Bomba & Susol, 2020). HACCP certification is essential for food safety and is required by law in many countries (Allam et al., 2023). HALAL certification is needed for food products consumed by Muslims worldwide (Shuhaimi et al., 2022). Organic certification is mainly needed for producing vegetables, fruits, meat, and dairy products that are not made with chemicals. It is also required for biodiversity and environmentally friendly production (Nie et al., 2022).

Organic Certification

Organic certification is the most widely recognized form of private food certification, with global coverage (Nie et al., 2022). Although it constitutes less than 1% of the world's agricultural land (with a very asymmetric distribution), organic consumption has grown substantially in the last two decades. Organic certification prohibits the use of synthetic chemical inputs and genetically modified organisms. It also encompasses several animal welfare and environmental protection standards. The certifications of the private food labels are voluntary and establish quality attributes absent in unregulated markets. Organic products are often perceived as healthier, better for the environment, and more humane in animal treatment than conventional products (Aitken et al., 2020).

Organic certification is producer-based and establishes production standards verified through controls of the production process and periodic inspections of certified producers. In addition to quality, organic certification also affects food trade. In international trade, accredited certification bodies generally demonstrate compliance with the importing country's organic standard. This situation has led to the proliferation of country-specific organic standards and lists of approved certification bodies (Kumar et al., 2023). For exporters in developing countries, organic certification can be more expensive than certification to a private standard such as GlobalGAP, which allows self-declaration and third-party inspection of producer compliance at a lower cost.

Fair Trade Certification

Guaranteeing a minimum price for a commodity is an essential aspect of many certification schemes. The best-known certification scheme that does this is Fair Trade. Fairtrade guarantees a minimum price for commodity producers. This price is usually higher than the market equilibrium price, leading to an overproduction of Fair-Trade commodities if all producers adhere to the certification standards. Because not all producers can sell their production as certified, only a select group benefits from Fair Trade; these are those selling at or near the minimum price before certification was introduced. Producers who are not certified and do not belong to the selected group lose out. These are those for whom the minimum price level was prohibiting rather than enabling (Bennett & Grabs, 2024). It may even lead to a situation where non-certified producers are worse off after introducing certification systems. In contrast, the relative welfare gains of certified producers are not as significant as Fair Trade advocates would have us believe.

In order to have a bigger picture of how both of these types of certifications work, Table 1 gives an overlook of Fair Trade and Organic certifications.

Table 1. Comparative chart: Organic Certification vs. Fair Trade Certification

Aspect	*Organic Certification*	*Fair trade Certification*
Main focus	Environmental sustainability and chemical-free production	Social justice, fair wages, and equitable trade conditions
Target Beneficiaries	Consumers seeking health/sustainability; environmentally conscious farmers	Small-scale farmers, workers in the Global South
Market Orientation	Strong in high-income markets with health- conscious consumers	Emphasizes ethical consumption and solidarity economy
Certification costs	Often high; includes annual inspections, documentation, and transition periods	High; includes audits, minimum volumes, and compliance systems
Role of AI	AI can automate compliance checks, traceability, and satellite monitoring	AI can aid in monitoring labor conditions and verifying claims through blockchain
Role of Collective Intelligence	Can involve participatory standard-setting and farmer-led innovation	Enables worker cooperatives and community participation in auditing and governance
Risk of social exclusion	High; excludes smallholders (indigenous and low-income producers) due to complexity and technical requirements	High; excludes informal producers and non-unionized laborers or producers, due to organizational, volume or documentation requirements
Consumer transparency	Moderate; mainly focused on environmental compliance	High; emphasizes both social and environmental narratives
Traceability tools	Increasingly digitized via QR codes, blockchain, AI enabled sensors	Often includes digital tracking and participatory audits

Source: Author-created.

This demonstrates that although both systems are focused on creating more responsible food chains, they can perpetuate social exclusion, especially when access to certification is hindered by financial, technological, or institutional barriers. The current systems give Collective Intelligence and AI the potential to make both certifications more inclusive, adaptive, and trustworthy, as it becomes clear ahead in the chapter.

Key Organizations And Standards

Regarding food standards, the world's most recognized standard-setting bodies are the FAO/WHO Codex Alimentarius Commission (CAC), the International Organization for Standardization (ISO), and the International Electrotechnical Commission (IEC). These organizations develop global food standards that contribute to food safety and provide guidelines for governments to address safety issues and ensure fair practices in international food trade. The standards developed by ISO and IEC support these primary objectives to provide confidence in the quality, safety, and technology of food products. These standards are voluntary but are increasingly used to support regulations and conformity assessment procedures to address the growing need for food safety worldwide (Bevilacqua, 2020).

A clearer understanding of each of the organizations would be that CAC focuses on food safety and consumer protection, backed by FAO and WHO, making it particularly influential in shaping global food trade and public health policy. ISO provides broader, cross-sectoral standards that indirectly affect food systems through management, quality, and sustainability protocols. And IEC, focused on technological and electrotechnical standardization, including emerging issues like AI and automation, which are relevant to food traceability and smart supply chains (Figure 1)

Figure 1. Comparison of Key Organizations

Source: Author-created with information from CAC (2023), IEC (2022), and ISO (2021)

While the three organizations emphasize global harmonization, their inclusivity and accessibility vary. Codex offers structured support for developing countries and allows observer input, while ISO and IEC are more industry-driven, with participation often limited by technical and financial barriers. This difficulty in accessing organizations and their standards can reinforce social exclusion unless it is mitigated by participatory mechanisms and collective intelligence frameworks that broaden stakeholder involvement in standard-setting.

An example of certifications and social exclusion, even trying to include all, is the Agro-export Sector of Peru. The country has experienced significant growth since the early 2000s, becoming a leading exporter of avocados, asparagus, and blueberries. To access premium markets in North America and Europe, Peruvian medium-sized agro-enterprises adopted ISO 22000 (Food Safety Management Systems), while smaller actors relied on local cooperatives or government programs to undergo certification processes. Despite these supports, many smallholders were left behind due to the complexity of documentation and auditing, reinforcing a dual economy within the agro-export sector (Amézquita-Zegarra, 2021).

On the other hand, the Codex Alimentarius Commission´s standards – often transposed into national food safety laws – provided a more accessible baseline. The Peruvian government used Codex frameworks to design food safety regulations that apply to all formal exporters, while offering technical assistance to marginalized communities through programs supported by FAO. However, IEC standards, particularly those related to smart agriculture, such as precision irrigation systems and sensor-based quality control, remained out of reach to small-scale producers due to the high cost of infrastructure and lack of training (Mendoza-Pachas & Pumasunco-Silva, 2021).

This case illustrates the asymmetric inclusion patterns across standardization bodies. While Codex standards tend to offer broader inclusion, ISO and IEC standards entrench social exclusion unless participatory mechanisms and capacity-building programs are embedded in implementation strategies. To ensure that emerging standards in food safety and traceability do not exacerbate inequality, there is a pressing need to integrate collective intelligence. In doing so, international standardization can fulfill its promise to harmonize markets and technology and also advance in inclusive and sustainable food systems.

Global Impact Of Food Certifications

Certifications bring two effects: a "positive" effect due to increased global awareness of the quality of a certified product and a "market barrier" effect caused by the additional cost for a producer to achieve certification. It is estimated that existing certifications have exceeded their mission of ensuring food quality.

The upward trend of food certifications is deeply rooted in the market (Starobin, 2021). A wide variety of certified foods already exists. However, existing work broadly analyzes the effect of product certification at an insufficient level of generality, considering the accreditation of a single product and its limited local consumption. In the global economy, all goods have the potential to be consumed anywhere in the world.

Several local, national, and international companies manage and operate the food supply in large, open economies. The presence of diverse companies in the food sector improves economic efficiency. However, in the presence of food certifications, several tiny firms may not be able to afford these certifications. They may be forced out of the market, leaving the economic power of the food market in the hands of a few large firms (Starobin, 2021).

The consequence of this shift in the power of food supply to other nations is that the national economy will be deprived of the income generated by the production, processing, and sale of food. In other words, if a nation does not have the power to supply food to other nations to meet their domestic demand, revenues are transferred from the food-exporting countries to the importing country, as the demand for food is met by the supply from the exporting country. The overall effect of food certifications on global food consumption is that food certifications restrict food production, processing, and consumption, as any restrictions on food production and consumption will, in turn, limit a country's economic development (Starobin, 2021; Schleifer & Sun, 2020).

Food certifications have an impact on the food supply chain. These certifications are market barriers. Large corporations, which have the resources to comply with international standards, dominate the market, while small businesses are excluded. This phenomenon contributes directly to the social exclusion of small producers in developing economies or regions with less access to finance and technology. It affects producers and communities that depend on local food production for their economic livelihoods. Unable to access international markets due to these barriers, these small businesses miss out on financial opportunities, which can lead to a cycle of poverty and exclusion from the global economy (Alvarado, 2012).

Large companies' dominance of the certified food market can concentrate economic power in a few hands, excluding small businesses and reducing competition. This situation means that smaller national economies, especially in developing countries, are stripped of their ability to generate income through food production and processing as consumers turn to cheaper, but not necessarily sustainable, imported products.

It also generates dependence on external markets, which weakens the country's economic autonomy and amplifies social and economic inequalities within a nation. This inequality is more significant in tiny countries, regions characterized by hurricanes or significant droughts, and with production based on one or two products.

Social exclusion intensifies because vulnerable communities in food-exporting countries (often family farmers or small producers) are displaced by competition from large corporations with access to capital and resources. At the same time, domestic demand for local products is met by imported products from countries with greater certification capacity.

Food certifications restrict developing countries' ability to generate employment, improve agricultural productivity, and promote economic growth autonomously. When certifications raise production costs and exclude small producers, national economic development is limited, as food production and sales revenues do not stay within the country. Instead of investing in local economies, countries import food from other nations that can meet international standards, perpetuating global inequality (Alvarado, 2006).

Given this scenario, collective intelligence plays a crucial role in developing alternative certification models that are more accessible to small producers and local businesses. For example, regional or community certifications, which do not require the high costs of international certifications, can be a viable solution. Collaboration among governments, NGOs, and local producer groups has led to the development of more inclusive and accessible quality standards, while ensuring food safety and product quality. These models allow small producers to compete in international markets without being excluded due to economic barriers. Examples of this can be seen in the export of coffee, avocado, and Oleaginosa Paprika (Alvarado, 2012).

Digital platforms based on collective intelligence facilitate access to shared certifications. Through these platforms, small producers can come together to obtain lower-cost certifications and access global markets. For example, producers can share certification costs through cooperatives or associations, improving market access without assuming enormous individual costs.

Emerging technologies, such as blockchain and other traceability platforms, improve transparency in food certifications. Consumers and producers gain real-time information about the quality, origin, and processing of products through collective intelligence. This levels the playing field between large companies and small producers, generating greater consumer confidence in certified local products.

Collective intelligence is a powerful driver for public advocacy. Through networks of non-governmental organizations, producers, and consumer groups, they can promote policy reforms that reduce the barriers imposed by certifications. Collective pressure leads to the creation of policies that support small producers through subsidies or cost exemptions, allowing them to compete on a level playing field with large multinational companies. The dismantling of the European Union's Common Agricultural Policy is a clear example of this.

Knowledge sharing and training networks based on collective intelligence are fundamental resources to help small producers meet the quality standards required by certifications. These networks offer technical assistance, training, and guidance on enhancing product quality, streamlining production processes, and meeting international standards, all at a lower financial cost. The AL-Invest program, which the European Union has financed to support smaller companies in Latin America, is a clear example (Alvarado, 2021).

AL-Invest aims to enhance the competitiveness and international market access of these companies, providing them with tools and resources to improve their productive capacity, innovate, and increase their participation in global trade (Alvarado, 2003). In particular, it seeks to strengthen trade relations between Latin America and the European Union by facilitating the exchange of knowledge, technology, and best business practices.

Comparison of Certification Standards Between Countries

Standards are used in international trade to facilitate the exchange of goods and services between countries. A standard developed at the national level is used as a barrier to entry for foreign products and influencing the characteristics of Trade

(Ikram et al., 2020). To overcome the obstacles, countries agree to apply internationally harmonized standards, such as Codex Alimentarius.

The Codex Alimentarius, Latin for "food code," is a collection of international standards, guidelines, and codes of practice to ensure food safety, quality, and fairness in global food trade. It was created in 1963 by the Food and Agriculture Organization of the United Nations (FAO) and the World Health Organization (WHO). Its main objective is to protect consumers' health and ensure fair practices in the global food trade. (WHO, 2018)

The Codex Alimentarius is a set of international standards covering everything related to food, including production, processing, labeling, storage, distribution, and marketing. Committees and groups of experts in different areas, such as food safety, hygiene, food additives, contaminants, and sampling methods, create these standards (WHO, 2018).

Although the Codex Alimentarius is not binding since it does not oblige countries to adopt its standards, many governments and international organizations consider it an essential reference for national policies and global trade agreements. Many trade agreements, such as the WTO (World Trade Organization) Agreement on Agriculture, are based on Codex Alimentarius, significantly impacting global food trade regulation.

The Codex Alimentarius is crucial for resolving trade disputes at the international level, especially when it comes to non-tariff barriers related to food safety (Wehr, 2007). If a country imposes restrictions on food imports from another country for public health reasons, Codex can be a reference to determine whether these restrictions are scientifically justified.

Objectives of the Codex Alimentarius (WHO, 2018):

1. Protection of public health: Codex's primary mission is to protect consumers' health by establishing clear scientific standards to ensure that food is safe for human consumption.
2. Facilitating international Trade: By harmonizing international food standards, Codex helps reduce trade barriers, promote smoother trade between countries, and avoid disputes related to food safety.
3. Improving quality and equity in the food industry: Through standards and guidelines, Codex also seeks to ensure that food is of high quality, that processes are transparent, and that consumers receive products that meet specific standards.

Areas Covered by the Codex Alimentarius (WHO, 2018):

1. Food safety standards: Establish limits for contaminants such as heavy metals, pesticides, and antibiotic residues, as well as specifications for microbiological food safety (e.g., standards for Salmonella and E. coli).
2. Food additives: Codex regulates the use of additives, colorants, preservatives, and other chemicals in food, establishing maximum permitted levels to ensure they do not pose a health risk.
3. Food labeling: This section provides guidelines on labeling food products. This includes nutritional information, ingredients, origin, expiration date, and other alerts to protect consumers, especially those with food allergies or intolerances.
4. Food hygiene: To prevent contamination, establish standards for hygiene during food production, processing, and distribution.
5. Methods of sampling and analysis: Codex also defines the methods of sampling and analysis that must be used to ensure that foods meet established quality and safety standards.
6. Fairtrade Practices: This section provides guidelines to promote transparent and fair trade practices, prevent food fraud, and protect consumers from deceptive product marketing.

The Codex Alimentarius comprises a series of committees and subcommittees that deal with different aspects of the food system. Among the most important are (WHO 2018):

- Codex General Standards Committee: Establishes general guidelines on food safety and quality.
- Codex Committee on Food Additives: Regulates the additives allowed in food.
- Codex Committee on Food Hygiene: Develops hygiene regulations during production and processing.
- Codex Committee on Food Labeling: Regulates labeling practices to ensure consumers receive clear and accurate information.

Each of these committees comprises international experts who work together to develop standards based on scientific evidence and global best practices. The decisions made are considered highly relevant by member countries and international organizations. (WHO, 2018)

Given that the main objective of certification systems is to facilitate regulatory compliance, it follows that some requirements of certification systems are more regionally specific than those of a regulatory nature. Although regional differences in regulations can be identified in areas such as labeling requirements, food safety, and environmental standards, significant differences in areas still need to be regulated or in regional specificities superimposed on a common legislative framework. These areas include country of origin labeling, animal welfare, or genetically modified organisms (GMOs) (Reckinger, 2022).

Regional food producers often use these differences as a competitive advantage over food exporters from third countries. The biggest challenge faced by producers is not complying with certification requirements per se but deciding in which market to certify their products and which regulatory regime to adhere to.

CONSUMER TRUST AND BRAND REPUTATION

Food producers are interested in ensuring their suppliers use good food safety practices. If a farmer or input supplier offers products certified by a well-respected third-party certification scheme, a food producer is likelier to purchase those products. The key for a brand owner is to have a certification scheme that is recognized and respected in the industry (Yadav et al., 2021).

Consumer Behavior and Food Certifications

What consumers choose to eat is a complex interaction of prices, income, tastes, and preferences (Knorr & Augustin, 2021). While food market signals effectively communicate the costs of production and the price at which a product is available, they also need to convey other important attributes of food, particularly its environmental impact. The lack of information about the harms of food and their associated environmental impact means that consumers may choose to live in blissful ignorance.

In most food transactions, producers have a considerable information advantage over consumers regarding production processes and their effects. As a result, it is difficult for consumers to protect themselves against such risks, which decreases their willingness to purchase certain types of food.

The development of product certification and labeling reflects these concerns regarding food safety and quality, and its purpose is to signal that specific desired characteristics exist in foods (Meijer et al., 2021). With an appropriate certification system, producers credibly demonstrate that relevant food safety or quality attributes have been met, and such signals reduce the level of consumer uncertainty and reluctance to purchase food.

Many brands use certifications to demonstrate that their products are of good quality. These certifications also make it easier for consumers to make informed decisions, as they can quickly identify products that align with their values (Chkanikova & Sroufe, 2021). For example, some consumers value protecting animals from suffering. These consumers buy products with the Animal Welfare Certified seal without checking the producer's website for information on how animals are treated.

To maintain a good reputation, companies ensure they follow the rules associated with a certification. They will lose consumers' trust if the regulations related to the stakeholders discover that they need to follow the standards and that their products do not comply with the established values.

Benefits of Food Certifications

One benefit of certification is that it enables food producers to demonstrate compliance with national and international food safety regulations, as well as the requirements of food safety programs developed by supermarket chains. A third benefit is that certification promotes good agricultural and hygienic practices, which reduce the risk for both food producers and consumers (Hu, 2023; Overbosch & Blanchard, 2023). The main benefit of food certification for food producers is increased access to markets. For many, certification is practically mandatory.

Challenges of Food Certifications

One of the main challenges food producers face when implementing food safety management systems is the high costs involved. Certification costs constitute a significant burden.

Another major challenge for food business operators is the increasing demand from consumers for quality, safe, and environmentally friendly food that is also animal-friendly. It translates into increased interest in implementing voluntary standards in the food production sector (Hu, 2023). Companies require a specific standard to produce a defined marketable product, and compliance with one standard does not mean that producing products for other markets is possible. The problem is that these market standards require particular and detailed specifications, and many food companies find themselves entangled in a "web of standards." New standards, regulations, or customer complaints are another challenge that currently certified companies or those considering certification must address, as it is an ongoing process to obtain, implement, maintain, and renew certifications (Chkanikova & Sroufe, 2021).

CAN COLLECTIVE INTELLIGENCE MITIGATE SOCIAL EXCLUSION IN FOOD CERTIFICATIONS?

As reviewed, food certifications are essential tools in verifying product quality, production ethics, and environmental responsibility. However, the certification landscape often reinforces social exclusion for smallholders, indigenous communities, and informal producers who face high entry barriers (Blesh et al., 2023) due to challenges presented above. Moreover, certification systems have historically been designed by institutions with limited to no participation from local actors. This is where AI, as part of Collective Intelligence, can offer new alternatives to democratize food certification processes, making them more inclusive.

For example, administrative barriers can be reduced using AI technologies such as remote sensing, natural language processing, and machine learning. Such technologies help to automate and simplify data collection and compliance verification in certification schemes. Some applied examples of this include satellite imagery that can monitor land use changes to verify organic farming practices without incurring significant expenses for repeated field visits (Pande et al., 2024). Mobile apps enhanced with AI-powered data recognition can enable small producers to document their practices in real-time using photos, voice recordings, or even questionnaires. These tools can reduce the cost and complexity of certifications, enabling participation from some excluded actors (Hinrix, 2024).

In terms of decision-making processes, Collective Intelligence facilitates the development of decentralized and transparent verification systems, where farmers, auditors, consumers, and other stakeholders collectively monitor and validate claims. For instance, blockchain-based traceability platforms can be combined with crowd-verified data inputs to strengthen accountability and reduce fraud (Miri et al., 2023). All these systems can include peer-review mechanisms, where communities participate in validating each other´s compliance, reinforcing local norms while making certifications more participatory.

When it comes to making certifications more aligned to local realities, Collective Intelligence through participatory standard setting becomes a possibility. Digital forums, assemblies, and community-driven scorecards enable actors across various social groups to co-create context-sensitive criteria that reflect their distinct values and needs (Manning et al., 2022). In this scenario, indigenous farming groups can help define biodiversity and cultural sustainability indicators, which are often overlooked in traditional certification schemes. This would bring social legitimization and local relevance to certifications.

Finally, with the contribution of Collective Intelligence, an adaptive certification system could be created. This system could incorporate real-time consumer feedback and field-level data. AI algorithms can synthesize input from online platforms, social media, and citizen apps to target concerns, update risks, or even highlight exemplary practices (Vinuesa et al., 2020). This feedback supports more dynamic and responsive certifications, which evolve in response to consumer awareness, environmental changes, and producer innovations, thereby bridging the gap between global standards and local practices.

It is possible to make food certifications more inclusive through Collective Intelligence, and even make them more transparent and adaptable.

Marketing Strategies For Certified Foods

Providing information through labeling is the most direct way to communicate a product's certification to consumers (Chalupová et al., 2020). In addition to the mandatory labels, many other certification labels in most markets require or allow voluntary labeling.

One of the main criticisms of certified foods is that the numerous certification labels with varying standards can confuse consumers. The more complex the certification standards, the greater the effort required to explain certification to customers. Consequently, relatively simple and highly recognized certification systems that create a competitive advantage in the marketplace are more likely to succeed (Chkanikova & Sroufe, 2021). Mandatory labels may be sufficient in countries where organic certification is prevalent and legally enforced (Kumar et al., 2023).

Food labels serve several functions. First, they provide information on the product's identity and the manufacturer's name and address. Second, they must list ingredients, nutritional information, and any allergens in the product. Third, they sometimes include other dietary information, such as the presence of genetically modified organisms (GMOs) or whether the product is organic. Fourth, labels may contain different information or claims, such as marketing, promotional, or other branding elements (Rupprecht et al., 2020).

Food labels can also be a source of social exclusion, as some consumers have varying levels of nutrition education or literacy (Ayaz et al., 2021). Those who do not understand the information on labels may be excluded from choosing foods that align with their dietary needs, exacerbating health problems in underserved communities. On the other hand, labels that include information about allergens, GMOs, or ingredients can stigmatize certain foods (Potts & Nelson, 2008). This can lead some people to avoid necessary or accessible products, which can negatively impact their well-being.

In the face of these forms of exclusion, collective intelligence has responded through community groups that use label information to educate and share knowledge about healthy eating. By working together and sharing information, communities have made more informed decisions about their consumption.

In the indigenous peoples of Latin America, collective intelligence is utilized to identify and promote local, healthy products that meet nutritional standards and are accessible to their communities (Altieri & Toledo, 2011). This action will counteract social exclusion by improving access to quality food.

CONCLUSIONS

Social exclusion within food supply chains occurs at various levels, ranging from unequal access to safe food to the inability of small producers to meet international standards. However, collective intelligence emerges as a critical agent in addressing these inequalities, fostering global collaboration, increasing access to financing, improving practices, and implementing technologies that promote transparency. Through collaborative networks and digital platforms, it is possible to reduce exclusion, improve sustainability, and increase the participation of small producers in global trade, creating a more just and equitable food system.

Food producers need help in their efforts to comply with certification standards and obtain certification. Some of the main challenges include the interpretation of different standards, which are constantly changing and sometimes contradictory; the high costs of full accreditation with high price standards, including compliance with numerous previous standards; difficulties in selecting appropriate standards; lack of market demand for products conforming to the standards; the availability of an alternative sector offering competition; lack of technical and financial support; as well as difficulties in understanding and using documentation requirements.

Most food certification systems operating worldwide are described and classified according to the main implementing and/or standard-setting organization. Commonly used food certification systems are classified as first-, second, or third-party certification systems. First-party certification is generally implemented through an organization's internal quality management system. Second-party certification is implemented by a customer or other interested parties who verify or audit the supplier's food safety and quality systems. Third-party certification is implemented by an independent certification body that verifies a food producer's compliance with a specific standard; this is the most widely recognized and practiced certification system.

Across all stages of the food supply chain, AI has the potential to either reinforce or disrupt social exclusion. The difference lies in whether these systems are developed in isolation or through inclusive, participatory processes. Collective Intelligence offers a pathway to democratize AI development, ensuring that marginalized voices are not only heard but also instrumental in shaping technology.

For producers, certifications can confer a competitive advantage in the global marketplace and also serve as a form of constraint, but one that can enable them to overcome, at least temporarily, the pressures of a worldwide market that continually seeks to reduce the prices of their products.

For consumers, certifications provide assurance that food was produced or processed under specific and desired conditions, such as organic, humane treatment of the animals, or fair wages for the men and women who harvested the ingredients.

While food certifications are increasingly in demand worldwide, there are regional differences in the popularity and growth of these certifications. For example, Halal certification is more prevalent in the Middle East, while Kosher is more popular in Israel and among Jewish communities worldwide. In contrast, organic, non-GMO, and fair trade certifications are more commonplace in North America and Europe. These regional differences in certification preferences are likely due to the cultural and religious beliefs of the populations in those regions. However, the growing trend of the world's population becoming increasingly concerned about what they consume in terms of health, the environmental impact of production, and social responsibility is driving demand for these certifications across regional boundaries.

REFERENCES

Aitken, R., Watkins, L., Williams, J., & Kean, A. (2020). The positive role of labeling on consumers' perceived behavioral control and intention to purchase organic food. *Journal of Cleaner Production*, *255*, 120334. DOI: 10.1016/j.jclepro.2020.120334

Allam, M., Bazok, R., Bordewick-Dell, U., Czarniecka-Skubina, E., Kazimierczak, R., Laikoja, K., Luik, A., Fuka, M. M., Muleo, R., Peetsmann, E., Petroselli, V., Roasto, M., Średnicka-Tober, D., Veith, M., Mancinelli, R., & Trafialek, J. (2023). Assistance needed for increasing knowledge of HACCP food safety principles for the organic sector in selected EU countries. *Sustainability (Basel)*, *15*(8), 6605. DOI: 10.3390/su15086605

Altieri, M. A., & Toledo, V. M. (2011). The agroecological revolution in Latin America: Rescuing nature, ensuring food sovereignty and empowering peasants. *The Journal of Peasant Studies*, *38*(3), 587–612. DOI: 10.1080/03066150.2011.582947

Alvarado, T. E. (2021). The Al-Invest Contribution to the Resilience of the Chemical Company: Development Cooperation. *Journal of International Cooperation and Development*, *4*(2), 1. DOI: 10.36941/jicd-2021-0009

Alvarado, T. E. G. (2003). Al-Invest y los intereses comerciales proteccionistas de la Unión Europea hacia Argentina, Brasil y México. *Contaduría y Administración*, (210), 47–70.

Alvarado, T. E. G. (2006). *Desarrollo endógeno articulado con la red de cooperación empresarial internacional: el caso de México* (Doctoral dissertation, Universidad Complutense de Madrid).

Alvarado, T. E. G. (2012). Internacionalización de empresas y desarrollo económico en zonas pobres. *Universidad & Empresa*, *14*(23), 45–69.

Amézquita Zegarra, R. (2021). Certificaciones complementarias a global GAP: GRASP y BRCGS en el Perú. https://hdl.handle.net/20.500.12996/4901

Ayaz, A., Dedebayraktar, D., Inan-Eroglu, E., Besler, H. T., & Buyuktuncer, Z. (2021). How does nutrition education contribute to the consumers' use and attitudes towards food labels? *Nutrition & Food Science*, *51*(3), 517–528. DOI: 10.1108/NFS-05-2020-0174

Bennett, E. A., & Grabs, J. (2024). How can sustainable business models distribute value more equitably in global value chains? Introducing "value chain profit sharing" as an emerging alternative to fair trade, direct trade, or solidarity trade. *Business Ethics, the Environment & Responsibility*. Advance online publication. DOI: 10.1111/beer.12666

Bevilacqua, D. (2020). Global Food Safety Regulation and the Interplay between Global Standards and WTO Law: How to Close the Legitimacy Gap? In *The Legitimacy of Standardisation as a Regulatory Technique* (pp. 243-265). Edward Elgar Publishing. DOI: https://doi.org/DOI: 10.4337/9781789902952.00018

Blesh, J., Mehrabi, Z., Wittman, H., Kerr, R. B., James, D., Madsen, S., Smith, O. M., Snapp, S., Stratton, A. E., & Bakar, R. (2023). Against the odds: Neservesnd institutional pathways enabling agricult,uthereby diversification. *One Earth*, *6*(5), 479–491. DOI: 10.1016/j.oneear.2023.03.004

Bomba, M. Y., & Susol, N. Y. (2020). Main requirements for food safety management systems under international standards: BRC, IFS, FSSC 22000, ISO 22000, Global GAP, SQF. *Scientific Messenger of LNU of Veterinary Medicine and Biotechnologies. Series. Food Technology*, *22*(93), 18–25. DOI: 10.32718/nvlvet-f9304

Bracic, A. (2020). *Breaking the exclusion cycle: How to promote cooperation between majority and minority ethnic groups*. Oxford University Press. DOI: 10.1093/oso/9780190050672.001.0001

Brockie, T., Clark, T. C., Best, O., Power, T., Bourque Bearskin, L., Kurtz, D. L., Lowe, J., & Wilson, D. (2023). Indigenous social exclusion to inclusion: Case studies on Indigenous nursing leadership in four high income countries. *Journal of Clinical Nursing*, *32*(3-4), 610–624. DOI: 10.1111/jocn.15801 PMID: 33942940

Casey, D. (2007). Private Food Safety and Quality Standards and the WTO. Social Science Research Network. https://kar.kent.ac.uk/31704/

Chalupová, M., Rojík, S., Kotoučková, H., & Kauerová, L. (2020). Food labels (quality, origin, and sustainability): The experience of Czech producers. *Sustainability (Basel)*, *13*(1), 318. DOI: 10.3390/su13010318

Chkanikova, O., & Sroufe, R. (2021). Third-party sustainability certifications in food retailing: Certification design from a sustainable supply chain management perspective. *Journal of Cleaner Production*, *282*, 124344. DOI: 10.1016/j.jclepro.2020.124344

Clapp, J., Moseley, W. G., Burlingame, B., & Termine, P. (2022). The case for a six-dimensional food security framework. *Food Policy, 106*, 102164. DOI: 10.1016/j.foodpol.2021.102164

Codex Alimentarius Commission (CAC). (2023). *Codex texts and standards*. https://www.fao.org/fao-who-codexalimentarius

Davis, K. F., Downs, S., & Gephart, J. A. (2021). Towards food supply chain resilience to environmental shocks. *Nature Food, 2*(1), 54–65. DOI: 10.1038/s43016-020-00196-3 PMID: 37117650

Dhal, S. B., & Kar, D. (2024). Transforming Agricultural Productivity with AI-Driven Forecasting: Innovations in Food Security and Supply Chain Optimization. *Forecasting, 6*(4), 925–951. DOI: 10.3390/forecast6040046

Diekman, C., Ryan, C. D., & Oliver, T. L. (2023). Misinformation and disinformation in food science and nutrition: Impact on practice. *The Journal of Nutrition, 153*(1), 3–9. DOI: 10.1016/j.tjnut.2022.10.001 PMID: 36913465

Dos Santos, R. B., Torrisi, N. M., & Pantoni, R. P. (2021). Third party certification of agri-food supply chain using smart contracts and blockchain tokens. *Sensors (Basel), 21*(16), 5307. DOI: 10.3390/s21165307 PMID: 34450749

FAO. (2021). *The state of food security and nutrition in the world 2021*. Food and Agriculture Organization of the United Nations., DOI: 10.4060/cb4474en

Galesic, M., Barkoczi, D., Berdahl, A. M., Biro, D., Carbone, G., Giannoccaro, I., Goldstone, R. L., Gonzalez, C., Kandler, A., Kao, A. B., Kendal, R., Kline, M., Lee, E., Massari, G. F., Mesoudi, A., Olsson, H., Pescetelli, N., Sloman, S. J., Smaldino, P. E., & Stein, D. L. (2023). Beyond collective intelligence: Collective adaptation. *Journal of the Royal Society, Interface, 20*(200), 20220736. DOI: 10.1098/rsif.2022.0736 PMID: 36946092

Gerardi, A. (2023). Global Food Safety Initiative (GFSI): underpinning the safety of the global food chain, facilitating regulatory compliance, trade, and consumer trust. In *Present Knowledge in Food Safety* (pp. 1089-1098). Academic Press.

Gligor, D. M., Davis-Sramek, B., Tan, A., Vitale, A., Russo, I., Golgeci, I., & Wan, X. (2022). Utilizing blockchain technology for supply chain transparency: A resource orchestration perspective. *Journal of Business Logistics, 43*(1), 140–159. DOI: 10.1111/jbl.12287

González, T. E., & Martín, M. A. (2018). Redes de cooperación empresaria internacionales en el sector ambiental y cooperación triangular. *Revista Universidad y Empresa, 20*(35), 51–77. DOI: 10.12804/revistas.urosario.edu.co/empresa/a.5307

Hinrix, F., Sanghera, J. K., Pak, T., Pankaj, V., Palepu, U. S., Turner-Rahman, S., . . . Beyer, J. L. (2024). AI Applications for Small & Medium Sized Enterprises. https://static1.squarespace.com/static/66708a0c236025663ebcd96f/t/680f8af480ae1a52c5ed58a1/1745849082806/AI+Applications+EN+cover.pdf

Holah, J. (2023). Principles of hygienic practice in food processing and manufacturing. In *Food Safety Management* (pp. 587–613). Academic Press., DOI: 10.1016/B978-0-12-820013-1.00029-2

Hu, L., Zheng, Y., Woods, T. A., Kusunose, Y., & Buck, S. (2023). The market for private food safety certifications: Conceptual framework, review, and future research directions. *Applied Economic Perspectives and Policy*, *45*(1), 197–220. DOI: 10.1002/aepp.13226

Ikram, M., Sroufe, R., Rehman, E., Shah, S. Z. A., & Mahmoudi, A. (2020). Do quality, environmental, and social (QES) certifications improve international trade? A comparative grey relation analysis of developing vs. developed countries. *Physica A*, *545*, 123486. DOI: 10.1016/j.physa.2019.123486

International Electrotechnical Commission (IEC). (2022). *Smart agriculture standards and tools*. https://www.iec.ch

International Organization for Standardization (ISO). (2021). *ISO 22000: Food safety management systems*. https://www.iso.org/iso-22000-food-safety-management.html

Kao, A. B., Banerjee, S. C., Francisco, F. A., & Berdahl, A. M. (2024). Timing decisions as the next frontier for collective intelligence. *Trends in Ecology & Evolution*, *39*(10), 904–912. DOI: 10.1016/j.tree.2024.06.003 PMID: 38964933

Kaplinsky, R., & Kraemer-Mbula, E. (2022). Innovation and uneven development: The challenge for low-and middle-income economies. *Research Policy*, *51*(2), 104394. DOI: 10.1016/j.respol.2021.104394

Kenney, M., Serhan, H., & Trystram, G. (2020). Digitization and platforms in agriculture: Organizations, power asymmetry, and collective action solutions. *Power Asymmetry, and Collective Action Solutions (June 20, 2020).*

Knorr, D., & Augustin, M. A. (2021). Food processing needs, advantages and misconceptions. *Trends in Food Science & Technology*, *108*, 103–110. DOI: 10.1016/j.tifs.2020.11.026

Kovacs, I., & Keresztes, E. R. (2022). Perceived consumer effectiveness and willingness to pay for credence product attributes of sustainable foods. *Sustainability (Basel)*, *14*(7), 4338. DOI: 10.3390/su14074338

Kumar, D., Menon, M. K., Balasubramani, N., Sadalaxmi, A., & Banerjee, M. (2023). Certification of Organic Agriculture and Trade Issues. In *Transforming Organic Agri-Produce into Processed Food Products* (pp. 113-151). Apple Academic Press. eBook ISBN9781003329770 DOI: 10.1201/9781003329770-7

Lambert, R., & Frenz, M. (2021). The economic impact for manufacturing sites operating to BRCGS certification. Downloaded from: https://eprints.bbk.ac.uk/id/eprint/46546/

Lang, B., & Conroy, D. M. (2022). When food governance matters to consumer food choice: Consumer perception of and preference for food quality certifications. *Appetite*, *168*, 105688. DOI: 10.1016/j.appet.2021.105688 PMID: 34509543

Lugo-Morin, D. R. (2024). Artificial Intelligence on Food Vulnerability: Future Implications within a Framework of Opportunities and Challenges. *Societies (Basel, Switzerland)*, *14*(7), 106. DOI: 10.3390/soc14070106

Machin, J. E., Mirabito, A. M., Azzari, C. N., Crosby, E., & Adkins, N. R. (2024). Disadvantaged Consumers, Market Access, and Consumer Well-Being. In *Fostering Consumer Well-Being: Theory, Evidence, and Policy* (pp. 69–90). Springer Nature Switzerland. DOI: 10.1007/978-3-031-59144-0_5

Manning, L., Brewer, S., Craigon, P. J., Frey, J., Gutierrez, A., Jacobs, N., Kanza, S., Munday, S., Sacks, J., & Pearson, S. (2022). Artificial intelligence and ethics within the food sector: Developing a common language for technology adoption across the supply chain. *Trends in Food Science & Technology*, *125*, 33–42. DOI: 10.1016/j.tifs.2022.04.025

Martínez-Martínez, O. A., Gil-Vasquez, K., & Romero-González, M. B. (2023). Food insecurity and levels of marginalization: Food accessibility, consumption and concern in Mexico. *International Journal for Equity in Health*, *22*(1), 178. DOI: 10.1186/s12939-023-01977-5 PMID: 37667336

Mattsson, V. (2022). Thesis: Governing Data in a Worker Cooperative. *Management, 49*, 424-438. https://urn.fi/URN:NBN:fi:aalto-202302051941

Meijer, G. W., Detzel, P., Grunert, K. G., Robert, M. C., & Stancu, V. (2021). Towards effective labelling of foods. An international perspective on safety and nutrition. *Trends in Food Science & Technology*, *118*, 45–56. DOI: 10.1016/j.tifs.2021.09.003

Mendoza Pachas, C. J., & Pumasunco Silva, L. E. (2021). Conocimiento de los enfoques de gestión de calidad beneficiosos para alcanzar los estándares de certificación relevantes dentro del mercado estadounidense en el contexto agroexportador del Perú. http://hdl.handle.net/20.500.12404/19266

Miri, P., Stankovski, V., Kochovski, P., & Klun, M. (2023). Technological Solutions for Transparent Monitoring, Citizen Engagement, and Achieving the Sustainable Development Goals. https://www.researchgate.net/publication/372860663_Technological_Solutions_for_Transparent_Monitoring_Citizen_Engagement_and_Achieving_the_Sustainable_Development_Goals

Nie, Y. Y., Liang, A. R. D., & Wang, E. C. (2022). Third-party certification labels for organic food: Consumers' purchase choice and willingness-to-pay. *British Food Journal*, *124*(11), 3993–4008. DOI: 10.1108/BFJ-07-2021-0777

Nurse, K. (2016). Study on Alternative and Innovative Funding Mechanisms for ACP Cultural Industries. *Final Executive Summary. European Union and the ACP Secretariat, December.*

Overbosch, P., & Blanchard, S. (2023). Principles and systems for quality and food safety management. In *Food Safety Management* (pp. 497–512). Academic Press., DOI: 10.1016/B978-0-12-820013-1.00018-8

Pande, C. B., Srivastava, A., Moharir, K. N., Radwan, N., Mohd Sidek, L., Alshehri, F., Pal, S. C., Tolche, A. D., & Zhran, M. (2024). Characterizing land use/land cover change dynamics by an enhanced random forest machine learning model: A Google Earth Engine implementation. *Environmental Sciences Europe*, *36*(1), 84. DOI: 10.1186/s12302-024-00901-0

Pilcher, J. M. (2023). *Food in world history*. Routledge. DOI: 10.4324/9781003332039

Potts, M., & Nelson, R. (2008). Understanding the effect of stigmatization on food consumer knowledge, perception and behaviour in Northern Ireland. *International Journal of Consumer Studies*, *32*(4), 366–373. DOI: 10.1111/j.1470-6431.2008.00676.x

Prylipko, T. M., Kostash, V. B., Fedoriv, V. M., Lishchuk, S. H., & Tkachuk, V. P. (2021). Control and identification of food products under EC regulations and standards. *International Journal of Agricultural Extension*, *9*(5), 83–91. DOI: 10.33687/ijae.009.00.3964

Radu, E., Dima, A., Dobrota, E. M., Badea, A. M., Madsen, D. Ø., Dobrin, C., & Stanciu, S. (2023). Global trends and research hotspots on HACCP and modern quality management systems in the food industry. *Heliyon*, *9*(7), e18232. Advance online publication. DOI: 10.1016/j.heliyon.2023.e18232 PMID: 37539220

Raman, P. (2022). *The Role of Integrative Analytics in Knowledge Building: Supporting Practices of Care* (Order No. 29397271). Available from ProQuest One Academic. (2743512512). http://wdg.biblio.udg.mx:2048/login?url=https://www.proquest.com/dissertations-theses/role-integrative-analytics-knowledge-building/docview/2743512512/se-2

Rampa, F., Lammers, E., Linnemann, A., Schoustra, S., & de Winter, D. (2020). *Pathways to improved food and nutrition security of the poor: The promise of African indigenous foods and technologies*. NWO WOTRO.

Reckinger, R. (2022). Values-based territorial food networks: Qualifying sustainable and ethical transitions of alternative food networks. *Regions & Cohesion : the Journal of the Consortium for Comparative Research on Regional Integration and Social Cohesion*, *12*(3), 78–109. DOI: 10.3167/reco.2022.120305

Rupprecht, C. D., Fujiyoshi, L., McGreevy, S. R., & Tayasu, I. (2020). Trust me? Consumer trust in expert information on food product labels. *Food and Chemical Toxicology*, *137*, 111170. DOI: 10.1016/j.fct.2020.111170 PMID: 32014536

Schleifer, P., & Sun, Y. (2020). Reviewing the impact of sustainability certification on food security in developing countries. *Global Food Security*, *24*, 100337. DOI: 10.1016/j.gfs.2019.100337

Shuhaimi, A. A. M., Ab Karim, M. S., Fatimah, S., Mohamad, U. F. U. Z. A., & Arshad, M. M. (2022). A review on Halal and Kosher regulations, certifications, and industrial practices. *International Journal of Academic Research in Business & Social Sciences*, *12*(2), 182–192. DOI: 10.6007/IJARBSS/v12-i2/12175

Sorbo, A., Pucci, E., Nobili, C., Taglieri, I., Passeri, D., & Zoani, C. (2022). Food safety assessment: Overview of metrological issues and regulatory aspects in the European Union. *Separations*, *9*(2), 53. DOI: 10.3390/separations9020053

Stanciu, M., Popescu, A., Antonie, I., Sava, C., & Nistoreanu, B. G. (2022). Good practices on reducing food waste throughout the food supply chain. *Amfiteatru Economic*, *24*(60), 566. DOI: 10.24818/EA/2022/60/566

Starobin, S. M. (2021). Credibility beyond compliance: Uncertified smallholders in sustainable food systems. *Ecological Economics*, *180*, 106767. DOI: 10.1016/j.ecolecon.2020.106767

Starobin, S. M. (2021). Credibility beyond compliance: Uncertified smallholders in sustainable food systems. *Ecological Economics*, *180*, 106767. DOI: 10.1016/j.ecolecon.2020.106767

Steggemann, M. (2023). Collective Intelligence synergizing into Collective Resilience. Mercados y negocios, 24(49), 65-82.

Stein, A. J., & Santini, F. (2022). The sustainability of "local" food: A review for policy-makers. *Review of Agricultural, Food and Environmental Studies*, *103*(1), 77–89. DOI: 10.1007/s41130-021-00148-w PMID: 38624674

Taneja, A., Nair, G., Joshi, M., Sharma, S., Sharma, S., Jambrak, A. R., Roselló-Soto, E., Barba, F. J., Castagnini, J. M., Leksawasdi, N., & Phimolsiripol, Y. (2023). Artificial Intelligence: Implications for the Agri-Food Sector. *Agronomy (Basel)*, *13*(5), 1397. DOI: 10.3390/agronomy13051397

Warshawsky, D. N. (2024). *Food Waste, Food Insecurity, and the Globalization of Food Banks*. University of Iowa Press.

Wehr, H. M. (2007). Codex Alimentarius: What It Is and Why It Is Important. In *Microbial Food Contamination* (pp. 517-546). CRC Press.

WHO. (2018). *Understanding the Codex Alimentarius*. Food & Agriculture Org.

Xiao, G., Samian, N., Faizal, M. F. M., As'ad, M. A. Z. M., Fadzil, M. F. M., Abdullah, A., & Hermadi, I. (2024). A Framework for Blockchain and Internet of Things Integration in Improving Food Security in the Food Supply Chain. *Journal of Advanced Research in Applied Sciences and Engineering Technology*, *34*(1), 24–37. DOI: 10.37934/araset.34.1.2437

Yadav, D., Dutta, G., & Kumar, S. (2021). Food safety standards adoption and its impact on firms' export performance: A systematic literature review. *Journal of Cleaner Production*, *329*, 129708. DOI: 10.1016/j.jclepro.2021.129708

Yalamati, S. (2024). The Contribution of Artificial Intelligence to Foster Sustainable Food Systems in Agriculture. In *Artificial Intelligence and Machine Learning for Sustainable Development* (pp. 236–248). CRC Press., DOI: 10.1201/9781003497189-18

ENDNOTES

1 Social exclusión defined by FAO (2021) as a systemic marginalization of individual sor communities from access to resources, rights and opportunities.

2 AI is understood as part of Collective intelligence. As Ried et al. (2021) mention in their work, humans and machines working together create an enhanced capacity known as Collective Intelligence, this creates greater outcomes than the ones achieved individually.

Chapter 6
Machine Learning and Bias:
Creating Inclusive AI Systems for All

Mustafa Kayyali
https://orcid.org/0000-0003-3300-262X
Maaref University of Applied Sciences, Syria

ABSTRACT

As machine learning systems become increasingly embedded in our daily lives, the biases they inherit and perpetuate carry real-world consequences—often exacerbating the very inequities they claim to neutralize. This chapter examines the multifaceted nature of bias in machine learning, not as a technical glitch, but as a reflection of societal structures encoded into data, design, and deployment processes. It explores how exclusion happens invisibly—through underrepresentation, flawed assumptions, and biased benchmarks—and challenges dominant notions of "objectivity" in AI. By reframing fairness through the lens of inclusivity and social justice, the chapter outlines tangible steps toward building equitable systems. It calls for a reimagining of machine learning not simply as a tool for efficiency, but as a moral and social force shaped by choices—human ones. The path to truly inclusive AI lies in questioning who gets to decide what intelligence is, and for whom it works.

INTRODUCTION

When Fairness Becomes a Mirage: The False Neutrality of Machine Learning
It begins, perhaps deceptively, with a line of code. A dataset compiled. A model trained (Pruksachatkun et al, 2023). The assumption—quiet but powerful—is that

DOI: 10.4018/979-8-3373-2685-6.ch006

Copyright © 2026, IGI Global Scientific Publishing. Copying or distributing in print or electronic forms without written permission of IGI Global Scientific Publishing is prohibited.

the technology, by its nature, is neutral. It observes, it calculates, it learns. It does not judge. Yet here we are, standing in the midst of an AI revolution that, while hailed as objective and data-driven, continues to reflect, reproduce, and amplify the very human biases we had hoped it would eliminate.

This chapter begins with a simple yet uncomfortable truth: machine learning systems are only as fair as the societies that create them (Barocas et al, 2023). Far from being neutral arbiters, these systems often act as mirrors—subtly echoing back our collective histories of inequality, exclusion, and injustice, but encoded now in technical artifacts that are harder to question, let alone dismantle. What makes this dynamic especially insidious is its invisibility. Decisions once made in boardrooms or by bureaucrats are now carried out by algorithms, cloaked in a veneer of precision and inevitability. Predictive policing, hiring algorithms, healthcare diagnostics, loan approvals—each, in theory, a step toward efficiency; in practice, too often a step backward into old, unspoken hierarchies.

Bias in AI is not a bug. It is not simply the result of poor data hygiene or flawed modeling choices—although those play a role. It is the systemic consequence of how our digital infrastructure is designed, who designs it, and who gets left out of the design process. Marginalized communities—already underserved by public services, underrepresented in research, and oversurveilled by state systems—are now facing new forms of algorithmic discrimination (Chaka, 2022). And these harms often happen silently. There's no pop-up window announcing that a resume was rejected because the model learned to associate certain zip codes with low performance. No alert when a medical algorithm allocates fewer resources to patients from historically disadvantaged backgrounds.

What we are witnessing is a shift in the locus of discrimination—from the overt and legal to the covert and technical. And with that shift comes a corresponding challenge: **how do we ensure that machine learning works *for* people, not *against* them?** How do we build systems that reflect not only statistical accuracy but also moral and social accountability?

This chapter takes up that challenge. We will explore the historical roots and technical mechanisms of algorithmic bias, but also push beyond diagnosis to imagine what a more inclusive AI future could look like. We will ask uncomfortable questions: Who gets to decide what fairness means? Who benefits from the current definitions? And what would it take—not just technically, but culturally and politically—to create systems that genuinely serve all of us?

This is not a purely academic exercise. It is a call for reimagining. For taking seriously the ethical dimensions of code. For recognizing that inclusion is not a checklist or an optional add-on, but the very foundation of a just technological future.

THE ROOTS OF ALGORITHMIC BIAS: HISTORICAL AND TECHNICAL ORIGINS

It's tempting to imagine that machine learning emerged in a vacuum. That it bloomed suddenly from lines of code, pristine and untouched by history, culture, or ideology. But that fantasy is as seductive as it is dangerous. The reality is far messier. Machine learning—like all technologies—is born of human hands, shaped by human choices, and soaked in the sediments of historical bias (Spicer, 2023). It may deal in numbers and probabilities, but its architecture is laced with the stories we've long told about who matters, who belongs, and who doesn't.

To understand algorithmic bias, we have to rewind—not just to the moment the dataset was compiled or the model was deployed, but further back. Way back. Because the roots of the problem stretch deep, entangled with centuries of social, political, and economic hierarchies. Bias didn't hitch a ride on the back of a GPU; it came embedded in the worldview of those who built the system in the first place.

Let's start with something deceptively simple: data. The raw material of machine learning. We speak of it as though it's just "out there," waiting to be harvested, neutral and objective. But data is never neutral. What gets counted, what gets recorded, what gets discarded—these are all choices. Sometimes deliberate, sometimes unconscious, always consequential. The police records used to train predictive policing models, for instance, don't merely reflect crime rates; they reflect decades of over-policing in certain neighborhoods, racial profiling, socioeconomic disparities, and legislative priorities skewed by power (Patterson et al, 2025). Feed that data into a model, and you're not training it to predict crime—you're training it to replicate the biases of the criminal justice system.

The irony is thick: in our quest to automate decision-making, we've enshrined human prejudice inside a mathematical shell. And because the outputs are draped in the authority of computation, they appear indisputable. Unbiased. Scientific. But under the surface, they're anything but.

Bias has always been a quiet companion of classification systems. Think back to the early days of statistics and anthropology, where entire populations were reduced to typologies and bell curves. Racial science, phrenology, eugenics—all of them dressed up their biases in numbers, claiming neutrality while justifying oppression (Jones, 2024). Fast forward to the present, and you'll find similar logics playing out in algorithmic form: models that predict recidivism rates assigning higher risk scores to Black defendants; facial recognition systems failing more often on darker skin tones; language models that associate certain names or dialects with lower intelligence or criminality. It's the same dance, just with shinier tools. And then there's the issue of abstraction. One of the strange qualities of machine learning is its reliance on pattern recognition at scale. It doesn't need to "understand" context in the way humans do. It just needs enough statistical signal. But this is where things start to fray. When context is stripped away—when nuance is flattened into binary labels—bias creeps in through the cracks. Take resume screening tools, for example. If a model is trained on past hiring data that shows a preference for men in engineering roles, it may penalize applicants who attended all-women's colleges or participated in diversity programs. The algorithm doesn't know why. It doesn't hate women. It's just chasing patterns. But chasing patterns without understanding history is a recipe for exclusion.

Table 1. Types of Bias in Machine Learning

Type of Bias	Description	Impact
Sampling Bias	Occurs when training data is not representative of the population.	Leads to inaccurate or unfair predictions.
Label Bias	Happens when labels in the dataset reflect stereotypes or inaccuracies.	Reinforces existing social prejudices.
Exclusion Bias	Arises when important data is left out of the model.	Reduces the model's generalizability.
Measurement Bias	Results from inconsistent data collection methods.	Compromises data quality and fairness.

Even technical decisions that seem unrelated to ethics—like how to define "accuracy" or what constitutes "noise"—can have moral consequences (Stenseke, 2024). Suppose you're training a model to predict health outcomes. Do you optimize it for the general population, or do you ensure it's equally accurate across subgroups? If you choose the former, marginalized communities with different baselines or access to care may end up with worse predictions. If you choose the latter, you may face trade-offs in efficiency. These are not just engineering decisions; they're ethical ones. But too often, they're made without considering the ethical dimension at all.

The culture of tech doesn't help. For years, the field of AI was dominated by a kind of apolitical pragmatism: build the model, ship the product, move fast and break things. There was little room for reflection on social impact or historical responsibility. Computer science curriculums rarely taught ethics, let alone critical race theory or gender studies. The result? An ecosystem that treats fairness as a post-processing task, something to be tacked on after deployment—if at all. Inclusion becomes a checkbox, not a principle.

We also have to talk about who's building these systems. Diversity in tech isn't just a feel-good slogan. It's a structural necessity. When teams are homogenous—when the same demographic, cultural, and ideological perspectives dominate—blind spots multiply. Biases go unchallenged, not out of malice, but out of unfamiliarity (Thomas, 2022). You don't test a facial recognition system on dark-skinned faces if no one on your team thinks to ask why that matters. You don't question the default gender assumptions in a dataset if everyone on your team shares them. Inclusion in development isn't charity. It's damage prevention. But let's not mistake intention for immunity. Even well-meaning developers, trying to "de-bias" their models, can fall into traps. One of the most common is over-correction—assuming that equal outcomes across groups automatically mean fairness. But fairness isn't just about parity; it's about justice. It's about acknowledging structural disadvantage and accounting for it, not pretending it doesn't exist. A model that treats everyone "equally" in a deeply unequal world is, in effect, perpetuating the inequality.

Figure 1. Addressing Bias in Machine Learning

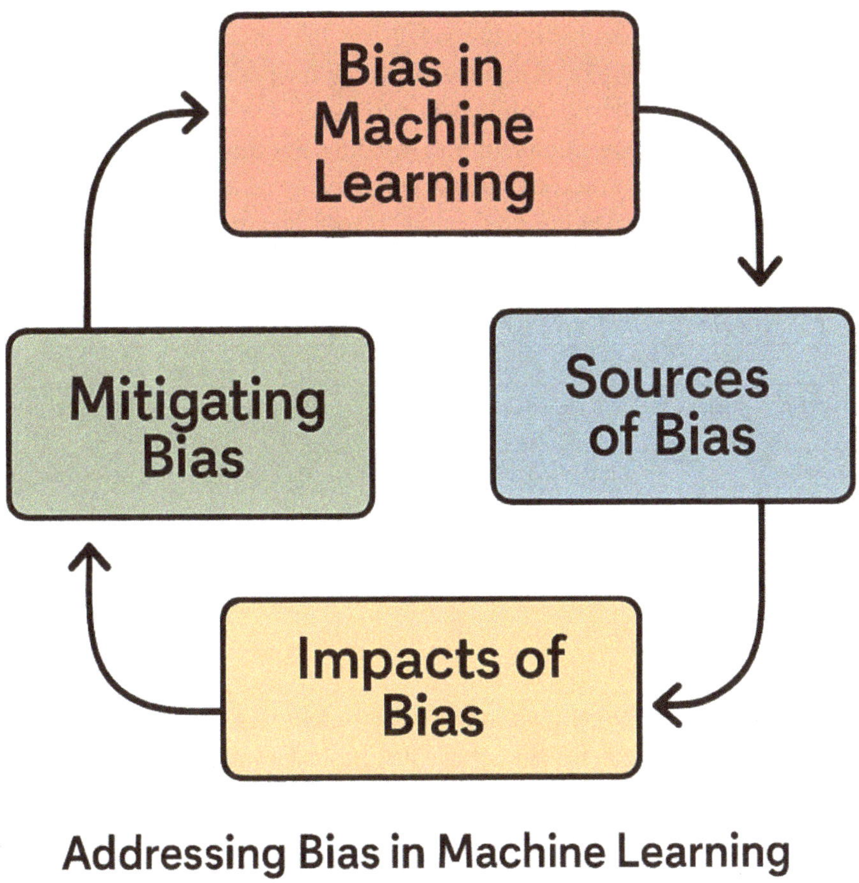

There's also the seductive pull of formalization. The belief that fairness can be reduced to a formula, a constraint to be optimized. But fairness is messy. Contextual. Sometimes contradictory. What's fair in one setting may not be in another. And the more we try to squeeze it into clean mathematical expressions, the more we risk flattening its complexity. It's not that technical tools are useless—far from it. But they're not enough. You can't debug injustice with code alone.

This is where historical literacy becomes essential. Not as a sidebar, but as a foundation. You can't design inclusive AI if you don't understand what exclusion has looked like. You need to know how redlining worked to grasp why housing algorithms might discriminate. You need to study colonial data practices to understand why Western datasets dominate. You need to listen to the communities who've borne the brunt of surveillance, automation, and digital neglect—not as subjects, but as co-creators (Hamid & Kuo, 2022). And yet, despite all of this, there's still hope. Because just as bias is human-made, so is the capacity to recognize it. To name it. To challenge it. We're seeing new interdisciplinary collaborations—between computer scientists, ethicists, sociologists, activists—that are pushing the conversation forward. We're seeing communities resisting algorithmic harms, demanding transparency, fairness, and accountability. We're seeing researchers turning the lens inward, asking harder questions, doing slower work. That matters.

Table 2. Strategies for Inclusive AI Design

Strategy	Goal	Implementation
Diverse Data Collection	Ensure representation of all user groups.	Gather datasets from varied demographics.
Bias Auditing	Identify and reduce harmful bias in models.	Use tools to measure and address fairness.
Transparent Reporting	Promote accountability in AI development.	Publish model behavior and limitations.
Inclusive Team Involvement	Reflect varied perspectives in AI systems.	Include experts from diverse backgrounds.

What if we treated fairness not as a constraint, but as a creative design principle? What if we built systems that didn't just avoid harm, but actively promoted equity? What if we understood that the goal of AI isn't just to predict what is, but to imagine what could be? The roots of algorithmic bias run deep. But roots can be unearthed. They can be studied. And—perhaps most importantly—they can be disrupted. Not by erasing the past, but by learning from it. Not by retreating into abstraction, but by grounding our work in the lived realities of those most affected. Bias may have been encoded into the early architecture of AI. But inclusion—real, robust, transformative inclusion—is still within reach. The question is not whether we can do it, but whether we will.

INVISIBLE EXCLUSIONS: HOW MACHINE LEARNING MARGINALIZES BY DESIGN

Exclusion, when it is visible, is at least negotiable. You can point to it, protest it, legislate against it (Browne et al, 2021). But when it's buried—when it's silent, technical, and normalized—then it becomes something far more dangerous: reality. That's where machine learning lives. It doesn't slam the door in your face. It just fails to see you at all. And there's no one to argue with. No clear act of discrimination. Just a blank screen, an unanswered application, an outcome you'll never know was denied. That's how marginalization happens now: invisibly. Not by intent, necessarily, but by design.

Let's begin here—at the subtle hinge between absence and erasure. Machine learning systems don't hate. They don't discriminate in the old-fashioned, overt sense of the word. They sort. They filter. They optimize. And in doing so, they quietly decide who counts and who doesn't. But the question they rarely ask—because their architects rarely ask it—is: *Who's missing?* Whose data never made it into the system? Whose reality is too complex, too irregular, too underrepresented to be legible to the algorithm?

Consider the training datasets that fuel most large-scale AI models today. These data reservoirs aren't gathered randomly; they're pulled from where data is plentiful, cheap, and easy to scrape. Which is to say—online, urban, English-speaking, majority-world-centric spaces. Social media profiles, e-commerce logs, digitized medical records from well-resourced hospitals (Periáñez et al, 2024). You don't often see data from remote rural clinics, undocumented workers, Indigenous communities, or the digitally excluded. Why? Because that data doesn't exist in clean, structured formats. Because it's messy, politically sensitive, or legally protected. Or simply because no one thought to look there. And when you're not seen, you're not learned from. When you're not learned from, you're not served. This is exclusion by omission. And it is *baked into the process*—not just the data, but the assumptions that determine what's relevant and what isn't. That's the cruel elegance of machine learning bias: it doesn't need to overtly discriminate to harm you. It just needs to pretend you don't exist.

Take the classic example of facial recognition technology. Study after study has shown that these systems perform significantly worse on darker-skinned faces, particularly Black women (Moore et al, 2021). The problem wasn't that someone programmed them to be racist. The problem was that the training sets were overwhelmingly white and male. It wasn't hatred. It was neglect. And that's often more insidious—because it's less obvious, easier to excuse, and harder to challenge in court.

Or consider natural language processing (NLP), the subfield behind chatbots, translation tools, and search engines (Lane & Dyshel, 2025). These systems learn from massive corpora of text—Reddit threads, Wikipedia pages, news articles, digitized books. Sounds comprehensive, right? But language is not neutral. It's loaded with social baggage. Historical texts are steeped in the values of their time. Modern texts reflect the voices of those who are literate, connected, and documented. Dialects, slang, minority languages—these get filtered out, tagged as "noise," or simply left out of the training pipeline. Which means the resulting models don't just echo mainstream values—they canonize them. They make dominant speech patterns seem like the only valid ones. And those who don't conform? They become unrecognizable. Uninterpretable. Unwelcome.

It's not just about race, or gender, or language. It's about how machine learning flattens complexity. Think about disability. Most models assume able-bodied norms unless told otherwise. Vision-based systems presume standard eyesight. Voice recognition presumes clear, fluent speech. Mobility tracking presumes conventional movement patterns (Rinelli, 2022). And if you don't fit those molds, the system might flag you as "anomalous," or worse—fraudulent. Not because it knows what disability is, but because it wasn't trained to expect you. And let's not forget trans and nonbinary individuals—often misgendered by systems trained on rigid binary labels. Or refugees without stable documentation, filtered out by ID-matching software. Or low-income users, whose behaviors diverge from the high-value customer profiles that financial AI systems are trained to favor.

Invisibility is not passive. It's constructed. Each design choice—each modeling decision, threshold setting, category definition—becomes a site of potential exclusion. The very act of labeling is political. Consider a machine learning model designed to detect "inappropriate" content. Who decides what's inappropriate? A group of engineers, perhaps, working off a rubric that reflects their own cultural sensibilities. Images of queer intimacy, Indigenous rituals, or political protest might be flagged not because they're harmful, but because they don't fit a particular vision of normalcy. And once they're flagged, they're hidden. Removed. Deleted. Exclusion becomes automated.

Then there's the issue of feedback loops. A biased system doesn't just reflect inequalities—it can reinforce and amplify them over time. Predictive policing is a stark example. If a neighborhood is over-policed, it generates more arrest records (Patterson, 2025). More records mean more data. More data means the model sees that area as a "hotspot," which leads to even more policing. The bias self-replicates. And the people inside that loop? They can't break free, because the system that governs them is convinced it's being objective.

Credit scoring, too, can trap people in invisible cages. If your financial history doesn't resemble the patterns of "creditworthy" users—if you pay rent in cash, if you don't have a credit card, if you switch jobs frequently—you may be penalized. Not because you're a risk, but because you don't fit the algorithm's model of stability. The result? Fewer opportunities, higher interest rates, fewer approvals. And the most painful part? You may never know why.

Transparency, as it turns out, doesn't come naturally to machine learning systems. They operate behind opaque mathematical veils—black boxes that are difficult to interpret even by their creators. For those affected by their decisions, there's rarely a clear path to recourse. If an AI system denies you a loan, who do you call? If a hiring algorithm filters out your résumé, who explains the reason? The opacity of machine learning doesn't just obscure error. It conceals accountability. And that's not a bug. It's a feature of design that prioritizes efficiency over justice. So how do we change this? How do we surface the exclusions that machine learning hides so well?

Figure 2. Sources of Algorithmic Bias in AI

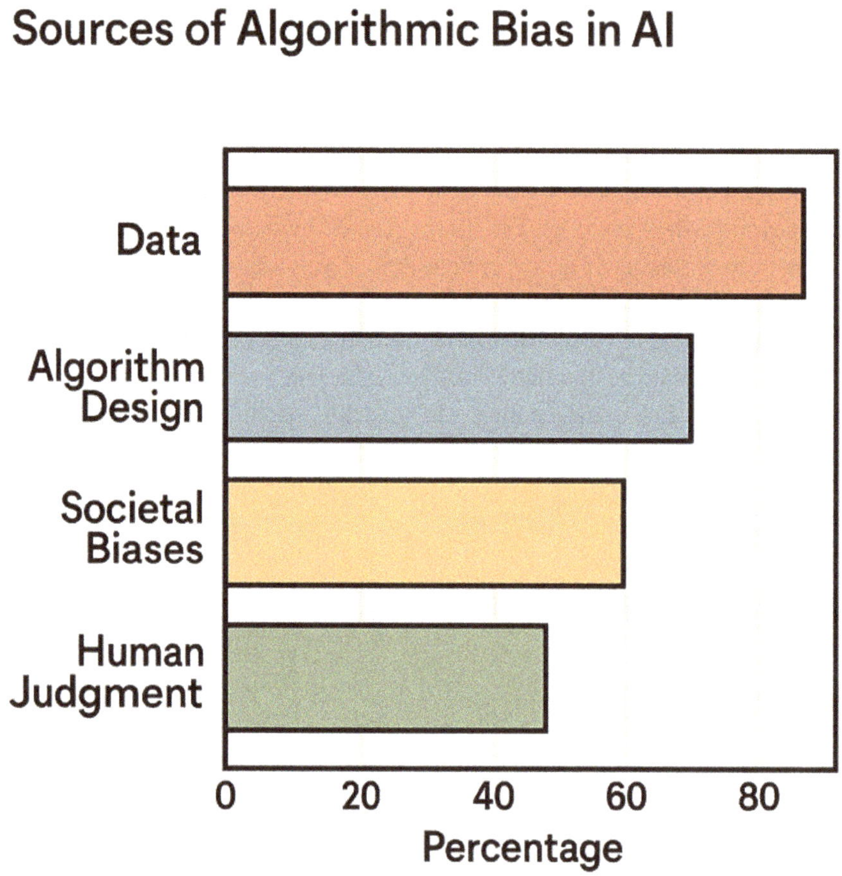

The answer, perhaps, begins with humility. A recognition that technology is not inherently fair, and that bias doesn't vanish just because decisions are made by machines (Broussard, 2023). We have to approach AI systems not as neutral arbiters, but as sociotechnical artifacts—products of human choices, embedded in human institutions, operating within human histories. That means rethinking everything—from data collection to model evaluation. It means asking: *Who benefits? Who gets harmed? Who is absent?* It means designing with and for marginalized communities, not just testing on them. It means being willing to slow down, to question assumptions, to complicate the clean lines of computational logic with the messy realities of lived experience. And it means creating channels for redress. Systems must be not just fair, but *contestable*. Users should have the right to know why decisions were made, to challenge those decisions, and to contribute to their revision. That's not just a technical problem—it's a democratic one.

Invisible exclusions are not inevitable. They are the result of habits—of how we define success, of whose input we value, of how we imagine the purpose of AI in society. To build systems that include, we must first learn to see what's been ignored. We must surface the silences. We must listen—not just to the data, but to the people the data forgets. In the end, inclusion isn't about being nice. It's about being just. It's about refusing to accept a future that looks too much like the past, just faster and harder to resist. Machine learning doesn't have to marginalize. But if we don't intervene—if we keep pretending it's objective—it will. Not because it intends to. But because that's what it's been trained to do.

REFRAMING FAIRNESS: RETHINKING METRICS, DATA, AND REPRESENTATION

Fairness—such a simple word. A moral comfort blanket, a metric we chase, a banner we wave when we say we want AI to be better, kinder, more just (Buttol, 2023). But fairness in machine learning? That's a trickier beast. It slips between definitions. It performs respectability in one model, betrayal in another. We say "fairness" like we all agree on what it means. We don't. And maybe that's the first problem: **we've mistaken measurement for morality**.

In the world of machine learning, fairness is often treated as an optimization goal—something you can compute, monitor, tweak. Flip a few switches. Adjust the thresholds. Add some demographic parity constraints. But when you peer into the logic behind these models, you start to see the fracture lines. You begin to understand that fairness is not just a variable in a loss function—it's a question about power, perspective, and who gets to define the norm.

There's this uneasy consensus among technical communities that fairness must be *quantified*—formalized into definitions that algorithms can understand. So, we get fairness through unawareness (just ignore sensitive attributes like race or gender). We get statistical parity (make outcomes equal across groups). We get equalized odds (make false positives and false negatives equal). These metrics are not wrong, per se. They're precise. They're mathematically elegant. But they're also sterile. Detached. As if harm and justice could be wrangled into tidy equations. But people aren't distributions. They're histories. They're context. They're contradiction. And yet, our models tend to flatten all that richness into clean, digestible bits of data—points plotted on a graph, stripped of their entanglements. It's not just reductive. It's dangerous. Because once we abstract human lives into numerical vectors, we risk making real suffering disappear behind the veil of computation.

Let's pause here, though, and ask a different question: **What are we trying to be fair *to*?** Fair to the data? Fair to the users? Fair to the system's performance? Or fair to the underlying inequalities that created the problem in the first place? This is where most fairness metrics fail. They don't interrogate the *origin* of the data—they assume it is trustworthy, clean, or at least fixable. But what if the data is a record of harm? What if it encodes decades of discrimination, structural violence, or epistemic exclusion? Are we still talking about fairness—or are we now talking about repair?

Data, as we often forget, is not collected in a vacuum. It's harvested through decisions—what to observe, how to classify, who to ignore (Muller & Strohmayer, 2022). What's labeled "ground truth" is often just someone's version of the truth, hardened into digital concrete. And when models learn from that, they don't just replicate the past—they re-legitimize it. They say, "This is normal." They say, "This is what the world looks like." And maybe that's the problem: **our models are too good at representing the world as it is**, not as it should be.

Representation, then, becomes a double-edged sword. On one side, there's the call for better inclusion in data—more voices, more faces, more languages, more bodies. And yes, that matters. Representation is a precondition for justice. But on the other side, there's a more uncomfortable truth: not all inclusion is liberatory. Sometimes, to be included in a dataset is to be commodified, surveilled, misunderstood. Just ask marginalized communities who've been overrepresented in policing data, medical experimentation, or poverty prediction models. Being seen by the system doesn't always mean being served by it.

So, when we talk about "rethinking representation," we have to go beyond diversity checklists. We have to ask: **Who is doing the seeing? Who is benefiting from this representation? And what is it costing those being represented?** Let's take a step back and look at the mechanics of labeling. Machine learning relies heavily on labeled data—training sets annotated by humans or heuristics (Geiger et al, 2021). But labels are not neutral. They often reflect biased taxonomies, outdated categories, or culturally loaded assumptions. For example, consider gender classification in facial recognition systems. Many of these systems force a binary: male or female. But gender is not binary for everyone. What happens to nonbinary individuals in such systems? They're either misclassified or erased entirely. And the model learns that erasure is accuracy.

So, what if instead of forcing the world to fit our labels, we reimagined our labels to fit the world? What if we designed systems to accommodate ambiguity, fluidity, and uncertainty—not as bugs to be fixed but as truths to be respected? It's possible. But it requires a radical shift in how we understand data—not as static, objective inputs but as living artifacts shaped by power, context, and culture. It requires us to treat data not as a given, but as a site of inquiry. Who collected it? Why? What was left out? Who decided what counts? This is why fairness isn't just a technical challenge—it's a political one. A cultural one. And any attempt to engineer fairness without engaging with the social realities that underpin our datasets will fall flat. Because fairness isn't about equalizing outputs in an unjust world. It's about transforming the world those outputs affect. That means embracing messiness. Embracing pluralism. It means rejecting the idea that there's a single "fair" model waiting to be discovered, and instead recognizing that fairness will look different in different contexts. That it's contested. That it needs to be negotiated—openly, transparently, and with those who are most affected at the center of the conversation.

Yes, we need technical tools. Fairness-aware algorithms. Bias audits. Inclusive benchmarks. But we also need more uncomfortable conversations (Emma, 2024). We need interdisciplinary teams that include ethicists, sociologists, activists, artists. We need frameworks that value lived experience as much as statistical rigor. We need humility—a rare commodity in the world of machine learning, where confidence often outpaces caution. And maybe we need to admit that some harms can't be solved with better code. That sometimes the fairest thing to do is not to build the system at all. Or to dismantle it. Or to build it differently—not for efficiency or profit, but for care, repair, and justice. What would it mean to center those values? To prioritize transparency, contestability, and community control over speed and scale? It would mean thinking of machine learning not as a product, but as a process—a process that requires reflection, iteration, and accountability.

Fairness, then, becomes less of a goal and more of a practice. Not something you achieve once and for all, but something you commit to continually (Abramovich & Vasiliu, 2023). A habit of mind. A way of seeing. A willingness to be wrong—and to listen when someone tells you you are. Maybe we stop asking whether the algorithm is fair, and start asking whether it *serves fairness*. Whether it contributes to a more just world, or merely simulates equity while preserving power. That's a harder question. It doesn't lend itself to easy answers or tidy metrics. But it's the question we need. Because the future of AI won't be shaped just by how clever our models are. It'll be shaped by the values we encode into them—explicitly or implicitly, consciously or not. If we want AI to be fair, we have to stop pretending that fairness is a mathematical ideal. It's not. It's a messy, moral, collective endeavor. And the only way to do it well is to do it together.

BUILDING INCLUSIVE SYSTEMS: ETHICAL, SOCIAL, AND POLICY INTERVENTIONS

You can't code your way out of injustice. That's the first thing we need to admit. Inclusion is not a feature. It's not a toggle. It doesn't live in the config file. Building inclusive systems isn't just about fixing models—it's about rethinking what we're building, why we're building it, and who gets to decide (DeMatthews, 2021). It's about creating something that doesn't just work technically, but resonates ethically, socially, and culturally. Something that doesn't just serve the system, but serves *people*—all people, especially those who've been left out, overlooked, misrepresented, or harmed. We start with a question—not "How do we make AI better?" but "Better for *whom*?" That shifts everything.

Too often, the conversation around AI fairness gets trapped in the model. The algorithm. The architecture. But fairness isn't born in the model; it begins long before. It begins in the way we define the problem, in the assumptions we carry into the data, in the choices about what matters and what gets measured. By the time we're "debiasing" a system, it may already be too late. Inclusion has to be designed from the ground up—not patched in at the end. So, what does that look like?

Let's talk ethics—not the checkbox kind, not the slide at the end of the pitch deck, but real, gut-level ethics. The kind that makes you pause. The kind that asks whether something *should* be built, not just whether it *can* be. The kind that slows things down. That invites discomfort. That replaces certainty with responsibility. Ethics, when it's real, doesn't just offer guidelines. It interrupts. It challenges. It insists on complexity. It asks: Who might be hurt? Who's missing from this conversation? What kind of world are we reinforcing with this design?

To embed that kind of ethical reflection into AI development, we need to reconfigure the pipeline (Vyhmeister et al, 2023). From ideation to deployment, there have to be ethical checkpoints—places where diverse stakeholders are not just consulted but empowered. That might mean ethics review boards with real veto power. It might mean participatory design workshops with communities affected by the technology. It might mean scrapping a project entirely if the risks outweigh the benefits. But ethics alone isn't enough. We need social scaffolding. Structures of accountability. Networks of care.

Building inclusive systems means embracing friction—inviting in voices that complicate the narrative (Portaankorva, 2024). It means letting impacted communities define the terms of inclusion. Not just bringing them into the room after the blueprint is drawn, but letting them co-create the blueprint itself. It means rejecting the logic that values scale above nuance, automation above humanity.

Let's be clear: community participation is not a branding tool. It's not about legitimacy optics. It's about shifting power. Because at the heart of exclusion is a power imbalance. And you can't fix that with better training data. You fix it by redistributing who gets to shape the system. So maybe inclusion starts with listening. Not token consultation. Not focus groups. Deep, sustained listening. Listening that doesn't just ask for feedback, but makes space for dissent. Listening that changes you (Welz et al, 2023). But listening won't mean much if there are no levers to pull. That's where policy steps in—not as a punitive force, but as a framework for justice. For setting the boundaries of what's acceptable. For protecting people from invisible harms and asymmetrical risks. And let's be honest—policy has a lot of catching up to do. The tech industry has moved fast, often too fast, and governance has stumbled behind, trying to make sense of the mess. But speed isn't always a virtue. Sometimes slowness is wisdom.

What we need are not just reactive policies, but visionary ones. Policies that don't just mitigate harm after the fact, but shape the conditions for more equitable systems from the start (Venet, 2023). That means regulation that enforces transparency—not just about how models work, but about how they're trained, what data they use, who gets to audit them. It means impact assessments that look beyond technical metrics and ask how communities are affected. It means legal frameworks that enshrine the right to explanation, the right to contest decisions, the right to *opt out*. It also means rethinking liability. When an algorithm denies someone a loan, or a diagnosis, or a job, who is accountable? The developer? The company? The data vendor? Right now, the chain of responsibility is murky by design. That needs to change. People deserve a system they can question. A system that answers back. And let's not pretend that global inclusivity can be built on Western ethics alone. The values baked into most AI systems today come from a narrow cultural bandwidth—rooted in Silicon Valley logics, neoliberal efficiency models, and individualistic notions of fairness. But fairness doesn't mean the same thing everywhere. Inclusion is not universal—it's contextual, local, evolving.

So, we need a pluralistic ethics. One that honors Indigenous knowledge systems, community-based models of consent, collective well-being. One that treats difference not as a complication, but as a condition for justice. This is especially urgent in a world where AI is being exported across borders, imposed on societies that had no say in its design (Crawford, 2021). Think about facial recognition systems sold to governments with long histories of surveillance. Think about biometric tools used to control refugee movements. Think about credit-scoring models used in development programs that penalize the very people they're meant to help. If inclusion is to mean anything, it must resist that kind of techno-colonialism. It must be rooted in sovereignty—data sovereignty, cultural sovereignty, epistemic sovereignty. It must center the right not just to be seen, but to self-determine how one is seen. And what about education? If we want more inclusive systems, we need more inclusive builders. That means training the next generation of developers not just in technical excellence, but in ethical imagination. It means interdisciplinary learning. It means rethinking what counts as "expertise." It means valuing community wisdom as much as academic prestige.

We also need institutions—real ones—with the courage to challenge the status quo. Public interest tech labs. Independent watchdogs. Ethical funding bodies. Coalitions of civil society groups that hold tech companies accountable (Charalabidis,

2022). These can't be feel-good accessories to the industry. They need teeth. They need funding. They need independence. And finally, we need stories. Not just data stories or design fictions, but *human stories*—the kind that make exclusion visible. Because what gets measured gets managed, yes. But what gets *felt* gets changed. When people see themselves in the story—when harm has a face, a name, a narrative—they're more likely to care. So maybe inclusion is also a narrative practice. A way of telling different futures into being. A way of saying: We could have built this differently. We *can* build this differently. And if there's one thing to hold onto, it's this: inclusion is not a destination. It's a commitment. A discipline. A constant act of reimagining. Not just adding more faces to the dataset, but changing the system that decides which faces matter.

We'll make mistakes. We'll fall short. We'll try and fail and try again. But that's okay. Because building inclusive systems isn't about getting it perfect. It's about refusing to settle for the exclusions that seem inevitable. It's about saying: *This is not good enough. And we can do better.* So, let's build. But let's build slow. Let's build with care. Let's build with people who've been told for too long that the system was never meant for them. Let's build something that *is*.

TOWARD A JUST AI FUTURE: COLLECTIVE RESPONSIBILITY AND HUMAN-CENTERED DESIGN

Somewhere along the way, we forgot to ask who technology is *for*. Or maybe we never asked at all. The allure of progress—quicker predictions, cleaner code, leaner pipelines—was too seductive. It promised us clarity. Optimization. Scalability. But it rarely promised justice. And now we find ourselves tangled in the consequences of that oversight: a world increasingly governed by systems that neither see everyone nor serve everyone equally. So, what does it mean to imagine a *just* future for AI?

Not a fair one. Not a "responsible" one. Not one that simply complies with regulation or passes an audit. But one that is built—intentionally, radically, continuously—around the full dignity of human life. One that makes room for complexity, contradiction, and care. One that doesn't just distribute harms and benefits more evenly but redefines what we value altogether.

To get there, we have to begin by shifting the center of gravity—from the system to the human. Not as a consumer or user or data point. As a person. A person with context. With history. With agency. It's about re-anchoring AI design in the messy realities of human life and resisting the cold convenience of abstraction. Human-centered design, when done with sincerity and not as a branding exercise, is fundamentally a political act (Rouse, 2024). It demands that we slow down, ask harder questions, and unlearn our assumptions about who belongs at the table. But let's not romanticize the phrase. "Human-centered" is often thrown around like a moral cure-all, as if merely invoking it dissolves power asymmetries. It doesn't. Because not all humans are treated equally in our systems—digital or otherwise. Centering the human must mean centering *those who have been dehumanized by default*. It means prioritizing the needs and voices of people who've historically been pushed to the margins of decision-making. It means asking what *they* want from technology—not what we think they should want.

Justice begins with listening. Deep listening. Not the kind that waits politely for its turn to speak, but the kind that risks being changed by what it hears. Listening to those who've been harmed by AI systems (Yin et al, 2024). Those who've been labeled "outliers," "noisy," "non-representative." Those whose suffering was dismissed as a trade-off for performance. It's not about asking permission to include them. It's about recognizing that no system is legitimate without them. But human-centered design doesn't just happen through workshops and empathy maps. It requires structures. Accountability mechanisms. Collective ownership. Because responsibility in AI can't live in the individual conscience of a developer alone (Griffin et al, 2024). The problems are too large, too distributed, too baked-in. If we want to build systems that are just, we need to share the weight of that work.

Collective responsibility is not a feel-good slogan. It's a framework. A way of understanding that every layer of the AI ecosystem—research, funding, policy, education, deployment—has a role to play. You can't expect a junior engineer to redesign fairness into a system that was architected by profit incentives. Nor can you expect a nonprofit to audit bias in tools they had no access to build. Responsibility has to be systemic. Interdependent. Reciprocal. That might mean tech companies opening up their models for independent scrutiny. It might mean governments investing in public AI infrastructure rather than outsourcing it to private monopolies. It might mean universities integrating ethics across disciplines, not siloed in a single semester. It might mean activist groups having veto power over the deployment of systems that affect their communities.

None of this is easy. Power rarely concedes itself willingly. But justice was never about convenience (Pushaw Jr & Silver, 2022). And inclusion—real inclusion—requires inconvenience. It requires reallocation. Reimagination. Resistance. And maybe also… repair. Because justice isn't just forward-facing. It's retrospective. It looks back. It acknowledges harm, names it, and works to make amends. Building just systems means reckoning with the damage already done. The job applications filtered out unfairly. The loan denials that deepened poverty. The prison sentences shaped by algorithmic risk scores. The communities over-surveilled. The identities misclassified or erased.

This isn't about guilt. It's about repair as a practice. As an ethic. As an orientation. It's about building AI that doesn't pretend it was born yesterday, but that holds memory—memory of who was harmed, and how, and why. That remembers the exclusions encoded in its early architectures and refuses to carry them forward without question. Human-centered design, in this context, becomes an act of refusal. Refusing to accept that what is efficient is always good. Refusing to accept that complexity should be optimized away (Glimcher, 2022). Refusing to reduce human life to probability distributions and behavioral predictions. It becomes a way of designing not just *for* users, but *with* them. Not just to solve problems, but to understand what problems are worth solving in the first place. And it also means recognizing that justice isn't static. It's not a feature we add once and move on. It's an ongoing negotiation. A constant recalibration. It asks us to remain open—open to critique, open to iteration, open to the idea that the best technology is the one that adapts not just to the market, but to moral clarity.

Can AI systems be just? That's not a technical question. It's a collective one. It depends on what we choose to care about. What we're willing to challenge. What we're willing to change. It depends on whether we're willing to let go of the illusion that the machine knows best, and return to the simple, radical truth: *the human must remain at the center*—not just the imagined user in a product flow, but the living, breathing human who carries the burden of our decisions. And yes, the path will be hard. Yes, we'll get it wrong. Yes, we'll be told it's too idealistic, too slow, too expensive. But what's the alternative? A future where AI systems quietly entrench the injustices we failed to address? A future where efficiency is bought at the cost of dignity? We can do better. We must. Let's stop asking whether AI can be fair (Rafanelli, 2022). Let's ask whether it can be *humble*. Whether it can be *kind*. Whether it can be built from a place of solidarity, not superiority. A just AI future is not inevitable. It must be imagined, insisted upon, and constructed—bit by bit, voice by voice, decision by decision. And it starts here. With us.

CONCLUSION

The journey to this point has required us to look critically, even painfully, at the structures underpinning our digital world. We have unmasked the illusion of objectivity in machine learning, interrogated the hidden ways exclusion is baked into data and design, and traced the impact of these systems on real human lives—particularly those already bearing the weight of marginalization. The question we must now face is not *whether* AI can be fair, but rather *how* we might cultivate fairness intentionally, meaningfully, and enduringly within systems that learn from us.

What becomes clear is that **inclusion cannot emerge from neutrality**. Inclusion demands taking a side. It requires acknowledging that the status quo—data, metrics, priorities—is not neutral terrain, but one shaped by power. To be inclusive, AI systems must actively push against the grain of inherited inequalities, rather than merely reflecting or even ignoring them. This means designing not just *for* users, but *with* them. It means centering the voices of those who have historically been excluded from the table—people whose stories are too often absent from datasets and whose perspectives are undervalued in boardrooms and research labs.

Technical fixes will only take us so far. We can tweak datasets, adjust weighting schemes, or diversify our training samples—but without structural and cultural change, these will amount to surface-level solutions. True inclusion requires a deeper reckoning. We must rethink who gets to define the problems we solve, what success looks like, and whose pain counts in our optimization functions. It means moving from a paradigm of *efficiency* to one of *equity*—and from *performance* to *participation*.

Let us also be honest about the road ahead. Creating inclusive AI systems is not easy. It means more than diversifying engineering teams or publishing fairness metrics. It calls for a radical shift in the values that guide technological development: from speed to care, from innovation for its own sake to innovation with purpose. And it asks each of us—researchers, developers, educators, policymakers—to act not just as technologists, but as stewards of the future. Because the systems we build today will shape what is possible—and for whom—tomorrow.

In the end, this is not merely about machines. It is about us. About whether we choose to encode our better angels or our deepest prejudices into the systems that increasingly govern our lives. Inclusion is not a feature to be toggled on or off. It is a philosophy. A practice. A commitment. And like all meaningful commitments, it begins with listening.

REFERENCES

Abramovich, N., & Vasiliu, A. (2023). Sustainability as fairness: A Rawlsian framework linking intergenerational equity and the sustainable development goals (SDGs) with business practices. *Sustainable Development (Bradford), 31*(3), 1328–1342. DOI: 10.1002/sd.2451

Barocas, S., Hardt, M., & Narayanan, A. (2023). *Fairness and machine learning: Limitations and opportunities*. MIT press.

Broussard, M. (2023). *More than a glitch: Confronting race, gender, and ability bias in tech*. MIT Press. DOI: 10.7551/mitpress/14234.001.0001

Browne, K., Banerjea, N., McGlynn, N., Bakshi, L., Beethi, S., & Biswas, R. (2021). The limits of legislative change: Moving beyond inclusion/exclusion to create 'a life worth living'. Environment and Planning C. *Politics and Space*, *39*(1), 30–52.

Buttol, V. (2023). Ethical implications of Artificial Intelligence: the relationship between algorithms and kindness.

Chaka, C. (2022). Digital marginalization, data marginalization, and algorithmic exclusions: A critical southern decolonial approach to datafication, algorithms, and digital citizenship from the Souths. Journal of e-Learning and Knowledge Society, 18(3), 83-95.

Charalabidis, Y. (2022). Artificial intelligence (AI). In *The Palgrave Encyclopedia of Interest Groups, Lobbying and Public Affairs* (pp. 43–50). Springer International Publishing. DOI: 10.1007/978-3-030-44556-0_129

Crawford, K. (2021). *The atlas of AI: Power, politics, and the planetary costs of artificial intelligence*. Yale University Press.

DeMatthews, D. (2021). Undoing systems of exclusion: Exploring inclusive leadership and systems thinking in two inclusive elementary schools. *Journal of Educational Administration*, *59*(1), 5–21. DOI: 10.1108/JEA-02-2020-0044

Emma, L. (2024). *The Ethical Implications of Artificial Intelligence: A Deep Dive into Bias*. Fairness, and Transparency.

Geiger, R. S., Cope, D., Ip, J., Lotosh, M., Shah, A., Weng, J., & Tang, R. (2021). " Garbage In, Garbage Out" Revisited: What Do Machine Learning Application Papers Report About Human-Labeled Training Data? arXiv preprint arXiv:2107.02278.

Glimcher, P. W. (2022). Efficiently irrational: Deciphering the riddle of human choice. *Trends in Cognitive Sciences, 26*(8), 669–687. DOI: 10.1016/j.tics.2022.04.007 PMID: 35643845

Griffin, T. A., Green, B. P., & Welie, J. V. (2024). The ethical agency of AI developers. *AI and Ethics, 4*(2), 179–188. DOI: 10.1007/s43681-022-00256-3

Hamid, S. T., & Kuo, R. (2022). (Forthcoming). Towards Collective Safety: Transformative Methodologies. First Monday. *Special Issue on Online Harm and Abuse.*

Jones, C. E. (2024). The Language of Medical Racism: Strategies for Anti-Oppressive Scientific Writing and Communication (Doctoral dissertation, Northeastern University).

Lane, H., & Dyshel, M. (2025). *Natural language processing in action.* Simon and Schuster.

Moore, K. R., Williams, D. R., & Baird, D. D. (2021). Disparities by skin color among young African-American women. *Journal of Racial and Ethnic Health Disparities, 8*(4), 1002–1011. DOI: 10.1007/s40615-020-00856-x PMID: 32888171

Muller, M., & Strohmayer, A. (2022, April). Forgetting practices in the data sciences. In *Proceedings of the 2022 CHI Conference on Human Factors in Computing Systems* (pp. 1-19).

Patterson, K. A. (2025). Predictive Policing Technology: Community Perceptions of ShotSpotter in West Denver (Master's thesis, University of Colorado Colorado Springs).

Periáñez, Á., Fernández Del Río, A., Nazarov, I., Jané, E., Hassan, M., Rastogi, A., & Tang, D. (2024). The digital transformation in health: How AI can improve the performance of health systems. *Health Systems and Reform, 10*(2), 2387138. DOI: 10.1080/23288604.2024.2387138 PMID: 39437247

Portaankorva, L. (2024). Values-Based Model to Foster Inclusive Organizational Culture.

Pruksachatkun, Y., McAteer, M., & Majumdar, S. (2023). *Practicing trustworthy machine learning*. O'Reilly Media, Inc.

Pushaw, R. J.Jr, & Silver, C. (2022). The Unconstitutional Assertion of Inherent Powers in Multidistrict Litigations. *BYU L. Rev., 48*, 1869.

Rafanelli, L. M. (2022). Justice, injustice, and artificial intelligence: Lessons from political theory and philosophy. *Big Data & Society, 9*(1), 20539517221080676. DOI: 10.1177/20539517221080676

Rinelli, L. (2022). Voice segmentation for early identification of neurodegenerative diseases (Doctoral dissertation, Politecnico di Torino).

Rouse, W. B. (2024). *From Human-Centered Design to Human-Centered Society: Creatively Balancing Business Innovation and Societal Exploitation*. CRC Press.

Spicer, T. (2023). *Man-Made: How the bias of the past is being built into the future*. Simon and Schuster.

Stenseke, J. (2024). On the computational complexity of ethics: Moral tractability for minds and machines. *Artificial Intelligence Review*, *57*(4), 105. DOI: 10.1007/s10462-024-10732-3

Thomas, J. J. (2022). Biases and Obstacles to Critical Thinking. In Developing Cross-Cultural Competence for Leaders (pp. 79-98). Routledge. DOI: 10.4324/9781003213352-7

Venet, A. S. (2023). *Equity-centered trauma-informed education*. Routledge. DOI: 10.4324/9781032677989

Vyhmeister, E., Castane, G., Östberg, P. O., & Thevenin, S. (2023). A responsible AI framework: Pipeline contextualisation. *AI and Ethics*, *3*(1), 175–197. DOI: 10.1007/s43681-022-00154-8

Welz, C., Ikonen, E., & Kristiansen, A. (2023). Learning through Listening and Responding: Probing the Potential and Limits of Dialogue in Local and Online Environments. *Religions*, *14*(2), 241. DOI: 10.3390/rel14020241

Yin, Y., Jia, N., & Wakslak, C. J. (2024). AI can help people feel heard, but an AI label diminishes this impact. *Proceedings of the National Academy of Sciences of the United States of America*, *121*(14), e2319112121. DOI: 10.1073/pnas.2319112121 PMID: 38551835

KEY TERMS AND DEFINITIONS

1. **Machine Learning:** A subset of artificial intelligence that enables systems to learn patterns from data and make predictions or decisions without explicit programming.
2. **Algorithmic Bias:** Systematic and repeatable errors in a computer system that create unfair outcomes, often disadvantaging certain groups.
3. **Data Imbalance:** A situation in which some categories or groups are under-represented in a dataset, leading to skewed model performance.

4. **Fairness in AI:** The principle of designing AI systems that treat all users equitably, regardless of race, gender, or background.

5. **Inclusive AI:** Artificial intelligence systems that are consciously designed to be accessible, representative, and non-discriminatory.

6. **Ethical AI:** The practice of ensuring that AI technologies align with human values, rights, and social good.

7. **Transparency in Algorithms:** The degree to which an AI system's decisions and operations can be understood and scrutinized by humans.

Chapter 7
Bridging the Gap:
How Global Value Chains Drive Inclusive Marketing Strategies

Parihar Suresh Dahake
https://orcid.org/0000-0002-2286-4120
Ramdeobaba University, Nagpur, India

Nihar Suresh Dahake
https://orcid.org/0009-0007-8971-9247
G.H. Raisoni College of Engineering, Nagpur, India

ABSTRACT

The ongoing globalization of markets has sparked a tremendous interest in emerging economies, particularly in the 'bottom of the pyramid' (BoP), prompting national corporations (MNCs) to address the unique marketing considerations for serving people experiencing poverty. Effective marketing for people experiencing poverty requires bridging the gaps in the conception of market offerings, information, physical access, price affordability, and distribution and service channels. These gaps are more pronounced in India, with its vast middle and lower-class population, and differing economic, cultural, and regulatory contexts, albeit with a rich pool of problems and opportunities. Using global value chain (GVC) analysis, marketing theory is expanded by increasing understanding of how gaps can be bridged and how these efforts facilitate development in emerging economies

DOI: 10.4018/979-8-3373-2685-6.ch007

Copyright © 2026, IGI Global Scientific Publishing. Copying or distributing in print or electronic forms without written permission of IGI Global Scientific Publishing is prohibited.

1. INTRODUCTION

The global marketplace presents a diverse mix of consumers with varied markets and traditions. To satisfy the varied and complex needs of global consumers, firms catering to these consumers need to adopt inclusive marketing strategies. Global Value Chains (GVCs) and Innovation Systems (IS) in developing countries, emphasizing the critical role of international knowledge exchange in fostering innovation(Pietrobelli & Rabellotti, 2011), India is the second-most populous country in the world and has the Fifth-largest economy. The Indian market has seen significant growth in the past 20 years due to increased disposable income from globalization. This growth has led to a significant change in consumer tastes and expectations. India's key role in value chains has impacted several sectors within the Indian economy, primarily enhancing the economy of certain cities and decreasing poverty. The global value chains, financialization, and new imperialism reshape industrial strategies, requiring pragmatic policy interventions(Chang & Andreoni, 2020), GVC is driven mainly by scale expansion over productivity(M. Niu et al., 2025).

Companies attribute a significant chunk of the increased innovation and competitiveness in the Indian market to the introduction of global value chains into the Indian business environment. These companies also examine the effect of global value chains on sales, product quality, and delivery to the buyer and find that global value chain-related activities lead to increases in sales. A value chain perspective, revealing fluctuating trends, major regional connections, and emissions driven by foreign final demand(Yang et al., 2025). With this growth, companies not only have to cater to a more sophisticated consumer, but one that is also more diverse both within different Indian markets and abroad due to the lasting effects of dual-income households.

Figure 1. Role of Global Value Chains Drive Inclusive Marketing

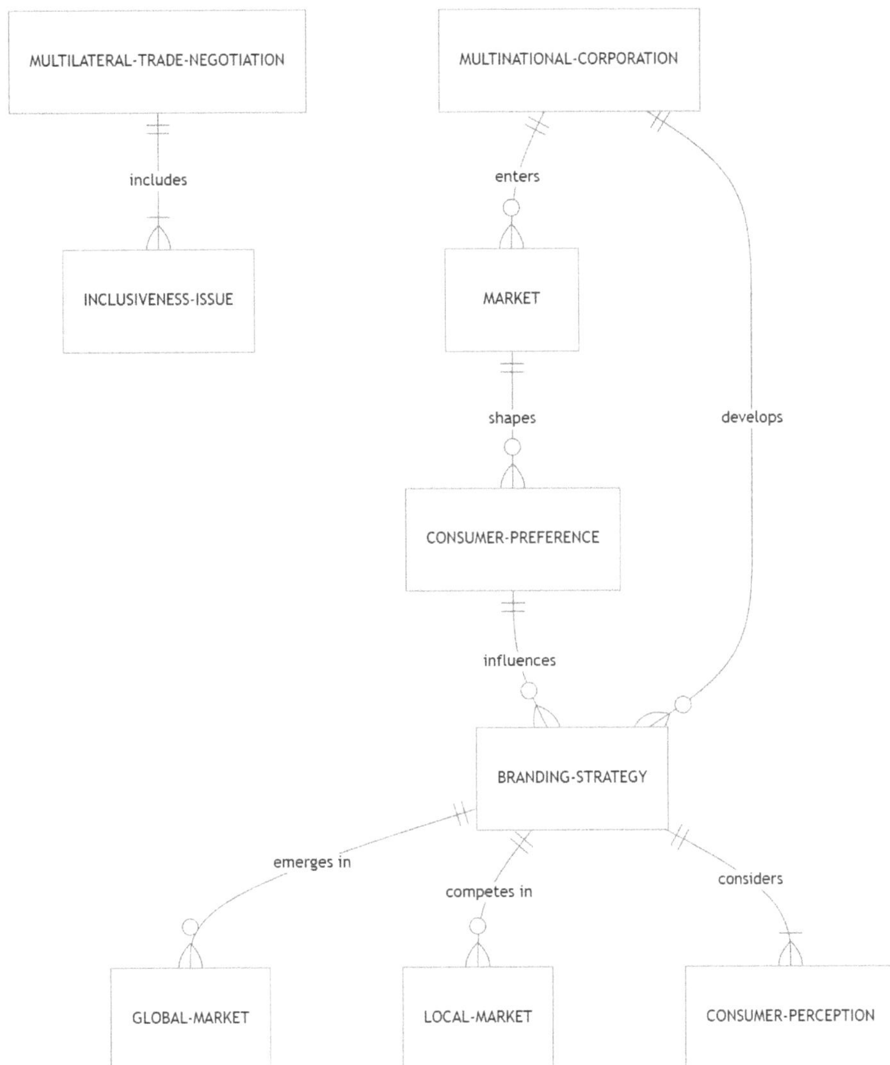

In this research, we explain the methods that firms follow to design and deliver inclusive marketing strategies. Foreign suppliers' technological choices significantly shaping global value chain dynamics and international trade competitiveness(DeStefano & Timmis, 2024).Business communities have historically played a central role in shaping India's character and ethos. As globalization deepens, there now exists a great opportunity in shaping business communities that can help embed industrialized norms of fair trade, workers' rights, environmental sustainability, and human development into their value chains. As uncertainty and automation drive reshoring, halting globalization(Faber et al., 2025). The Liberalism and realism offer differing predictions on future economic structures either fragmented linkages or concentrated blocs(Witt, 2019), New global value chains have the potential to build partnerships of prosperity that could also inform shifts in global economic governance. In such scenario Individuals will agree to relax voting requirements in a democracy only if compensated by decreased decision costs or other organizational costs, equal to or greater than the expected increase in external costs(Boss, 1974).In contrast, the dilemmas facing the governance and effectiveness of global institutions are well noted, and the lack of inclusiveness is seen as a major hurdle in multilateral trade negotiations. The debate over branding strategy has grown in significance with the emergence of global markets and competition from local as well as international markets. The decisions over branding strategy have taken into account a broader range of factors, including consumer perception of global versus local brands, and country-of-origin effect. The Coca-Cola versus Pepsi tussle or the Euro Disney versus Disneyland tussle exemplifies the significance of branding strategies in mass marketing in international markets. As more multi-national corporations enter new markets in different countries; to establish their presence, they need to develop branding strategies based on the understanding of consumers' preference for global brands versus local brands. Consumers from nations ranging from being underdeveloped to matured economies hold significantly varying perceptions of global brands versus local brands. There is a paucity of academic literature assessing this phenomenon for the Indian market(Sengupta, 2014)

The current study investigates the impact of the economic environment of the target market, the ethnocentric bias of the consumers, the demographic characteristics of the consumers, and the type of product and product familiarity on consumers' preference for foreign brands or domestic brands in the Indian apparel consumer market. Each of the above-mentioned factors is analyzed and multiple research questions are framed on the basis of it. There are a plethora of information available in the form of articles, books, journals and case studies on the Indian consumer market. As competition in the Indian apparel consumer market is rising, the scope for study is vast. This consumer market analysis would be of great help to the brands that are relatively new entrants in the market.

Countries like India, Brazil, China and Indonesia have witnessed a significant change in socio-economic conditions over the last one and half decades. The growing affluence and globalization have led to the emergence of fast-growing sizable consumer groups across these countries, which are viewed as potential buyers of global brands (both niche and mass).

These groups have

(i) Been annexed with rising middle class;
(ii) Graduated out of mass consumerism;
(iii) Witnessed a surge in spending on international brands; and
(iv) Evolved as both aspirational and exclusive consumers of global brands.

The emergence of a sizable middle class in these countries wielding substantial purchasing power along with the salient increase in media exposure and mounting fashion consciousness has been responsible for progressively altering the consumer needs and the consequent brand offers. Global value chains are governed by transaction complexity, codification ability, and supply-base capabilities, leading to five types of governance: hierarchy, captive, relational, modular, and market(Gereffi et al., 2005).The Indian economy, one of the largest economies of the world, is an emerging one with an aspiration of becoming sustainable. A sustained level of growth is important to reduce poverty levels and ensure a better quality of living for its residents and immigrants alike. Sustainable development is likely to succeed with the participation of the people of the country irrespective of their gender, caste, class, ethnicity, social status, or age(Sengupta, 2014). Marketing strategies should also appeal to them and cater for their needs. Conventional marketing strategies target mainly the influential, affluent, and well-connected people, leaving out a huge proportion of the population. The inclusive growth agenda has recently led to attempts to market to the 'bottom of pyramid' (BOP) consumers which is differently a challenge for brand owners. Industrial clusters' insertion into global value chains can enable or hinder local-level upgrading efforts, with developing country firms selling to large global buyers facing unique challenges(Humphrey & Schmitz, 2002).

An emerging economy like India however presents a challenge of multiple levels of economic and social development along with deprivation and destitution. Near-shoring increased for strategic industries(Freund et al., 2024), So while the BOP is desired as consumers, it is nebulous and fragmented. A GVC, GPN perspective is resourcefully used to explore the information asymmetries in GSP market thereby limiting inclusive strategies by big brands. In spite of the challenges and dilemmas, it is found that both local and global brands grapple with innovative marketing strategies, some of them being promising. Value chain, value shop, and value network models help analyze firm-level value creation logic across various industries and firms, aiding in competitive advantage diagnosis(Stabell & Fjeldstad, 1998).The findings open avenues for further academic research and provide implications for practitioners, global brands, local brands, NGOs, and civil organizations facilitating inclusive brands, developments, and growth in other emerging countries. It also suggests ways for the Indian government to develop goods and labor market policy to ensure sustainable growth without inflation. The Indian apparel industry is one which has enjoyed global value chain participation since ages and domestically since the last decade. MNCs can successfully enter low-income markets by leveraging existing market strengths and developing relationships with non-traditional partners, co-inventing custom solutions, and building local capacity(London & Hart, 2004). It offers market space for both big and local brands to compete passionately at varying consumer segments. It is an important growth sector for the Indian economy providing lot of opportunities and employment generation. The apparel industry faces challenges in sourcing of raw materials, employment rigidity, ensuring a minimum level of quality without being exorbitantly priced, supply chain and infrastructure constraints.

2. GLOBAL VALUE CHAINS: AN OVERVIEW

Global value chains (GVCs) are internationally fragmented production processes, with simple linkages between exporting and importing countries(S. Nefedov & Yu. Panibratov, 2017), GVCs offer researchers a conceptual framework for lifestyle rise/ demise, from coffee to car parts. balanced linkages, foreign, domestic, and indirect exports, drive sustainable economic growth, enhance competitiveness, and optimize development benefits in GVC(Moussir, 2025) but exchange rate volatility affects short-term growth(Utouh & Kitole, 2024), They allow a competitive-product-safe-product-country change/flight study. The driving question is about minimum corporate social responsibility (CSR) standards in GVC management and reconfiguration in commodity booms, when patching is cheap and possible.In value chain integration, with developing economies relying more on backward linkages, while advanced nations dominate forward connections, reshaping global economic interactions(Mancini et al., 2024).Eventually Higher domestic risk in inland regions, global exposure in coastal areas, **and** greater demand-side vulnerabilities across high-tech industries and major trade hubs(Hongfu et al., 2024)

3. UNDERSTANDING INCLUSIVE MARKETING

To the extent that MNCs advance their ethical efforts in low-income markets, collaborative service views of corporations, NGOs, and governments as facilitators of an inclusive market economy emerge. Large retailers dominate the market, driving tighter supply chains and quality-focused competition(Dolan & Humphrey,

2004) and firms increasingly restructure production, focusing on core competencies while maintaining profit margins through offshoring(Milberg, 2008).The Vertical integration and specialization stratcgics can enhance efficiency and effectiveness in knowledge-intensive industries(Mudambi, 2008) and,SME strategic sustainability behaviors range from resistant to anticipatory, and interacting with external actors can increase their innovative capacity for sustainability-oriented innovations(Klewitz & Hansen, 2014).Value-based strategies, which involve both supplier and buyer relations, can create positive added value for firms(Brandenburger & Stuart, 1996), Assessing these efforts at the bottom of the pyramid has global implications for the credibility of multinational corporations attempting to bridge the gap between rich nations and developing or emerging markets. Adaptive marketing capabilities, including vigilant market learning, adaptive experimentation, and open marketing, are crucial for organizations to effectively respond to market complexity and adapt to new media and social networking technologies(Day, 2011).

Figure 2. Inclusive Marketing strategy

Could it set a precondition for broader market access for MNCs in more discretionary markets? Ethical brand advocates must increasingly question whether humanitarian ambition masks profit motives, leaving consumers skeptical even in less developed economies. Reconceptualizing consumer protection goals to oppose unnecessary market access might stymy efforts to improve basic quality of life through profit-maximizing business models. If MNCs are perceived as benefitting less fortunate consumers solely as a business strategy, the reputation of multinational firms as altruistic entities might be irreparably damaged (Santos & Laczniak, 2009). This lack of inclusion limits an escalating market potential for mass consumption. At best, MNC focus has been limited to the modestly poor, who comprise only 3% of the world market. Examples of previous brands seized market opportunities amongst the featured aspirational segment must expand inclusively. And environmental costs in global value chains(Meng et al., 2018). MNCs must investigate ways to remove obstacles for mass consumption markets with emerging income growth potential. Proactive efforts to reach low-income households willing but unable to procure offerings through affordable marketing might eventually prevent brand failure, damaging reputational risks for perceived exploitative corporations with a long-term consequence hence Entrepreneurial orientation and marketing strategy play crucial roles in improving firm performance among SMEs affected by globalization(G. Knight, 2000).

4. REVIEW OF LITERATURE:

The advantages of global value chains (GVCs) extend beyond cost competitiveness. In addition, MNCs must explore how GVCs influence inclusive marketing strategies in emerging nations. GVC coordination, end-market transformations, and value chain concentration reshape development strategies(Gereffi, 2014), Along with the established market position, marketers must encounter existing and emerging barriers to serving the market at the base of the pyramid (BOP) (González-Torres et al., 2020). In addition, GVCs are expected to be the enabler of effective inclusive marketing strategies. A literature search assimilated GVCs and inclusive marketing. The synthesis will be useful for MNCs marketing managers who are pursuing sustainable prospects in emerging nations.

Figure 3. All Keywords Analysis by VosViewer

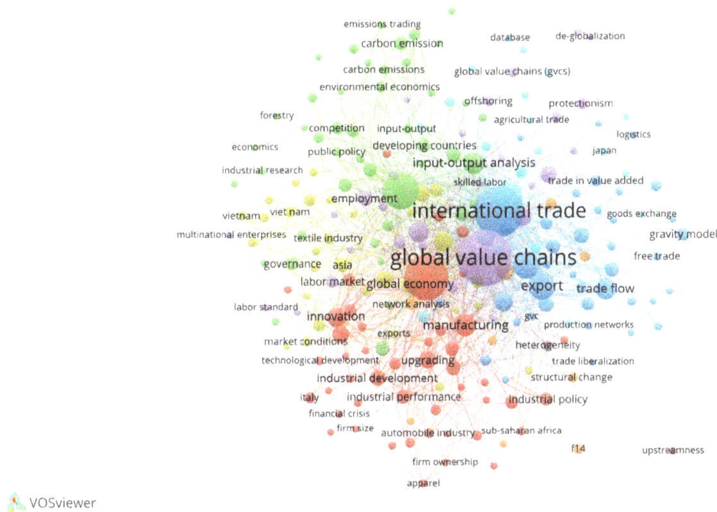

The paper is structured as follows. First, the methods employed to conduct the literature search and synthesis will be detailed. Next, key findings will be highlighted, addressing the research questions and the scope for further research. The paper will conclude, highlighting the paper's contributions and implications for marketing managers. To identify the papers for review, keywords were used to help choose keyword search terms in scholarly research databases. These terms derived from the literature review mentioned above. The keywords included "GVCs," "Global Value Chains," "inclusive marketing," "prospect at the base of the pyramid (BOP)," "bottom of the pyramid (BoP)," "bottom of the pyramid (BOP) marketing," and "inclusiveness." Using only the first five keywords, the initial search resulted in 87 indexes in a Scopus database citation report. The following results were found: two papers in 2001, one in 2003, in 2007, and two in 2010; five papers in 2012 and 2013, respectively; four in 2014, six in 2015, eight in 2016, and nine in 2017; 15 papers in 2018; and 11 in 2019. In 2020, there are six, and the most recent paper was published in 2021,2022,2023,2024 & 2025.

Figure 4. Author Keywords Analysis by VosViewer

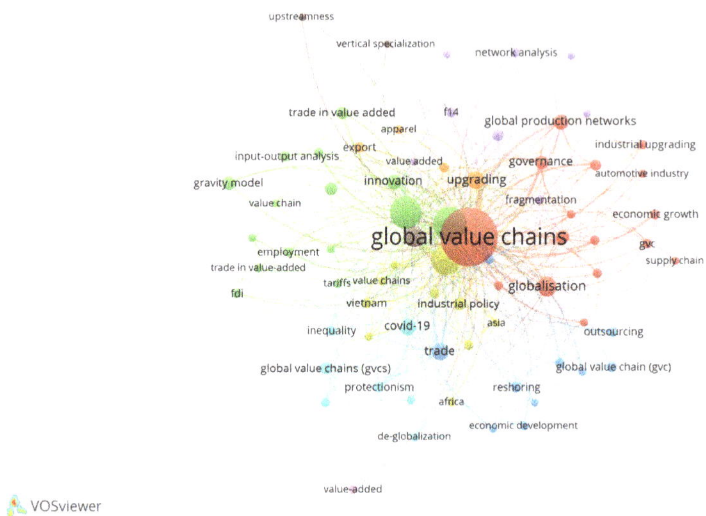

The 132 keywords were filtered from the 355 articles. The keywords co-occurrence matrix was imported to software. The option "Create a map based on the network data from an external source" was selected. The normalized co-occurrence data were derived from the co-occurrence matrix. The fractions option was selected under the "Weighting" option. The "layout" option was chosen as "iterative" in the provided settings. The inclusion threshold for each of the simplex option was set to 2. The keywords mapping can be interpreted is like there is Color which is responsible for the subdivision and clustering of keywords. The network consists of 5 clusters. Red cluster maps positional and territorial exclusive the economics of GVCs. It also maps several words used in clustering ownership and blockage behavior on GVCs, for instance, pathway, unbundling economist, frictions, dependency and prioritization placed. Blue cluster maps the theory of institutions, consumption and governance and education explicitly related to GVCs. However, the keywords with more connections revolve around the exclusive territorial level manner such as vertical specialization, market size, position, bottom-up. The inclusion of external participants is excluded in the research Cyan cluster maps the GVCs sourcing and marketing inclusiveness and exclusion., Yellow cluster maps the corporate social responsibilities and collaborative networks related to GVCs. And Green cluster maps the marketing strategies in GVCs while focusing on cooperated networks. The time-series animation can be built in software. The time span of the browsing starts from 2001 and ends in 2025 with the time interval by years. The time range was set according to the first time the keywords index and database words time creation.

The viewing task of There is One private cluster. Only method modalities can be preset and color can be specified with respect to the time stamps tagged. It can be observed that the globalization keyword first appeared in 2001. It can be interpreted as it was the first time to categorize the scientific and technical topics in the new area. The broadened empirical bases and breadth in keywords tagged were widened in 2001 and 2010. This phenomenon implies the micro-upward movement of there-meta and the applied inclusivity theories. Even though GVCs globalization process was incendiary in 2001, the conceptualization remained obligation or compliance based pop was created. The visualization of accessibility or inclusiveness omission in GVCs drivers or marketing strategies was invented in a short sight. Such omitted word usage must be involved in GVCs consumption or governance mechanism from developed countries or viewpoints such as cost, and lead firm dominations on GVCs.

Figure 5. Index Keywords Analysis by VosViewer

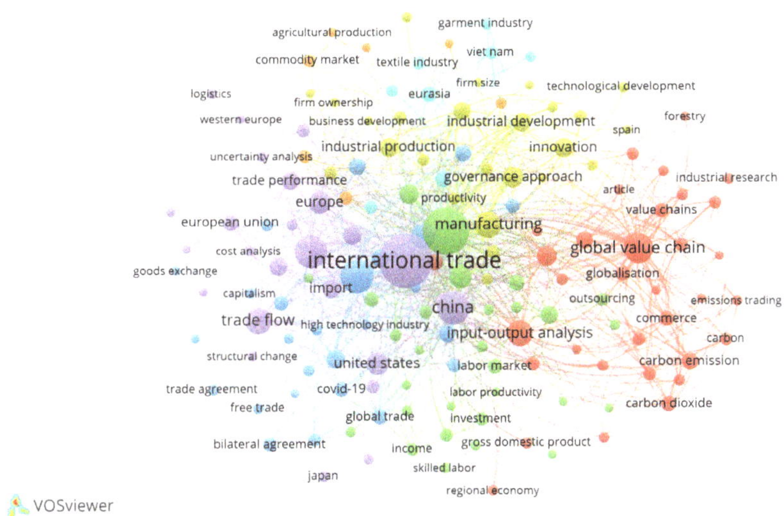

Map based bibliometric analysis on cooccurrence of index keywords was carried out and presented in the Figures 3. The key words were selected from the search of the title to include in the entries. Authors made two observations from the analysis of the keyword cooccurrence analysis. Top 20 Global Value Chain (GVC) indicators that have highest definition question were selected and analysed. More than half indicators proposed by different researchers were not represented in the definition question. The other observations were explained in detail.

The global value chain (GVC) locations of all components involved in GVC exporting within each of the 35 industries were estimated. Location quotient (LQ) was applied to decompose the GVC trade indices (GVC-TI) and GVC jobs indices (GVC-JI) in a structural way by tracking the domestic, upstream and downstream sources and destinations in the two indices. Lastly, a GVC collaboration network that analyzed the node centrality and community was represented at the industry level as an informative tool for further expansion connections by exporting and investment. Various estimation procedures and prior studies were invoked to derive these indicators. The substantial contributions of China to the world economy are gradually being realized, and they can also be found in GVC and HC. Meantime, many debates are triggered regarding the changing GVCs and HCs, as well as the strategies accompanied to optimize such changes.

Thorough investigations on how India's GVC participation is determined, its implications on human capital development and the resulting new perceptions on inclusion would benefit from the GVC, including all sectors but only its manufacturing and premanufactured goods sectors being examined. On the other hand, after eliminating the econometric inconsistency that restricted research on the relationship between GVC and HC, the complicated two-way influences between them deserved to be further studied. A Survey of marketing strategies viewed by practitioners through the lens of marketing strategy, an analytic perspectives on enhancing the service chains value of the platform.

The relationship between global value chains (GVCs) and inclusive marketing strategies has garnered increasing attention in academic literature, particularly as the dynamics of globalization continue to reshape market landscapes. The foundational work by (Vermeulen et al., 2008) emphasizes the necessity for businesses to understand the entire supply chain, as consumer demands for quality and safety are now pivotal in the agrifood sector. They argue that the success of small-scale producers hinges on their ability to adapt to the intricate demands of modern retail and agribusiness, highlighting the importance of integrating producers into evolving market frameworks. Building on this premise, (Vallet-Bellmunt et al., 2011)delve into the complexities of supply chain integration, identifying strategic marketing as a critical factor in navigating the challenges faced by firms within the fresh produce sector. Their analysis underscores the need for effective vertical coordination in supply chains, suggesting that successful integration can enhance both operational efficiency and market responsiveness. In addition to this (Kano et al., 2020)finds that governance issues at different levels micro, GVC, and macro have been unevenly explored, prompting future research directions. Key results suggest emerging topics such as GVC mapping, digitization, protectionism, value creation, financialization, and chain-level performance management.(BUCIUNI et al., 2013)further this discussion by exploring how manufacturers, specifically in the furniture industry, are reconfiguring their supply chains in response to global competition. Their findings illustrate the need for firms to align marketing and operations strategies to create value across the supply chain, a theme that resonates with the broader implications of GVCs in fostering inclusive marketing practices. (Kazekula, 2014)provide a case study of small-scale farmers in Zambia, illustrating the potential of GVCs as vehicles for pro-poor initiatives. They highlight that understanding the intricacies of GVCs is essential for small producers to engage economically viable practices, thereby linking their development to global market opportunities. However, (Dufour et al., 2025) highlights challenges in integrating planned economies into global value chains, emphasizing the need for cooperation rather than complete autarky. Furthermore, (Masoumik et al., 2014)introduce the concept of strategic green supply chain management, emphasizing the competitive advantages that can be gained through environmentally conscious practices. In addition to this(Conteduca et al., 2025) revealing selective decoupling, persistent dependencies, and complex supply chain reconfigurations, particularly involving China, the US, and the EU Their work suggests that sustainable strategies can enhance the alignment of marketing efforts with consumer expectations, particularly as sustainability becomes a key driver in consumer purchasing decisions.(Zhu et al., 2014)contribute to the discourse by mapping the topological properties of GVCs, offering insights into how value-added contributions are distributed across industries. This empirical approach enriches the understanding of GVCs and sets the stage for further exploration of their implications for marketing strategies. Triggered by this (Lowitt et al., 2015) advocate for integrating communities of practice within value chain development, emphasizing the role of social interactions among actors in enhancing resilience and performance in food-related value chains. Their findings suggest that fostering collaboration and knowledge transfer can significantly impact the effectiveness of inclusive marketing strategies. Significantly (Sinkovics et al., 2015) propose a reconceptualization of social value creation, arguing for a broader understanding of corporate social responsibility in the context of multinational enterprises. This perspective aligns with the notion that inclusive marketing strategies must account for the social impacts of business operations, particularly in emerging markets., Consequently, (St. Petersburg State University et al., 2017) examine the institutional dimensions of GVCs, highlighting how companies from developing markets can navigate complexities to integrate into global chains.

Their insights underscore the importance of understanding governance structures in shaping effective marketing strategies that resonate with diverse consumer bases. Over and above that, (Gürhan-Canli et al., 2018)synthesize research on consumer-brand relationships, emphasizing the need to adapt marketing strategies to align with evolving cultural and technological landscapes. Their findings suggest that as digitalization and sustainability trends rise, inclusive marketing strategies must evolve to meet new consumer expectations. In conjunction with this, (Morgan et al., 2018) analyze food value chains through the lens of nutrition goals, illustrating how value chain interventions can enhance dietary diversity and health outcomes. This research supports the argument that inclusive marketing strategies can play a crucial role in addressing public health challenges. in the same way (Beverelli et al., 2019) explore the relationship between domestic and global value chains, providing empirical evidence that domestic value chains can facilitate GVC integration. Their findings suggest that inclusive marketing strategies must consider the interconnectedness of local and global markets.

Moreover, (Ridoutt et al., 2019)review the impact pathways of value chains on diet quality, emphasizing the importance of aligning marketing strategies with consumer education and behavior. Their research indicates that effective value chain management can lead to improved nutritional outcomes, reinforcing the need for inclusivity in marketing approaches.For this reason, (Von Delft et al., 2019)discuss the role of global knowledge in business model innovation, advocating for the integration of supply chain strategies that leverage global insights. This approach underscores the importance of adaptive marketing strategies in responding to diverse consumer needs across markets. However, (Aslam et al., 2025) address the challenges facing the food supply chain amid climate change, emphasizing the need for innovative business models that can enhance resilience and sustainability. Their insights highlight the critical role of inclusive marketing strategies in ensuring food security and meeting consumer demands.But conversely, (Lavassani & Movahedi, 2021)explore how centrality in supply chain networks influences firm performance, suggesting that firms must strategically position themselves within the GVC to enhance their market presence. This research emphasizes the importance of aligning marketing strategies with supply chain positioning.As depicted, (Fernández, 2023) provides a systematic review of innovation in international business, arguing for the integration of global strategies to enhance competitive advantage. This perspective reinforces the notion that inclusive marketing strategies must be informed by global dynamics and innovation trends. To illustrate all of this, (Navaratne & Anthony, 2023) investigate the interplay between market orientation and supply chain strategy, suggesting that effective customer integration is essential for achieving superior performance. Their research highlights the need for inclusive marketing strategies that consider the diverse needs of customers across different markets.

5. RESEARCH METHODOLOGY

The bibliometric analysis on Global Value Chains and Inclusive Marketing Strategies was conducted using 355 documents in the Web of Science Core Collection database and the VOSviewer software. The analysis focused on the most prolific authors, sources, countries, institutions, and keywords, as well as the temporal evolution of the research field under analysis. Data Collection. To obtain the analysed documents, the search was established in the WoS Core Collection database using the following query: TS = ("Global Value Chain*" OR "Global Value Networks" OR "Global Product Chain*" OR "International Value Chain*" OR "International Value Networks" OR "International Product Chain*" OR "Global Supply Chain*" OR "Value Chain*" OR "Value Network*" OR "Value Web*" OR "Value Stream*") AND TS = ("Marketing" OR "Market" OR "Strategic Market" OR "Marketing Strategy*" OR "Positioning" OR "Market Selection" OR "Market Targeted*" OR "Market Entry" OR "Market Channel*" OR "Market Identification" OR "Market Adaptation" OR "Market Product*") AND Language = (English). The search was limited to articles published from 2017 until April 15th, 2025. The records were exported as a plain text file, including full records and cited references, using the bibtex format. After removing duplicates, a total of 355 documents were selected for analysis with VOSviewer software. The software allows for overlay visualizations of network data, which presents information over time in different colours representing specific years.

VOSviewer. To conduct the analysis, the software's full network visualisation function was implemented, allowing for the selection of various ways to create a visualisation based on the entirety of the dataset. As a result, the analysis sheds light on 155 bibliometric network visualisations, representing the dimensional characteristics of the current literature on Value Chains and Inclusive Marketing Strategies. Subsequent steps revealed clusters of co-authorship, co-citation, co-occurrence of keywords, and bibliometric maps that illustrate impacts and trends across countries and institutions.

6. THE INDIAN MARKET LANDSCAPE

Unlike Western markets, which are characterized by an abundance of resources to create products and sell them later to consumers, developing markets like India are resource constrained. They are at the bottom of the pyramid (BOP), where the population needs goods and services much cheaper than in developed economies if at all. The BOP is over four billion people, living in less than one dollar per day in purchasing power parity. This faceless, mass-market segment is usually underserved and shunned as a waste of time by brand managers, although this bottom billion is hugely untapped and the world's largest, poorest, most underserved market (Sun et al., 2009).The economic opportunities through diversified supplier networks, influencing trade redistribution amid geopolitical tensions(Khorana et al., 2022).

The Indian consumer is price driven with purchase triggers that are different from the developed world. conventional export-based indicators overestimate economic strength, necessitating new measures like global value chain (GVC) income(Timmer et al., 2013). Products catered to these new Indian consumers need to explore and exploit the psychologies peculiar to the Indian market. Above all digital platforms reshape producer-driven and buyer-driven chains, favoring direct consumer access and reinforcing existing corporate power(Gereffi, 2001). Global value chains are increasingly buyer-driven due to the embedding of complex quality information into widely accepted standards and codification and certification procedures(Ponte & Gibbon, 2005). If marketers can get inside the consumer's head and understand their values, needs, and purchase triggers, huge opportunities will be uncovered for marketers to tap mass markets with branded, affordable and accessible products(Malhotra, 2015).The increased trade uncertainties, multilateral institution challenges, and reshoring trends, emphasizing a shift toward localized supply chains rather than deeper global integration(Ciravegna & Michailova, 2022). Thus Conceptual explorations of how different industries can serve the consumers in mass markets need to be developed and researched. Similarly, understanding how mass consumers are attracted towards brands and explore innovative ways to create brand equity will cross borders.

7. THE ROLE OF GLOBAL VALUE CHAINS IN INDIA

Global Value Chains (GVCs) have emerged as a potent force in the global economy. In recent decades trade has been unbundled, leading to an increase in intra-firm and intra-industry trade, which has increased the importance of cross-border flows of intermediate goods, knowledge and services. Best value supply chains excel at cost, quality, speed, and flexibility, achieving competitive advantages and superior performance compared to traditional supply chains(Ketchen & Hult, 2007). GVCs are now a defining feature of globalization: they have become the dominant form of production in many sectors, accounting for 67 per cent of the global trade in goods (Meagher, 2019).GVCs are complex, multi-tiered systems of firms and institutions from different countries, composed of a lead firm enacting control in order to minimize costs and, thus, gain a competitive advantage. The marginal trade risks, adaptability, and economic rationales favoring cross-border collaboration, emphasizing that emerging technologies and strategic flexibility sustain global value chains despite rising nationalism(Contractor, 2022). The governance structures in supply chains, commodity chains, and production networks lack integration of sustainability principles(Bush et al., 2015) because Understanding globalization through value chains is crucial for developing countries to participate and gain access to skills, competences, and supporting services(Gereffi et al., 2001).It has been argued that the growth of GVCs represents an unprecedented opportunity for less developed countries to develop their economies. While firm-led GVCs may impose exclusion and inequalities, institutional-led inter-firm networks may enable developing country firms and workers to move up GVCs (, 2018). This depends on the degree of complementarity and cross-ownership between foreign and domestic firms, and the resources and capabilities of local economic actors. Awareness of both the opportunities and limitations of the GVC literature for inclusive development programming has been growing. The emerging GVC literature emphasizes the importance of upstream and downstream linkages connecting economic actors, which gives prominence to the role of marketing strategies requisite for positioning products in high-value-added market segments. But developing economies face low-end locking, limiting climate gains(Wang et al., 2022), GVC strategies are configured along the marketing axis of the chain in evolving contexts of competition and demand: namely, the arrival of mass-marketing or generic brands, the development of differentiated market segments and the rise of visibility-driven foreign direct investment (FDI). All these developments have become manifest in India in the past two decades. However, marketing investments are notoriously risky, uncertain and hard to measure, particularly in cases of innovation, non-price competition and behavioural conditioning as is required for the design and roll out of inclusive marketing-place products.

8. HISTORICAL CONTEXT

In the context of economic growth, India has a significance of its own because of its demographic structure, particularly a huge untapped consumer market with increasing purchasing power(Scaini, 2018), India is still considered a developing country, where nearly half of the population is illiterate and consuming traditional products such as handmade or home-made products. However, organized retailing is gradually growing as the existing players offer improved quality products at comparable prices and conduct aggressive marketing practices and promotional activities. Rural India has remained alien to the modern trade and shopping. Less than 1 percent of retailing is organized and there are no national chains of grocery stores or supermarkets. However, experts say that this is a potentially huge market that will see changes that are comparable with those experienced earlier in the urban area's presence of young population and huge number of first-time buyers having a very strong aspirational value. Policy changes undertaken by Government on Foreign Direct Investment (FDI) in the retail sector have also enthused this market. It is recorded that during the last census period, rural India (which constitutes about 69 percent of the country's population) has contributed more to the additional population than urban India and this trend is expected to continue. It is applicated by The GMS, a broad conceptualization of global marketing strategy, positively impacts a firm's global market performance by integrating standardization, configuration-coordination, and integration perspectives(Zou & Cavusgil, 2002).Notably the **cross-industry** collaborations, reshaping supply chain strategies(Gereffi et al., 2022) As opposed to the homogeneous urban environment, rural India represents a complex structure comprising a large number of states, cultures, languages, ethnicities, traditions and lifestyles adding their diversity.

Challenges related to communicating the relevance of non-consumption and low-consumption segments in these markets will need to be addressed proactively. Segmentators will need to communicate a relatively simple product offering to these segments and build awareness slowly both through push and pull. In many cases, existing communication media may not be effective. Participation in local festivals, village ballets, and street plays may need to be constructed and executed to build brand familiarity among these audiences. Because balanced climate of trust and power in strategic supply chains can lead to competitive advantage for firms by fostering cultural competitiveness and fostering joint entrepreneurship and learning(Ireland & Webb, 2007). While there are new opportunities through new mediums of advertising, safety, privacy and language issues will need to be addressed proactively to avoid social backlashes.

9. CURRENT TRENDS

In recent years, Corporate Social Responsibility (CSR) has emerged as one of the most discussed topics in the field of business. Notably for this, The GVC framework helps understand global industries, allowing policy makers to address development issues and adapt to emerging global realities(Gereffi, n.d.). A business that ignores its corporate obligations creates a firm that cannot be sustained for long. The factor endowments, trade policies, political stability, and FDI as key drivers of global value chain participation(Fernandes et al., 2022).Multinational companies recognize India's potential as a huge market for their goods and services, and with threats come opportunities. Some global corporations, with their bottomless pockets, have chosen to take the 'easy option': purchase local companies in their entirety. In a culture rich in social nuances, with the family as the focal point of life, marketers here face a challenge of dissecting a kaleidoscope of individual, family, caste, and religion-oriented lifestyle choices which will define future consumption choices. It must be remembered that the majority of consumers in India are at the low-income level(Bose & Chatterjee, 2008). Lower-income consumers exhibit a strong desire to improve their lives through the purchase of branded products. Western companies often interpret this as a desire for Western product values to meet consumer aspirations. It is not Western values aspirational for lower income consumers. They are massive and rich in gestures, sound, writing, artworks, architecture, and so on. In a poor but communicatively rich culture, the aspirations of lower income consumers will be largely symbolic rather than about functionality. Again, it must be remembered that 721 million people in India live in villages. Before the arrival of mass media and commercial television semi-arid masses knew very little about life outside of their own social conditions. There is a cultural void between modernity and tradition in which companies, advertising agencies and firms all operate.Also historical parallels, warning against repeating past mistakes, emphasizing multilateral cooperation to mitigate geopolitical tensions and trade disruptions(Mariotti, 2022).

The optimal allocation of ownership rights along the global value chain depends on the relative position of suppliers in the production line, with integration incentives varying based on the supplier's position and demand elasticity(Antràs & Chor, 2012).This gulley is also one of the greatest opportunities for marketing. The new global brands entering India are investing heavily to find a place in the hearts of consumers who are usually suspicious of new entrants. In leveraging opportunities in this market, there is typically an over-dependence on standardization of retail environments, product, and advertising communication. Developing this approach can often lead to confusion and produce a negative impression of what the brand means and how this product can improve the consumer's quality of life. This leads to disconnect, wastage, and diminished returns on advertising spend. However, a solution for bridging this gap between modernity and tradition lies in the growing importance of 'viral' marketing - brand and convergence producers becoming content producers.

10. CHALLENGES IN IMPLEMENTING INCLUSIVE MARKETING STRATEGIES

Several challenges need to be addressed in order to ensure the successful implementation of inclusive marketing strategies in emerging economies.

Figure 6. Challenges in Implementing Inclusive Marketing Strategies

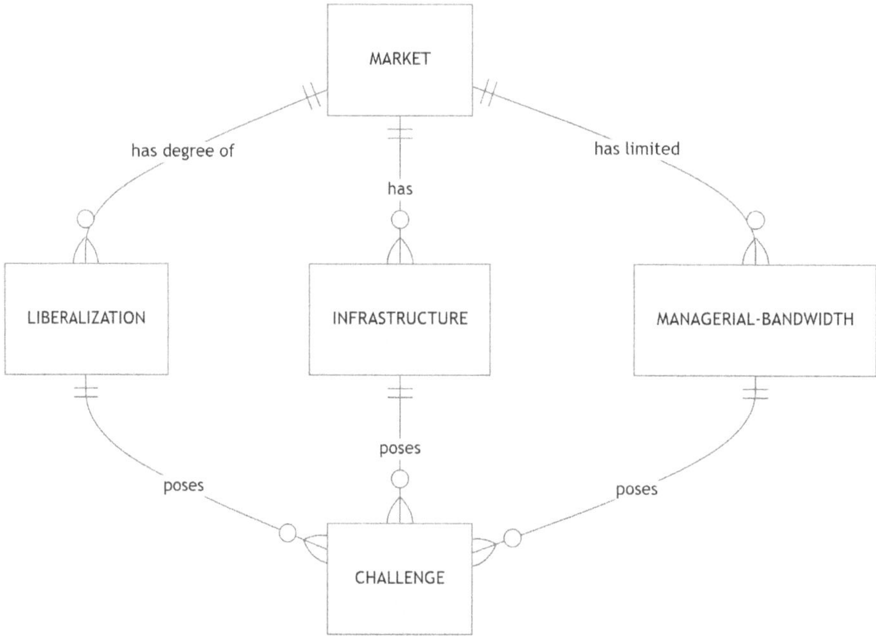

These challenges can restrict, delay or even derail the design and implementation of inclusive marketing strategies. Based on insights obtained from executives, three key challenges are discussed;

(1) Degree of liberalization of the mass market;
(2) Inadequate physical and institutional infrastructure; and
(3) Limited managerial bandwidth.

Managers of MNCs should understand that the business environment in lower-income countries differs from both their own home and emerging market operations. Stricter consumer protection laws, a more intense and restrictive scrutiny of marketing practices, and a strong lobbying by domestic players characterize these environments as compared to high-growth and emerging markets. An excessive focus on growth in base-of-the-pyramid markets is likely to backfire and Open innovation research needs to include diverse perspectives, strategy formulation, and customer co-creation, with potential applications in marketing, organizational behavior, and management(Randhawa et al., 2016). As Integrating social responsibility and business ethics into strategic marketing planning can help close the gap between concept and application(Robin & Reidenbach, 1987). Devising culturally nuanced strategies for engaging local communities and consumer segments would go a long way in ensuring sustained brand equity. Marketing messages that promote consumption-related behaviors, such as healthy eating or personal hygiene should be disseminated. The automation-driven transformations, influencing internationalization strategies and economic interdependencies, requiring firms to adapt through digital integration and flexible market structures(Castagnoli et al., 2022).

As target consumers in emerging markets are typically low-literate and use multiple local dialects, their engagement requires innovative ways of communicating. TV and print media which are the core of the marketing mix in developed countries, do not have huge impacts. While some MNCs have adapted their media strategy to include vernacular radio and cinema, more effort is needed. Most inclusive marketing strategies are complex, multifaceted and require cooperation from multiple divisions/stakeholders. Given the existing heavy workload, short- to medium-term pressures to develop growth strategies for other countries may sideline the focus on inclusive marketing efforts. Where shareholder returns are the only focus, it is far more difficult to make inclusive marketing strategies succeed. Hence successful inclusive marketing strategies require a genuine commitment to social action on the part of MNCs, which would be aided by bringing the planning and implementation of these strategies under the purview of the CEO. Because GVC governance has been interpreted as driving, coordination, and normalization, and while it is possible to reconcile different approaches within a unified paradigm, GVC analysis is best understood as a methodological approach that can be mobilized within various theoretical perspectives(Gibbon et al., 2008).The supply chain effects had the most severe impact, followed by output losses, while demand-side effects remained insignificant(Hayakawa & Mukunoki, 2021).

11. CULTURAL BARRIERS

A significant problem may arise due to differences in long-term orientation, acceptance for uncertainty, and individualism. Other striking features of a culture in which team members expect group equality include an emphasis on coastal geographies, strong reliance on interpersonal relationships and personal acquaintances, strong merchandising orientation, harmony and consensus-seeking, relatively close friendships, and stronger trust in recommendations from social contacts. People in a culture of individualism tend to work independently rather than collaboratively in teams, resulting in an avoidance of frequent and productive interaction with people of the organization's other generations. Teams in a more collectivist culture are expected to answer a question with a more integrated opinion to promote social harmony. In this sense, a team climate may be less well established, and disagreement may be perceived as disruptive.Optimal disaggregation and global dispersion of a firm's value chain can lead to benefits and increased complexity, but also increased complexity and costs(Contractor et al., 2010).

People with less uncertainty avoidance tend to work spontaneously, making it difficult to arrange meetings, which is one reason for the rare Asian meetings. An evaluation exercise should be both qualitative and quantitative to embrace the Middle-Eastern culture. A failure to bring future benefits from iGOAL means that those people with a higher long-term orientation may prioritize other activities that are easier to manage and are expected to bring more security in the future. One way to mitigate technology-related risks is to lower the level of hypermodernity of a consumption technology. The higher the complexity of the technology, the lower the acceptance. The more complex a technology, the more uncertain it is how much time and effort it takes to learn. Investment or trial-and-error strategies will gradually and collectively motivate users to acquire it. But Integrating corporate social responsibility in global value chains and industrial clusters leads to a new form of "synergistic governance" involving private, social, and public governance(Gereffi & Lee, 2016). Strategies for developing human resource skills, including the availability of trainers and access to training, play a role in the degree of power distance. Uncertainty about the positive impact of training can discourage participation(Nurhas et al., 2020)

12. ECONOMIC CONSTRAINTS

Low levels of literacy, especially among women, coupled with varying dialects, religious practices and social customs lead to differential education of communication and comprehension abilities specifying the need of innovatively tackling economic constraints before undertaking a mainstream approach. Customizing marketing communication to reach the rural women effectively will involve at first gaining their attention and subsequently holding it long enough to understand clearly the socio-economic educational and commercial points of the promotional info(Rao, 2014)Without an innovative ideal method these barriers prevent effective grasping of the multimedia marketing communication info. Penetration of low-cost digital media offers greater promise to overtake these barriers. Main borrowed practices in this regard involve storing of info through spread of micro and nano entrepreneurship-based user businesses. Game based experiential marketing strategies being formulated for the same are being innovated keeping all relevant factors in mind including comprehension ability kind and setting of promotions used and construct and type brand/ services being promoted etc. The digitalization reshapes global production, balancing reshoring expectations with fragmentation realities. Automation and digital logistics enable localized manufacturing(Butollo, 2021) Nurturing trust-based relationships with last mile user businesses is crucial for effectiveness of the method. Innovation is limited to enhancing understanding of digital media by customizing conventional aspects for grasping their uniqueness and pace of ease in current development by micro and nano entrepreneurship. Understanding of prior anchoring aspects too is being innovated with caution co-development and diffusion to gain scale and long-term sustainability. Middle millstone user businesses turn as lower reach focusing brand as well as advertisement niche market segment. These innovations too pioneer firm establishing better understanding of the rural advertising space in North India. Together with economic constraints level and quality of ease in current affordability they affect speed of communication. The significant influence of level of awareness indicates potential for rising communication effectiveness by upscaling awareness. Peer support construct too reveals the rich fabric of group facilitation nature and structure in rural market. The need of wholesome understanding and communication of all aspects impacting farming management are emphasized. On understanding development comprehension and externality factors a viable strategy was presented to enhance effectiveness of the whole chain. Customizing communications to public advance rural agriculture effectively involves addressing all factors concurrently. Improving branding credence on the internet being purchased by prior awareness about it offers a potential blue sea.

13. REGULATORY ISSUES

The regulatory issues related to GVCCs are, firstly, the treatment of companies by municipalities and states in developing economies. Local governments may impose varying regulations on companies involved with GVCs. GVCs are a means of production by which firms integrate or source their production overseas; countries wish to control their incoming GVCs in an attempt to encourage local firms to undertake value-adding activities or to develop capabilities. This may lead to rigidities in global investment regulations and FDI-related conditions, which may constrain the international expansion of MNEs and firms. The entrepreneurs engaged in GVCs are generally confronted with regulations that are administrative, exclusionary, or asymmetric, owing to the treatment of MNEs by the local authorities(Egede, 2013). The second issue is that MNEs may engage in supplier discrimination, although it may be the consumer some firms receive an end-price discount. MNEs bound by a buyer-driven GVC may obtain a special price discount on their product inputs, as part of their negotiation with suppliers. The upstream import expansion, stable export positioning, and greater domestic value-added reveal productivity gains and deeper supply chain integration(Chor et al., 2021). This may put suppliers in developing economies in disadvantage, particularly suppliers from poorer countries(Santos & Laczniak, 2009). Those not operating in such GVCs may be excluded from their supplier chain. Local suppliers in less-developed economies may be discriminated against even within a GVC by MNEs, particularly if they operate in markets with low entry costs against peers based in emerging economies with free entry.

14. STRATEGIES FOR LEVERAGING GLOBAL VALUE CHAINS

MD companies are aware of the opportunities in Indian markets, which have plenty of untapped potential. This was evaluated on the basis of the following interviewed and surveyed states. A short overview of the findings and how they could serve as inputs for analysed marketing strategies are elaborated on. To put MD companies in a position to seize the opportunity of markets and the incoming potential in India, ideas were formulated for possible marketing strategies. Bridging the gap between isolationist and global approaches in studying systemic risk requires encompassing theoretical models and improved data disclosure(Benoit et al., 2015). Starting from the definition that a global marketing strategy is the aggregate of global targeted markets and the marketing mix, specific strategies are discussed at three levels: worldwide, regional and local. These are complemented with a check list containing a suggested set of actions at the level of local firms. The proposed strategies are based on the findings of the previous session. However, this does not imply that all MD companies can and should adopt all these strategies. The options represent alternatives from which companies can select.

Figure 7. Strategies for Leveraging Global Value Chains

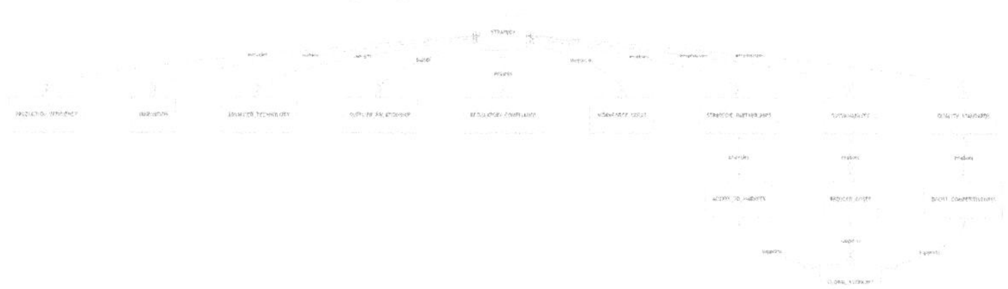

The global value chain concept has become popular for analyzing international expansion and geographical fragmentation of supply chains, with China playing a key role in value creation and capture(Gereffi & Lee, 2012). At the worldwide level, five strategies are proposed. The first is to globally direct, coordinate and observe international marketing efforts on a generic basis. A second option is to globally develop and build more of an in-house staff and culture with a local relevant profile. Thirdly, marketing capabilities development or improvement is not only worldwide but also through a local off-shoring route within India itself. Fourthly, an in-house scouting facility should be established that can provide marketing technology findings that are relevant for application in other markets. The fifth is to play a leading role in the development of an open intra-sectoral platform for modelling management and control tools, with the express purpose of enabling application and innovation opportunities to be accelerated. International entrepreneurial orientation and key strategic activities significantly improve the international performance of SMEs(G. A. Knight, 2001). At a regional level, the first suggested strategy is to initiate cooperation with surrounding non-conflicting MD companies, investigating opportunities for partnerships to facilitate growth. The second recommendation is to generate relevant publicity on the availability and application possibilities of MD technology aimed at expansion and innovation through targeted information campaigns, exhibitions and workshops. A third option is to sponsor and/or cooperate with an important agricultural or horticultural fair in the Asia Pacific region in general or in India in particular with the scope of generating international display opportunities. The final recommendation is to promote free and open availability of data and models in the framework of the agricultural and horticultural modelling benchmarks.Sustainable strategies in SMEs can increase value creation, attract investment, create competitive networks, and improve global supply chain sustainability(Moore & Manring, 2009).

15. PARTNERSHIPS WITH LOCAL BUSINESSES

The Global Value Chain is one of a national economy's ways of integration into the world economy. The global value chains impact emerging market firms' sustainability(Golgeci et al., 2021).Small and medium enterprises have special importance in economic growth and export promotion in both developed and developing countries due to their inherent strengths in developing one or more niche areas. There is also a lot of awareness as well as concern regarding the rapidly emerging small and medium enterprises' sector, popularly known as SMEs, and its implications on the national economies.

Figure 8. Strategies for the Partnerships with Local Businesses

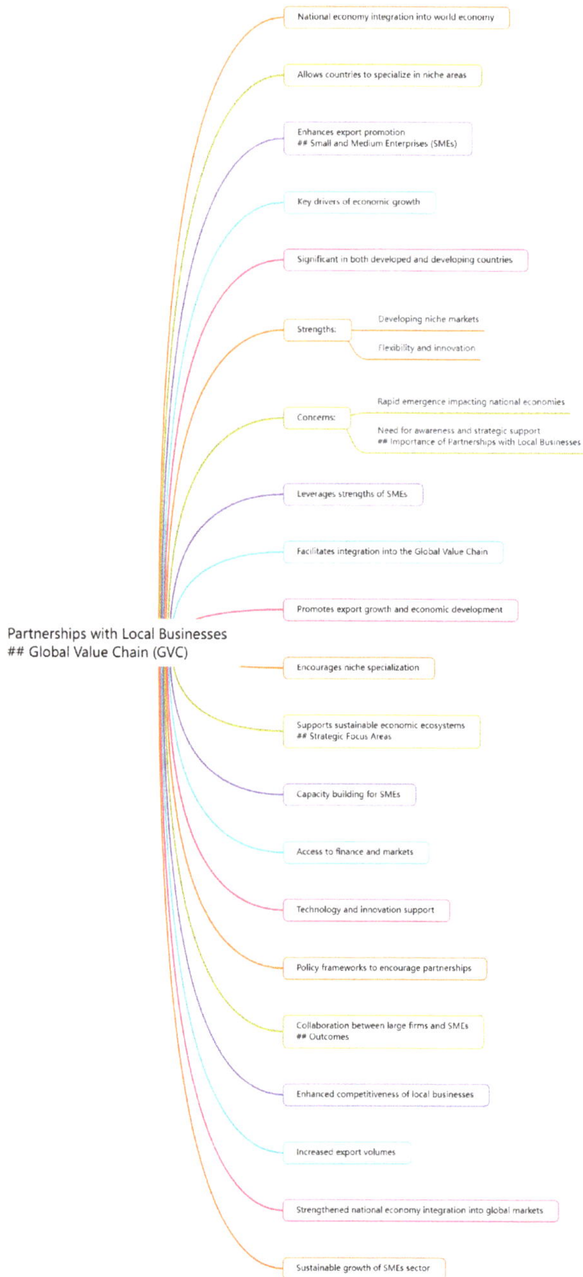

These concerns primarily revolve around the potential of SMEs in advancing national goals of eradicating poverty and achieving income equity, creating more jobs, and reducing the exodus of youth into urban slums from rural areas. On the other hand, most of the attention of the multi-lateral agencies is concentrated on the large corporations despite their adverse effects in terms of increasing age-old structural inequalities and concentration of wealth and power. Policies/laws should make it mandatory for large firms to share more of their profits with other local suppliers through actions that implement GVC initiatives undertaken by them. Enhancing industry level co-ordination and collaboration on global competitiveness, modernization, quality, training, research and development to create Malaysia as an internationally recognized brand. Local industry associations should function on a 'non-partisan approach' involving interaction of all industry associations and the trade diplomacy efforts. Working with financing institutions to create and deliver "entrepreneurial funding" as different instruments with government sponsored guarantee. Active public relations campaigns should be designed for government programs. Different training programs and trade diplomats training programs should be conceptualized, developed and implemented as GVC enactors. The findings substantiate the need for a casual analysis, resulting in a GVC model and related GVC initiatives which need to be implemented for a more impactful and effective promotional effort for more inclusive global marketing strategy.

16. KEY PERFORMANCE INDICATORS

Most of the models are related to the agriculture, fruit or vegetable products, industrial products or services and soft drinks available in the Indian market. The literature of minor products, especially beverages is lacking. The objective of this paper is to explore and evolve a continuous canvas/driving models for building international positioning strategies for Indian soft drink product(s) especially on the Indian soft drink market. This paper has three parts, the introduction, the drawing model in detailing forces shaping the international positioning of Indian soft drink beverage products, and the conclusion with future directions(Sharma, 2014).Marketing of financial services intrinsically appears to be quite different from marketing of soft drink products. The reasons for this are severalfold. The most important one being that the soft drink products are physical ones and hence do possess tangible features, both malleability and visibility which the financial services do not possess. In other words, soft drink products can be fabricated and manufactured by the marketing firm before selling them as finished products. As a consequence, the price, packaging, size and model of soft drinks can be designed by the marketer according to the demands of the target consumer. This is not the case with the financial service products.

An exhaustive literature review is necessary in the first stage of research process to understand the whole subject area, its scope and to identify gaps in research for subsequent investigations leading to contributions to knowledge. A literature review seeks to find material relevant to the area of study, analyse, evaluate and synthesise the above material. Systematic literature review attempts to explain how literature review study process is designed and conducted.

17. EMERGING MARKETS

Emerging Markets Are Hot, But Hard. But Why? Characteristics of Emerging Markets Emerging markets are made up of the current generation of developing economies. They were addressed in 1981 as "newly-industrialized countries," and the subsequent expansion of large-scale and/or rapid economic growth represented by "highflying Asian Tigers," such as South Korea and Taiwan. Over a short period of time, they moved from underdeveloped to industrialized and advanced economies. Extensive literature exists on newly-industrialized economies; it is, however, now a good time to take stock of emerging markets. Emerging markets can be characterized in different ways(Egede, 2013) here are two viewpoints: expected per capita growth vs. current per capita income, and geographical and cultural/market based positioning. Emerging markets are demanding Emerging markets are difficult and perhaps the most demanding markets. First, they are very demanding culturally and with respect to marketing. Needed is the understanding of the culture, which is difficult due to its complex and multi-layered nature. Consumer behavior is governed not just by taste and income, but also by social and cultural factors and even religious beliefs. Opening up and directly confronting a culture may lead to a reaction akin to a lion's ferocity, not even matching one's own understanding. Cultural/religious variation in taste also creates difficult class and adaptation challenges for marketing strategies. For example, the use of images of women is sensitive in Islam. Therefore, between Islamic and non-Islamic markets, this difference should be considered and marketing strategies effectively applied. Another question to consider is how to position the product and the firm/brand in the eyes of consumers in newly emerging markets full of non-trust. No knowledge, either local or global, creates great anxiety among consumers.

Emerging Markets Are Fragmented Emerging markets are fragmented, without any major national market. Per capita GDP in U.S. dollars varies from a few hundred in some parts of Africa to about 7,000 in Chile. This poses a big problem, not just in terms of local culture/language adaptations needed of the marketing mix, but also because of the vast geographical size and may remain so for the foreseeable future. Even India, which is continuously hailed as a huge single market comparable in size to China, falls short of this view. It is projected to have an unfulfilled market potential more than 600 million people, which suggests extreme inequality in wealth distribution.

18. SUSTAINABILITY CONSIDERATIONS

Logistics performance significantly boosts global value chain trade, with partner country logistics playing a bigger role than domestic logistics(Zaninović & Bugarčić, 2023). Environmental marketing can be termed as a special application of societal marketing to reduce the depletion of natural resources and to increase the well-being of the ecosystem(University of Lucknow, Department of Business Administration & Trivedi, 2015). Environmental marketing can be defined with the help of two concepts: green marketing and society marketing. Collaboration through intelligent e-business networks is crucial for supply chain management, enabling all participants to thrive and grow in a competitive global market(Horvath, 2001). It is the holistic policy of an enterprise concerning the evolution and commercialization of an innovative kind of product giving a functional value to customers while satisfying their in-use requirements using and bringing into service different kinds of goods without inappropriate detrimental consequences to the personal environment or the ecosystem. The holistic policy of an enterprise concerning the production and commercialization of a product giving a functional value to customers while satisfying their product requirements with a process having a minimum supply of environmental resources and production-caused detrimental consequences and the product having a possibly environmentally friendly technology of recycling(Oates et al., 2016),An energy-efficient refrigerator has an innovative structure giving the customer a higher utility and saving a considerable amount of energy compared with the old commonly used one.

19. POLICY RECOMMENDATIONS FOR STAKEHOLDERS

The implications of this research must move beyond the realm of academia and marketing managers to the consideration of multiple stakeholders including societal interest groups, governments, governmental organizations, and non-governmental organizations. Each of these stakeholders plays a crucial role in either supporting or obstructing marketers' long-term visions for serving poorer consumers in India. These organizations are ideally positioned to stimulate and facilitate conditions leading to broader and deeper engagement with impoverished consumer segments. Sustainable supply chain management in global supply chains involves greater connections between firms and multi-tier suppliers, with governance mechanisms playing a key role in sustainability outcomes(Koberg & Longoni, 2019). At the broadest level, they serve as a very important social good by creating a fair playing field through policy and a just marketplace to protect marginalized consumers. Well-intentioned marketers ready to move to engage the marginalized may need incentives or supporting policy for them to do so (J. C. Santos & R. Laczniak, 2009). Because Demand chain management is a new business model that combines marketing and supply chain competencies to create value in the marketplace by effectively meeting customer needs(Jüttner et al., 2007). Hence, productive partnerships that enable marketers to assist marginalized consumers more effectively are crucial. Family members and children should be involved in consumer education initiatives. The overarching goals of policy intervention should be the provision of both safety and education, allowing impoverished consumers to make fair and informed choices in the marketplace. These policies must either mandate or encourage marketers to understand better and assist these consumers more effectively while also ensuring that their interests are represented and protected. On the other hand, there are also dangers that policy interventions may be misguided or that unintended consequences may emerge. Therefore, monitoring must accompany policy encouragement. Some firms have responded to broad strokes policies that would legally encourage them to target poorer consumers by merely upselling their existing lower-tier offerings for greater margins. Their actions have merely preempted continued access to these offerings through threats of boycott. The key to successful policy intervention would be to know how engagement with markets at the bottom of the pyramid may serve the long-term interests of all stakeholders including firms. Affluent stakeholders must be educated on how their long-term interests will be better served through enhancing the marketing efforts targeted at the impoverished. Thus, this research aims to widen the debate by creating a better conceptual understanding of how the major stakeholders influence this under-researched area of marketing ethics. The outcome is a framework in which varying stakeholder interests influencing how marketers enter the marketplace to better serve their poorer consumers are delineated. Insights into how this entry process may stimulate broad forms of engagement which may maximize welfare for wider society at large are carefully illustrated. Consideration of how the engagement process may be dissuaded or derailed through poor ally choice or predatory practices are also detailed.

20. PRIVATE SECTOR ENGAGEMENT

Building on best practices learned from the global and Indian contexts, there are six key approaches corporates can adopt that will shift from exclusion to empowerment. GVC participation accelerates technology transfer in developing economies, especially via foreign licensing(Rigo, 2021), Capitalize on Alternative Technologies and Delivery Channels. Different technologies such as mobile telephony, rechargeable point-of-sales systems, solar lamps, portable clean water systems and affordable hybrid seed apply to and resonate with rural markets. For these technologies, product adaptations are necessary, followed by pilot testing. Less traditional delivery channels such as second sales force, service-oriented companies, cooperatives, village-based entrepreneurs and even self-help groups (SHGs) can form effective partnerships which offer the last mile a direct as well as indirect channel for contact and engagement. Create New Pricing and Payment Models. Various rural communities have shown a readiness to pay for empowerment and access. For this market, separate standard pricing and payment models are appropriate. regional trade protections, South African investment flows, and wage disparities drive supply chain configurations, influencing firms' strategic sourcing and economic integration(Pasquali et al., 2021). Furthermore, partial grants or government incentives overcome the affordability barrier. However, incumbents must retain sufficient pricing margins for financial viability, sustainability and continuous improvement. Re-Design Demand Creation Approaches. Effective demand creation goes beyond marketing gimmicks and offers a solution reflecting a deep understanding of the last mile's needs. adaptation in exports by mid-2020 but persistent import declines, highlighting long-term trade vulnerabilities amid crises(Amador et al., 2023).

Figure 9. Private Sector Engagement in Global Value Chain

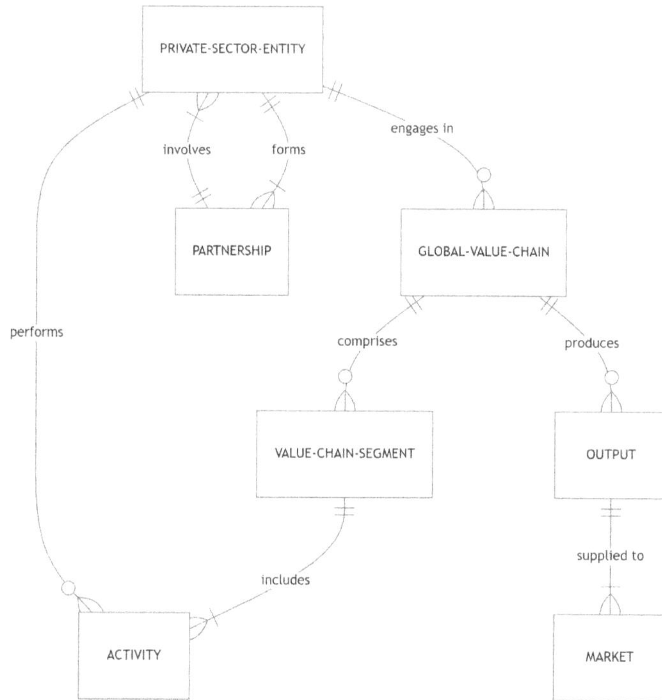

The financial market imperfections impact production organization, restricting firms from pursuing more profitable opportunities and informing trade policy decisions(Manova & Yu, 2016) and hence Financial independence of outreach is critical; either the last mile absorbs outreach costs through higher margins or local businesses attend to outreach to create an even larger, more accessible pie. Develop Multi-faceted Engagement Platforms. The bundling of multiple services is needed at the last mile, especially in rural villages, where form and use aggregately deny access to parts of the market. However, the question remains: who bundles these multiple services? Companies, NGOs, SHGs and cooperatives could play this role. Their activity must be sufficiently scaled and exposed for interpretation as market-making. In the intermediary phase, facilitators or public-private joint platforms help in linking and trust-building between sectors. Facilitate Non-linear Acquisition of Skills and Establish Frontiers. Finding such companies willing to help refers to the last mile's interests and the first mile's cost structure. Only when both are addressed will co-investment take place. The counterparts willing to assist need to be incentivized, rewarded, anchored and tracked. Finding funding partners based on their projected returns is necessary to enable the co-investments that will empower communities. Build on the Start-up Ecosystem. With an emerging mature startup ecosystem in India, rural empowerment systems should also be able to tap its potential. Public-private partnerships would benefit from this outside knowledge and experience, which could be less rigid in execution and would balance the need for impact with the need for returns and an exit option(Rao, 2014).

21. RESULT & DISCUSSION BASED ON THE LITERATURE

The thrust of globalization is perceptible globally as well as nationally. However, a general perception is that Homo sapiens, the rulers of the earth, has viewed this thrust with dubiousness with respect to its nation-states. In a country like India, poverty, illiteracy, overpopulation, corruption, and the usage of caste, creed, and religious affiliations for political gain are stupendous hindrances in gaining the prolific benefits of globalization. backward participation remains dominant, while forward support varies by scale effect(W. Niu et al., 2023) The credible external regulations reduce the need for direct buyer governance, transforming industry standards and developmental policies(Humphrey & Schmitz*, 2001). dominant currency pricing limits export competitiveness, but global value chains enable adaptation, reshaping trade responses to interest rate shifts(Cook & Patel, 2023). Nevertheless, it has succeeded in forming a market economy, and there is a current permeability of walls against the ingress of products from international players. This has not only altered the direction of marketing but has also initiated a new set of auxiliary problems. Oft-seized nations are discerning the uncontrolled clout of this product, its surpassing branding strategies, and its coercive promotional mixes on a diverse range of local consumer segments. combining vertical and horizontal aspects of value chains enhances understanding of how restructuring influences local economies, social relations, and ecological sustainability(Bolwig et al., 2010). However, the brunt is most crushed by the developing nations like India. This attempts to highlight the efforts made by global competitors in aspects such as advertising, sales promotion, publicity, and public relations to create a mark among the Indian consumers. The thrust of globalization is perceptible globally as well as nationally. final product trade becomes increasingly less environmentally effective, highlighting the complex environmental effects of different trade patterns(Zhang et al., 2017), The trade and industrial policies favoring processing trade contribute to these disparities, emphasizing the need to distinguish between processing and non-processing exporters in global value chain analyses(Dai et al., 2016), In a country like India, poverty, illiteracy, overpopulation, corruption, the usage of caste, creed, and religious affiliations for political gain are stupendous hindrances in gaining the prolific benefits of globalization. beyond acting as a facilitator, states increasingly function as regulators, producers, and buyers, shaping economic development(Horner, 2017), Nevertheless, it has succeeded in forming a market economy and there is a current porosity of walls against the ingress of products from international players. This has not only altered the direction of marketing but has also initiated a new set of auxiliary problems. Oft-seized nations are discerning the uncontrolled clout of this product, its surpassing branding strategies, and its coercive promotional mixes on a diverse range of local consumer segments. However, the brunt is most crushed by the developing nations like India. Production share revealing strengthened intra-regional forward linkages(Marcato, 2023) This attempts to highlight the efforts made by global competitors in aspects such as advertising, sales promotion, publicity, and public relations to create a mark among the Indian consumers.

22. CONCLUSION

By all objective measures, the BOP (bottom of the pyramid) is an enormous market, with approximately 4 trillion USD of daily consumer expenditures. For decades, the BOP market was ignored by marketers, correctly regarded as too poor for any meaningful retail engagement. However, the opportunity is real because many FMGCs (fast-moving consumer goods companies) are now actively describing their engagement with impoverished marketing segments underdeveloped markets. The regional trade agreements complement rather than threaten global trade, evolving beyond tariff preferences to deeper economic integration(Pomfret, 2021). Poor people want to buy soap that is less than a dollar, but soap that is more than a dollar goes unsold. An educational program encouraging BOP residents to improve everyday hygiene could easily double this market. MNC projections imply that the BOP is a distinct marketing segment with unique preferences and beliefs. Segments are marketing's fundamental unit of analysis, the building blocks on which many of marketing's concepts and theories are developed. These segments emerge from and are predicated on the existence of differences in the degree to which certain individuals control or possess scarce resources needed for shaping a BOP market. The requisite deployments of these resources are the modes used to reach and to serve BOP consumers. Transparency enhances accountability and environmental governance, its future effectiveness depends on strategic institutional arrangements that balance consumer empowerment and corporate interests(Mol, 2015),Understanding GVCs (global value chains) can enhance the development of an emerging market by recognizing how MNCs (multinational corporations) think and propose strategies to compete for investment in the national economy. On top of it it is notable that, rising geographic and organizational concentration in GVCs creates uneven upgrading opportunities, favoring dominant firms while limiting smaller suppliers(Lee & Gereffi, 2015), Other linkages contribute less or not at all. In an era of growing nationalism, several implications for action and research address the need of integrating emerging economies into GVCs, in consideration of the preceding differences in degrees(Rao, 2014). MNC subsidiaries in emerging economies provide full information and sensitivity analyses to parent firms concerning the relevance of the available services in producing for GVCs. No doubt a global value chains create uneven power dynamics, affecting labor relations and market transactions(Carr et al., 2000), Also sector-level disparities, where technology-intensive industries benefit more, reinforce policies that promote GVC engagement and domestic capacity-building for sustained growth(Jangam & Rath, 2021).A more inclusive siting policy adopts a broader definition of benefit, going beyond job creation. This ensures managers agree on a definition of what is economic development and sustainably development as a means to attract GVCs. At an academic level, when encountering better documented cases, theory can sometimes be refuted. Even without comparative labor cost advantages, some countries have acquired GVCs and the associated benefits, hence questioning the received theory. There can be mechanisms enabling such countries to jump start a GVC presence, but normal GVC logic does not operate. Entering and sustaining a GVC can be highly susceptible to firms in a developing country building on political ties or using bribery, something which is typically viewed as anti-competitive. Hence, basic and applied research sweeping in the other direction is necessary.

23. FUTURE DIRECTIONS FOR INCLUSIVE MARKETING IN INDIA

Corporate philanthropy with a profit motive is necessary but not sufficient to address the last mile. The difference between social and commercial motives is not just terminology. The former incorporates an exclusivity of intent that while focused on social good, ignores an entire market that does not meet the social performance criteria. This new class will be born and imbued with beliefs that personal hygiene which brings health, happiness, and respect is worth the investment. At that rate, social capital is built. But these bleached pastes or cakes or powders will remain beyond the reach of the current household. A co-operative model like Amul, e-choupal scale knowledge capacity building initiative with crucial density of intervention for a sustainable income and improvement will become increasingly necessary. To get there, it is necessary to engage fully with the existing and invaluable unbranded WASH knowledge, and its attendant bureaucratic nightmare, to strike the right balance between social assumptions and business targets. GVCs that are not as soft as surely will be able to negotiate this tension. They have time. The new whites have no childhood. This too is humanitarian enforcement therefore beware. GVC has dual role as a supplier of intermediate inputs globally and a production hub regionally, reinforcing its strategic importance in trade(Araújo et al., 2021).The industry-driven certifications dominating over consumer-facing labels, emphasizing global value chain dynamics shaping regulatory standards beyond national political economies(Mook & Overdevest, 2021).

To sustainably build markets in rural areas, attention has to shift from supply to demand. Positive demand again cannot be assumed. Addressing awareness, affordability, distribution, and varied new offerings for every customer is a long hard labor. GVC integration influences EU policy, while anti-globalization pressures reshape trade governance, requiring nuanced strategies to maintain economic stability, Considering the muscular WASH beginnings of their businesses, it is ironically illuminating that the hardest work has been without the brown and pink bars, the clear liquids and the blue gels that are seen peddled so cheaply by enterprising unbranded competitors in urban areas. Based on decades of careful work in building rural markets, these consumption choices and routines are suggested. Hence, industrial policy's role in reshoring, emphasizing supplier diversification to enhance resilience against future crises and reduce dependence on concentrated production hubs(Coveri et al., 2020). Major important gaps for these segments are personal cleansing from petrichor, flesh debris, and food particle terms misunderstood in trade parlance; village-based health, happiness, and dignity enhancement houses for browning, wheeling, and wrinkling; and answer which went to the bodies built without eyes from Waterloo, Toronto, and the Pyramids. Nonprofit-MA/profit-MB huge adaptive organizations hybridizing human and machine.

24. FUTURE SCOPE OF THE STUDY

This study exposes a broader theoretical perspective driving inclusive marketing strategies across the globe. Further research is warranted to test the applicability of the theoretical framework among developing nations not involved in the 2020 Pandemic. In addition, to determine how the framework can be operationalized and the unique factors in each region/market that need to be accounted for in inclusive marketing strategy efforts (Sengupta, 2014). Longitudinally testing the model, to devise new points of inclusion and exclusion, would be valuable for managers and scholars alike. Guidelines for how social fabric and networking can be regained in vulnerable times and be utilized for resolving exclusion are also critical, and warrant more pointed research. Similar efforts can be made to conduct experimentation on the proposed frameworks. This would help managers channel their efforts accordingly, as some of the initiatives may be easier to enact, less resource-intensive, or may yield quicker returns than others. The sectoral variations in GVC integration, showing supply and demand perspectives influence trade structures, impacting responses to trade wars and economic disruptions(Xiao et al., 2020).In turn, this would augment theory on the role of brands in public health and emergency circumstances worldwide.

In global marketing research, this study opens a new fertile ground for research on the impact of GVCs on inclusive marketing. Because corporations today are no longer bound by national borders, questions of local marketing and adaptation can now take on broader views. Heterogeneity not just among countries but also among the employees and producers of each chain can be studied in relation to consumer markets and attitudes. Furthermore, this study enriches marketing strategy discussions by enhancing the understanding of the sources behind co-branded inclusive marketing. Finally, as the number of brands and GVC driven marketing initiatives grows, so does the need for frameworks on co-branding, alliances, and political marketing specifically in the context of the Global South.

REFERENCES

Amador, J., Melo Gouveia, C., & Pimenta, A. C. (2023). COVID-19, lockdowns and international trade: Evidence from firm-level data. *Empirical Economics*, *65*(5), 2427–2466. DOI: 10.1007/s00181-023-02421-x PMID: 37361946

) Antràs, P., & Chor, D. (2012). *Organizing the Global Value Chain* (No. w18163; p. w18163). National Bureau of Economic Research. DOI: 10.3386/w18163

Araújo, I. F. D., Perobelli, F. S., & Faria, W. R. (2021). Regional and global patterns of participation in value chains: Evidence from Brazil. *Inter Economics*, *165*, 154–171. DOI: 10.1016/j.inteco.2020.12.009

Aslam, H., Waseem, M., Muneeb, D., Ali, Z., Roubaud, D., & Grebinevych, O. (2025). Customer integration in the supply chain: The role of market orientation and supply chain strategy in the age of digital revolution. *Annals of Operations Research*, *348*(3), 2145–2169. DOI: 10.1007/s10479-023-05191-y PMID: 36846244

Benoit, S., Colliard, J.-E., Hurlin, C., & Perignon, C. (2015). Where the Risks Lie: A Survey on Systemic Risk. SSRN *Electronic Journal*. DOI: 10.2139/ssrn.2577961

Beverelli, C., Stolzenburg, V., Koopman, R. B., & Neumueller, S. (2019). Domestic value chains as stepping stones to global value chain integration. *World Economy*, *42*(5), 1467–1494. DOI: 10.1111/twec.12779

Bolwig, S., Ponte, S., Du Toit, A., Riisgaard, L., & Halberg, N. (2010). Integrating Poverty and Environmental Concerns into Value-Chain Analysis: A Conceptual Framework. *Development Policy Review*, *28*(2), 173–194. DOI: 10.1111/j.1467-7679.2010.00480.x

Bose, S. K., & Chatterjee, J. (2008). CHALLENGES FACED BY THE INDIAN TINPLATE PACKAGING INDUSTRY. *Analysis*, •••, 13.

Boss, M. (1974). Economic theory of democracy: An empirical test. *Public Choice*, *19*(1), 111–115. DOI: 10.1007/BF01718551

Brandenburger, A. M., & Stuart, H. W.Jr. (1996). V alue-based B usiness S trategy. *Journal of Economics & Management Strategy*, *5*(1), 5–24. DOI: 10.1111/j.1430-9134.1996.00005.x

Bush, S. R., Oosterveer, P., Bailey, M., & Mol, A. P. J. (2015). Sustainability governance of chains and networks: A review and future outlook. *Journal of Cleaner Production*, *107*, 8–19. DOI: 10.1016/j.jclepro.2014.10.019

Butollo, F. (2021). Digitalization and the geographies of production: Towards reshoring or global fragmentation? *Competition & Change*, *25*(2), 259–278. DOI: 10.1177/1024529420918160

Carr, M., Chen, M. A., & Tate, J. (2000). Globalization and Home-Based Workers. *Feminist Economics*, *6*(3), 123–142. DOI: 10.1080/135457000750020164

Castagnoli, R., Büchi, G., Coeurderoy, R., & Cugno, M. (2022). Evolution of industry 4.0 and international business: A systematic literature review and a research agenda. *European Management Journal*, *40*(4), 572–589. DOI: 10.1016/j.emj.2021.09.002

Chang, H., & Andreoni, A. (2020). Industrial Policy in the 21st Century. *Development and Change*, *51*(2), 324–351. DOI: 10.1111/dech.12570

Chor, D., Manova, K., & Yu, Z. (2021). Growing like China: Firm performance and global production line position. *Journal of International Economics*, *130*, 103445. DOI: 10.1016/j.jinteco.2021.103445

Ciravegna, L., & Michailova, S. (2022). Why the world economy needs, but will not get, more globalization in the post-COVID-19 decade. *Journal of International Business Studies*, *53*(1), 172–186. DOI: 10.1057/s41267-021-00467-6 PMID: 34511653

Conteduca, F. P., Giglioli, S., Giordano, C., Mancini, M., & Panon, L. (2025). Trade fragmentation unveiled: Five facts on the reconfiguration of global, US and EU trade. *Economia e Politica Industriale*. Advance online publication. DOI: 10.1007/s40812-024-00337-w

Contractor, F. J. (2022). The world economy will need even more globalization in the post-pandemic 2021 decade. *Journal of International Business Studies*, *53*(1), 156–171. DOI: 10.1057/s41267-020-00394-y PMID: 33551513

Contractor, F. J., Kumar, V., Kundu, S. K., & Pedersen, T. (2010). Reconceptualizing the Firm in a World of Outsourcing and Offshoring: The Organizational and Geographical Relocation of High-Value Company Functions. *Journal of Management Studies*, *47*(8), 1417–1433. DOI: 10.1111/j.1467-6486.2010.00945.x

Cook, D., & Patel, N. (2023). Dollar invoicing, global value chains, and the business cycle dynamics of international trade. *Journal of International Economics*, *145*, 103839. DOI: 10.1016/j.jinteco.2023.103839

Coveri, A., Cozza, C., Nascia, L., & Zanfei, A. (2020). Supply chain contagion and the role of industrial policy. *Economia e Politica Industriale*, *47*(3), 467–482. DOI: 10.1007/s40812-020-00167-6

Dai, M., Maitra, M., & Yu, M. (2016). Unexceptional exporter performance in China? The role of processing trade. *Journal of Development Economics*, *121*, 177–189. DOI: 10.1016/j.jdeveco.2016.03.007

Day, G. S. (2011). Closing the Marketing Capabilities Gap. *Journal of Marketing*, *75*(4), 183–195. DOI: 10.1509/jmkg.75.4.183

DeStefano, T., & Timmis, J. (2024). Robots and export quality. *Journal of Development Economics*, *168*, 103248. DOI: 10.1016/j.jdeveco.2023.103248

Dolan, C., & Humphrey, J. (2004). Changing Governance Patterns in the Trade in Fresh Vegetables between Africa and the United Kingdom. *Environment and Planning A. Environment & Planning A*, *36*(3), 491–509. DOI: 10.1068/a35281

Dufour, M., Elias-Pinsonnault, S., & Tremblay-Pepin, S. (2025). An international interface: Democratic planning in a global context. *Competition & Change*, *29*(1), 83–100. DOI: 10.1177/10245294231212681

Egede, E. A. (2013). International and National Marketing Channel Decisions For Emerging Markets. *Developing Country Studies*, *3*(10), 149.

Faber, M., Kilic, K., Kozliakov, G., & Marin, D. (2025). Global value chains in a world of uncertainty and automation. *Journal of International Economics*, *155*, 104079. DOI: 10.1016/j.jinteco.2025.104079

Fernandes, A. M., Kee, H. L., & Winkler, D. (2022). Determinants of Global Value Chain Participation: Cross-Country Evidence. *The World Bank Economic Review*, *36*(2), 329–360. DOI: 10.1093/wber/lhab017

Fernández, I. A. (2023). Innovation and international business: A systematic literature review. *Heliyon*, *9*(1), e12956. DOI: 10.1016/j.heliyon.2023.e12956 PMID: 36704276

Freund, C., Mattoo, A., Mulabdic, A., & Ruta, M. (2024). Is US trade policy reshaping global supply chains? *Journal of International Economics*, *152*, 104011. DOI: 10.1016/j.jinteco.2024.104011

Gereffi, G. (2001). Beyond the Producer-driven/Buyer-driven Dichotomy *The Evolution of Global Value Chains in the Internet Era. IDS Bulletin*, *32*(3), 30–40. DOI: 10.1111/j.1759-5436.2001.mp32003004.x

Gereffi, G. (2014). Global value chains in a post-Washington Consensus world. *Review of International Political Economy*, *21*(1), 9–37. DOI: 10.1080/09692290.2012.756414

Gereffi, G. (n.d.). GLOBAL VALUE CHAIN ANALYSIS. *PRiMER: Peer-Reviewed Reports in Medical Education Research.*

Gereffi, G., Humphrey, J., Kaplinsky, R., & Sturgeon, T. J. (2001). Introduction: Globalisation, Value Chains and Development. *IDS Bulletin*, *32*(3), 1–8. DOI: 10.1111/j.1759-5436.2001.mp32003001.x

Gereffi, G., Humphrey, J., & Sturgeon, T. (2005). The governance of global value chains. *Review of International Political Economy*, *12*(1), 78–104. DOI: 10.1080/09692290500049805

Gereffi, G., & Lee, J. (2012). Why the World Suddenly Cares About Global Supply Chains. *The Journal of Supply Chain Management*, *48*(3), 24–32. DOI: 10.1111/j.1745-493X.2012.03271.x

Gereffi, G., & Lee, J. (2016). Economic and Social Upgrading in Global Value Chains and Industrial Clusters: Why Governance Matters. *Journal of Business Ethics*, *133*(1), 25–38. DOI: 10.1007/s10551-014-2373-7

Gereffi, G., Pananond, P., & Pedersen, T. (2022). Resilience Decoded: The Role of Firms, Global Value Chains, and the State in COVID-19 Medical Supplies. *California Management Review*, *64*(2), 46–70. DOI: 10.1177/00081256211069420

Gibbon, P., Bair, J., & Ponte, S. (2008). Governing global value chains: An introduction. *Economy and Society*, *37*(3), 315–338. DOI: 10.1080/03085140802172656

Golgeci, I., Makhmadshoev, D., & Demirbag, M. (2021). Global value chains and the environmental sustainability of emerging market firms: A systematic review of literature and research agenda. *International Business Review*, *30*(5), 101857. DOI: 10.1016/j.ibusrev.2021.101857

González-Torres, T., Rodríguez-Sánchez, J.-L., Montero-Navarro, A., & Gallego-Losada, R. (2020). Visualizing Research on Industrial Clusters and Global Value Chains: A Bibliometric Analysis. *Frontiers in Psychology*, *11*, 1754. DOI: 10.3389/fpsyg.2020.01754 PMID: 32793074

Gürhan-Canli, Z., Sarial-Abi, G., & Hayran, C. (2018). Consumers and Brands across the Globe: Research Synthesis and New Directions. *Journal of International Marketing*, *26*(1), 96–117. DOI: 10.1509/jim.17.0063

Hayakawa, K., & Mukunoki, H. (2021). Impacts of COVID -19 on Global Value Chains. *The Developing Economies*, *59*(2), 154–177. DOI: 10.1111/deve.12275 PMID: 33821021

Hongfu, N., Daocheng, Z., & Siyi, P. (2024). A new method for measuring industrial chain risk exposure: A regional perspective in China. *Journal of Economic Surveys*, *38*(5), 1760–1794. DOI: 10.1111/joes.12626

Horner, R. (2017). Beyond facilitator? State roles in global value chains and global production networks. *Geography Compass, 11*(2), e12307. DOI: 10.1111/gec3.12307

Horvath, L. (2001). Collaboration: The key to value creation in supply chain management. *Supply Chain Management, 6*(5), 205–207. DOI: 10.1108/EUM0000000006039

Humphrey, J., & Schmitz, H. (2002). How does insertion in global value chains affect upgrading in industrial clusters? *Regional Studies, 36*(9), 1017–1027. DOI: 10.1080/0034340022000022198

Ireland, R. D., & Webb, J. W. (2007). A multi-theoretic perspective on trust and power in strategic supply chains. *Journal of Operations Management, 25*(2), 482–497. DOI: 10.1016/j.jom.2006.05.004

Jangam, B. P., & Rath, B. N. (2021). Do global value chains enhance or slog economic growth? *Applied Economics, 53*(36), 4148–4165. DOI: 10.1080/00036846.2021.1897076

Jüttner, U., Christopher, M., & Baker, S. (2007). Demand chain management-integrating marketing and supply chain management. *Industrial Marketing Management, 36*(3), 377–392. DOI: 10.1016/j.indmarman.2005.10.003

Kano, L., Tsang, E. W. K., & Yeung, H. W. (2020). Global value chains: A review of the multi-disciplinary literature. *Journal of International Business Studies, 51*(4), 577–622. DOI: 10.1057/s41267-020-00304-2

Kazekula, H. (2014). *A global value chain perspective to understanding and unpacking the development trajectory of the horticultural industry in Zambia: The case of small-scale farmers based in Lusaka*. https://www.academia.edu/90102473/A_global_value_chain_perspective_to_understanding_and_unpacking_the_development_trajectory_of_the_horticultural_industry_in_Zambia_the_case_of_small_scale_farmers_based_in_Lusaka

Ketchen, D. J.Jr, & Hult, G. T. M. (2007). Bridging organization theory and supply chain management: The case of best value supply chains. *Journal of Operations Management, 25*(2), 573–580. DOI: 10.1016/j.jom.2006.05.010

Khorana, S., Escaith, H., Ali, S., Kumari, S., & Do, Q. (2022). The changing contours of global value chains post-COVID: Evidence from the Commonwealth. *Journal of Business Research, 153*, 75–86. DOI: 10.1016/j.jbusres.2022.07.044 PMID: 35996441

Klewitz, J., & Hansen, E. G. (2014). Sustainability-oriented innovation of SMEs: A systematic review. *Journal of Cleaner Production, 65*, 57–75. DOI: 10.1016/j.jclepro.2013.07.017

Knight, G. (2000). Entrepreneurship and Marketing Strategy: The SME under Globalization. *Journal of International Marketing*, *8*(2), 12–32. DOI: 10.1509/jimk.8.2.12.19620

Knight, G. A. (2001). Entrepreneurship and strategy in the international SME. *Journal of International Management*, *7*(3), 155–171. DOI: 10.1016/S1075-4253(01)00042-4

Koberg, E., & Longoni, A. (2019). A systematic review of sustainable supply chain management in global supply chains. *Journal of Cleaner Production*, *207*, 1084–1098. DOI: 10.1016/j.jclepro.2018.10.033

Lavassani, K. M., & Movahedi, B. (2021). Firm-Level Analysis of Global Supply Chain Network: Role of Centrality on Firm's Performance. *International Journal of Global Business and Competitiveness*, *16*(2), 86–103. DOI: 10.1007/s42943-021-00026-8

Lee, J., & Gereffi, G. (2015). Global value chains, rising power firms and economic and social upgrading. *Critical Perspectives on International Business*, *11*(3/4), 319–339. DOI: 10.1108/cpoib-03-2014-0018

London, T., & Hart, S. L. (2004). Reinventing strategies for emerging markets: Beyond the transnational model. *Journal of International Business Studies*, *35*(5), 350–370. DOI: 10.1057/palgrave.jibs.8400099

Lowitt, K., Hickey, G. M., Ganpat, W., & Phillip, L. (2015). Linking Communities of Practice with Value Chain Development in Smallholder Farming Systems. *World Development*, *74*, 363–373. DOI: 10.1016/j.worlddev.2015.05.014

Malhotra, D. (2015). Social paradigms of the digital marketing- an Indian perspective of Social Media Marketing. *MPRA Paper*, Article 66405. https://ideas.repec.org//p/pra/mprapa/66405.html

Mancini, M., Montalbano, P., Nenci, S., & Vurchio, D. (2024). Positioning in Global Value Chains: World Map and Indicators, a New Dataset Available for GVC Analyses. *The World Bank Economic Review*, *38*(4), 669–690. DOI: 10.1093/wber/lhae005

Manova, K., & Yu, Z. (2016). How firms export: Processing vs. ordinary trade with financial frictions. *Journal of International Economics*, *100*, 120–137. DOI: 10.1016/j.jinteco.2016.02.005

Marcato, M. B. (2023). Regional Dynamics in Global Production Sharing: Evidence from "Factory South America.". *European Journal of Development Research*, *35*(5), 1173–1196. DOI: 10.1057/s41287-022-00572-8 PMID: 36573215

Mariotti, S. (2022). A warning from the Russian–Ukrainian war: Avoiding a future that rhymes with the past. *Economia e Politica Industriale*, *49*(4), 761–782. DOI: 10.1007/s40812-022-00219-z

Masoumik, S. M., Abdul-Rashid, S. H., & Olugu, E. U. (2014). Gaining Competitive Advantage through Strategic Green Supply Chain Management: From a Literature Review towards a Conceptual Model. *International Journal of Supply Chain Management*, *3*(3), 3. Advance online publication. DOI: 10.59160/ijscm.v3i3.964

) Meagher, K. (2019). Working in Chains: African Informal Workers and Global Value Chains. *Agrarian South: Journal of Political Economy: A Triannual Journal of Agrarian South Network and CARES*, *8*(1–2), 64–92. DOI: 10.1177/2277976019848567

Meng, B., Peters, G. P., Wang, Z., & Li, M. (2018). Tracing CO2 emissions in global value chains. *Energy Economics*, *73*, 24–42. DOI: 10.1016/j.eneco.2018.05.013

Milberg, W. (2008). Shifting sources and uses of profits: Sustaining US financialization with global value chains. *Economy and Society*, *37*(3), 420–451. DOI: 10.1080/03085140802172706

Mol, A. P. J. (2015). Transparency and value chain sustainability. *Journal of Cleaner Production*, *107*, 154–161. DOI: 10.1016/j.jclepro.2013.11.012

Mook, A., & Overdevest, C. (2021). What drives market construction for fair trade, organic, and GlobalGAP certification in the global citrus value chain? Evidence at the importer level in the Netherlands and the United States. *Business Strategy and the Environment*, *30*(7), 2996–3008. DOI: 10.1002/bse.2784

Moore, S. B., & Manring, S. L. (2009). Strategy development in small and medium sized enterprises for sustainability and increased value creation. *Journal of Cleaner Production*, *17*(2), 276–282. DOI: 10.1016/j.jclepro.2008.06.004

Morgan, E. H., Hawkes, C., Dangour, A. D., & Lock, K. (2018). Analyzing food value chains for nutrition goals. *Journal of Hunger & Environmental Nutrition*, *14*(4), 4. Advance online publication. DOI: 10.1080/19320248.2018.1434106

Moussir, C.-E. (2025). Morocco's Economic Prospects: A Dynamic ARDL Simulation on Global Value Chain Integration. *ECONOMICS*, *13*(1), 179–196. DOI: 10.2478/eoik-2025-0009

Mudambi, R. (2008). Location, control and innovation in knowledge-intensive industries. *Journal of Economic Geography*, *8*(5), 699–725. DOI: 10.1093/jeg/lbn024

Navaratne, A., & Anthony, J. O. M. (2023). Methods of Incorporating Sustainability Contexts in Marketing and the Expected Response–A Fuzzy Approach. SocArXiv, Article kec8w_v1. https://ideas.repec.org//p/osf/socarx/kec8w_v1.html DOI: 10.31235/osf.io/kec8w

Niu, M., Wang, Z., Zhang, Y., & Mao, Y. (2025). The chasing dragon: To what extent and how does China catch up with USA under global value chains? *Applied Economics*, *57*(8), 839–852. DOI: 10.1080/00036846.2024.2309460

Niu, W., Xu, Z., Liu, B., & Liu, C. (2023). INTERNATIONALIZATION OF THE CONSTRUCTION INDUSTRY IN THE GLOBAL VALUE CHAIN. *Technological and Economic Development of Economy*, *29*(4), 1336–1352. DOI: 10.3846/tede.2023.19426

Nurhas, I., Aditya, B. R., Geisler, S., & Pawlowski, J. (2020). Why Does Cultural Diversity Foster Technology-enabled Intergenerational Collaboration? DOI: 10.48550/ARXIV.2001.07630

Oates, C., Alevizou, P., & McDonald, S. (2016). Challenges for Marketers in Sustainable Production and Consumption. *Sustainability (Basel)*, *8*(1), 75. DOI: 10.3390/su8010075

Pasquali, G., Godfrey, S., & Nadvi, K. (2021). Understanding regional value chains through the interaction of public and private governance: Insights from Southern Africa's apparel sector. *Journal of International Business Policy*, *4*(3), 368–389. DOI: 10.1057/s42214-020-00071-9

Pietrobelli, C., & Rabellotti, R. (2011). Global Value Chains Meet Innovation Systems: Are There Learning Opportunities for Developing Countries? *World Development*, *39*(7), 1261–1269. DOI: 10.1016/j.worlddev.2010.05.013

Pomfret, R. (2021). 'Regionalism' and the global trade system. *World Economy*, *44*(9), 2496–2514. DOI: 10.1111/twec.13155

Ponte, S., & Gibbon, P. (2005). Quality standards, conventions and the governance of global value chains. *Economy and Society*, *34*(1), 1–31. DOI: 10.1080/0308514042000329315

Randhawa, K., Wilden, R., & Hohberger, J. (2016). A Bibliometric Review of Open Innovation: Setting a Research Agenda. *Journal of Product Innovation Management*, *33*(6), 750–772. DOI: 10.1111/jpim.12312

Rao, S. (2014). The Last Mile: Gateway to rural empowerment in India. *Field Actions Science Reports. The journal of field actions, Special Issue 12*, Article Special Issue 12. https://journals.openedition.org/factsreports/3711

Ridoutt, B., Bogard, J. R., Dizyee, K., Lim-Camacho, L., & Kumar, S. (2019). Value Chains and Diet Quality: A Review of Impact Pathways and Intervention Strategies. *Agriculture*, *9*(9), 185. DOI: 10.3390/agriculture9090185

Rigo, D. (2021). Global value chains and technology transfer: New evidence from developing countries. *Review of World Economics*, *157*(2), 271–294. DOI: 10.1007/s10290-020-00398-8

Robin, D. P., & Reidenbach, R. E. (1987). Social Responsibility, Ethics, and Marketing Strategy: Closing the Gap between Concept and Application. *Journal of Marketing*, *51*(1), 44–58. DOI: 10.1177/002224298705100104

Santos, N. J. C., & Laczniak, G. R. (2009). Marketing to the Poor: An Integrative Justice Model for Engaging Impoverished Market Segments. *Journal of Public Policy & Marketing*, *28*(1), 3–15. DOI: 10.1509/jppm.28.1.3

Scaini, L. (2018). The Way How Anthropological Culture Shapes Consumes: An Exploratory Comparative Study. *European Scientific Journal*. Advance online publication. DOI: 10.19044/esj.2018.c3p6

Sengupta, A. (2014). Brand Analyses of Global Brands Versus Local Brand in Indian Apparel Consumer Market. *Theses and Dissertations--Retailing and Tourism Management*. https://uknowledge.uky.edu/mat_etds/6

Sharma, S. K. (2014). Drawing Modelling Canvas For The International Positioning Of Indian Beverage Products. *Industrial Engineering Letters*, *4*(7), 30.

Sinkovics, N., Sinkovics, R. R., Hoque, S. F., & Czaban, L. (2015). A reconceptualisation of social value creation as social constraint alleviation. *Critical Perspectives on International Business*, *11*(3/4), 340–363. DOI: 10.1108/cpoib-06-2014-0036

St. Petersburg State University. Nefedov, K. S., Panibratov, A. Yu., & St. Petersburg State University. (2017). Global value chain analysis: Main dimensions and further research agenda. *Vestnik of Saint Petersburg University. Management, 16*(3), 364–397. DOI: 10.21638/11701/spbu08.2017.302

Stabell, C. B., & Fjeldstad, Ø. D. (1998). Configuring value for competitive advantage: On chains, shops, and networks. *Strategic Management Journal*, *19*(5), 413–437. DOI: 10.1002/(SICI)1097-0266(199805)19:5<413::AID-SMJ946>3.0.CO;2-C

Sun, Q., Sridhar, N., & O'Brien, M. (2009, April). *Consumer Perception Of Product Stimuli: An Investigation into Indian Consumer Psychology and its Implications for New Product Development, Process and Strategy*. D2B2: the 2nd Tsinghua International Design Management Symposium, Tsinghua University, Beijing, China. https://eprints.hud.ac.uk/id/eprint/5273/, https://www.hud.ac.uk/news/

The Last Mile: Gateway to rural empowerment in India. (n.d.). Retrieved May 18, 2025, from https://journals.openedition.org/factsreports/3711

Timmer, M. P., Los, B., Stehrer, R., & De Vries, G. J. (2013). Fragmentation, incomes and jobs: An analysis of European competitiveness. *Economic Policy*, *28*(76), 613–661. DOI: 10.1111/1468-0327.12018

Trivedi, P.University of Luckno. (2015). Department of Business Administration, & Trivedi, P. (2015). A conceptual model for driving green purchase among indian consumers. *Journal of Marketing and Consumer Behaviour in Emerging Markets*, *2015*(2), 49–59. DOI: 10.7172/2449-6634.jmcbem.2015.2.4

Utouh, H. M. L., & Kitole, F. A. (2024). Forecasting effects of foreign direct investment on industrialization towards realization of the Tanzania development vision 2025. *Cogent Economics & Finance*, *12*(1), 2376947. DOI: 10.1080/23322039.2024.2376947

Vallet-Bellmunt, T., Martínez-Fernández, M. T., & Capó-Vicedo, J. (2011). Supply chain management: A multidisciplinary content analysis of vertical relations between companies, 1997–2006. *Industrial Marketing Management*, *40*(8), 1347–1367. DOI: 10.1016/j.indmarman.2011.03.002

Vermeulen, S., Woodhill, A. J., Proctor, F., & Delnoye, R. (2008). *Chain-wide learning for inclusive agrifood market development: A guide to multi-stakeholder processes for linking small-scale producers to modern markets*. International Institute for Environment and Development. https://research.wur.nl/en/publications/chain-wide-learning-for-inclusive-agrifood-market-development-a-g

Von Delft, S., Kortmann, S., Gelhard, C., & Pisani, N. (2019). Leveraging global sources of knowledge for business model innovation. *Long Range Planning*, *52*(5), 101848. DOI: 10.1016/j.lrp.2018.08.003

Wang, S., Wang, X., & Chen, S. (2022). Global value chains and carbon emission reduction in developing countries: Does industrial upgrading matter? *Environmental Impact Assessment Review*, *97*, 106895. DOI: 10.1016/j.eiar.2022.106895

Witt, M. A. (2019). De-globalization: Theories, predictions, and opportunities for international business research. *Journal of International Business Studies*, *50*(7), 1053–1077. DOI: 10.1057/s41267-019-00219-7

Xiao, H., Meng, B., Ye, J., & Li, S. (2020). Are global value chains truly global? *Economic Systems Research*, *32*(4), 540–564. DOI: 10.1080/09535314.2020.1783643

Yang, Z., Fang, G., & Sun, W. (2025). Embodied carbon emissions and their transfer pathways in global aluminum trade: The value chain perspective. *Journal of Cleaner Production*, *494*, 145057. DOI: 10.1016/j.jclepro.2025.145057

Zaninović, P. A., & Bugarčić, F. Ž. (2023). THE EFFECTS OF INTERNATIONAL LOGISTICS IN GLOBAL VALUE CHAIN TRADE. *Journal of Business Economics and Management*, *24*(5), 841–856. DOI: 10.3846/jbem.2023.20443

Zhang, Z., Zhu, K., & Hewings, G. J. D. (2017). A multi-regional input–output analysis of the pollution haven hypothesis from the perspective of global production fragmentation. *Energy Economics*, *64*, 13–23. DOI: 10.1016/j.eneco.2017.03.007

Zhu, Z., Puliga, M., Cerina, F., Chessa, A., & Riccaboni, M. (2014). *Global Value Trees*. DOI: 10.48550/ARXIV.1410.4694

Zou, S., & Cavusgil, S. T. (2002). The GMS: A Broad Conceptualization of Global Marketing Strategy and Its Effect on Firm Performance. *Journal of Marketing*, *66*(4), 40–56. DOI: 10.1509/jmkg.66.4.40.18519

Chapter 8
Reconfiguring Human-Car Relations in Software-Defined Vehicles:
Dynamic Capabilities for Mitigating Technological Exclusion

Haomin Fu
https://orcid.org/0009-0003-6658-669X
Kyushu University, Japan

ABSTRACT

This chapter examines how dynamic capabilities can be used to address technological exclusion in SDVs, where algorithm-driven features and data-centric business models increasingly reshape human-car relations. Drawing on the theoretical framework established by Teece and Eisenhardt, the chapter explores how sensing, seizing, and reconfiguring capabilities can be strategically utilized to mitigate algorithmic bias, enhance data transparency, and foster inclusive innovation. It analyzes how firms can shift from reactive adaptation to proactive governance by integrating ethical foresight and inclusive design into their dynamic capabilities framework. The chapter also discusses global regulatory discrepancies and cross-industry collaborations as key elements in establishing equitable algorithmic governance in the SDV era. Ultimately, the chapter argues that firms strategically aligning dynamic capabilities with ethical governance can transform algorithmic control into a mechanism for inclusive mobility, positioning themselves as leaders in a rapidly

DOI: 10.4018/979-8-3373-2685-6.ch008

Copyright © 2026, IGI Global Scientific Publishing. Copying or distributing in print or electronic forms without written permission of IGI Global Scientific Publishing is prohibited.

evolving automotive landscape.

1. INTRODUCTION

On a cold winter morning in 2024, Parker, a San Francisco resident, rushed to his car, eager to attend an important business meeting. As he settled into his seat and prepared to start the navigation, the vehicle's dashboard suddenly flashed a message: "Automated Driving Assistance has been disabled; please visit our website to subscribe to this service." Parker stared in disbelief. The feature had worked flawlessly since he purchased the used vehicle months earlier. Now, without prior notice or explanation, a critical feature he relied on suddenly vanished, leaving him disoriented and frustrated. Parker's feelings of betrayal and confusion illustrate a growing phenomenon in today's automotive landscape, highlighting the tension between technological advancement and consumer trust.

Parker's experience is not isolated but emblematic of a broader global trend: the rapid rise of SDVs, which are fundamentally reshaping the relationship between humans and automobiles. SDVs are marked by their significant reliance o software to control vehicle functionality, which is significantly impacting technological development and business models within the automotive industry. AI-driven algorithms have taken over essential driving tasks such as environmental perception, route planning, and decision-making processes, promising road safety and operational efficiency improvements. These advancements are highlighted as crucial for tackling increasing urban congestion and pollution, positioning SDVs as vital solutions for sustainable mobility in rapidly urbanizing global populations.

Nevertheless, the rapid integration of AI into vehicles brings significant management and ethical complexities. Consumer skepticism toward fully autonomous driving systems remains strong; surveys show that more than half of drivers express anxiety or fear about using fully autonomous vehicles (The Dallas Morning News, 2025). Conversely, research by the National Highway Traffic Safety Administration (NHTSA, 2015) indicates that over 90% of traffic accidents are attributed to human error, suggesting that substantial safety improvements are attainable if AI systems can effectively support or even replace human drivers. However, to achieve these benefits, automotive manufacturers must overcome technical challenges and build public trust in AI systems and their decision-making abilities. This task is complicated by recent studies that reveal how biases embedded in algorithmic systems disproportionately affect marginalized groups, worsening existing inequalities and raising urgent questions about ethical responsibility in AI implementation.

The global automotive industry is undergoing a profound technological revolution, driven by significant investments in SDV technology (Ordóñez, 2024). Recent analysis from the Boston Consulting Group (Koster et al., 2023) highlights that the world's leading automotive manufacturers collectively invest over $80 billion annually in SDV-related research and development, exceeding the GDP of many mid-sized economies. The industry frames this technological shift as the start of an AI-driven mobility era, promising transformative impacts through autonomous driving, adaptive software architectures, and highly personalized vehicle experiences. However, the business models supporting these advances often depend heavily on subscription-based services, where core vehicle functionalities become contingent upon ongoing payments. This shift transforms the traditional one-time purchase model into a continuous monetization scheme, raising significant concerns regarding equitable access and consumer rights.

Yet beneath the optimistic promises lies an emerging ethical challenge: technologies initially intended to promote inclusivity and democratize access to mobility instead worsen exclusion through mechanisms such as algorithmic gatekeeping and digital paywalls (Vincent, 2022). For example, automated vehicle features already integrated within the vehicle hardware may be activated or deactivated remotely based on subscription models, turning basic automotive functions into exclusive commodities. This practice highlights a broader industry trend prioritizing technological agility and profit maximization over social equity and inclusivity. Such practices have drawn significant consumer backlash and regulatory scrutiny, fueling intense debates about the ethical implications of automotive innovation.

Central to this ethical dilemma is a significant gap in modern management theory and practice. Specifically, the Dynamic Capabilities Theory (Teece et al., 1997), which is widely used in analyzing transformations in the automotive industry, highlights firms' abilities to sense market changes, seize emerging opportunities, and reconfigure internal resources to sustain competitive advantages. In the realm of SDVs, carmakers indeed demonstrate dynamic capabilities by utilizing real-time data insights, rapidly implementing software updates and subscription models, and strategically adjusting vehicle features as market opportunities emerge. However, the conventional dynamic capabilities framework primarily focuses on agility and market performance, often neglecting or sidelining ethical considerations and social implications. This limitation makes it insufficient when compared to more ethically focused frameworks like 'Responsible Innovation' or 'Fairness in AI,' which call for embedding social values into technology from the design phase. While Dynamic Capabilities theory excels at explaining *how* firms adapt to competitive landscapes, it is less equipped to prescribe *what* they should adapt for in terms of societal good. Frameworks for Responsible Innovation, for instance, explicitly call for anticipatory governance, reflexive monitoring of impacts, and inclusive deliberation with stakeholders—dimensions largely absent from the traditional DC perspective. Similarly, the field of Fairness, Accountability, and Transparency (FAT) in AI provides concrete technical and procedural tools to address bias, which the high-level strategic focus of DC theory does not encompass. As a result, while firms effectively capitalize on short-term revenue opportunities, such as subscription-based features, they risk alienating consumers who are unable or unwilling to bear additional costs.

Furthermore, dynamic capabilities theory typically does not explicitly incorporate mechanisms to identify and address social or ethical risks linked to technological advancements. This gap in the theory becomes especially concerning in the era of SDVs, where the consequences of algorithmic decision-making and software-controlled vehicle functionalities directly affect consumer trust and societal equity. Expanding dynamic capabilities to include proactive ethical assessments can help automotive companies better anticipate exclusionary practices, integrate fairness into business strategies, and enhance consumer confidence, ultimately bolstering their market positions in ethically sensitive environments.

Addressing these critical issues requires explicitly rethinking the dynamic capabilities framework to include ethical dimensions. This redefinition would necessitate that carmakers proactively identify exclusion risks during the sensing phase, ensure universal accessibility in the value-capture phase, and incorporate community-driven co-design principles during resource reconfiguration. By directly embedding ethical considerations into dynamic capabilities, SDVs can shift from reinforcing existing inequalities to becoming platforms that truly promote equitable and inclusive mobility.

Ultimately, the implications of this discussion extend far beyond strategic corporate management; they determine the future role of AI in transportation, whether AI will act as an equalizing force or further entrench existing social and economic divisions. The central argument of this chapter is that while the foundational principles of the Dynamic Capabilities framework remain robust, their effective application in the SDV era necessitates a new interpretation—one that expands the focus from a purely firm-centric perspective to encompass the broader socio-technical system in which the firm is embedded. This interpretation emphasizes that in a world of connected vehicles and ongoing user relationships, capabilities related to managing human-car relations, ethical governance, and platform ecosystems are not peripheral concerns, but have become central to the successful enactment of sensing, seizing, and reconfiguring.

To develop this argument, the chapter is structured as follows. Section 2 will establish the context by detailing the business models and profound ethical implications of the SDV transformation. Section 3 delves into the reconfigured human-car relations under algorithmic control, focusing on the user experience. Section 4 then applies the dynamic capabilities framework to this new context, presenting a systematic comparative analysis of how Tesla and incumbent OEMs manifest these capabilities differently. Finally, Section 5 synthesizes these insights to articulate a human-centric interpretation of dynamic capabilities and concludes by discussing the theoretical contributions, managerial implications, and directions for future research.

2. SOFTWARE AS THE NEW ENGINE: BUSINESS MODELS AND ETHICAL IMPLICATIONS IN SDVS

2.1. The Architectural Shift: From Hardware to Dynamic Platforms

In recent decades, the automotive sector has transformed from primarily hardware-driven engineering to increasingly software-centric designs (Szalavetz, 2024). Historically, automotive innovation was rooted in mechanical advancements, with vehicle performance and features closely linked to physical components and configurations. However, starting in the late 2010s, SDVs emerged prominently, marking a fundamental shift in which software broadly defines vehicle functionality, performance, and consumer experience (Liu et al., 2022).

SDVs represent a fundamental reimagining of vehicle architecture, where software dictates not only key functionalities but also the user experience, operational efficiency, and lifecycle management of vehicles. Unlike traditional vehicles, where software primarily served as a supportive function to hardware, SDVs elevate software to a central, defining role (Vdovic et al., 2019), encompassing aspects such as real-time diagnostics, predictive maintenance, and advanced driver assistance systems (ADAS). As McKinsey (2023) reports, the average SDV now operates with over 200 million lines of code, a figure expected to increase exponentially as more features are developed and refined over-the-air (OTA).

This paradigm shift in vehicle architecture redefines the boundaries of vehicle development, positioning software as the primary driver of value creation. In conventional vehicles, hardware was both a necessary and sufficient condition for delivering core functionalities, with software serving merely as an auxiliary support system. However, in SDVs, hardware has become a critical but no longer sufficient condition; instead, software has taken on the role of an adequate condition, shaping not only vehicle functions but also the consumer experience and service delivery throughout the vehicle's lifecycle (Liu et al., 2022).

Additionally, the transition to SDVs has significant implications for business models and value chains. In traditional automotive structures, the value of products was primarily derived from physical components and hardware configurations. In contrast, SDVs are organized around software ecosystems that facilitate continuous updates and feature enhancements via OTA. This model aligns with the observations of Pérez-Moure et al. (2024), who note that digitalization is compelling automotive manufacturers to explore new business models to meet future challenges. This capability effectively extends the lifecycle of vehicles, transforming them from static products into dynamic platforms that can evolve in response to both technological advancements and consumer preferences (Zhao et al., 2022).

However, this evolution is not without its challenges. While SDVs offer opportunities for recurring revenue through software subscriptions and service-based monetization, they also introduce significant complexities related to data security, algorithmic integrity, and the standardization of design interfaces. The absence of universally accepted technical standards hinders the complete separation of hardware and software, leaving OEMs and suppliers to navigate fragmented development environments with differing strategies and interpretations of SDV architecture. More critically, this transformation does not occur in a vacuum. It carries significant environmental and socioeconomic impacts, such as the growth of electronic waste from frequent hardware obsolescence, massive energy use for the data centers that support cloud processing, and a deepening dependence on rare earth elements needed for chips and batteries. The mining of these materials, such as cobalt and lithium, is often concentrated in countries of the Global South, raising profound ethical questions about labor practices, environmental degradation, and the equitable distribution of wealth generated by this technological shift. These issues introduce an often-overlooked ethical layer to this technological paradigm shift, demanding that the discussion of dynamic capabilities be linked to broader concerns of sustainability and global supply chain equity, as noted by Pérez-Moure (2025) who identifies sustainability, digitalization, and dynamic capabilities as pillars of the new dimension of mobility companies. Thus, as carmakers embrace SDVs, they must navigate complex intersections of technological innovation, commercial strategy, and ethical responsibility.

Thus, as carmakers embrace SDVs, they must navigate complex intersections of technological innovation, commercial strategy, and ethical responsibility. Among these intersecting challenges, the shift in business models stands out as the most immediate and tangible force reshaping the human-car relationship. While technical and environmental issues present long-term structural problems, it is the commercial strategy of monetizing software that directly impacts consumer rights, ownership concepts, and social equity on a daily basis. Foremost among these new strategies is the rise of subscription-based services. The following section will therefore delve deeply into this specific phenomenon, analyzing how the subscription model functions as a primary engine of value creation for manufacturers, and simultaneously, as a powerful mechanism that can create a new and profound "digital divide" among users.

2.2. The Subscription Model and the Rise of the Digital Divide

The rise of SDVs has not only transformed vehicle architectures but also redefined the revenue models for carmakers (Rísquez Ramos & Ruiz-Gálvez, 2024). As vehicles evolve into platforms for continuous software updates, the traditional one-time sales model gradually gives way to subscription-based services. This shift is driven by the opportunity to monetize vehicle functionalities over the entire lifecycle, rather than solely at the point of sale. Subscription models enable manufacturers to generate ongoing revenue by locking or unlocking vehicle features based on user payments. ADAS, heated seats, remote start, and enhanced infotainment systems are increasingly offered as pay-to-use services, accessible only through a monthly or annual fee (Levin, 2022). In this model, software becomes the linchpin of revenue generation, allowing manufacturers to control access to once standard functionalities, thereby shifting the economic dynamics of the automotive market.

While the subscription model presents compelling financial incentives for carmakers, it also introduces critical concerns regarding consumer rights, accessibility, and economic stratification. By converting essential vehicle functions into paywalled services, manufacturers risk creating a two-tiered access system wherein those with greater financial resources can access advanced safety and convenience features. At the same time, economically disadvantaged consumers may find themselves excluded from fundamental functionalities. This dynamic effectively transforms standard features—such as adaptive cruise control, lane-keeping assistance, and remote vehicle diagnostics—into premium commodities accessible only through ongoing payments.

The implications of such stratification extend beyond initial purchasers to the used vehicle market, where new owners might need to pay extra fees to activate functionalities that were originally included in the vehicle's base package. This practice raises concerns about fairness and transparency, as features that were initially advertised as part of the vehicle may become inaccessible without additional financial expenditure. Furthermore, it complicates the resale value of vehicles, as potential buyers must factor in the ongoing costs of maintaining access to essential functions.

Additionally, subscription-based services challenge traditional ideas of vehicle ownership. If software becomes the main factor in vehicle functionality, the idea of ownership is effectively redefined. Consumers who have fully paid for a vehicle may find themselves unable to access essential features without ongoing financial commitments, effectively turning vehicle ownership into a continual service contract. This trend resonates with the future envisioned by Ida Auken (2020) in her Forbes article, "Welcome to 2030: I own nothing, have no privacy, and life has never been better," where access to products supplants ownership of them. This raises fundamental legal and ethical questions: How much control should manufacturers keep over vehicle functions after the sale? To what extent can they decide access to features that already exist in the vehicle but are locked behind software paywalls?

Furthermore, the blurring of ownership boundaries could lead to new forms of digital disenfranchisement, where lower-income consumers, unable to afford recurring fees, are systematically excluded from essential safety and convenience features. Thus, as SDVs reshape the automotive industry's economic landscape, they also create new forms of exclusion and digital inequity. The implications are economic and societal, as access to advanced vehicle functionalities increasingly hinges on financial capability rather than technological availability. In this evolving landscape, algorithmic gatekeeping effectively determines who can afford to access certain features, raising concerns about digital divides and consumer autonomy in a software-defined automotive ecosystem. This section makes clear that while SDVs enable innovative business models, these models risk creating systemic exclusion if not ethically integrated with a firm's dynamic capabilities.

3. HUMAN-CAR RELATIONS: THE RISE OF ALGORITHMIC CONTROL

The advent of SDVs has radically transformed how control is allocated between drivers and carmakers. In traditional cars, once a customer drove off the lot, the physical features and capabilities of the vehicle were largely fixed – the owner had complete, autonomous control over the machine's functions. SDVs disrupt this balance. By equipping vehicles with cloud connectivity and updatable software, manufacturers maintain centralized algorithmic control—defined as the ability to manage, restrict, or modify vehicle functionalities through remotely deployed software and automated decisions—over many aspects of the car long after the purchase. Features are no longer strictly hardware-bound; they can be remotely activated, modified, or disabled by software commands from the manufacturer. This means that carmakers (or their algorithms) can effectively reach into an owned vehicle and alter its behavior or capabilities at will via OTA updates. One notable example involved an EV maker remotely disabling advanced driver-assistance features (like Autopilot) on a used car after it was resold, claiming that the new owner hadn't paid for the software package – a move that "yank[ed] access to software features" the vehicle was initially equipped with (Statt, 2020). Such incidents vividly illustrate how power dynamics are shifting: manufacturers now wield post-sale control in ways that were impossible in the pre-connected era.

From the carmakers' perspective, this centralized control opens profitable opportunities. The industry is racing toward a future of continuous monetization through software—an ecosystem often compared to "a future full of microtransactions" for car features (Vincent, 2022). Analysts indicate that software-based services could generate immense value for carmakers, with one estimate projecting over $650 billion in new value by 2030 from the shift to software-defined vehicles (BCG, 2023). Carmakers worldwide are eager to capitalize on this value by utilizing software locks and subscriptions as new revenue streams. Crucially, this strategy reconfigures the human-car relationship: the vehicle increasingly acts not as a personally owned asset under the driver's complete control, but as a platform "managed" by the manufacturer's algorithms. Routine decisions about what the car can or cannot do may be dictated by remote software policies rather than the driver's immediate preferences. This centralization of decision-making authority in the hands of code and corporations raises concerns about user agency. Owners find themselves having to implicitly ask for permission from an algorithm (or pay a fee) to access features already integrated into their car. Consequently, the balance of power shifts away from the human in the driver's seat toward the distant software controllers. The result is an asymmetrical relationship: the company maintains an active governing presence in the vehicle's operation while the user's autonomy is correspondingly reduced. These dynamics set the stage for tensions around control, trust, and fairness in the era of algorithmically mediated automobility.

3.1 Algorithmic Gatekeeping Mechanisms

The abstract concept of algorithmic control is made concrete through an array of technical and commercial mechanisms that manufacturers are increasingly deploying. These mechanisms function as digital gatekeepers, governing a user's access to and experience of their own vehicle. Three primary forms of this gatekeeping are particularly salient: software-based feature locking, remote management via over-the-air updates, and dynamic, algorithm-driven pricing models.

The most fundamental mechanism is the use of software locks to unlock or restrict access to physical hardware. Carmakers can install features in every vehicle but restrict access via software until the owner pays for activation. For example, a luxury carmaker infamously offered heated seats only via a monthly software subscription, even though "the hardware for this feature [was] already installed in the vehicle." Drivers already owned the seat heaters physically, yet the company placed a digital lock on their use until an $18/month fee was paid. Such paywalls can apply to amenities (heated steering, infotainment apps) and even safety or performance options. This approach effectively turns built-in functions into rentals, enforced by code. Owners have bristled at the notion of paying recurrently for things sitting dormant in their cars, calling it out as a greedy, exploitative practice. Indeed, "charging more for high-end features feels different when you already own them" – the dynamic changes fundamentally when software (not physical capability) is the limiting factor. The carmaker, not the owner, holds the keys – literally digital keys – to the car's full functionality.

This control is further extended through the capability for over-the-air (OTA) updates and remote feature management. OTA updates allow manufacturers to modify a vehicle's behavior anytime post-sale. While this can be positive—delivering improvements and new features—it also enables unilateral feature removal or downgrades. The remote disabling of a driver-assistance suite after resale (mentioned earlier) is one extreme example. More routinely, companies can decide to unlock extra performance or introduce new pay-per-use options via software downloads. The vehicle thus becomes a constantly evolving product, tethered to the carmaker's servers. This means critical functions now depend on the manufacturer's ongoing support and policies. If a company chooses, it can deactivate or alter features through an OTA patch as an enforcement tool (for instance, disabling functionality when a subscription lapses, or conducting a "software audit" of second-hand cars to ensure new owners pay for previously enabled options). This persistent algorithmic gatekeeping, this power to remotely reach into cars and "update" what an owner can or cannot do, fundamentally weakens the notion that the buyer has final say over their machine.

Finally, the most advanced form of this control involves dynamic pricing and pay-per-use models driven by algorithms. Alongside static subscriptions, companies are experimenting with flexible pricing schemes where usage data can feed into pricing decisions, opening the door to usage-based fees or even surge pricing for features. An owner might be offered a day-pass to use autonomous driving on a long trip or be charged per hour for a performance boost mode. While not yet widespread, the infrastructure of SDVs makes such dynamic feature pricing feasible: the car itself can meter feature usage and bill, accordingly, making certain high-end functions analogous to on-demand utilities. From the user's standpoint, this adds uncertainty and potential cost, turning the personal car experience into something resembling a rental or ride-hailing service where every added convenience has a metered price. The psychological shift is non-trivial, as ownership begins to feel like a continual transaction. Despite strong consumer resistance (Rodríguez, 2023), the potential for recurring revenue may lead carmakers to continue pushing this model, especially as younger drivers show higher tolerance for subscription-based digital life.

Together, these three mechanisms—software locks, OTA control, and algorithmic pricing—represent a profound shift in the automotive business model, blurring the line between product and service. They create a system of persistent algorithmic gatekeeping where the car's behavior is contingent on code and corporate policy, not just the mechanical will of its driver. By detailing these foundational mechanisms, we can now proceed to analyze their deeper implications for personal autonomy, privacy, and the very nature of ownership in the sections that follow.

3.2 Personalization, Data, and the Erosion of User Autonomy

SDVs don't just change the available features; they also profoundly influence how those features operate through algorithmic decision-making and personalization. Modern vehicles are essentially computers on wheels, continuously gathering data on driving behavior, location, vehicle usage patterns, biometric indicators (via in-cabin cameras), and more. This data fuels personalized driving experiences—seemingly a benefit of smart vehicles. For example, AI algorithms might automatically adjust settings to suit a driver's preferences, provide customized route suggestions, or proactively recommend maintenance based on telemetry. In theory, such personalization enhances comfort and convenience. In practice, however, the same data-driven mechanisms can undermine user autonomy and privacy, as decisions are made for drivers (or about them) by unseen algorithms. The car and its backend systems begin to act as algorithmic intermediaries in every interaction between humans and vehicles.

A key concern is the opacity and scope of data collection in connected cars. Studies have concluded that "cars are the worst product category... for privacy," with new vehicles tracking extensive personal data without clear user awareness (SAE Media, 2023). The vehicle's myriad sensors and apps may record everything from a driver's real-time location and driving style to in-cabin conversations. This information is transmitted back to manufacturers or third-party service providers under connectivity and personalization. Yet drivers often have "no way... to know how the collected data is being used or if it's even possible to turn it off." Thus, driving an SDV may inadvertently mean consenting to continuous surveillance. The algorithms that enable personal convenience features simultaneously to feed a growing appetite for data monetization. As one digital privacy expert observed, companies have "an extreme desire to collect as much data as they can... to build products around that data, or to sell that data" (SAE Media, 2023). Personalized services therefore come at the cost of pervasive data gathering, creating a power imbalance in information: the car (and, by extension, the manufacturer) knows everything about the user's behavior, whereas the user remains in the dark about how this knowledge is utilized.

This dynamic has direct implications for power and autonomy. With vehicles algorithmically tailoring responses, drivers may find their choices subtly directed or restricted by what the system considers optimal or profitable. For example, an in-car navigation system might prioritize routes that benefit the carmaker's charging network or partner businesses, rather than providing a neutral option—essentially an algorithm guiding the driver's decision under the guise of assistance. More starkly, data-driven profiles could result in differential treatment: a driver labeled as "high risk" by an insurance-linked algorithm might have certain high-performance modes automatically limited, or a driver flagged for aggressive driving might start receiving frequent safety interventions from the car's ADAS. While some interventions can enhance safety, they also position the vehicle as an algorithmic "nanny" monitoring and correcting the human. In extreme cases, an SDV could refuse to activate certain features based on sensor data or backend decisions—effectively overriding the driver's commands. This represents a new kind of autonomy trade-off: the vehicle's autonomy (through AI decision-making) can encroach on the human's autonomy to operate the vehicle as they prefer.

Another aspect of this issue is algorithmic bias and differential outcomes. If the algorithms controlling personalization and oversight are not carefully designed, they may not serve all users equally. Evidence suggests that some automotive AI systems perform unevenly across different demographic groups. For instance, vision algorithms used in self-driving or driver-assistance systems are less accurate in detecting dark-skinned pedestrians (Harding, 2023). In one significant study, camera-based detection systems – increasingly utilized for emergency braking and driver monitoring – struggled to recognize darker-skinned individuals, highlighting the broader bias issues in facial recognition technology. This bias isn't merely a technical flaw; it reduces safety or functionality for specific users. A car that "sees" a Black pedestrian a split second later (or not at all) puts those lives at greater risk, effectively excluding them from the full potential of the technology. Similarly, suppose in-cabin monitoring (used to ensure driver alertness in semi-autonomous modes) has more false negatives or false positives for certain ethnicities or body types. In that case, those drivers may find the feature unusable or intrusive. Algorithmic decision-making can thus inadvertently marginalize groups of users – a high-tech echo of existing social biases. Without explicit efforts towards fairness, personalization might mean that some experience a superior, seamless interaction while others face glitches or denial of service based on their identity. These examples underscore that user autonomy in the age of algorithmic control is not just about individual freedom from corporate interference; it's also about equitable treatment by the algorithms themselves.

Finally, the data-driven nature of SDVs has captured the interest of law enforcement and governments, raising civil liberty concerns. Vehicles with constant connectivity and abundant data streams effectively become rolling data collectors that can be used for surveillance. Recent reports indicate that police agencies are eager to utilize the "data trails generated by a surge of new internet-connected vehicle features," and that subscription-based features (which enhance connectivity) "drastically" increase the data accessible to investigators (Cameron, 2025). Consequently, opting into these services could make drivers more visible to external monitoring, an outcome most drivers did not foresee when activating a convenience feature. This highlights a loss of autonomy in a broader sense – the car that serves you is simultaneously sharing your data with others, without detailed consent. In summary, while algorithmic enhancements in SDVs promise personalization and smarter assistance, they are intertwined with pervasive data extraction and delegated decision-making that collectively undermine the driver's autonomy and privacy. The human-car relationship is increasingly mediated by a layer of algorithms that decide, nudge, and even constrain behind the scenes. As we address issues of ownership and access, it becomes evident that such algorithmic control not only impacts individual users in the present but also carries implications throughout the vehicle's lifespan and across different segments of society.

3.3 Ownership, Consent, and Differential Access

The rise of algorithmic control in vehicles compels us to confront a fundamental question: what does it mean to "own" a car in the software-defined era? Traditional notions of ownership grant buyers the rights to use and modify their property as they wish. However, with critical functionalities locked behind proprietary software, car owners often find they possess only partial ownership—typically of the vehicle's physical shell—while the manufacturer effectively retains ownership of the digital "soul." This ambiguity has practical consequences. Consumers are discovering that buying a car doesn't always guarantee unfettered access to all its capabilities; instead, it often confers a license governed by terms of service that allow the vendor to intervene. Legal experts are beginning to question the validity of this model. In contract law, a deal requires an exchange of value on both sides, yet "the important legal question boils down to: How can an auto manufacturer justify a subscription fee for something that a vehicle buyer already owns and that works by pushing a button? (Beaver, 2024)" If an owner has paid for the hardware, demanding additional payment to "unlock" its use may not provide new value—a point that could render such arrangements unenforceable under traditional notions of consideration. As simply put by one consumer advocate, "I own [the car] outright. What right do they have to turn things on or off in a car that I have just purchased?" This evolving tussle between user property rights and manufacturer control rights is redefining ownership in practice and is being tested in courts and public opinion.

Issues of consent are intertwined with this ambiguity. Many drivers are not fully aware, at the time of purchase, of the extent to which their vehicle's features can be remotely governed or altered. Often, the details are buried in dense end-user license agreements or fine-print disclosures. For instance, some subprime financing agreements have required the installation of GPS-enabled starter interrupt devices – essentially kill switches that a lender can activate if the buyer misses a payment. Frequently, borrowers consent without a clear understanding, or they have little choice if they need the loan. The result can be harrowing: drivers have been left stranded when their cars were remotely disabled for a missed payment, sometimes in dangerous situations. In one documented case, a young driver in North Carolina found that her used car would not start and emitted only a beeping sound; unbeknownst to her, the dealer had installed a kill switch and activated it after a payment was late. She had to plead for the car to be briefly reactivated just to get home (Povich, 2018b). This example highlights how consent at signing (often under economic pressure) can translate into a serious loss of agency later. The broader point is that SDV features – whether related to a finance-related kill switch or a carmaker's OTA update – may be enacted without granular, real-time consent from the user at the moment of action. A manufacturer doesn't typically ask a second-hand owner, "May we disable Feature X on your car?" before proceeding; it is carried out unilaterally under the earlier umbrella agreement. This lack of ongoing consent mechanisms contributes to feelings of helplessness and mistrust. It also disproportionately affects those with fewer resources: financially vulnerable consumers are more likely to face invasive forms of control (like mandatory kill switches or strict subscription requirements for basic functions) as they navigate lower-priced markets and used car lots.

The second-hand market indeed highlights many of these issues. When a software-defined car changes hands, what exactly does the buyer receive? Cases have shown that features the original owner paid for can be wiped or locked for the next owner unless they pay again to re-enable them (Statt, 2020). This was virtually unheard of with purely mechanical features – a used car with premium hardware would simply pass those benefits to the new owner. Now, a used car might come de-equipped despite having all the necessary parts, because the software license didn't transfer. This creates a new kind of inequality in access. Buyers in secondary markets, who are often more cost-conscious, might find themselves with a materially capable but artificially limited vehicle unless they spend additional funds. The burden of digital paywalls thus cascades downstream. Moreover, if a manufacturer discontinues support or goes out of business, second-hand owners could be left with features that no one can activate or repair, a situation analogous to having a sophisticated device with no available software keys. These uncertainties undermine the long-term value of ownership and particularly impact markets in the Global South that rely heavily on imports of used vehicles. In countries where a manufacturer's subscription services or mobile connectivity may not be operational, imported SDVs could permanently lose functions with no way to restore them, effectively delivering second-class technology to those regions. This digital divide in automotive features is a growing global concern. Research indicates that lower-income consumers already hesitate to adopt software-heavy vehicles due to fear of losing access to features behind paywalls (Aylmer, 2024; Rodríguez, 2023), and this hesitancy can slow the dissemination of advanced vehicle technologies in those communities.

Finally, we are witnessing early regulatory and policy responses aimed at mitigating the excesses of algorithmic control. Several jurisdictions have moved to curb the most egregious practices: for instance, states like New York and New Jersey have enacted laws requiring explicit disclosure of any kill-switch device in a car and, in some cases, limiting their use due to safety concerns (Povich, 2018a). There are calls in Europe and beyond to clarify the rights of car owners regarding software – including proposals to ensure that certain core features (especially those related to safety) remain freely accessible as a matter of consumer protection (Chee, 2025; Katta, 2025). The Right to Repair movement is also extending into the digital realm, advocating for legislation that would provide owners and independent shops with the necessary data and tools to service and unlock vehicle software on fair terms. All these efforts highlight the growing recognition that "Whose car is it, anyway?" is no longer just a rhetorical question – it demands an answer in policy. The ambiguity of ownership and uneven access created by software-defined vehicles have made it clear that new governance frameworks are crucial to protect consumers from technological exclusion. When some owners can afford full feature access while others cannot, or when manufacturers can selectively grant or withhold functionalities, the outcome is a stratified mobility landscape. This contrasts sharply with the early promise that digital vehicle innovations would democratize and enhance transportation for everyone. Instead, without intervention, we risk a future where an individual's experience of a car is heavily influenced by their ongoing ability to pay and adhere to corporate rules, rather than merely by the car they choose to buy.

4. APPLYING THE DYNAMIC CAPABILITIES FRAMEWORK IN THE SDV CONTEXT

Building upon the previous discussion of algorithmic control in SDVs, we now focus on the dynamic capabilities framework as a perspective for managing rapid technological change. Dynamic capabilities refer to an organization's ability to adapt by continuously renewing its skills and resources. Teece et al. (1997) famously define dynamic capabilities as "the firm's ability to integrate, build, and reconfigure internal and external competencies to address rapidly changing environments." In a complementary view, Eisenhardt and Martin (2000) describe them as the firm's "processes to integrate, reconfigure, gain, and release resources – to match or even create market change." Essentially, dynamic capabilities enable corporate agility: the ability to sense emerging threats or opportunities, seize them through action, and reconfigure assets as needed.

The SDV era heightens the necessity for such adaptability. SDVs are "an ecosystem that continually delivers new value and experiences to users by updating features through software at its core (PwC, 2024)." Unlike traditional vehicles with fixed features, SDVs can acquire or lose capabilities overnight through over-the-air updates. This volatility in software-based feature design means companies face constantly changing user expectations and technical possibilities. A feature adjustment intended to delight drivers might inadvertently introduce a bug or bias, leading to immediate backlash. Indeed, carmakers have already seen how software changes can trigger consumer backlash. For instance, one famous carmaker abruptly abandoned its plan to charge a monthly fee for heated seats, directly citing consumer resistance to the subscription model (Bierenkoven, 2023). Such incidents highlight that companies must be prepared to identify and address public concerns in a software-driven market swiftly.

Additionally, as SDVs depend on complex algorithms (such as those for driver assistance, personalization, etc.), they become susceptible to algorithmic bias. Biases embedded in training data or design can result in certain user groups being unfairly excluded or disadvantaged by vehicle features. A recent analysis of autonomous vehicle systems cautions that treating disabled individuals as "edge cases" in algorithm design embeds unequal treatment and ableist assumptions into the software (Moura, 2022). If left unaddressed, such technological exclusion can erode trust and incite regulatory scrutiny. Dynamic capabilities are essential for SDV companies to maneuver through these challenges. They offer the meta-skills needed for continuous learning and adaptation—detecting problems like bias or discontent early on and proactively adjusting strategies before minor issues escalate into reputational crises. In summary, dynamic capabilities provide a pathway for organizations to thrive in the fluid, feedback-rich landscape of software-defined vehicles, rather than being destabilized by it. The following sections explore how the three pillars of this framework—sensing, seizing, and reconfiguring (Teece, 2007)—can assist in mitigating technological exclusion in human–car relations.

4.1 Sensing: Identifying Technological Exclusion and Algorithmic Bias

The first component of dynamic capabilities, sensing, involves scanning the environment to detect subtle changes, emerging risks, or unmet needs. In the context of SDVs, effective sensing enables firms to identify technological exclusion and algorithmic bias before these issues solidify into crises. This capability centers on organizational awareness – recognizing market blind spots, ethical concerns, and patterns of exclusion that might otherwise remain unnoticed in a rapidly changing landscape.

According to Teece (2007), sensing involves processes to gather and filter information from both inside and outside the firm. Internally, self-driving vehicle companies must promote open feedback loops and audits that identify problems early on. For instance, regular algorithmic audits can help reveal whether an AI model in the vehicle's system mistreats certain inputs or performs inadequately for specific groups. Researchers define algorithm auditing as assessing, monitoring, and ensuring an algorithm's behavior aligns with safety, legal, and ethical standards, drawing a clear parallel to sensing within the dynamic capabilities framework (Koshiyama et al., 2024). By institutionalizing such audits, a company can continually sense whether its self-driving or driver-assistance features show bias (for example, failing to recognize darker-skinned pedestrians or wheelchair users as consistently as others). Similarly, diverse test cohorts and inclusive design reviews function as internal sensors: if a feature is tested by individuals of various ages, abilities, and backgrounds, the company is more likely to detect usability or accessibility issues that uniform teams would overlook. In summary, fostering a diverse internal knowledge base and feedback culture boosts a firm's "capacity to learn quickly" – a requirement that Teece argues is foundational to dynamic capabilities.

External sensing mechanisms are equally vital. SDV companies operate among vigilant stakeholders – tech-savvy customers, regulators, and advocacy groups – who will voice concerns about exclusion or unfairness. Leading companies establish channels to listen to these perspectives actively. For instance, user feedback platforms and communities can be monitored to detect complaint patterns (e.g., reports that a navigation system consistently misroutes drivers in specific neighborhoods). Social media monitoring might highlight a potential backlash regarding a new feature that some demographics find problematic. Engaging with external experts is another approach: a carmaker might partner with disability rights organizations or ethicists to review its forthcoming driver-assistance AI, benefiting from "outside-in" perspectives on bias and exclusion. Such collaborative sensing aligns with what Augier and Teece (2009) emphasize as a key managerial role – identifying emerging strategic issues by looking beyond the firm's four walls. It also reflects the notion that dynamic capabilities require leveraging internal expertise and external knowledge to perceive what's on the horizon truly.

By investing in robust sensing capabilities, SDV firms can identify market blind spots and emerging ethical concerns early. For instance, a lack of representation in data is a blind spot that can lead to discriminatory outcomes. One study noted that the "insufficient representation of disabilities within datasets" for AV algorithms poses significant risks of harm to disabled individuals as these vehicles are introduced (Moura, 2022). A company aware of such warnings might proactively enhance its training data diversity or modify its computer vision algorithms before deployment. In terms of dynamic capabilities, this involves sensing and shaping opportunities and threats in real time, where a threat (algorithmic bias) is perceived and reframed as an opportunity for improvement (a safer, more inclusive product). Without strong sensing, companies risk being caught off guard by issues of technological exclusion, only realizing them after they have sparked public outcry or injustice. Therefore, sensing is the essential first step that informs the other dynamic capabilities: what isn't seen cannot be seized or reconfigured.

4.2 Seizing: Transforming Exclusion into Strategic Opportunity

Once a potential issue or unmet need is sensed, dynamic firms must seize it – that is, act on it—mobilizing resources and making strategic decisions based on insight. In the SDV era, seizing often involves reframing exclusionary risks as opportunities for innovation and differentiation. Instead of perceiving technological exclusion or algorithmic bias merely as compliance issues or public relations risks, progressive firms view them as catalysts for new inclusive offerings that can broaden markets and increase brand value.

Dynamic capabilities theory connects seizing to entrepreneurial action: it involves committing to a direction and investing in solutions once an opportunity is identified (Augier & Teece, 2009). In practice, if sensing reveals that a specific customer segment is overlooked or treated unfairly by current vehicle software, an agile firm will strategize on how to address that gap in a manner that also strengthens its competitive position. One approach is developing tiered services or alternative access models. For instance, consider an SDV feature that relies on costly data plans or the latest smartphones, effectively excluding lower-income users. A company might seize this exclusionary risk as an opportunity to create a tiered service offering: a basic version of the service that operates offline or with older devices (perhaps with slightly reduced functionality) alongside the premium version. By doing so, the firm not only mitigates the equity issue but also taps into an underserved customer base. This method reflects the idea in dynamic capability research that firms should exploit opportunities by reconfiguring offerings to fit diverse market segments better (Salvato, 2021).

Another example is pricing strategy. Equitable pricing can transform a critique into a selling point. Suppose consumer backlash arises because specific safety or comfort features (like emergency braking or heated seats) are paywalled in high-end trims or subscriptions. In that case, a bold firm can respond by making those features standard or more affordable, thus seizing goodwill and market share. When that famous carmaker faced criticism over its subscription-based heated seats, the company's ultimate decision to include the feature without extra fees was a reactive move (Bierenkoven, 2023). However, a truly dynamic-capability-driven firm might have anticipated such backlash and proactively structured pricing to avoid perceived double charges – or even used inclusive pricing as a marketing differentiator ("no extra charge for safety and comfort basics"). In terms of dynamic capabilities, this exemplifies opportunity exploitation: leveraging what was a reputational threat (the exclusion of some customers) and transforming it into an opportunity for positive differentiation in the market.

Strategic management literature highlights that seizing opportunities often requires committing resources and sometimes adjusting business models (Helfat & Raubitschek, 2018). In the SDV context, seizing an inclusion opportunity could involve reallocating the R&D budget to develop a new interface for elderly drivers uncomfortable with touchscreens. The firm might pilot a voice-assistant feature designed for those with limited tech literacy, transforming a known pain point (older adults feeling excluded by modern car interfaces) into a new product feature. If successful, this initiative not only brings a marginalized user group into the fold but can also give the company a first-mover advantage in an emerging niche, such as adopting a brand ethos of "vehicles friendly for all ages." Similarly, addressing algorithmic bias can drive innovation that benefits everyone. A navigation system improved to better serve rural or minority communities (perhaps by incorporating local input and avoiding biases in point-of-interest data) could ultimately prove superior for all users in terms of accuracy and trustworthiness. Thus, what starts as a solution for exclusion can evolve into a general quality improvement – a classic example of inclusive innovation.

Seizing also involves timing and boldness. Dynamic capability scholars note that opportunities are perishable—once sensed, they must be seized quickly before competitors or context shifts make them obsolete. In SDVs, technology and consumer sentiment evolve rapidly. For instance, public awareness of algorithmic bias is increasing; a company that swiftly seizes the chance to brand itself as the "fair AI" carmaker could secure a reputational advantage. Moreover, dynamic seizing may involve a strategic renewal of a firm's direction (Augier & Teece, 2009). If certain legacy practices (such as designing for an "average" user while overlooking edge cases) are found to be exclusionary, an SDV manufacturer might pivot its strategy to emphasize personalized, user-centric design as a core value. This shift could be reflected in everything from marketing messages to the organization of product development teams, effectively transforming a new ethical stance into a strategic opportunity for renewal and brand revitalization.

In summary, seizing capabilities enable SDV firms to transform awareness into action. By viewing technological exclusion not merely as a risk to be mitigated but as a strategic opportunity, companies can develop new products, services, or business models that cater to a wider audience. This aligns with the dynamic capability ethos of constantly adapting the organization to its environment in a proactive manner. The ability to seize opportunities for inclusive innovation will distinguish the industry leaders from laggards in the era of software-defined vehicles.

4.3 Reconfiguring: Adaptive Architectures for Inclusive Innovation

Seizing an opportunity is not the end of the story; organizations must then reconfigure themselves to support and sustain the innovations they commit to. The third pillar of dynamic capabilities – sometimes referred to as transforming or reconfiguring – involves adapting organizational structures, resources, and processes to ensure that new strategies (such as inclusive offerings or ethical safeguards) are effectively implemented.

At its core, reconfiguring involves realigning the company's tangible, intangible, and human asset base to fit a new direction. Helfat et al. (2007) emphasize that a dynamic capability is the ability "to purposefully create, extend, or modify [the firm's] resource base." In our context, this may mean restructuring R&D routines, reassigning talent, or upgrading technical systems to prioritize inclusion and fairness. For instance, if a manufacturer decides to build "fairness-by-design" into its SDV software updates, it may need to reconfigure its development process by introducing new steps for ethical review in the software lifecycle, establishing cross-functional committees to vet AI changes, or retraining engineers in bias mitigation techniques. These changes often require breaking old routines. An organization might need to shift from a traditional automotive testing regime, which focuses mainly on performance and safety, to an expanded regime that also tests for equity outcomes—e.g., does the voice recognition work equally well for different accents? Does the pedestrian detection avoid systematic blind spots? Such process innovation reflects what Teece (2018) argues about dynamic capabilities, enabling firms to adjust not just their products but also their business models and ecosystems (Helfat & Raubitschek, 2018). To truly institutionalize inclusive innovation, an SDV firm may reconfigure partnerships by building an ecosystem that includes atypical partners (consider accessibility consultants, civil rights groups, open-source AI communities). These partners can provide expertise and accountability, effectively becoming part of the firm's extended resource base for ethical innovation.

Adaptive reconfiguration also encompasses organizational culture and metrics. Companies may need to evolve their KPIs and incentive structures to reward teams for achieving inclusion goals rather than solely technical accomplishments or sales targets. For example, a unit responsible for the in-car user interface could have a KPI focused on accessibility scores or user diversity, ensuring that design decisions consider a broader range of users. When equity outcomes are weighted in performance evaluations, employees throughout the hierarchy are more likely to prioritize them. This thorough integration of new values often requires commitment from top management—what dynamic capabilities scholars refer to as orchestrating assets in support of strategic change. Leadership might establish a dedicated role such as a Chief Ethical Innovation Officer or empower a task force to reform practices that unintentionally reinforce bias. The dynamic capabilities framework recognizes that such high-level reconfiguration is challenging yet essential; it depends on managerial vision to "orchestrate complementary assets" and realign the organization with its environment.

Technologically, SDV firms can also reconfigure their software architectures to be more adaptable and inclusive. A rigid, monolithic software stack might hinder quick fixes or improvements related to bias. In contrast, a modular architecture (where, for instance, the algorithm for image recognition can be updated independently) allows for faster iteration on problematic components. If an issue is sensed in one module (e.g., the vision system struggles with certain lighting conditions that affect neighborhoods disproportionately), a modular, microservices-style architecture enables engineers to implement targeted updates without overhauling the entire system. This agility represents a form of technical reconfigurability that complements organizational reconfigurability. It embodies the continuous upgrading and protection of the asset base that Teece (2007) associates with dynamic capabilities. By designing software platforms that can evolve and integrate new modules (perhaps a plugin for bias correction or an API for external ethical checkers), firms create an inclusion architecture that can absorb improvements continuously.

A real-world example of adaptive reconfiguration is the increasing trend among carmakers to deliver features through software updates and feature toggles. This technical arrangement was not common in legacy vehicle programs, but companies have revised their IT and electrical/electronic architectures to accommodate it. Now, if a particular feature is causing exclusion or dissatisfaction, it can be patched or modified in weeks instead of waiting for the next year's model. Some carmakers have even reshaped their partnership networks to address ethical challenges better—for instance, joining industry consortia on AI ethics or co-developing standards for data privacy in connected cars. Teece (2018) points out that building ecosystems and alliances allows firms to create and capture value in modern environments. Here, collaborating with external groups for inclusive innovation (such as sharing best practices on algorithmic fairness across companies) can elevate the baseline for the entire industry and prevent a "race to the bottom" on ethics. It's a collective approach to reconfiguring the competitive landscape to prioritize inclusion.

4.4 A Comparative Application: Tesla vs. Incumbent OEMs

To illustrate how the interpretation of dynamic capabilities shifts in the SDV context, it is useful to systematically compare the approaches of a disruptor, Tesla, with those of incumbent OEMs. The following table organizes the examples discussed throughout this chapter to highlight how the manifestation of these classic capabilities differs (see Table 1).

Table 1. A Comparative Application of Dynamic Capabilities in the SDV Context

Dynamic Capability	Incumbent OEMs	Tesla	Explanatory Gap in Traditional DC
Sensing	Focus on traditional market research, competitor analysis, and existing customer surveys.	Focus on real-time fleet data analysis and direct feedback from a dedicated user community.	The shift from sensing static market data to sensing dynamic, real-time user ecosystem data.
Seizing	Focus on unbundling features and creating new revenue streams via paywalls (e.g., heated seat subscriptions).	Focus on enhancing the overall user experience through continuous OTA updates, building long-term loyalty and trust.	The shift from a product-centric, feature-monetization logic to a service-centric, experience-curation logic.
Reconfiguring	Focus on internal restructuring by creating siloed software divisions, often facing cultural clashes with legacy hardware departments.	Focus on holistic, integrated reconfiguration of an entire hardware-software platform from the ground up.	The shift from reconfiguring siloed organizational assets to reconfiguring an integrated platform architecture.

Source. Author's elaboration

This comparison demonstrates that the core concepts of sensing, seizing, and reconfiguring remain robust. However, the nature of these activities is fundamentally altered by the socio-technical context of the SDV. The most effective sensing now involves tapping into a user ecosystem; the most effective seizing involves curating an experience rather than just monetizing features; and the most effective reconfiguring involves managing an integrated platform. This new context does not limit the theory, but rather enriches our understanding of its application.

In summary, reconfiguring capabilities enables SDV organizations to consolidate the benefits of sensing and seizing. This phase focuses on institutionalizing change—transforming the organizational DNA to ensure that new inclusive strategies remain sustainable. It requires structural flexibility: routines must be adaptable, teams easily re-deployed, and systems able to be updated. The literature points out that dynamic reconfiguration often necessitates deliberate design by management and may face internal resistance. However, when executed successfully, the firm becomes significantly more resilient and responsive. It can continuously "create, extend, upgrade, and protect" its assets and processes in alignment with its values and the changing market. For an SDV manufacturer, this could mean the difference between a one-time effort toward inclusion and a long-term competitive advantage built on consistently delivering equitable innovation.

Yet, a critical question remains: can SDV companies move beyond reactive adaptation to truly proactive strategies that anticipate and prevent technological exclusion from the outset? Dynamic capabilities provide organizations with the tools to respond and evolve, but the next section examines whether that is sufficient. How can firms preempt algorithmic biases and prioritize inclusion from the start, so that mitigation becomes less necessary? In other words, having learned to dance with change, can the industry also learn to lead the dance regarding equitable innovation?

5. A NEW INTERPRETATION: TOWARDS HUMAN-CENTRIC AND ECOSYSTEM-ORIENTED DYNAMIC CAPABILITIES

The discussion thus far demonstrates how dynamic capabilities can be applied to mitigate exclusion. However, a truly resilient strategy requires moving from a reactive posture to one of proactive foresight. In the context of SDVs, this means that the same organizational abilities used to innovate technology can also be applied to promote inclusion and fairness as strategic priorities. Instead of viewing measures like accessibility features or unbiased algorithms as temporary solutions, companies are starting to see them as investments in long-term resilience. Inclusion and algorithmic fairness are becoming essential pillars of future competitiveness, especially as the automotive industry transitions to data-driven, subscription-based service models that require ongoing customer trust.

This evolution gives rise to what can be termed 'Dynamic Inclusion Capabilities'—an organization's higher-order ability to purposefully and continuously integrate ethical and inclusive principles into its core processes of sensing, seizing, and transforming. Rather than being an afterthought, inclusion becomes a foundational element of how the firm innovates and competes. This goes beyond simple market sensing and involves a deep, normative commitment to shaping markets responsibly.

One element of this evolution is the emergence of preventive algorithmic audits. Companies are beginning to conduct regular reviews of the AI and algorithmic systems in their vehicles for bias, fairness, and safety prior to any complaints or accidents necessitating such scrutiny. To be effective, these audits must be rigorous, incorporating clear fairness metrics (e.g., demographic parity, equal opportunity, equalized odds), standardized demographic testing protocols across various intersecting identities (race, gender, age, disability), and benchmarking against industry best practices and emerging regulatory standards (Koshiyama et al., 2024). By institutionalizing such audit routines, firms create a continuous feedback loop that reinforces algorithmic fairness as a sustained quality, not a one-time check.

Ethical foresight also involves broadening the scope of dynamic capabilities through cross-sector partnerships and stakeholder engagement. The complex challenges SDVs pose—ensuring accessibility for people with disabilities, aligning autonomous decision-making with social norms, and others—cannot be solved by engineers alone. Leading companies have started to incorporate outside perspectives into their innovation processes. For example, one autonomous vehicle developer collaborated with disability advocacy groups to co-design features for riders with disabilities, embedding inclusive thinking into the innovation process (Canter, 2025). This type of collaboration enables companies to identify usability issues or ethical concerns that in-house teams might overlook while building goodwill with communities and regulators.

However, a critical aspect that deserves further examination is how these manufacturers respond differentially to legislation across regions. While countries in the Global North adhere to stricter regulations regarding security, data privacy, and sustainability, countries in the Global South often benefit from more lax or poorly standardized regulatory frameworks. This creates a risk of a "double standard," where inclusive and ethical innovations are deployed in highly regulated markets, while less protected markets receive older or less equitable technologies. A truly resilient dynamic inclusion capability must therefore involve a commitment to globally consistent ethical standards, resisting the pressure to exploit regulatory gaps for short-term commercial advantage. This requires a level of corporate stewardship that transcends national borders and acknowledges a universal responsibility to all users.

Ultimately, embracing inclusive innovation offers benefits that significantly outweigh the costs. Designing products and services to be accessible and fair expands the addressable market and minimizes the risk of public relations crises or legal challenges. Studies have shown that when algorithms in services are perceived as biased or exclusionary, even advantaged users lose trust and become less likely to engage (Draws et al., 2021). Conversely, providing equitable access and clear, fair value propositions can boost customer loyalty and enhance brand differentiation. Business strategists increasingly note that inclusion is not an ethical nicety but a source of sustainable value: companies that embed inclusivity into their offerings and culture gain a competitive edge (Ludke, 2020).

6. CONCLUSION

The transition to the Software-Defined Vehicle represents a crucible for the automotive industry, testing not only its technological prowess but also its strategic acumen. This chapter has argued that navigating this turbulent environment requires a renewed and sophisticated application of the Dynamic Capabilities framework. The analysis has demonstrated that while the foundational pillars of sensing, seizing, and reconfiguring are as relevant as ever, their successful enactment is now deeply intertwined with a firm's ability to understand and manage complex human-car relations, ethical responsibilities, and platform ecosystems. The key takeaway is that in the digital age, a firm's adaptive capacity is inseparable from its socio-technical orientation.

The primary contribution of this chapter is the articulation of a human-centric and ecosystem-oriented interpretation of dynamic capabilities within the specific context of a major industrial transformation. Rather than proposing a new theory, this work enriches the existing one by demonstrating its elasticity and continued relevance. It answers the call to bring socio-technical perspectives into strategic management by illustrating how classic capabilities manifest differently when confronted with challenges like algorithmic control, data ethics, and platform-based business models. This chapter, therefore, serves as a detailed case study in the contemporary application of a canonical theory, highlighting the necessity of a nuanced, context-sensitive reading.

For practicing managers, this analysis offers a clear, actionable insight: competitive advantage in the SDV era is built on the quality of relationships, not just the quality of products. This translates into three key imperatives. First, sensing must evolve from passive market analysis to active ecosystem listening, treating user data as a source of insight for co-creation, not merely as a resource to be monetized. Second, seizing opportunities must be balanced with the imperative of building trust; short-term gains from aggressive subscription models may lead to long-term erosion of brand loyalty. Third, reconfiguring requires more than creating a software division; it demands fostering an integrated platform culture that breaks down the historical silos between hardware, software, and service.

This conceptual analysis opens several avenues for future empirical inquiry. There is a compelling need for large-scale quantitative research to investigate the correlation between ecosystem-oriented capabilities and firm performance metrics, such as customer loyalty and lifetime value. Rich, longitudinal case studies tracking the multi-year transformation efforts of specific incumbent OEMs would provide invaluable, fine-grained insights into the organizational challenges of adopting this new interpretation. Finally, future research could fruitfully apply this human-centric lens to the study of dynamic capabilities in other industries, such as healthcare and finance, that are also grappling with their own profound software-defined transformations. In doing so, a more generalized understanding of how classic strategic principles adapt to the socio-technical realities of the 21st century can be achieved.

REFERENCES

Augier, M., & Teece, D. J. (2009). Dynamic Capabilities and the Role of Managers in Business Strategy and Economic Performance. *Organization Science*, *20*(2), 410–421. DOI: 10.1287/orsc.1090.0424

Auken, I. (2020, November 11). Welcome to 2030: I own nothing, have no privacy, and life has never been better. Forbes. https://www.forbes.com/sites/worldeconomicforum/2016/11/10/shopping-i-cant-really-remember-what-that-is-or-welcome-to-2030-i-own-nothing-have-no-privacy-and-life-has-never-been-better/

Aylmer, J. (2024, October 14). Carmakers locking basic features behind paid subscription services. Straight Arrow News. https://san.com/cc/carmakers-locking-basic-features-behind-paid-subscription-services/

BCG. (2023, September 2). Rewriting the Rules of Software-Defined Vehicles. BCG Global. https://www.bcg.com/publications/2023/rewriting-rules-of-software-defined-vehicles

Beaver, H. D. (2024, January 2). Automakers' Added Subscription Fees Raise Legal Questions. Kiplinger. https://www.kiplinger.com/personal-finance/automakers-added-subscription-fees-raise-legal-questions

Bierenkoven, C. (2023, September 27). BMW's Heated Seat Subscription Is Dead; Others Live On. Edmunds. https://www.edmunds.com/car-news/bmw-relents-on-heated-seat-subscription.html

Cameron, D. (2025, April 28). Car Subscription Features Raise Your Risk of Government Surveillance, Police Records Show. Wired. https://www.wired.com/story/police-records-car-subscription-features-surveillance/

Canter, E. (2025, March 27). NCIL Welcomes Waymo to Washington, DC; Advocates for Inclusive Innovation in Autonomous Transportation. National Council on Independent Living. https://ncil.org/news/announcements/waymo-dc/

Chee, F. Y. (2025, March 5). EU plans law to give car services groups access to vehicle data. Reuters. https://www.reuters.com/business/autos-transportation/eu-plans-law-give-car-services-groups-access-vehicle-data-2025-03-04/?utm_source=chatgpt.com

Draws, T., Szlávik, Z., Timmermans, B., Tintarev, N., Varshney, K. R., & Hind, M. (2021). *Disparate Impact Diminishes Consumer Trust Even for Advantaged Users* (Vol. 12684)., DOI: 10.1007/978-3-030-79460-6_11

Eisenhardt, K. M., & Martin, J. A. (2000). Dynamic Capabilities: What Are They? *Strategic Management Journal*, *21*(10/11), 1105–1121. DOI: 10.1002/1097-0266(200010/11)21:10/11<1105::AID-SMJ133>3.0.CO;2-E

Harding, X. (2023, August 7). Facial Recognition Bias: Why Racism Appears In Face Detection Tech. Mozilla Foundation. https://www.mozillafoundation.org/en/blog/facial-recognition-bias/

Helfat, C. E., Finkelstein, S., Mitchell, W., Peteraf, M., Singh, H., Teece, D., & Winter, S. G. (2007). *Dynamic Capabilities: Understanding Strategic Change in Organizations*. John Wiley & Sons.

Helfat, C. E., & Raubitschek, R. S. (2018). Dynamic and integrative capabilities for profiting from innovation in digital platform-based ecosystems. *Research Policy*, *47*(8), 1391–1399. DOI: 10.1016/j.respol.2018.01.019

Katta, S. (2025, March 11). The EU Data Act: A catalyst for change. Smartcar. https://smartcar.com/blog/eu-data-act

Koshiyama, A., Kazim, E., Treleaven, P., Rai, P., Szpruch, L., Pavey, G., Ahamat, G., Leutner, F., Goebel, R., Knight, A., Adams, J., Hitrova, C., Barnett, J., Nachev, P., Barber, D., Chamorro-Premuzic, T., Klemmer, K., Gregorovic, M., Khan, S., & Chatterjee, S. (2024). Towards algorithm auditing: Managing legal, ethical and technological risks of AI, ML and associated algorithms. *Royal Society Open Science*, *11*(5), 230859. DOI: 10.1098/rsos.230859 PMID: 39076787

Koster, A., Lang, N., Collie, B., Xie, A., & Hagenmaier, M. (2023). Software-Defined Vehicles Will Create a More Than $650 Billion Value Potential for the Auto Industry by 2030. https://www.bcg.com/press/7september2023-software-defined-vehicles-create-650-billion-value-potential

Levin, T. (2022, November 22). Car companies want to make billions by charging monthly fees for features like heated seats, but buyers won't pay up. Business Insider. https://www.businessinsider.com/car-feature-subscriptions-add-ons-bmw-ford-toyota-gm-2022-2

Liu, Z., Zhang, W., & Zhao, F. (2022). Impact, Challenges and Prospect of Software-Defined Vehicles. *Automotive Innovation*, *5*(2), 180–194. DOI: 10.1007/s42154-022-00179-z

Ludke, R. (2020). Competitive, Integrated Employment: A Driver of Long-Term Value Creation. The Harkin Institute for Public Policy & Citizen Engagement. https://harkininstitute.drake.edu/wp-content/uploads/sites/103/2022/06/Harkin-Disability_Inclusion_and_Long_Term_Value_Creation-design_Final-6.6.22.pdf

McKinsey & Company. (2023). Automotive software electronics market 2030. https://www.mckinsey.com/industries/automotive-and-assembly/our-insights/mapping-the-automotive-software-and-electronics-landscape-through-2030

Media, S. A. E. (2023, October 10). The Chaos of Automotive Data Privacy. https://www.mobilityengineeringtech.com/component/content/article/49351-sae-ma-07256

Moura, I. (2022, November 7). Addressing Disability and Ableist Bias in Autonomous Vehicles: Ensuring Safety, Equity and Accessibility in Detection, Collision Algorithms and Data Collection. Disability Rights Education & Defense Fund. https://dredf.org/addressing-disability-and-ableist-bias-in-autonomous-vehicles-ensuring-safety-equity-and-accessibility-in-detection-collision-algorithms-and-data-collection/

NHTSA. (2015). Critical Reasons for Crashes Investigated in the National Motor Vehicle Crash Causation Survey (DOT HS 812 115; TRAFFIC SAFETY FACTS). https://crashstats.nhtsa.dot.gov/Api/Public/ViewPublication/812115

Ordóñez, S. (2024). Global Production Networks and Dynamic Cores in the World's Main Nodes: The Technological-Productive Transition of the Automotive Industry. *World Review of Political Economy*, *15*(1), 46–81. DOI: 10.13169/worlrevipoliecon.15.1.0046

Pérez-Moure, H. (2025). The new dimension of mobility companies: Dynamic capabilities, sustainability, and digitalization. *Suma de Negocios*, *16*(34), 10–20. DOI: 10.14349/sumneg/2025.V16.N34.A2

Pérez-Moure, H., Ochoa-Urrego, L. C., & Arbelaez-Giraldo, M. (2024). Mobility business models toward a digital tomorrow: Challenges for automotive manufacturers. *Futures*, *156*, 103309. DOI: 10.1016/j.futures.2023.103309

Povich, E. S. (2018a, November 27). Late Payment? A 'Kill Switch' Can Strand You and Your Car. Stateline. https://stateline.org/2018/11/27/late-payment-a-kill-switch-can-strand-you-and-your-car/

Povich, E. S. (2018b, December 2). States Look at "Kill Switches" Used to Disable Cars With Late Payments. Route Fifty. https://www.route-fifty.com/management/2018/12/kill-switch-payments/153205/

PwC. (2024, October 3). What is an SDV (Software Defined Vehicle)? Defining SDVs beyond just vehicles. PwC. https://www.pwc.com/jp/en/knowledge/column/definition-of-sdv.html

Rísquez Ramos, M., & Ruiz-Gálvez, M. E. (2024). The transformation of the automotive industry toward electrification and its impact on global value chains: Inter-plant competition, employment, and supply chains. *European Research on Management and Business Economics*, *30*(1), 100242. DOI: 10.1016/j.iedeen.2024.100242

Rodríguez, J. J. (2023, March 7). Survey: 69% Of Americans Don't Want Subscription-Based Options In Their Cars. Jalopnik. https://www.jalopnik.com/car-buyers-dont-want-subscription-based-options-survey-1850194708/

Salvato, C. (2021). Dynamic Capabilities and Routine Dynamics. In Feldman, M. S., Pentland, B. T., D'Adderio, L., Dittrich, K., Rerup, C., & Seidl, D. (Eds.), *Cambridge Handbook of Routine Dynamics* (1st ed., pp. 460–480). Cambridge University Press., DOI: 10.1017/9781108993340.039

Statt, N. (2020, February 7). Tesla remotely disables Autopilot on used Model S after it was sold. The Verge. https://www.theverge.com/2020/2/6/21127243/tesla-model-s-autopilot-disabled-remotely-used-car-update

Szalavetz, A. (2024). In-house software development for software-defined vehicles: Major changes ahead in automotive value chains? *International Journal of Automotive Technology and Management*, *24*(5), 22–39. DOI: 10.1504/IJATM.2024.142127

Teece, D. J. (2007). Explicating dynamic capabilities: The nature and microfoundations of (sustainable) enterprise performance. *Strategic Management Journal*, *28*(13), 1319–1350. DOI: 10.1002/smj.640

Teece, D. J. (2018). Tesla and the Reshaping of the Auto Industry. *Management and Organization Review*, *14*(3), 501–512. DOI: 10.1017/mor.2018.33

Teece, D. J., Pisano, G., & Shuen, A. (1997). Dynamic capabilities and strategic management. *Strategic Management Journal*, *18*(7), 509–533. DOI: 10.1002/(SICI)1097-0266(199708)18:7<509::AID-SMJ882>3.0.CO;2-Z

The Dallas Morning News. (2025, February 25). Americans Don't Trust Self-Driving Cars Says AAA Survey. CPA Practice Advisor. https://www.cpapracticeadvisor.com/2025/02/25/americans-dont-trust-self-driving-cars-says-aaa-survey/156524/

Vdovic, H., Babic, J., & Podobnik, V. (2019). Automotive Software in Connected and Autonomous Electric Vehicles: A Review. *IEEE Access : Practical Innovations, Open Solutions*, *7*, 166365–166379. DOI: 10.1109/ACCESS.2019.2953568

Vincent, J. (2022, July 12). BMW starts selling heated seat subscriptions for $18 a month. The Verge. https://www.theverge.com/2022/7/12/23204950/bmw-subscriptions-microtransactions-heated-seats-feature

Zhao, F., Song, H., Liu, Z., Zhao, F., Song, H., & Liu, Z. (2022, January 31). Identification and Analysis of Key Technical Elements and Prospects for Software-Defined Vehicles. SAE 2021 Intelligent and Connected Vehicles Symposium Part II. https://doi.org/DOI: 10.4271/2022-01-7002

Chapter 9

The AI Bias and Its Implications for the Future Business Context:

A Cross-Cultural Study With a Focus on the Mobility Sector

Hugo Pérez-Moure
https://orcid.org/0000-0002-2233-0057
University of Vigo, Spain

Kiyoshi Murata
https://orcid.org/0000-0002-5632-8078
Meiji University, Japan

Yasunori Fukuta
Meiji University, Japan

Miguel Crespo-Velando
https://orcid.org/0009-0004-4011-9580
University of Vigo, Spain

ABSTRACT

A new industrial revolution is transforming nearly all sectors. One of the most strategic is mobility, where AI plays a key role by enabling connected and autonomous vehicles. AI is now widely adopted—75% of employees already use it—but firms may misinterpret its outputs or overlook opportunities due to its limitations. This chapter explores bias in generative AI applied to mobility, focusing on economic-geographical bias, business model bias, and representation bias. The methodology

DOI: 10.4018/979-8-3373-2685-6.ch009

Copyright © 2026, IGI Global Scientific Publishing. Copying or distributing in print or electronic forms without written permission of IGI Global Scientific Publishing is prohibited.

is novel, employing and comparing responses from three AIs—ChatGPT, DeepSeek, and Gemini. Findings reveal inclusion-related biases, a focus on efficiency and Industry 4.0 logic over Industry 5.0 values, and underrepresentation of key regions and sustainable models. Results suggest AI and ethics should be addressed as Dynamic Capabilities that shape competitive advantage. Yet, without critical oversight, AI may hinder long-term strategies and reinforce exclusion. Practical implications urge ethical, inclusive, and context-aware use of AI for fair, human-centric mobility systems.

1. INTRODUCTION

A new industrial revolution is occurring, transforming value chains, business models, and consumer interactions. Companies and society must adapt to this shift from Industry 4.0 to Industry 5.0 (Pérez-Moure et al., 2025). This transformation is driven by digitalization, although the term alone does not fully capture the current landscape. Recent technologies, such as Big Data, Blockchain, and Business Intelligence, remain limited in democratization; their lack of widespread adoption restricts disruptive potential (You et al., 2022; Hoover & Lee, 2015; Coccia, 2010).

Historically, each industrial revolution is characterized by key technologies and uncertainty. Currently, machine learning-based artificial intelligence (AI) epitomizes these characteristics, driving productivity, innovation, and societal transformation. Given AI's novelty, its implications must be studied comprehensively.

Generative AI, in particular, demonstrates significant democratization (Chiu, 2023; Mannuru et al., 2023). OpenAI reported nearly 15.5 million paid ChatGPT subscribers in 2024, excluding free users and other AI platforms like Copilot, Gemini, and DeepSeek (The Information, 2024). Microsoft found 75% of workers already use generative AI professionally (Microsoft, 2024).

Despite its benefits (Csaszar et al., 2024; Liu et al., 2024; Sawhney, 2022; Sullivan & Wamba, 2024), AI also presents challenges, described as digitalization's "dark side" (Belanche et al., 2024; Barari et al., 2024; Mikalef et al., 2022). In B2B industrial markets, characterized by trust-based, long-term relationships, poorly implemented AI risks harming human interactions essential for negotiations and collaboration (Pérez-Moure et al., 2025; Belanche et al., 2024). Issues of plagiarism, originality, and opaque decision-making further complicate AI's integration.

AI raises significant ethical and exclusion concerns. Overreliance on AI-generated information could lead to missed market opportunities or generic strategies lacking analytical depth. Moreover, since AIs reflect inherent human biases from training data, regions with greater digital access disproportionately influence AI outputs

(Bender et al., 2021). Pérez-Moure et al. (2025) emphasizes the growing importance of AI-driven business models and data privacy (Fukuta et al., 2020).

Although several regulations and normative frameworks addressing the ethical and responsible use of artificial intelligence have emerged in recent years (such as the AI Act in the European Union and various data privacy and governance initiatives) their development and implementation still present notable limitations. As recent studies indicate and reviewers have highlighted, there remains a significant gap between current regulatory proposals and the actual needs arising from rapid technological advances, particularly within dynamic and sensitive sectors like New Mobility (Zhou et al., 2024; Taeihagh, 2025).

Within this dynamic context, AI is the most democratized emerging technology (Stahl, 2025). However, improper use poses risks linked to embedded biases (Stahl & Eke, 2024). This chapter focuses on the New Mobility sector, significantly impacted by digitalization, Industry 5.0, and innovative business models (Lampón et al., 2023). Mobility is strategically critical for countries including Japan, Spain, France, the US, Mexico, China, and Germany, and it has been extensively studied across various dimensions (Rísquez-Ramos & Ruiz-Gálvez, 2024).

Traditional mobility firms (OEMs) currently face transformative pressures. AI and data management are pivotal in navigating emerging business models like carsharing (You et al., 2022; Leminen et al., 2022). OEMs must strategically adapt to emerging competitors, such as Chinese manufacturers and tech giants (Google, Amazon, Microsoft), as well as specialized mobility-focused startups (Steinberg et al., 2022; Athanasopoulou, 2019).

As vehicles become increasingly intelligent and data-intensive, AI-driven services, like Honda's crime-predictive vehicle, illustrate new possibilities (Pérez-Moure et al., 2023). However, significant concerns persist regarding data ownership, privacy, and ethical use (Pérez-Moure et al., 2024; Fukuta et al., 2020; Murata & Orito, 2020). Mismanagement or biases in AI could undermine trust and lead to misguided investments.

This chapter examines AI bias using an innovative methodology involving direct interactions with AI platforms, highlighting potential impacts on corporate strategy. It stresses the necessity for a human-centric approach, balancing efficiency and societal considerations, with ethics and values playing key roles. Through critical analysis, the chapter explores AI's ethical implications and strategic use in mobility.

The structure is as follows: First, the theoretical framework outlines Industry 5.0, AI in New Mobility and business models, AI ethics, and Dynamic Capabilities theory. Then, a case study involving direct queries to AI platforms is presented, followed by concluding reflections.

2. LITERATURE REVIEW

2.1. The New Industry 5.0 and AI

The concept of industrial revolution has evolved significantly over time, driven by technological advances that have transformed production, trade, and society. In recent years, the Industry 4.0 paradigm—based on digitalization, automation, and data usage—has dominated the business landscape. However, this vision, focused on efficiency and process optimization, has given way to a broader and more human-centered approach: Industry 5.0 (Liu et al., 2024; Xu et al., 2021; Loureiro, 2018). To understand how AI is affecting companies, it is essential to grasp this new paradigm and how it differs from the previous one.

Industry 4.0 is characterized by the pursuit of efficiency and production optimization, thanks to technologies such as IoT, Cloud Computing, Big Data, and AI (Murtaza et al., 2024). These tools enable real-time communication, remote diagnostics, and automated logistics. In this context, AI has primarily served as a means of automating processes and generating large volumes of data to enhance operational performance. One of the most relevant outcomes has been the rise of servitization, where digital solutions support value-added services (Leng et al., 2024). Moreover, although there is a certain degree of collaboration within Industry 4.0, it tends to remain within the boundaries of the value chain and is often oriented towards technological efficiency rather than social impact. As a result, people are often sidelined in this paradigm, and technology is frequently seen as an end in itself (Huang et al., 2022; Deguchi et al., 2020).

In contrast, Industry 5.0 redefines the relationship between humans and technology (Huang et al., 2022). This emerging paradigm emphasizes human-centricity, sustainability, and social resilience, aligning with the vision of Society 5.0, where technology serves human and societal well-being. It actively promotes eco-design, the circular economy, and multisectoral collaboration—bringing together actors from different industries that share common goals in sustainability (Deguchi et al., 2020; Del Giudice et al., 2023; Golavianko et al., 2023). While Industry 4.0 focused on optimizing internal processes, Industry 5.0 aims to build inclusive and cooperative ecosystems across sectors.

Although both paradigms currently coexist, recent studies show a clear shift towards Industry 5.0 (Pérez-Moure et al., 2025). This shift is driven in part by the rise of generative AI, which expands the role of artificial intelligence from simple automation to strategic and creative support. AI is no longer just a productivity tool; it is increasingly being integrated into strategic decision-making and the execution of complex tasks (Liu et al., 2023; Leng et al., 2024). However, this also brings ethical risks, such as algorithmic bias, transparency concerns, and the potential loss of trust

(Stahl & Eke, 2024). Consequently, many companies are adopting a glocalization approach—adapting AI tools to local cultural contexts to reduce exclusion based on age, gender, race, or ethnicity (Pérez-Moure et al., 2025).

The transformation towards Industry 5.0 also implies profound changes in business models. AI enables new ways of generating value, especially through hyper-personalization. This has fostered the growth of subscription-based and pay-per-use services. Furthermore, the concept of AI-as-a-service has emerged, making powerful AI tools widely accessible, even to small businesses and individuals (Li et al., 2021; Okuda et al., 2018). In such a competitive and democratized environment, companies and workers alike require dynamic capabilities such as adaptability, resilience, critical thinking, ethical awareness, and cross-sector collaboration (Pinto et al., 2025).

Table 1. Industry 4.0 vs. Industry 5.0

	Industry 4.0	**Industry 5.0**
Main Focus	**Efficiency and productivity**	**Human-centric and sustainability**
Additional focus	Automation and digitalization	Resilience and well-being
Goal	Supply chain optimization and cost reduction	Create sustainable and inclusive value
AI Role	Task automation and data processing	Generative AI, decision support and creativity
Key Technologies	IoT, big data, robotics, cloud computing	Human-machine collaboration, AI ethics, green tech
Relevance of Collaboration	Relevant mainly within industry	Strongly relevant across sectors and society
Societal Integration	Limited	Closely aligned with Society 5.0 vision
Human Role	Operator and overseer of machines	Co-creator, strategic partner, empowered contributor
Ethical Dimension	Not explicitly addressed	Central: ethics, privacy, fairness in AI use
Environmental Impact	Often secondary	Proactively minimized (eco-design, circular economy)
Customization	Mass customization	Hyper-personalization
Skills required	Digital and technical skills	Tech + creativity, ethics, adaptability and analysis

continued on following page

Table 1. Continued

	Industry 4.0	Industry 5.0
Approach to Globalization	Global efficiency and offshoring	Glocalization and cultural adaptation
Contextual Environment	Technological acceleration and economic optimization	Complex, volatile, uncertain context, with societal and ethical challenges

Source: Author's elaboration

As summarized in Table 1, the transition towards Industry 5.0 requires not only a technological transformation but also an ethical, organizational, and cultural shift. In this paradigm, AI must be understood as a tool for promoting diversity, sustainability, and shared value, especially in fields like new mobility, where its impact is particularly significant.

2.2. The New Mobility, New Business Models and AI

Industry 5.0, along with the implementation of new technologies, has resulted in a radical transformation of the automotive sector. Traditionally, the automotive industry followed a clear structure and set of objectives: to develop a product (the vehicle) for mass markets by offshoring activities based on labor costs and the value they added. In other words, decisions were based on cost-benefit analyses, with OEMs holding full control and power over production, while the rest of the suppliers (Tier 1, 2, 3… n) were positioned at the corresponding levels of the value chain. These suppliers generally had very limited bargaining power and did not control their own activities, among other reasons, because their contributions were of low added value (Lampón et al., 2022; Lampón et al., 2024). However, the emergence of new business models, digitalization, and the implementation of Industry 5.0 have caused the traditional automotive industry to evolve into what is now known as New Mobility (Zhang & Kamargianni, 2023).

Whereas mobility was previously understood purely as the movement of someone or something, it is now regarded as an industry that goes beyond vehicle production and connects different sectors such as transport, urban planning, and technology. The emergence of technology—and in particular, AI—has fundamentally changed the paradigm. New Mobility shifts the focus from the vehicle as a product to services that place the user at the core (Pérez-Moure et al., 2023). This transformation is not only visible in the production of the final product, but also in how technology is integrated at all levels. In the traditional automotive industry, technology was employed exclusively for production purposes, whereas in the new mobility paradigm, vehicles are now highly connected—generating, capturing, and processing data (Leminen et al., 2022).

This change has redefined accessibility. While in the traditional industry mobility was a private service reserved for certain segments of society, in New Mobility it becomes democratized and accessible to everyone. Multimodality and car-sharing promote a more inclusive approach (Pérez-Moure et al., 2024). As a result, the concept of ownership is being redefined, favouring circular and shared economies in which the value lies in the service itself (Cabanelas et al., 2023). At the same time, sustainability has become a fundamental pillar, not only through shared-use models but also through the shift towards more environmentally friendly technologies such as electric vehicles or hydrogen-based propulsion systems (Athanaspoulou et al., 2019). This evolution has led to the emergence of software-defined vehicles (SDVs), where software governs much of the vehicle's functionality, enabling real-time or over-the-air (OTA) updates, personalization, and integration with broader digital ecosystems (Keskar, 2019).

New Mobility also pursues broader goals such as reclaiming urban spaces by reducing the number of circulating vehicles and lowering emissions (Zhang & Kamargianni, 2023); offering more personalized and adapted mobility services, including rural mobility and the inclusion of people with reduced mobility; reducing inequalities through accessible transport; and promoting citizen participation in the design of mobility policies (You et al., 2022). If inclusion is one of the core principles of New Mobility, it would be contradictory for these new business models and technologies to generate exclusion. In this regard, the emergence of CASE (Connected, Autonomous, Shared, and Electric) vehicles carries significant implications at the business, political, and social levels (Lampón & Muñoz-Dueñas, 2023). Figure 1 presents the areas covered by New Mobility and how they are interconnected.

Figure 1. New Mobility Pyramid

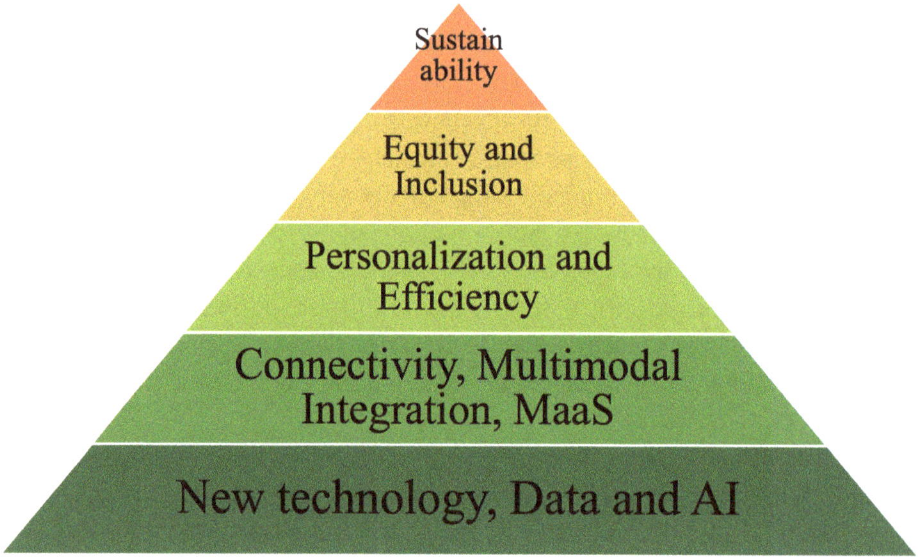

Source: Author's elaboration

Several authors have attempted to categorize the different business models emerging around New Mobility, although there is no clear consensus. Some have proposed classifications based on value propositions (Cabanelas et al., 2023), while others have sought to categorize them based on common patterns (Pérez-Moure et al., 2025; Pérez-Moure et al., 2023). However, there is still a lack of research identifying the most promising business models. In general, though, most studies have highlighted those related to AI, data, sustainability, and personalization.

Therefore, without technology, data, or AI, neither connected nor autonomous mobility can be developed, nor can advanced services be offered. For this reason, real-time data analysis and the integration of autonomous vehicles have become one of the main goals. These types of vehicles require a high level of connectivity—not only among themselves, but also with a range of infrastructures and actors such as pedestrians or other vehicles—an interaction known as vehicle-to-everything (V2X) (Gschwendtner et al., 2021). Similarly, the connectivity enabled by new technology makes it possible to offer services instead of products, aiming to integrate all modes of transport into a single platform or provide on-demand transport. This is known as mobility as a service (MaaS) (Liu et al., 2024).

This degree of servitization, data management, and connectivity enables improved traffic management, route optimization, personalized and subscription-based services—all based on user data—enhancing the overall experience, reducing travel time, and allowing for lower costs (Zhang & Kamargianni, 2023). Moreover, well-developed infrastructure and new technologies make it possible to design on-demand routes for rural areas, provide accessible vehicles for people with reduced mobility, or offer personalized pricing based on income levels (Steinberg et al., 2022). AI and data should be able to detect inequalities and offer fairer solutions. All of this promotes sustainability and urban transformation, contributing to a cleaner, more human, and a more human environment, thanks to shared and predictive systems empowered by the base of the pyramid.

In general, all of New Mobility is framed and conditioned by the proper management of data and AI. Although this may work well in theory, it can present serious challenges in practice (Kassens-Noor et al., 2021). A clear example of this is connected and autonomous vehicles (CAVs), which, despite years of development and the existence of prototypes, still cannot operate on motorways or highways. In fact, they are facing serious ethical issues due to AI hallucinations that pose risks to pedestrians (Ma et al., 2025). Similarly, AI uses information about users' habits to provide better services and greater equity. However, this also raises ethical concerns, as control over mobility data can seriously compromise individuals' privacy and integrity (Fukuta et al., 2017; Orito et al., 2014; Fukuta et al., 2020). Through these data, knowing where people go, how long they stay, how often they move, who they are with, or even their mood could pose a threat to individuals if not managed ethically (Fukuta et al., 2017; Orito et al., 2014; Fukuta et al., 2020).

2.3. Ethical Issues in AI Computing

The full-fledged use and proliferation of AI systems has led to a wide recognition of various ethical issues, including potential ones, raised by the development, operation and use of the systems. The issues recognized thus far can be classified into the following five categories.

(a) Discrimination generated by biases lurking in machine learning data and algorithms: This issue was first widely perceived when the AI-based face recognition system used for Google Photos labeled a photo of a black couple as "Gorillas" (Zhang, 2015). It was reported that a predictive AI system used in the United States to support probation and parole officers to judge the risk of recidivism tended to incorrectly place black defendants at higher risk of recidivism than white defendants (Larson et al., 2016). Large language models (LLMs) allegedly have this problem, as well. Bender et al. (2021) described that LLMs learn the hegemonic worldview holed up in their training data, and reproduce and even amplify the biases pertaining to such a worldview. Inclusive AI thus has become one of the most important AI ethics research areas.

(b) Negative impacts on employment: Since Frey & Osborne (2013) pointed out the substantial influence of AI over jobs many people engaged in, the social concern that the technology is causing job losses has been generated mainly in industrialized countries. The pros and cons of introducing a universal basic income system are being debated, and the meaning of labor for human beings is being questioned anew.
(c) Ethicality of the intended use of AI systems: The development and use of lethal autonomous weapons (LAWs), for example, have been considered ethically problematic. Many insist that AI robots should be regulated so that they never kill opposing soldiers or enemy civilians based on their autonomous decisions (e.g.: Trager & Luca, 2022). Another example is the use of AI in the sex industry (Palma, 2021). While this would contribute to the diversification of sexual orientation and gender identity, it would also have a profound impact on the role and shape of the family and society.
(d) Manipulation of human psychological states and behaviors brought about by autonomous decisions and judgments made by AI systems and the resultant loss of individual autonomy: AI-based microtargeting systems can provide individuals with elaborated personalized information or recommendations which intend to control their mental status and behavior—in many cases without their being aware of the intent—to attain a certain purpose. This kind of system was used for political objectives by Cambridge Analytica, a British political consulting firm, before a United Kingdom national referendum on membership of the European Union and a United States presidential election in 2016 (Kaiser, 2019), and this case let many people realize that such a system would seriously deteriorate democracy. In fact, the phenomena of filter bubble (Pariser, 2011) and echo chamber (Nguyen, 2018) have been caused by an operation of such microtargeting systems online platform companies adopt, resulting in group polarization and social segmentation (Murata, 2022), which raise a concern about undermining the fundamental principles of democracy (Coeckelbergh, 2024). Because the personalized recommendation provision presupposes the collection and use of a massive amount of personal data and can intervene personal decisions and psychological status, this issue is often discussed in the context of an invasion of personal privacy.
(e) A vacuum of responsibility/accountability in AI computing: AI-based systems tend to function as black boxes because their autonomous behavior, based on machine learning, is unintelligible and inexplicable, as well as unpredictable and uncontrollable even by the engineers who develop and operate the systems. These characteristics are inseparable from the benefit of contemporary AI computing, which is that it provides knowledge and findings human beings could never extract. When AI-based systems are networked to interact with

other AI-based systems, such characteristics are exacerbated. The operation of autonomous systems featuring AI technology encourages normally responsible people to claim "it's the system's fault", to evade accountability for harm. The abovementioned character of AI-based systems tends to justify this. In addition, machine-learning algorithms developed by outside parties are often available by means of application programming interfaces, and free/libre open-source software (FLOSS) is often incorporated into AI-based systems. Open-source and outsourced datasets are commonly used to train machine learning models. Consequently, the problem of many hands, one of the four barriers to accountability in computing (Nissenbaum, 1996), becomes worse, and it can be very difficult to ensure accountability in AI computing (Murata, 2022). When it comes to mobility, it is in fact very difficult to clarify who is responsible when an autonomous vehicle has an accident. Responsible, explicable and transparent AI have actively been explored to fill the vacuum.

The advent of generative AIs, which create variety kinds of new contents such as texts, codes, pictures and videos responding to prompts, has added several issues to the AI ethics agenda. Copyright infringement can be induced by using such AI systems, because there is the potential for unauthorized copying of others' original work when generating a new content through combining information from existing literature or online materials. The conceptual muddles (Moor, 1985) of "creation", "originality", "plagiarism" and so on caused by the spread of generative AIs have indeed been considered problematic in the educational and academic fields. Is it permissible to name ChatGPT as a co-author of an academic research paper?

A LLM training requires a huge amount of energy, and the amount of power needed to train AI models is growing exponentially. This means that the development and use of such a generative AI directly contributes to global warming (Ceurstemont, 2025). Given that those who enjoy benefits of the generative AIs are different from those who suffer the effects of climate change, LLM-driven environmental racism has been occurring (Bender et al., 2021).

2.4. Dynamic Capabilities and AI

The new Industry 5.0 paradigm, the emergence of AI, and consequently the rise of new business models, compel companies to engage in a constant search for information to ensure corporate survival. In this context, the Theory of Dynamic Capabilities emerges. This theory focuses on a firm's ability to adapt, innovate, and compete in constantly changing environments by integrating and reconfiguring its resources and competencies, with the aim of achieving a sustainable competitive advantage (Cabanelas et al., 2023), avoiding core rigidities (Leonard-Barton, 1992).

Therefore, dynamic capabilities are grounded in a firm's core competencies and, through improvement and change, can alter its competitive position in the short term while establishing long-term advantages (Cabanelas et al., 2023; Teece, 2020). Since its introduction, the theory has undergone significant and ongoing evolution (Ghosh et al., 2022; Yuan & Cao, 2022). Moreover, it is important to consider that a competitive advantage must be sustainable over time and provide real value. Thus, in the context of globalization, uncertainty, and multiple scenarios, it becomes essential to carefully select which capabilities should be developed (Yuan & Cao, 2022).

Capabilities within an organization can be classified at different levels: ordinary capabilities, micro foundations, and, finally, dynamic capabilities (Teece, 2020). Ordinary capabilities refer to those emerging from the company's daily operational processes. While they are necessary, they do not provide any form of competitive advantage. Micro foundations are more specialized capabilities resulting from external alliances or the development of new products and innovations. Finally, dynamic capabilities represent key strategic abilities for a company's long-term adaptation and survival in a constantly changing environment (Ferigotti et al., 2020). This classification of capabilities is shaped by other key elements such as the availability of resources, strategic orientation, market competition, and the role of public institutions (Teece, 2014).

The role that new technologies and AI may play remains unexplored. Decisions based on AI can compromise the functioning of the company, as well as the appropriate selection of capabilities to be developed (Liu et al., 2024). Likewise, it may undermine inclusion and lead to flawed development of new products, investments, or partnerships, thereby compromising the firm's micro foundations, which could later evolve into dynamic capabilities (Sullivan & Wamba, 2024). AI could almost be considered a dynamic capability in itself, as it can be sustainable over time, add value, enable companies to adapt strategically, and ultimately ensure their survival (Pérez-Moure et al., 2025). Currently, there is uncertainty about which productive model, technologies, and business models will prevail. In this context, the Theory of Dynamic Capabilities has become essential in the mobility industry to cope with rapid technological change, the rise of AI, and emerging models such as the sharing economy, all of which are reshaping competition and requiring continuous adaptation (Teece, 2017; Cabanelas et al., 2023).

Moreover, in line with the principles of Industry 5.0, the growing concern for sustainability and the urgent need to reduce carbon emissions have brought energy efficiency and the adoption of cleaner mobility solutions to the forefront (Pérez-Moure et al., 2023). The complexity and diversity of international regulations add another challenge, requiring greater flexibility and adaptability from companies

(George et al., 2020). Finally, the convergence with the technology sector has led to the development of specialized dynamic capabilities (Cabanelas et al., 2023).

Integration of AI into business processes and models is conditioned by ethical issues that may affect the development of dynamic capabilities (Sjödin et al., 2023; Mikalef et al., 2021). Therefore, there is a growing need to develop dynamic capabilities that respond not only to efficiency and competitiveness, but also to equity, inclusion, and transparency, aligned with the principles of Industry 5.0, where people occupy a central role.

In this sense, if human oversight mechanisms or proper data management are not incorporated, automated decision-making could reproduce biases or compromise key business data. This ethical dimension could directly affect capability development, undermining the sustainability of competitive advantage if it is not aligned with emerging social or regulatory values (Floridi, 2023; Stahl, 2025). Thus, incorporating ethics as a strategic component in the development of dynamic capabilities may be essential to ensure their effective performance.

3. EXPLORING BIAS, EXCLUSION AND ETHICS IN PRACTICE: AN AI EXPERIMENT

3.1. Methodology

In line with the theoretical framework and the reviewed literature, this chapter adopts an exploratory methodological design to assess potential bias in generative AI systems and its ethical implications within the mobility sector. As artificial intelligence increasingly shapes business models and policy decisions, particularly in the context of New Mobility, it is essential to examine the risks of exclusion embedded in the narratives these technologies produce.

Although the approach is relatively novel, it follows established methodological guidance for both case studies and exploratory experiments. While AI bias has been explored in fields such as healthcare, its analysis in business and ethics remains limited. This study contributes to addressing that gap by applying a hybrid methodology that combines two techniques: the case study approach described by Meyer (2001), and the exploratory experiment framework outlined by Lin (2004).

The case study approach is justified by the focus on a specific sector, New Mobility, and the aim to analyse a defined phenomenon in depth. The objective is to generate rich and context-specific insights that may support theoretical reflection and practical understanding, rather than produce statistical generalizations.

In parallel, the design also includes an exploratory experiment. A predefined set of inputs was submitted to different AI platforms, followed by a systematic observation and interpretation of outputs. Although there is no control group or quantification, the method involves the structured manipulation of variables linked to the bias dimensions under study. The hypotheses guiding the analysis are presented in the following section.

3.1.1 Hypotheis Development

Based on previous research, we propose that generative AI systems may reproduce certain biases related to geography, business models, and social representation. These biases could compromise the inclusive and sustainable goals that Industry 5.0 and New Mobility aim to promote. Based on existing literature, we formulate the following hypotheses guiding this research:

H1: Generative AI tends to highlight economic and geographical actors concentrated in specific regions (e.g., the United States, Europe, Japan), overlooking other relevant contributors (Signh, 2024; Li & Sinnamon, 2024).
H2: Generative AI prioritizes business models aligned with Industry 4.0 logics (profitability, efficiency), while underrepresenting Industry 5.0 principles such as sustainability, human-centered approach, personalization or adaptability (Doron et al., 2024; Ghobakhloo et al., 2024).
H3: Generative AI favors user profiles associated with high purchasing power, often from the Global North, neglecting a broader, more inclusive representation of users and urban contexts (Zhou et al., 2024; Taeihagh, 2025; Sadeghiani, 2024).

3.1.2 Procedure

This experiment involved submitting a series of questions (inputs) to three generative AI platforms: ChatGPT, Gemini, and DeepSeek. ChatGPT was selected for its popularity, flexibility, and pioneering role; Gemini, Google's model, for its image generation capabilities and widespread adoption; and DeepSeek, a fast-growing Chinese platform, for its advanced computing capacity and relevance beyond linguistic performance. Including a Chinese-developed AI also helps mitigate cultural bias and geographical imbalance in the analysis.

Free versions of all three platforms were used, as they are the most accessible to both the general public and businesses. The models employed were ChatGPT-4, Gemini 2.0, and DeepSeek V3. Following recommendations for case study research, three platforms were selected to balance information richness and analytical manageability.

Each AI was asked the same set of questions. To avoid cross-contamination, a new chat was initiated for each analytical dimension, and every question was submitted three times to control for variation in responses. The questions, derived from the literature and directly related to the study's hypotheses, aimed to detect potential biases in three areas: economic-geographical focus, business model orientation, and user representation.

Responses were qualitatively analysed to identify patterns of inclusion or omission. Although the approach is exploratory, it offers valuable insight into the narratives these technologies may reinforce.

The case study focuses on New Mobility, a sector undergoing rapid transformation and of strategic relevance for industrial policy. This focus enables greater analytical depth, though cross-sectoral implications may also arise.

The Table 2 outlines the three dimensions of analysis, the types of questions posed to each AI, and the expected patterns of response based on prior literature and theoretical assumptions.

Table 2. Bias resume and questions

	Economic-Geographical Bias
Sample Questions	**- Who are the main or key actors developing the future of mobility?** **- Which countries or cities lead the development of autonomous mobility?** **- What are the main initiatives in new mobility and who leads them?**
Expected Bias	- Focus on US, Japan, and Western Europe. - Omission of Southeast Asia, Israel, or emerging countries.
	Business Model Bias
Sample Questions	- What are the most profitable business models in the mobility sector? - How do companies monetize their mobility services? - How is data used to offer new products and services?
Expected Bias	- Emphasis on corporate, scalable, for-profit models. - Limited mention of cooperative or public-sector alternatives. - Focus on revenue generation rather than user benefit or ethical management.
	Representation Bias
Sample Questions	- What type of consumer will benefit most from new mobility services and vehicles? - Generate an image of a city in the future. - Generate an image of a person using a smart mobility system.
Expected Bias	- Focus on affluent, urban users from developed countries. Limited consideration of marginalized groups. - Possibly clean, smart cities based on Western models, omitting informal or diverse urban contexts. - Likely to depict tech-savvy, able-bodied individuals with high purchasing power.

Source: Authors' elaboration

3.2. Results and Discussion

After submitting the questions to the different generative AI platforms, the responses were analyzed and compared. The results are presented according to the dimensions examined.

3.2.1 Economic-Geographical Bias

Overall, the AIs correctly identified various mobility stakeholders, reflecting a sense of inclusiveness by mentioning not only companies but also society and government. However, there was no consensus among platforms regarding which actors were included, nor a shared classification framework. The logic appeared to follow sustainability criteria, mostly limited to electric vehicles (EVs).

Some actors were included or omitted depending on the platform. For example, only Gemini mentioned universities, while only DeepSeek referred to companies focused solely on autonomous vehicles. Notably, DeepSeek excluded society as a key actor, potentially indicating bias. These differences may reflect each model's institutional origin. Gemini, developed by Google, is closely tied to academic and research networks, possibly explaining the inclusion of universities. DeepSeek may omit societal actors due to the lower civic emphasis within China's political model.

Regarding countries and cities, our findings align with Li and Sinnamon (2024), as both Gemini and ChatGPT focused on dominant economies such as the United States, China, Germany, Japan, South Korea, and the United Kingdom. DeepSeek also included Israel and Singapore, while ChatGPT briefly mentioned the United Arab Emirates. At the city level, ChatGPT was the most limited, listing only cities from those same countries. In contrast, Gemini and DeepSeek provided more varied examples. Gemini cited Abu Dhabi, Dubai, Rotterdam, and Albertslund, while DeepSeek mentioned cities in Canada and Sweden.

These results overlook several countries that play a critical role in the development of New Mobility, including Italy, Spain, Portugal, India, Brazil, Mexico, France, and Turkey. These countries are essential in both current strategies and future scenarios (Lampón et al., 2024b). As Hensher et al. (2020) emphasize, an inclusive assessment of future mobility must account for territorial diversity, including transitioning or intermediate regions. None of the AIs addressed this adequately.

Most AIs portrayed the race for autonomous driving as centred on the United States, Germany, and China. However, this view neglects strategic alliances that shape the sector. Toyota leads key projects like Woven City in Japan and collaborates with firms such as Pony.ai. Similarly, Volkswagen has partnered with Mobileye in Israel. These examples show a tendency of AIs to prioritise dominant powers while ignoring broader industry dynamics (Pérez-Moure et al., 2025a; Sawhney, 2022; Zhang and Kamargianni, 2022).

When asked about leading initiatives, AIs gave structurally diverse but thematically similar responses. Cities such as Barcelona and Paris were linked to micromobility, Helsinki and Vienna to MaaS, and Milan and Bogotá to regulation and planning. Yet, all AIs showed a limited understanding of MaaS, focusing mainly on intermodality or shared mobility, without aligning with recent academic definitions. They also omitted key concepts like urban or inclusive mobility, despite their importance in literature (Lyons et al., 2020; Hensher et al., 2020; Pangbourne et al., 2020). Moreover, none highlighted user data, a core component in current mobility models (Pérez-Moure et al., 2023).

3.2.2 Business Model Bias

In this case, all three AIs identified the same initiatives as the most profitable business models in mobility. This represents a significant limitation, as many other business models have been overshadowed or directly contradict existing academic research (Athanasopoulou et al., 2019). One example is car-sharing platforms, which, despite being highly profitable, currently face a saturated market and significant barriers to entry—even for OEMs (Pérez-Moure et al., 2024a). The same can be said for charging infrastructure and electric vehicles, which, except in China, still do not represent fully consolidated opportunities. Furthermore, although ChatGPT did not explicitly highlight it, the other AIs did recognize data monetization and subscription-based models as the most profitable—an assessment that does align with recent studies. In other words, mobility companies are indeed commercializing their customers' data.

On the other hand, only DeepSeek mentioned alternative or niche business models such as air mobility. Most of the models emphasized by the three AIs—such as logistics, B2B autonomous vehicles, or car-sharing—focus mainly on product efficiency, rather than on sustainability or social dimensions. This confirms hypothesis H2 and aligns with other authors who argue that AI tends to prioritize business models rooted in the principles of Industry 4.0 rather than those of Industry 5.0 (Huang et al., 2022; Deguchi et al., 2020). Moreover, the results not only confirm this hypothesis but also suggest that AI focuses on business models that prioritize short-term efficiency and profitability, while overlooking those based on sustainability, inclusiveness, or rural mobility. Additionally, key features of future business models—such as servitization and personalization (Pérez-Moure et al., 2024a)—are largely absent, possibly once again due to the lack of human-centered logic in the systems.

Finally, regarding the use of data by companies, all three AIs agreed that data are used both internally and externally. However, there is a notable difference in focus between ChatGPT and Gemini on one side, and DeepSeek on the other—likely due to regional policy influences. While the first two AIs stated that data are used to increase profitability—for example, by offering personalized services, dynamic pricing, or customized route suggestions—DeepSeek emphasized data use oriented towards the user. This includes increasing battery life, enhancing connectivity with the city, optimizing fleet performance, or even improving insurance efficiency.

3.2.3 Representation Bias

Regarding representation bias, the results are varied. On the one hand, it is true that the AIs identified elderly individuals and people with limited mobility as among the groups that could benefit most from New Mobility. However, neither ChatGPT nor Gemini considered peri-urban residents. All three AIs highlighted the following groups as the main beneficiaries: urban residents, younger generations, environmentally conscious consumers, cost-sensitive users, and—paradoxically—tourists. This presents some contradictions: for example, residents are expected to benefit from cleaner, less stressful, and less congested cities, yet the promotion of tourism through increased multimodal travel could, in fact, negatively impact on those very same residents.

Moreover, none of the AIs mentioned low-income populations or rural communities—groups that are central to current debates on inclusive mobility. Nor did they mention women, who could benefit from safer last-mile transport options such as autonomous vehicles. Furthermore, the initiatives suggested by the AIs have all focused on autonomous or electric vehicles from a product-efficiency perspective, without considering alternative approaches—such as the business model being developed by Toyota to deliver medical services or food via autonomous vehicles. Interestingly, DeepSeek stated that rural areas and low-income populations would benefit the least from New Mobility, which contradicts findings in previous research. This aligns with earlier studies that highlight the representation bias of AI and its alignment with the logic of Industry 4.0.

Additionally, to confirm this representation bias, each AI was asked to generate specific images[1].

Following the request to generate images, it became clear—consistent with the findings of authors such as Stahl & Eke (2024)—that AI systems exhibit significant forms of exclusion. Regarding the representation of cities, the images did not reflect the principles of New Mobility. In fact, the only noticeable differences were an increase in the number of roads and the size of buildings, along with more green areas. Rural elements were not included, and overall, the generated cities could be understood as predominantly Western, based on Western models, omitting informal or diverse urban contexts. However, what was expected was the depiction of a connected or smart city, which was not the case.

As for the people shown using New Mobility systems, important exclusion biases were observed. One of the most evident was gender bias, as all the generated individuals were men. In addition, they were all middle-aged, employed, and of a certain purchasing power. This indicates the presence of both age bias and class bias. Finally, regarding ethnicity, in almost all the cases, the generated were white Western men, with very few representations of other ethnic groups. Therefore, the exclusion of key social groups based on age, ethnicity, gender, purchasing power, or geographic origin is confirmed. These patterns are consistent with previous studies such as Zhou et al. (2024) and Sadeghiani (2024).

In addition, our research has highlighted other representational gaps, including the omission of individuals with limited mobility, people from lower income groups, and rural populations. Moreover, the cities generated clearly reflected a U.S.-influenced urban model. It is also noteworthy that, while previous textual responses from the AIs had mentioned a variety of business models, in this case such models were almost entirely omitted—except for micromobility and autonomous mobility.

4. IMPLICATIONS AND CONCLUSIONS

The analysis inidicates notable biases in AI responses, particularly regarding representation and the exclusion of certain groups. Biases and omissions also emerged in the treatment of business models, regions, and industries, with user-centred and sustainability-focused approaches often overlooked. AI systems failed to reflect Industry 5.0 principles or the broader socio-political context of mobility, frequently omitting key countries. While some differences were observed among the three platforms, none was free of bias. DeepSeek provided the most balanced responses overall, although it also showed limitations, especially in areas such as data policy.

4.1 Theoretical Implications

This research presents important theoretical implications, not only at a conceptual level but also methodologically. On the one hand, considering the biases identified, the study has demonstrated the relevance of introducing AI and ethics as Dynamic Capabilities. This is because the use of AI can create a sustainable competitive advantage over time, as well as streamline processes and generate value when used correctly, allowing companies to easily present new proposals, identify investment opportunities, or develop new projects. Furthermore, ethics also becomes essential, as through improvement and change, it can alter a firm's competitive position in the short term while establishing long-term advantages in a world where data management is fundamental.

In addition, the use of AI may affect which Dynamic Capabilities are activated or inhibited, since depending on the questions asked, the information retrieved, and the AI's own bias, it may favor the activation of those capabilities that are explicitly mentioned and oriented toward immediate benefits, rather than those focused on long-term competitive advantage. Therefore, although AI can function as a Dynamic Capability in itself, it may also act as a barrier to the proper development of truly strategic capabilities.

Regarding the impact of AI on New Mobility or on Industry 5.0 itself, the research has demonstrated that AI exhibits bias, which may have significant consequences in the way future narratives are shaped. This influence is particularly relevant in the context of mobility, where such biases could reinforce existing inequalities and distort the direction of innovation and policy development. Although this issue might initially appear to be merely a technical or practical limitation, it in fact goes much further: it reflects a structural dimension with deep organizational, political, and social implications. Therefore, AI possesses the capacity to shape how New Mobility evolves by downplaying or even disregarding its fundamental principles, such as inclusion and accessibility. Moreover, AI tends to overlook the relevance of urban policies and real-world contexts, which are essential to the equitable and sustainable development of mobility systems. As a result, its use may contribute to the reproduction of exclusionary frameworks, particularly if these biases are not recognized and addressed through critical, ethical, and context-aware approaches.

On the other hand, a new methodology has been implemented in which AI is used as the focus of study, following a hybrid approach that combines elements of experiment, case study, and in-depth interviews. While this methodology has proven functional, it also presents limitations similar to those of qualitative approaches. In this sense, future studies aiming to use AI as an object of analysis are advised to formulate questions in several languages, replicate the study multiple times — as it is often carried out only once — and incorporate as many AIs as possible, following the case study principle (no fewer than two and no more than five).

Finally, although AI is widely accessible and used by a large part of the population, this does not necessarily imply real impact, contrary to what is often claimed. That is, while access to AI may be open, it does not guarantee real inclusion in the representations generated or in the resulting business models. In this regard, literature points out that the user-AI relationship is not reciprocal, which constitutes a serious flaw and leads to the continued underrepresentation of vulnerable groups — even when they are the ones using these tools. Thus, the notion of technological democratization often reflects a simplistic view that focuses solely on access and not on impact. Moreover, no substantial differences were found among the AIs analyzed, suggesting deficient or selective training by the developing companies.

4.2 Practical Implications

This chapter presents significant implications for companies, public actors, and society at large. The research has shown that AI is far from neutral and presents notable biases.

4.2.1 Implications for Firms

AI has limited the business models and actors it mentions, prioritizing those that offer immediate returns while ignoring a wide range of other relevant factors. Therefore, companies should use AI appropriately; otherwise, they may miss opportunities, conduct flawed analyses, adopt short-term perspectives, or fail to align with the current objectives of society and governments.

In contrast, when used correctly, AI can enhance companies' Dynamic Capabilities, allowing them to improve quickly in the marketplace, identify hidden opportunities, or access specific knowledge in a rapid and efficient manner. In other words, although AI may have a dark side, its impact will ultimately depend on how it is used.

It is recommended that companies provide training and educate their employees on the proper use of AI to take full advantage of its potential. One possible strategy to mitigate AI bias—and thus avoid missing opportunities or neglecting specific market segments—would be to use multiple AIs or implement internal best-practice protocols for AI usage within the company to minimize impact. Overall, a systematic evaluation protocol for AI outputs should be established as part of the decision-making process. AI should be treated like any other employee—subject to being overruled or questioned by other parts of the organization.

4.2.2 Implications for Government

Governments may see their public policies limited if generative AI is used in decision-making processes, as this could perpetuate existing issues and increase the social divide between different groups. For instance, rural mobility has not been highlighted by the AIs analyzed, which suggests that relying on AI for policymaking could further deepen the divide between urban areas and rural environments. In this regard, it is recommended that all available options be thoroughly evaluated and that governments always consult genuine experts before implementing any measures.

Furthermore, new legislation should be developed concerning data usage and AI training, alongside the creation of ethics observatories for AI. Lastly, governments bear the responsibility of educating the public on the importance of digital literacy, ensuring that the population is aware of the ethical and practical implications associated with the use of AI.

4.2.3 Implications for Society

From a societal perspective, it is essential to be aware of the ethical dimension of AI and how it, along with mobility systems, uses personal data and the consequences this entails. While ChatGPT and Gemini have been more transparent about how data is used, DeepSeek has not demonstrated the same level of clarity, potentially placing users at risk of exposing sensitive information unknowingly.

Of course, as long as the data is anonymized and used to improve social welfare, there should be no major concerns. However, current mobility companies are using data to develop new products and services and, in general, to gain such deep insights into users that they can deliver highly individualized offers. Therefore, society must use AI with full awareness of the ethical frameworks and data practices behind it—just as companies and governments must do.

4.2.4 Implications for AI Developers and Academia

This situation reveals a deeper issue: the disconnect between AI systems and academic knowledge. In all cases analysed, the AIs made classification errors or omitted information that has been thoroughly addressed in the literature. This includes misclassifying business models, failing to identify key actors in New Mobility, and overlooking representational bias. These findings highlight the need to ground AI training in high-quality, peer-reviewed research.

Bridging the gap between academia and AI development could resolve many of the previously identified issues. AI should be trained to reflect diverse social realities, including differences in age, ethnicity, gender identity, income levels, and cultural context, even when users do not specify them explicitly.

Developers and system managers play a critical role in this process, not only for companies but for society more broadly. Teams should be multidisciplinary and inclusive, incorporating ethical audits and human feedback mechanisms to address challenges that go beyond programming. Training should also integrate a wide range of cultural, linguistic, and value-based perspectives.

These challenges pose serious risks. The way AI is trained today will influence how society functions tomorrow. As AI systems become more rigid and logic-driven, they may promote inflexible attitudes in both companies and individuals. This threatens to undermine the human-centric vision of Industry 5.0. If ethical and inclusive principles are not prioritised, AI could contribute to a more dehumanised future. Ultimately, the design, training, and use of AI will shape not only how we move, but how we relate to one another as a society.

REFERENCES

Athanasopoulou, A., de Reuver, M., Nikou, S., & Bouwman, H. (2019). What technology enabled services impact business models in the automotive industry? An exploratory study. *Futures*, *109*, 73–83. DOI: 10.1016/j.futures.2019.04.001

Barari, M., Ferm, C. L. E., Quach, S., Thaichon, P., & Ngo, L. (2024). The dark side of artificial intelligence in marketing: Meta-analytics review. *Marketing Intelligence & Planning*, *42*(7), 1234–1256. DOI: 10.1108/MIP-09-2023-0494

Belanche, D., Belk, R. W., Casaló, L. V., & Flavián, C. (2024). The dark side of artificial intelligence in services. *Service Industries Journal*, *44*(3–4), 149–172. DOI: 10.1080/02642069.2024.2305451

Bender, E. M., Gebru, T., McMillan-Major, A., & Shmitchell, S. (2021). On the dangers of stochastic parrots: can language models be too big? *FAccT '21: Proceedings of the 2021 ACM Conference on Fairness, Accountability, and Transparency*, 610–623. DOI: 10.1145/3442188.3445922

Cabanelas, P., Parkhurst, G., Thomopoulos, N., & Lampón, J. F. (2023). A dynamic capability evaluation of emerging business models for new mobility. *Research in Transportation Business & Management*, *100964*, 100964. Advance online publication. DOI: 10.1016/j.rtbm.2023.100964

Ceurstemont, S. (2025). Controlling AI's growing energy needs. *Communications of the ACM*, *68*(3), 15–17. DOI: 10.1145/3703788

Chiu, T. K. F. (2023). The impact of Generative AI (GenAI) on practices, policies and research direction in education: A case of ChatGPT and Midjourney. *Interactive Learning Environments*, *32*(10), 6187–6203. DOI: 10.1080/10494820.2023.2253861

Coccia, M. (2010). Democratization is the driving force for technological and economic change. *Technological Forecasting and Social Change*, *77*(2), 248–264. DOI: 10.1016/j.techfore.2009.06.007

Coeckelbergh, M. (2024). *Why AI Undermines Democracy and What To Do about It*. Polity Press.

Csaszar, F. A., Ketkar, H., & Kim, H. (2024). Artificial Intelligence and Strategic Decision-Making: Evidence from Entrepreneurs and Investors. *Strategy Science*, *9*(4), 322–345. Advance online publication. DOI: 10.1287/stsc.2024.0190

Deguchi, A., Hirai, C., Matsuoka, H., Nakano, T., Oshima, K., Tai, M., & Tani, S. (2020). *What is Society 5.0?* En Society., DOI: 10.1007/978-981-15-2989-4_1

Del Giudice, M., Scuotto, V., & Papa, A. (2023). Knowledge Management and AI in Society 5.0. https://doi.org/DOI: 10.4324/9781003258056

Doron, G., Genway, S., Roberts, M., & Jasti, S. (2024). Generative AI: Driving productivity and scientific breakthroughs in pharmaceutical R&D. *Drug Discovery Today, 104272*. Advance online publication. DOI: 10.1016/j.drudis.2024.104272 PMID: 39675517

Ferigotti, C. M. S., da Cunha, S. K., & dos Santos, J. S. (2020). Dynamic capabilities and business model in the transition to sustainability: The case of Bosch/Curitiba-Brazil. *International Business, Trade and Institutional Sustainability*, 81-95. https://doi.org/DOI: 10.1007/978-3-030-26759-9_5

Floridi, L. (2023). AI as Agency Without Intelligence: On ChatGPT, Large Language Models, and Other Generative Models. *Philosophy & Technology*, *36*(1), 15. Advance online publication. DOI: 10.1007/s13347-023-00621-y

Frey, C. B., & Osborne, M. (2013). The Future of employment: How susceptible are jobs to computerisation? https://www.oxfordmartin.ox.ac.uk/publications/the-future-of-employment

Fukuta, Y., Murata, K., & Orito, Y. (2020). Perceived Risk and Desired Protection: Towards A Comprehensive Understanding of Data Sensitivity. In Societal Challenges in the Smart Society (pp. 573-586). Universidad de La Rioja.

George, G., Lakhani, K. R., & Puranam, P. (2020). What has changed? The impact of Covid pandemic on the technology and innovation management research agenda. *Journal of Management Studies*, *57*(8), 1754–1758. DOI: 10.1111/joms.12634

Ghobakhloo, M., Fathi, M., Iranmanesh, M., Vilkas, M., Grybauskas, A., & Amran, A. (2024). Generative artificial intelligence in manufacturing: Opportunities for actualizing Industry 5.0 sustainability goals. *Journal of Manufacturing Technology Management*, *35*(9), 94–121. DOI: 10.1108/JMTM-12-2023-0530

Ghosh, S. K., Hughes, M., Hodgkinson, I. R., & Hughes, P. (2022). Digital transformation of industrial businesses: A dynamic capability approach. *Technovation*, *113*, 102414. DOI: 10.1016/j.technovation.2021.102414

Gschwendtner, C., Sinsel, S. R., & Stephan, A. (2021). Vehicle-to-X (V2X) implementation: An overview of predominate trial configurations and technical, social and regulatory challenges. *Renewable & Sustainable Energy Reviews*, *145*, 110977. DOI: 10.1016/j.rser.2021.110977

Hoover, S., & Lee, L. (2015). Democratization and Disintermediation: Disruptive Technologies and the Future of Making Things. *Research Technology Management*, *58*(6), 31–37. DOI: 10.5437/08956308X5806069

Huang, S., Wang, B., Li, X., Zheng, P., Mourtzis, D., & Wang, L. (2022). Industry 5.0 and Society 5.0—Comparison, complementation and co-evolution. *Journal of Manufacturing Systems*, *64*, 424–428. DOI: 10.1016/j.jmsy.2022.07.010

Kaiser, B. (2019). *Targeted: My Inside Story of Cambridge Analytica and How Trump, Brexit and Facebook Broke Democracy*. HarperCollins.

Kassens-Noor, E., Siegel, J., & Decaminada, T. (2021). Choosing Ethics Over Morals: A Possible Determinant to Embracing Artificial Intelligence in Future Urban Mobility. *Frontiers In Sustainable Cities*, *3*, 723475. Advance online publication. DOI: 10.3389/frsc.2021.723475

Keskar, A. (2019). Exploring business models for software-defined vehicles: Subscription-based paradigms and their impact on automotive innovation and consumer adoption. *World Journal of Research and Review*, *1*(2), 61–77. DOI: 10.30574/wjarr.2019.1.2.0004

Lampón, J. F., Carballo-Cruz, F., & Velando-Rodríguez, M. (2024a). The irruption of autonomous and connected vehicle technologies and the repositioning of the periphery in the European automotive industry. *Kybernetes*. Advance online publication. DOI: 10.1108/K-02-2024-0447

Lampón, J. F., & Muñoz-Dueñas, P. (2023). Are sustainable mobility firms reshaping the traditional relationships in the automotive industry value Chain? *Journal of Cleaner Production*, *413*, 137522. DOI: 10.1016/j.jclepro.2023.137522

Lampón, J. F., Pérez-Moure, H., Carballo-Cruz, F., & Velando-Rodríguez, M. E. (2024b). New mobility technologies and regional status in the automotive industry value chain: The case of Spain and Portugal. *Technology in Society*, *78*, 102624. DOI: 10.1016/j.techsoc.2024.102624

Larson, J., Mattu, S., Kirchner, L., & Angwin, J. (2016). How we analyzed the COMPAS recidivism algorithm. ProPublica, 23 May. https://www.propublica.org/article/how-we-analyzed-the-compas-recidivism-algorithm

Leng, J., Zhu, X., Huang, Z., Li, X., Zheng, P., Zhou, X., Mourtzis, D., Wang, B., Qi, Q., Shao, H., Wan, J., Chen, X., Wang, L., & Liu, Q. (2024). Unlocking the power of industrial artificial intelligence towards Industry 5.0: Insights, pathways, and challenges. *Journal of Manufacturing Systems*, *73*, 349–363. DOI: 10.1016/j.jmsy.2024.02.010

Leonard-Barton, D. (1992). Core capabilities and core rigidities: A paradox in managing new product development. *Strategic Management Journal, 13*(S1), 111–125. DOI: 10.1002/smj.4250131009

Li, M., Yin, D., Qiu, H., & Bai, B. (2021). A systematic review of AI technology-based service encounters: Implications for hospitality and tourism operations. *International Journal of Hospitality Management, 95*, 102930. DOI: 10.1016/j.ijhm.2021.102930

Lin, Y., Mistree, F., Allen, K. J., Tsui, K., & Chen, P. C. V. (2004). A Sequential Exploratory Experimental Design Method: Development of Appropriate Empirical Models in Design. *International Design Engineering Technical Conferences in Computers and Information in Engineering Conference, DETC2004-57527*, 1021-1035. https://doi.org/DOI: 10.1115/DETC2004-57527

Liu, P., Lai, Y., & Liu, D. (2024). Artificial intelligence research in organizations: A bibliometric approach. *Cogent Business & Management, 11*(1), 2408439. Advance online publication. DOI: 10.1080/23311975.2024.2408439

Liu, Y., Guo, M., Han, Z., Gavurova, B., Bresciani, S., & Wang, T. (2023). Effects of digital orientation on organizational resilience: A dynamic capabilities perspective. *Journal of Manufacturing Technology Management, 35*(2), 268–290. DOI: 10.1108/JMTM-06-2023-0224

Loureiro, A. (2018). There is a fourth industrial revolution: The digital revolution. *Worldwide Hospitality and Tourism Themes, 10*(6), 740–744. DOI: 10.1108/WHATT-07-2018-0044

Ma, H., Qian, C., Li, L., Qu, X., & Ran, B. (2025). Risk quantification based Adaptive Cruise control and its application in approaching behavior at signalized intersections. *Accident; Analysis and Prevention, 212*, 107939. DOI: 10.1016/j.aap.2025.107939 PMID: 39879919

Mannuru, N. R., Shahriar, S., Teel, Z. A., Wang, T., Lund, B. D., Tijani, S., Pohboon, C. O., Agbaji, D., Alhassan, J., Galley, J., Kousari, R., Ogbadu-Oladapo, L., Saurav, S. K., Srivastava, A., Tummuru, S. P., Uppala, S., & Vaidya, P. (2023). Artificial intelligence in developing countries: The impact of generative artificial intelligence (AI) technologies for development. *Information Development, 0*(0), 02666669231200628. Advance online publication. DOI: 10.1177/02666669231200628

Meyer, C. B. (2001). A Case in Case Study Methodology. *Field Methods, 13*(4), 329–352. DOI: 10.1177/1525822X0101300402

Mikalef, P., Conboy, K., & Krogstie, J. (2021). Artificial intelligence as an enabler of B2B marketing: A dynamic capabilities micro-foundations approach. *Industrial Marketing Management*, *98*, 80–92. DOI: 10.1016/j.indmarman.2021.08.003

Mikalef, P., Conboy, K., Lundström, J. E., & Popovič, A. (2022). Thinking responsibly about responsible AI and 'the dark side' of AI. *European Journal of Information Systems*, *31*(3), 257–268. DOI: 10.1080/0960085X.2022.2026621

Moor, J. H. (1985). What is computer ethics? *Metaphilosophy*, *16*(4), 266–275. DOI: 10.1111/j.1467-9973.1985.tb00173.x

Murata, K. (2022). Post-truth: Organisational social responsibility in an AI-driven society. In Bounfour, A. (Ed.), *Platforms and Artificial Intelligence: The Next Generation of Competences* (pp. 269–281). Springer., DOI: 10.1007/978-3-030-90192-9_13

Murata, K., & Orito, Y. (2020). Rethinking the concept of the right to information privacy: a Japanese perspective. In Routledge eBooks (pp. 215-227). https://doi.org/ DOI: 10.4324/9781003075011-16

Murtaza, A. A., Saher, A., Zafar, M. H., Moosavi, S. K. R., Aftab, M. F., & Sanfilippo, F. (2024). Paradigm Shift for Predictive Maintenance and Condition Monitoring from Industry 4.0 to Industry 5.0: A Systematic Review, Challenges and Case Study. *Results in Engineering*, *102935*, 102935. Advance online publication. DOI: 10.1016/j.rineng.2024.102935

Nguyen, C. T. (2018). Echo chambers and epistemic bubbles. *Episteme (Edinburgh)*, *17*(2), 141–161. DOI: 10.1017/epi.2018.32

Nissenbaum, H. (1996). Accountability in a computerized society. *Science and Engineering Ethics*, *2*(1), 25–42. DOI: 10.1007/BF02639315

Okuda, T., & Shoda, S. (2018). AI-based Chatbot Service for Financial Industry. *Fujitsu Scientific and Technical Journal*, *54*(2), 4–8.

Orito, Y., Fukuta, Y., & Murata, K. (2014). *I Will Continue to Use This Nonetheless: Social Media Survive Users' Privacy Concerns.* International Journal Of Virtual Worlds And Human Computer Interaction., DOI: 10.11159/vwhci.2014.010

Palma, M. (2021). Artificial intelligence enhances the sex industry. Predict, 27 February. https://medium.com/predict/artificial-intelligence-enhances-the-sex-industry-7294cf80dd16

Pariser, E. (2011). *The Filter Bubble: What the Internet Is Hiding from You.* Penguin Press.

Pérez-Moure, H., Lampón, J. F., & Cabanelas, P. (2024a). Mobility business models toward a digital tomorrow: Challenges for automotive manufacturers. *Futures, 156*, 103309. DOI: 10.1016/j.futures.2023.103309

Pérez-Moure, H., Lampón, J. F., & Cabanelas, P. (2024b). Collective Intelligence Approach for New Mobility. In Advances in business information systems and analytics book series, 149-174. https://doi.org/DOI: 10.4018/979-8-3693-7272-2.ch006

Pérez-Moure, H., Lampón, J. F., Velando-Rodriguez, M., & Rodríguez-Comesaña, L. (2023). Revolutionizing the road: How sustainable, autonomous, and connected vehicles are changing digital mobility business models. *European Research on Management and Business Economics, 29*(3), 100230. DOI: 10.1016/j.iedeen.2023.100230

Sawhney, N. (2022). Contestations in urban mobility: Rights, risks, and responsibilities for Urban AI. *AI & Society, 38*(3), 1083–1098. DOI: 10.1007/s00146-022-01502-2

Sjödin, D., Parida, V., & Kohtamäki, M. (2023). Artificial intelligence enabling circular business model innovation in digital servitization: Conceptualizing dynamic capabilities, AI capacities, business models and effects. *Technological Forecasting and Social Change, 197*, 122903. DOI: 10.1016/j.techfore.2023.122903

Stahl, B. C. (2025). Locating the Ethics of ChatGPT—Ethical Issues as Affordances in AI Ecosystems. *Information (Basel), 16*(2), 104. DOI: 10.3390/info16020104

Stahl, B. C., & Eke, D. (2024). The ethics of ChatGPT – Exploring the ethical issues of an emerging technology. *International Journal of Information Management, 74*, 102700. DOI: 10.1016/j.ijinfomgt.2023.102700

Sullivan, Y., & Wamba, F. S. (2024). Artificial intelligence and adaptive response to market changes: A strategy to enhance firm performance and innovation. *Journal of Business Research, 174*, 114500. DOI: 10.1016/j.jbusres.2024.114500

Taeihagh, A. (2025). Governance of Generative AI. *Policy and Society, 44*(1), 1–22. Advance online publication. DOI: 10.1093/polsoc/puaf001

Teece, D. (2014). A dynamic capabilities-based entrepreneurial theory of the multinational enterprise. *Journal of International Business Studies, 45*(1), 8–37. DOI: 10.1057/jibs.2013.54

Teece, D. (2020). Hand in glove: Open innovation and the dynamic capabilities framework. *Strategic Management Review, 1*(2), 233–253. DOI: 10.1561/111.00000010

Teece, D. J., & Linden, G. (2017). Business models, value capture, and the digital enterprise. *J Org Design, 6*(1), 8. DOI: 10.1186/s41469-017-0018-x

Trager, R. F., & Luca, L. M. (2022). Killer robots are here—And we need to regulate them. *Foreign Policy*, *11*(May). https://foreignpolicy.com/2022/05/11/killer-robots-lethal-autonomous-weapons-systems-ukraine-libya-regulation/

Xu, X., Lu, Y., Vogel-Heuser, B., & Wang, L. (2021). Industry 4.0 and Industry 5.0—Inception, conception and perception. *Journal of Manufacturing Systems*, *61*, 530–535. DOI: 10.1016/j.jmsy.2021.10.006

Zhang, M. (2015). Google Photos tags two African-Americans as gorillas through facial recognition software. *Forbes*, *1*(July). https://www.forbes.com/sites/mzhang/2015/07/01/google-photos-tags-two-african-americans-as-gorillas-through-facial-recognition-software/

Zhang, Y., & Kamargianni, M. (2022). A review on the factors influencing the adoption of new mobility technologies and services: Autonomous vehicle, drone, micromobility and mobility as a service. *Transport Reviews*, *43*(3), 407–429. DOI: 10.1080/01441647.2022.2119297

Zhou, M., Abhishek, V., Derdenger, T., Kim, J., & Srinivasan, K. (2024). Bias in Generative AI. arXiv (Cornell University). https://doi.org//arxiv.2403.02726DOI: 10.48550

ENDNOTE

1 In this case, DeepSeek's AI is continued under development and therefore the generated images haven't enough quality for being included in the research, and the other Chinese AI have geographical restrictions.</unknown>

Chapter 10

The Effect of Citizen Participation on the Culture of Peace and Its Relationship With Social Innovation: An Analysis of the Communities of the ZMG

César Omar Mora-Pérez
https://orcid.org/0000-0002-3917-1144
University of Guadalajara, Mexico

Gustavo Vaca Medina
https://orcid.org/0000-0001-7823-3582
University of Guadalajara, Mexico

Jesús Vaca Medina
https://orcid.org/0000-0002-2860-109X
University of Guadalajara, Mexico

ABSTRACT

This document examines the impact of citizen participation on the culture of peace and its connection to social innovation. These three linked elements empower society to tackle environmental issues actively, focusing on peace and coexistence. A quantitative methodology was employed, involving the distribution of a collection instrument to 230 individuals across 10 communities in the metropolitan area of

DOI: 10.4018/979-8-3373-2685-6.ch010

Copyright © 2026, IGI Global Scientific Publishing. Copying or distributing in print or electronic forms without written permission of IGI Global Scientific Publishing is prohibited.

Guadalajara. The results, which underscore the crucial role of citizen participation in the culture of peace and the significant relationship between these elements and social innovation, are of paramount importance. They not only highlight the potential impact of this research on social innovation and peace-building but also inspire optimism for the future.

INTRODUCTION

The concept of a culture of peace is becoming increasingly important today. It must be understood as a way of thinking and acting that focuses on preventing violence, promoting peaceful conflict resolution, and fostering equality. When people and communities adopt a culture of peace, they are less likely to resort to violence and more open to working together to resolve conflicts in a peaceful manner. This collective effort results in a significant reduction in violence and an improvement in the quality of life for all parties involved.

Promoting a culture of peace is a challenge that demands the active participation of all sectors of society. Citizen participation, understood as the active involvement of individuals in decision-making and the implementation of public policies, is not just beneficial but necessary in building and maintaining a culture of peace (Putnam, 2000). Existing literature suggests that citizen participation can strengthen democratic legitimacy, increase trust in institutions, and foster social cohesion —essential elements for a culture of peace (Fung, 2006; Lederach, 1997). However, it has also been noted that citizen participation is not only beneficial but also necessary when implemented inclusively and equitably (Cornwall, 2008). This highlights the importance and responsibility of each individual in fostering a culture of peace.

Analyzing this relationship is relevant both theoretically and pragmatically. Theoretically, it contributes to a deeper understanding of the processes and mechanisms that underpin sustainable peace. Literature in this field has highlighted the importance of citizen participation in building peaceful societies, but there is a need for empirical studies that examine these relationships in different contexts and using various methods (Harris, 2009; Galtung, 1996). Mora et al. (2024) establish that creating spaces that allow civil society participation in public decision-making guarantees constant monitoring of public exercise. Pragmatically, it enables the identification of the most influential citizen participation mechanisms, and understanding the conditions that favor them can help policymakers, civil society organizations, and community actors design and implement more effective strategies to promote a culture of peace (Wampler, 2012; Baiocchi & Ganuza, 2014). Furthermore, in a global context where violence and conflict continue to be prevalent, understanding how citizen participation can contribute to peace is of utmost importance for formulating local and international intervention strategies (Tarrow, 2005).

Social innovation is another element that underlies this relationship. It is defined as new ideas that work to satisfy social needs (Mulgan, 2006). These ideas can manifest in products, services, organizational models, or new forms of cooperation and governance. Unlike technological or market innovations, social innovation places a strong emphasis on social objectives, seeking solutions to problems such as poverty, social exclusion, inequality, and environmental sustainability (Phills et al., 2008).

In this context, social innovation emerges as a critical element that can enhance the positive effects of citizen participation in the culture of peace by focusing on the development of new ideas, concepts, and strategies that address social needs and improve the well-being of communities, through collaborative and participatory approaches (Murray et al., 2010).

However, although the importance of citizen participation in the theory and practice of peacebuilding has been widely recognized, there is still a lack of clear understanding of how and to what extent this participation effectively contributes to the culture of peace. Therefore, it is essential to investigate how the different mechanisms of citizen participation impact the culture of peace and what conditions are necessary for these mechanisms to be effective, triggering guiding approaches to social innovation.

Currently, violence and conflict are a threat to the stability and well-being of people. Therefore, the culture of peace seeks to address these problems with respect, tolerance, and cooperation. In Mexico, particularly in Jalisco, there are high rates of conflict and insecurity; according to the National Urban Public Security Survey (INEGI, 2024), between 62% and 75% of the population perceive an environment of insecurity. However, women feel more insecure than men. Furthermore, 72% and 91% stated that they had had a conflict in their community (in the Guadalajara Metropolitan Area), mainly due to excessive noise, garbage, parking, or domestic animals; between 23% and 50% had consequences such as shouting or insults.

Regarding Jalisco's electoral participation, according to the Electoral and Citizen Participation Institute (IEPC, 2021), the participation rate in the 2021 process was 47.5% for deputies and 47.84% for municipalities. Regarding participation mechanisms, the consultation on the fiscal pact in 2021 had a turnout of only 7% of the electoral roll, well below the 33% required for the result to be binding. Another indicator is the eighth Citizen Perception Survey on Quality of Life of "Jalisco, ¿Cómo Vamos?" (2022), which indicates that 70% of the population has little or no interest in public affairs and politics, only 36% of the population is willing to sign petitions, 25% are willing to share on social networks and only 16% to protest or demonstrate. This indicates the low level of citizen participation in our state.

For this reason, this document proposes to determine the effect of citizen participation in the culture of peace through an analysis of various communities of the Guadalajara Metropolitan Area and to link these results to social innovation. The concepts of culture of peace, citizen participation, and their relationship will be theoretically analyzed, along with the influence of social innovation on these concepts. It is proposed that this document contributes to the debate and academic reflection on the importance of these three elements and their interrelation, promoting citizen participation, a culture of peace, and an approach oriented to social innovation.

The Culture of Peace

The concept of a culture of peace has evolved significantly in recent decades, gaining global relevance as a means of promoting peace and resolving conflicts. UNESCO defines the culture of peace as a set of values, attitudes, and behaviors that reflect respect for life, human dignity, and equality and promote the nonviolent resolution of conflicts (UNESCO, 1999). This approach is based on the idea that peace is not just the absence of conflict but an active state of social justice.

Theoretically, the concept of a culture of peace is linked to various disciplines, including philosophy, sociology, psychology, and education. Authors such as Galtung (1996) defined negative peace as the absence of direct violence, while positive peace refers to social justice, equity, and well-being. For its part, UNESCO (1999) has promoted a comprehensive vision of the culture of peace, emphasizing the importance of education, intercultural dialogue, the promotion of human rights, and the peaceful resolution of conflicts.

Numerous studies have demonstrated that peace education is essential for constructing more just and equitable societies. Studies have explored various dimensions and approaches, particularly how educational practices can contribute to sustainable peace. Cremin and Bevington (2017) explore the role of mediation and conflict resolution in promoting a culture of peace.

Promoting a culture of peace is based on various mechanisms that act in an integrated manner to promote values, attitudes, and behaviors that promote peaceful coexistence and the nonviolent resolution of conflicts. These mechanisms include peace education, mediation and conflict resolution, community participation, inclusive governance, and the role of international organizations.

Education plays a crucial role in a culture of peace based on principles such as respect for human rights, democracy, gender equality, and solidarity. Harris (2009) states that peace education transforms attitudes and behaviors by promoting conflict resolution skills, empathy, and cooperation. Educational programs in various contexts have proven effective in reducing violence, promoting a culture of peace among young people, reducing school violence, and promoting peaceful student relationships (Bar-tal, 2022; Salomon & Nevo, 2002).

In addition to education, community participation is essential for building a culture of peace. Lederach (1997) argues that sustainable peace can only be achieved through the active participation of local communities in peacebuilding processes. Gaventa (2009) argues that participatory processes empower communities, allowing them to influence policies and programs that affect their lives. Participatory budgeting initiatives and community forums exemplify how citizen participation can build a Culture of peace (Cornwall, 2008). A holistic approach that integrates social, economic, and political aspects, empowering individuals and communities to be agents of change and fostering a sense of belonging and shared responsibility.

Mediation and conflict resolution are crucial mechanisms facilitating dialogue between conflicting parties to reach mutually beneficial agreements. Lederach (1997) emphasizes the significance of mediation in fostering sustainable peace, as it addresses the root causes of conflicts and enhances relationships between the parties involved. Training in mediation skills and establishing community-level conflict resolution centers are effective strategies for promoting a culture of peace (Galtung, 1996).

The role of institutions is also fundamental, as governance and social justice are pillars of a culture of peace, by fostering trust in institutions and the rule of law. According to Hegre *et al.* (2001), governance and transparency reduce social tensions and prevent the outbreak of conflicts. Implementing policies that promote gender equality, human rights, and social justice is crucial to building a sustainable culture of peace (Galtung, 1996). For Galtung (1996), positive peace is achieved through equity, inclusion, and justice, reducing the' structural causes of conflicts.

International organizations play a crucial role in promoting a culture of peace. The UN and UNESCO have played vital roles in disseminating peace values and practices globally. We seek to integrate peace and justice into global development through initiatives such as the 2030 Agenda for Sustainable Development. In particular, Sustainable Development Goal 16 promotes peaceful and inclusive societies, access to justice for all, and the building of effective, accountable, and inclusive institutions (UN, 2015). Furthermore, the UNESCO Declaration and Program of Action on a Culture of Peace (1999) establishes a framework for promoting peace through education, international cooperation, and sustainable development.

In the current context, marked by global challenges such as the COVID-19 pandemic, climate change, and armed conflicts, promoting a culture of peace is more relevant than ever. International cooperation and global solidarity are crucial for addressing these challenges and fostering a more peaceful and just world. According to the UN (2020), the global response to the pandemic has demonstrated the importance of cooperation and solidarity in overcoming crises and promoting resilience and peace.

Citizen Participation

Citizen participation is a vital component of modern democracies, promoting greater inclusion and representation in decision-making processes. This approach is defined as the process through which individual and collective citizens exercise their right to influence the formulation, execution, and monitoring of public policies (Gaventa, 2009). This concept has evolved significantly from electoral consultation and participation to active involvement in various forms of participatory governance (Arnstein, 1969).

The theoretical framework of citizen participation is based on several fundamental principles. Firstly, participation is seen as a fundamental human right. The Universal Declaration of Human Rights, adopted in 1948, recognizes all people's right to participate in their country's government, directly or through freely chosen representatives (UN, 1948). This right has been reaffirmed in numerous international treaties and conventions, underscoring the importance of inclusion and participation in democratic processes.

In terms of theories of democracy, citizen participation is crucial for democratic legitimacy. Participatory democracy, defended by authors such as Pateman (1970), argues that direct citizen participation in public affairs strengthens democracy by fostering greater accountability and transparency in governance. This approach improves the quality of political decisions, empowers citizens, and strengthens the social fabric.

Furthermore, citizen participation is essential for effective governance and sustainable development; by implementing participatory processes, governments can better capture citizens' needs and priorities, leading to more effective and equitable policies (Fung, 2006). Participation also fosters a greater sense of ownership and commitment towards the implemented policies, facilitating their implementation and long-term sustainability (Cornwall, 2008).

Citizen participation also has a notable impact on social cohesion and the construction of resilient communities. Through local initiatives and community decision-making, citizens develop a greater sense of belonging and solidarity (Putnam, 2000), thereby improving the community's ability to face collective challenges, such as natural disasters or economic crises.

However, citizen participation has challenges and criticism. Some studies indicate that participatory processes may be biased towards specific groups, excluding minorities and marginalized populations (Cooke & Kothari, 2001). Furthermore, participation can be used as a legitimation tool for decisions that have already been made, rather than genuinely influencing policy (Arnstein, 1969). Therefore, it is crucial to design inclusive and transparent participation mechanisms that guarantee equitable representation of all sectors of society.

The mechanisms of citizen participation have undergone considerable evolution in recent decades, adapting to the sociopolitical transformations of modern societies. These mechanisms are crucial for strengthening democracy, promoting inclusivity, and enhancing the quality of political decisions.

Electoral participation is one of the most traditional and fundamental mechanisms of citizen participation. Through voting, citizens can elect their representatives and express their political preferences. This mechanism is essential for democratic legitimacy and the accountability of rulers (Dahl, 1998). However, electoral participation faces challenges such as apathy and abstentionism, which can undermine the representativeness and quality of democracy (Lijphart, 1997).

Consultation and deliberation processes are another critical mechanism for citizen participation. These processes enable citizens to express their opinions and contribute to the formulation of public policies. Public consultations and forums, such as citizen juries and deliberative assemblies, are examples of how citizens can be involved in decision-making (Fishkin, 2011). These mechanisms promote informed debate and can improve the legitimacy and acceptance of policies (Gastil & Levine, 2005).

Participatory budgets are an innovative form of citizen participation that allows citizens to directly decide how to allocate a portion of the public budget. This mechanism originated in Brazil in the 1980s and has proven effective in promoting transparency, accountability, and social inclusion (Wampler, 2012). Through participatory budgets, citizens can identify and prioritize community projects, thereby strengthening the relationship between the government and its citizens (Baiocchi & Ganuza, 2014).

Public hearings are a mechanism for citizens to evaluate and supervise public policies. At these hearings, citizens can directly present their opinions, complaints, and suggestions to decision-makers. This mechanism promotes transparency and accountability and can influence the modification of policies and programs (Fung, 2006).

Citizen legislative initiatives allow citizens to propose new laws or modify existing ones. This mechanism strengthens direct democracy, allowing citizens' demands to be translated into concrete legislative proposals. Collecting signatures and presenting initiatives to parliaments empower citizens and can lead to significant changes in legislation (Serdült & Welp, 2012).

Digital participation platforms have radically transformed citizen participation mechanisms in the digital era. These platforms allow for broader and more accessible participation, facilitating virtual consultation, debate, and decision-making

(Peixoto & Fox, 2016). Information and communication technologies (ICT) have opened new opportunities for participation, although they also present challenges such as the digital divide and data protection (Chadwick, 2009).

Transnational citizen participation has gained significance in the current context, characterized by globalization and increased interconnection. Citizens and civil society organizations participate in global governance processes, influencing decisions that transcend national borders. Examples of this are the global mobilizations for climate change and human rights, which demonstrate the power of citizen participation at the international level (Tarrow, 2005). Furthermore, civic education and participation training are crucial mechanisms to foster informed and effective citizen participation. Educational programs that teach civic skills and promote civic engagement can strengthen individuals' ability to participate actively in political and community life (Michels & De Graaf, 2010).

Citizen Participation And The Culture Of Peace

Citizen participation plays a crucial role in promoting and sustaining a culture of peace by promoting inclusion, dialogue, cooperation, and social justice. By involving citizens in decision-making and the implementation of public policies, an environment of peace can flourish.

The relationship between citizen participation and the culture of peace has been widely studied and documented in academic literature. This highlights the importance of citizens' active inclusion in decision-making processes and its impact on promoting and sustaining a peaceful society. Putnam (2000) argues that citizen participation is crucial for building social capital, fostering social cohesion, and mitigating community tensions. Putnam argues that when citizens actively engage in community life, they develop networks of trust and reciprocity essential to a culture of peace.

Fung (2006) also highlights the diversity of citizen participation mechanisms and their impact on democratic governance. Fung proposes that participatory mechanisms, such as participatory budgeting and public consultations, not only increase the legitimacy of political decisions but also foster inclusion and equity, contributing to social peace. Empirical studies support this view, demonstrating that well-designed participatory processes can lead to a more equitable distribution of resources and the satisfaction of community needs (Wampler, 2012).

The relationship between citizen participation and the culture of peace has also been explored in the context of peace education. Ian Harris (2009) emphasizes the significance of civic education and training in conflict resolution skills, promoting active and engaged citizenship. Harris argues that educational programs that integrate citizen participation and peace education can transform attitudes and behaviors, promoting values of dialogue, cooperation, and mutual respect —essential components of a culture of peace.

Lederach (1997) highlights the importance of community participation in mediation and conflict resolution processes. Lederach maintains that community participation in conflict resolution is crucial to addressing the roots of conflict and building sustainable relationships, leading to more lasting and acceptable solutions for all parties involved (Lederach, 1997).

Fishkin (2011) examines how deliberative processes enable citizens to express their opinions and engage in informed debates on issues of common interest. Fishkin argues that public deliberation fosters mutual understanding and tolerance, as citizens can listen to and consider different perspectives, contributing to social cohesion and reducing polarization (Fishkin, 2011).

Participatory budgeting, a specific form of citizen participation, has also been widely studied for its impact on social peace. Allegretti and Herzberg (2004) highlight in their study on participatory budgeting in Europe how these processes can empower citizens and improve transparency and accountability in public administration. By allowing citizens to decide on the allocation of public resources, participatory budgeting can contribute to a more equitable distribution of resources and the satisfaction of basic community needs, thus reducing inequalities and preventing conflicts (Allegretti & Herzberg, 2004).

Finally, Peixoto and Fox (2016) highlight that digital platforms can facilitate broader and more diverse participation, allowing citizens to engage in online debates and consultations. Although ICTs present challenges such as the digital divide, their potential to include more citizens in decision-making is significant, thus contributing to social peace (Peixoto & Fox, 2016).

Innovation and Its Relationship With Citizen Participation And The Culture Of Peace

Academic literature has identified several critical dimensions of social innovation. First, there is the aspect of novelty, which involves the creation of original solutions or the novel application of existing solutions to new contexts or problems (Murray et al., 2010). Second, effectiveness refers to the ability of these innovations to produce tangible results and improve social well-being. Third, inclusion and participation highlight that social innovations must involve communities and beneficiaries in their design and implementation to be effective and sustainable (Nicholls & Murdock, 2012).

Prominent examples of social innovation include participatory budgeting, which enables citizens to decide on the allocation of public resources directly. This mechanism has been implemented in various cities worldwide, demonstrating its ability to improve transparency, accountability, and equity in the distribution of resources (Wampler, 2012). Another example is microcredit, popularized by the Grameen Bank in Bangladesh. It has provided millions of people excluded from the traditional banking system access to financing, promoting entrepreneurship, and reducing poverty (Yunus, 2007).

Social innovation theory also connects to complex systems theory, which views social innovations as emerging from dynamic interactions between diverse actors within a social system. This approach emphasizes the significance of networks, cross-sector collaboration, and adaptability in achieving the success of social innovations (Westley et al., 2006).

Putnam (2000) argues that citizen participation strengthens social capital, essential for social cohesion and conflict reduction. Interaction and collaboration between citizens build networks of trust and reciprocity, promoting values of cooperation and mutual understanding that are fundamental to a culture of peace.

Social Inclusion As An Element Of Active Citizenship And The Culture Of Peace In Contexts Of Social Innovation

Social inclusion, understood as the full incorporation of marginalized people and communities into decision-making processes, is both a condition and a result of active citizenship and a culture of peace strengthened through social innovation. In this sense, in contexts where institutions innovate through participatory approaches, it is observed that the effective inclusion of vulnerable groups enhances democratic legitimacy, reinforces social cohesion, and multiplies the impact of the innovations implemented.

Recent literature provides solid evidence of this link. In the case of Europe, it examines how social integration programs for migrants can be successful when based on participatory social innovation approaches, that is, when the communities involved are not only recipients of policies but also active agents in their design and implementation (Cuconato, 2023). These types of experiences, which prioritize inclusive participation, generate not only functional integration but also mutual trust, community resilience, and peaceful relations between diverse social actors. Additionally, the Organization for Economic Cooperation and Development (OECD, 2024) has noted that inclusion-oriented public innovation enables the reconstruction of the “social contract” between governments and citizens. In its study applied to Latin America, the OECD identifies that inclusion should not be conceived as a welfare policy, but as a structural principle that, when integrated into public policies, improves institutional efficiency, transparency, and the equity of results.

Furthermore, participatory tools specifically designed to include disadvantaged populations have proven more effective in promoting civic culture and social peace. For example, citizen assemblies and social innovation laboratories that integrate inclusive deliberative mechanisms (such as participation quotas for vulnerable groups, accessible language, and safe spaces) achieve more sustainable results in terms of social cohesion and political legitimacy (García-Espín, 2023). In these environments, deliberation not only distributes symbolic power but also builds empathy, promotes collective agreements, and reduces social tensions.

Finally, a recent meta-analysis on open social innovation highlights that systemic approaches that combine collaborative governance, technology, and community engagement are only practical if they are anchored in structural inclusion as a guiding principle (Pacheco et al., 2025). This finding is critical, as it demonstrates that innovation without inclusion can generate new inequalities or reinforce existing ones. In contrast, inclusive innovation tends to strengthen the democratic fabric and prevent conflict.

METHODOLOGY

The present study employs a primarily quantitative and exploratory approach, developing a measurement scale based on theoretical elements to investigate the relationship between citizen participation and the culture of peace. The validity and reliability of the instrument were assessed using the Statistical Package for the Social Sciences (SPSS) software. Its application to the target population was carried out personally in March and April 2024 in 10 communities within the Guadalajara Metropolitan Area (comprising Guadalajara, Zapopan, Tlaquepaque, Tonalá, and Tlajomulco), resulting in 230 valid questionnaires. Based on the obtained information, descriptive and inferential analyses were conducted.

The variables that were used were:

Table 1. Variables and indicators to use in research

Variable	Items	Sense	Guy
Culture of peace	12	-	Dependent
Citizen participation	10	+	Independent
Social Innovation	12	-	Complementary

Source: self-made.

The following figure shows the relationships between the analyzed variables:

Figure 1. Variable relationship model

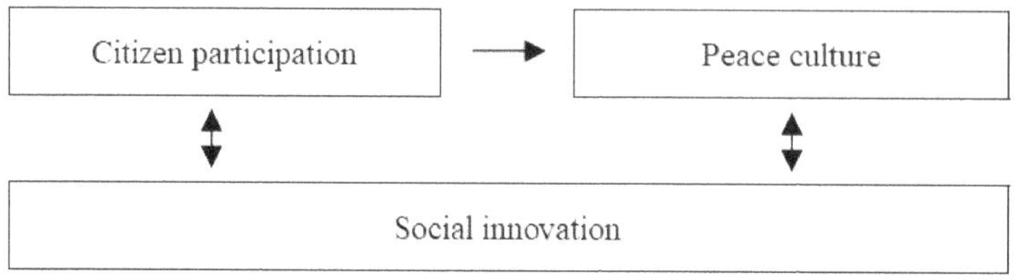

Source: self-made.

Table 2. Research congruence matrix

Research objective	Research question	Variables	Hypothesis
Determine the effect of citizen participation on the culture of peace in ZMG communities and its relationship with social innovation.	What is the effect of citizen participation in the culture of peace? What is the relationship of social innovation with citizen participation and the culture of peace?	Social Innovation Citizen participation Culture of peace	H1: Promoting citizen participation in communities has a positive influence on promoting a culture of peace H2: There is a positive relationship between social innovation, citizen participation, and the culture of peace

Source: self-made.

This research is proposed as another contribution to the academic debate on the effect of citizen participation in the culture of peace and its relationship with social innovation. Once the data structuring phase was completed, the indicators were coded using the SPSS statistical package (Statistical Package for Social Sciences).

To purify the database and detect possible errors in its transcription, descriptive techniques were employed, calculating the frequency distribution of each variable to verify that all variable codes fell within the possible values. The analysis was conducted to determine the effect of the independent variable (citizen participation) on the dependent variable (Culture of peace), as well as the correlation between both variables and the complementary variable (social innovation).

ANALYSIS OF RESULTS

In principle, we analyzed the results with descriptive statistics to verify that all the information had been analyzed. We found all the data for the 230 surveys applied and a Cronbach's Alpha of .928, a KMO of .890, and a significance of .000 throughout the model:

Table 3. Summary of case processing

		N	%
Cases	Valid	230	100.0
	Excluded [a]	0	.0
	Total	230	100.0

a. List elimination based on all variables in the procedure.
Source: elaboration with SPSS data.

Subsequently, an analysis is conducted using the correlation coefficient to examine the relationships between the variables. The results show significant correlations between the variables and in the direction proposed for each one:

Table 4. Correlation Analysis

		Citizen participation	**Culture of peace**
Citizen participation	Pearson correlation	1	.453 **
	Sig. (bilateral)		,000
	N	230	230
Culture of peace	Pearson correlation	.453 **	1
	Sig. (bilateral)	,000	
	N	230	230

**. The correlation is significant at the 0.01 level (two-sided).
Source: elaboration with SPSS data.

Once the previous exercise has been carried out, an analysis will be applied using the following regression model:

Equation 1. Regression model

$$Y' = a + b_1X_1 + b_2X_2$$

The first analysis of the model indicates that the two introduced variables were analyzed:

Table 5. Analysis of Variables

Variables introduced/removed[a]			
Model	**Introduced variables**	**Eliminated variables**	**Method**
1	Citizen participation [b]	.	Introduce

a. Dependent variable: Culture of peace
b. All requested variables entered.
Source: elaboration with SPSS data.

The following table provides information on the regression line's ability to explain the total variation in the dependent variable. As can be seen, the R-squared value is 0.205, indicating that a considerable percentage of the total variation has been explained. Additionally, this model summary indicates whether the variables are relevant to the regression model:

Table 6. Summary of the Regression Model

Model	R	R squared	corrected R-squared	Typical error of the estimate
1	.453 [a]	.205	.202	.69522

a. Predictor variables: (Constant), Citizen participation
Source: own elaboration with SPSS data.

In the table below, the ANOVA results demonstrate that the regression model is statistically significant, at least at the 99% confidence level. Consequently, the null hypothesis is rejected for all estimated parameters equal to zero.

Table 7. ANOVA analysis

ANOVA [a]						
Model		**Sum of squares**	**gl**	**mean square**	**F**	**Next.**
1	Regression	28,477	1	28,477	58,918	·000[b]
	Residual	110,200	228	.483		
	Total	138,678	229			

a. Dependent variable: Culture of peace
b. Predictor variables: (Constant), Citizen participation
Source: own elaboration with SPSS data.

The coefficients of the most significant variables are presented in the following table, based on the results from the previous table. According to the results, all the coefficients of the variable “Citizen Participation” are statistically significant, as the T values (in absolute value) are greater than 1.96. Likewise, the independent variables have significance values less than 0.05, so they are accepted.

Table 8. Analysis of coefficients

Coefficients [a]						
Model		Unstandardized coefficients		Standardized coefficients	t	Next.
		b	Typical error	Beta		
1	(Constant)	2,080	.181		11,525	,000
	Citizen participation	.374	.049	.453	7,676	,000

a. Dependent variable: Culture of peace
Source: elaboration with SPSS data.

The statistical results show that "Citizen participation" positively affects the dependent variable "Culture of peace." This implies that when the different mechanisms of citizen participation are strengthened, the various ways of promoting a culture of peace are also strengthened. Therefore, the first hypothesis is verified. It is essential to note that, although studies have established that the values of the determination coefficients for economic-administrative models should be greater than 60% (Estrada & Vargas-Hernández, 2018), the high sensitivity of the model is taken into consideration, providing a different approach to understanding this relationship.

A final analysis was conducted to determine the relationship between social innovation, citizen participation, and the culture of peace through the correlation coefficient. The results show significant correlations between the variables and the direction proposed for each one.

Table 9. Analysis of correlations between variables

		Citizen participation	Culture of peace	Social Innovation
Citizen participation	Pearson correlation	1	.453 **	.335 **
	Sig. (bilateral)		,000	,000
	N	230	230	230
Culture of peace	Pearson correlation	.453 **	1	.343 **
	Sig. (bilateral)	,000		,000
	N	230	230	230

continued on following page

Table 9. Continued

		Citizen participation	Culture of peace	Social Innovation
Social Innovation	Pearson correlation	**.335** **	**.343** **	1
	Sig. (bilateral)	,000	,000	
	N	230	230	230

**. The correlation is significant at the 0.01 level (two-sided).
Source: elaboration with SPSS data.

Due to the above, the positive relationship between social innovation and citizen participation, as well as the culture of peace, is verified, thus supporting the second hypothesis.

CONCLUSIONS

This document has captured the importance of social innovation, citizen participation, and the culture of peace as a dynamic and multifaceted relationship. Active and equitable citizen participation strengthens social cohesion, reduces conflict, and fosters social innovation by enabling citizens to experiment with new ideas and approaches to address social problems. The implementation of digital technologies, peace education, and community mediation is an example of how social innovation can enhance the positive effects of citizen participation in promoting a culture of peace. This interconnection underscores the need for integrated and collaborative approaches to address contemporary social challenges and promote more just and peaceful societies.

In addition, participation allows for interaction with people of diverse origins and perspectives, enabling citizens to challenge prejudices, foster empathy, and identify commonalities. This collaborative spirit fosters a sense of community and belonging, which is crucial for preventing conflict and promoting peaceful coexistence. However, the relationship between citizen participation and the culture of peace is not without challenges, as unequal access to resources and power can hinder the meaningful participation of marginalized groups. Additionally, manipulation by political elites or the spread of misinformation can prevent constructive dialogue and hinder progress towards a culture of peace.

Another key element to highlight is the importance of a culture of peace, particularly as a mindset and approach that fosters peaceful coexistence and justice. However, this process requires the active participation of all social actors, underscoring the crucial role of citizen participation. This active participation means that citizens participate in decision-making processes, hold authorities accountable, and advocate for policies that promote peace and social justice, fostering a sense of belonging and responsibility.

A third element is evident: in communities where violence and conflict are recurrent, implementing citizen participation mechanisms helps strengthen the culture of peace and promotes social innovation. Therefore, proximity public policies should focus on these mechanisms and principles of participatory governance.

With these results, the proposed hypotheses are verified, and the research questions are answered, leaving it up for discussion to concentrate on other elements to measure the effective involvement of the population in each of the variables.

The results highlight that a culture of peace is reinforced by an active citizenry and strong participatory mechanisms, as evidenced statistically by a model in which citizen participation explains 20.5% of the variability in the culture of peace. However, social inclusion remains a latent, implicit variable, but is not directly addressed. This represents an opportunity to make the proposed model more complex in future empirical work, incorporating dimensions such as gender equity, digital accessibility, and the participation of historically excluded groups.

In this sense, it can be affirmed that social inclusion should be understood not only as a desirable outcome but also as a dynamic and interdependent process that fosters a culture of peace and social innovation. The positive correlation between innovation, a culture of peace, and participation suggests that an open, inclusive, and collaborative social environment facilitates innovative practices with greater collective impact. In turn, more inclusive communities tend to build denser social networks, fostering civic trust and resilience in the face of conflict (Torres & Ramírez, 2023). Therefore, social inclusion is both a condition and a consequence of democratic participatory systems oriented toward collective well-being.

REFERENCES

Allegretti, G., & Herzberg, C. (2004). *Participatory budgets in Europe. Between efficiency and growing local democracy*. Transnational Institute. TNI Briefing Series.

Arnstein, S. R. (1969). A Ladder of Citizen Participation. *Journal of the American Institute of Planners*, *35*(4), 216–224. DOI: 10.1080/01944366908977225

Baiocchi, G., Ganuza, E. (2014). Participatory Budgeting as if Emancipation Mattered. 29-50. .DOI: 10.1177/0032329213512978

Bartal, D. (2022). The elusive nature of peace education. In Salomon, G., & Nevo, B. (Eds.), *Peace education: The concept, principles, and practices around the world* (pp. 27–36). Lawrence Erlbaum Associates Publishers.

Chadwick, A. (2009). Web 2.0: New Challenges for the Study of E-Democracy in an Era of Informational Exuberance. A Journal of Law and Policy for the Information Society, pp. 9-41. .DOI: 10.7551/mitpress/9006.003.0005

Cooke, B., & Kothari, U. (2001). *Participation: The New Tyranny*. Zed Books.

Cornwall, A. (2008). Unpacking 'Participation': Models, meanings, and practices. *Community Development Journal: An International Forum*, *43*(3), 269–283. DOI: 10.1093/cdj/bsn010

Cremin, H., & Bevington, T. (2017). *Positive Peace in Schools: Tackling Conflict and Creating a Culture of Peace in the Classroom*. Routledge., DOI: 10.4324/9781315304236

Cuconato, M. (2023). Participation and Social Innovation as a Compass towards Integration: The Rationale behind the INTE-great Project. *Societies (Basel, Switzerland)*, *13*(6), 145. DOI: 10.3390/soc13060145

Dahl, R. (1998). *On Democracy*. Yale University Press.

Fishkin, J. (2011). *When the People Speak: Deliberative Democracy and Public Consultation*. Academic., DOI: 10.1093/acprof:osobl/9780199604432.001.0001

Fung, A. (2006). Varieties of Participation in Complex Governance. *Public Administration Review*, *66*(s1), 66–75. DOI: 10.1111/j.1540-6210.2006.00667.x

Galtung, J. (1996). *Peace by peaceful means: Peace and conflict, development and civilization. International Peace Research Institute Oslo*. Sage Publications. DOI: 10.4135/9781446221631

García-Espín, P. (2023). Class Inequalities and Participatory Democracy: Assessing the Impact of Social Inclusion Tools in Citizens' Assemblies. *Political Studies Review*, *22*(3), 585–607. DOI: 10.1177/14789299231179081

Gastil, J., & Levine, P. (2005). *The Deliberative Democracy Handbook: Strategies for Effective Civic Engagement in the Twenty-First Century*. Jossey-Bass.

Gaventa, J. (2009). Finding the Spaces for Change: A Power Analysis. *IDS Bulletin*, *37*(6), 23–33. DOI: 10.1111/j.1759-5436.2006.tb00320.x

Harris, I. (2009). History of Peace Education.

Hegre, H., Ellingsen, T., Gates, S., & Gleditsch, N. (2001). Toward a Democratic Civil Peace? Democracy, Political Change, and Civil War, 1816-1992. *The American Political Science Review*, *95*(1), 33–48. https://www.jstor.org/stable/3117627. DOI: 10.1017/S0003055401000119

IEPC. (2021). Results of the Local Electoral Process. Obtained from https://www2.iepcjalisco.org.mx/tablero-electoral-2021/?page_id=1307

INEGI. (July 24, 2024). National Urban Public Security Survey (ENSU). Obtained from https://www.inegi.org.mx/contenidos/programas/ensu/doc/ensu2024_junio_presentacion_ejecutiva.pdf

Lederach, J. P. (1997). *Building Peace: Sustainable Reconciliation in Divided Societies*. United States Institute of Peace Press.

Lijphart, A. (1997). Unequal Participation: Democracy's Unresolved Dilemma. *The American Political Science Review*, *14*(1), 1–14. Advance online publication. DOI: 10.2307/2952255

Michels, A., De Graaf, L. (2010). Examining Citizen Participation: Local Participatory Policy Making and Democracy. Local Government Study, 477-491, http://.DOI: 10.1080/03003930.2010.494101

Mora, C. O., Ortíz, K. H., & Silva, R. (2024). Fortalecimiento de la transparencia en México: Responsabilidad social y participación ciudadana como impulsores de democracia y eficiencia gubernamental. *Revista Venezolana de Gerencia*, *29*(106), 581–592. DOI: 10.52080/rvgluz.29.106.8

Mulgan, G. (2006). The Process of Social Innovation. *Innovations: Technology, Governance, Globalization*, *1*(2), 145–162. DOI: 10.1162/itgg.2006.1.2.145

Murray, R., Caulier-Grice, J., & Mulgan, G. (2010). *The Open Book of Social Innovation*. Nesta.

Nicholls, A., & Murdock, A. (2012). *Social Innovation: Blurring Boundaries to Reconfigure Markets*. Palgrave Macmillan. DOI: 10.1057/9780230367098

OECD. (2024). Public Innovation for Social Inclusion in Ibero-America. OECD. https://www.oecd.org/en/publications/public-innovation-for-social-inclusion-in-ibero-america_97d84618-en.html

Pacheco, J. N., Turro, A., & Urbano, D. (2025). Open social innovation: A systematic literature review and future research agenda. *Technological Forecasting and Social Change*, *V-216*, 124160. Advance online publication. DOI: 10.1016/j.techfore.2025.124160

Pateman, C. (1970). *Participation and Democratic Theory*. Cambridge University Press., DOI: 10.1017/CBO9780511720444

Peixoto, T., Fox, J. (2016). When Does ICT-Enabled Citizen Voice Lead to Government Responsiveness? Opening Governance, 21-32. .DOI: 10.19088/1968-2016.104

Phills, J., Deiglmeier, K., & Miller, D. (2008). Rediscovering Social Innovation. Stanford Social Innovation Review, 34–43. DOI: 10.48558/GBJY-GJ47

Putnam, R. D. (2000). *Bowling alone: The collapse and revival of American community*. Touchstone Books/Simon & Schuster., DOI: 10.1145/358916.361990

Salomon, G., & Nevo, B. (2002). *Peace education: The concept, principles, and practices around the world*. Lawrence Erlbaum Associates Publishers.

Serdült, U., & Welp, Y. (2012). Direct Democracy Upside Down. Taiwan journal of democracy, 69-92. DOI: 10.5167/UZH-98412

Tarrow, S. (2005). *The New Transnational Activism*. Cambridge University Press. DOI: 10.1017/CBO9780511791055

UN. (1948). *Universal Declaration of Human Rights*. United Nations.

UN. (2015). *Transforming our world: the 2030 Agenda for Sustainable Development*. United Nations.

UN. (2020). *UN Comprehensive Response to COVID-19: Saving Lives, Protecting Societies, Recovering Better*. United Nations.

UNESCO. (1999). *Declaration and Program of Action on a Culture of Peace*. UNESCO.

Wampler, B. (2012). Participatory Budgeting: Core Principles and Key Impacts. Journal of Deliberative Democracy, doi https://doi.org/.DOI: 10.16997/jdd.138

Westley, F., Zimmerman, B., & Patton, M. (2006). *Getting to Maybe: How the World is Changed*. Random House Canada.

Yunus, M. (2007). *Creating a World Without Poverty: Social Business and the Future of Capitalism*. Public Affairs.

Chapter 11
Trend of Sustainable Supply Chain Management Research: Bibliometric Analysis 2007-2023

Marco Alberto Valenzo-Jiménez
https://orcid.org/0000-0001-6155-5948
Universidad Michoacana de San Nicolás de Hidalgo, Mexico

Arcadio González-Samaniego
https://orcid.org/0000-0003-2640-4495
Secretaría de Ciencia, Humanidades, Tecnología, e Innovación, Mexico

Cinthya Zaragoza Ortiz
https://orcid.org/0009-0009-1102-5143
Universidad Michoacana de San Nicolás de Hidalgo, Mexico

ABSTRACT

The globalization of supply chains has intensified their interaction and impact on the surrounding environment. Companies committed to sustainability increasingly recognize their responsibility toward the societies affected by their operations. The sustainability of focal firms is influenced by economic, social, and environmental dimensions, collectively known as the Triple Bottom Line. Sustainable Supply Chain Management (SSCM) integrates these three dimensions and has played a crucial role in enhancing organizational competitiveness. This study aimed to conduct a bibliometric analysis of SSCM. The 1.242 documents were retrieved from the Web of Science and Scopus databases. The findings reveal a growing scholarly interest in SSCM, reflected in the upward trend of related publications. Sustainability and the various approaches to addressing it have become a fundamental component of

DOI: 10.4018/979-8-3373-2685-6.ch011

Copyright © 2026, IGI Global Scientific Publishing. Copying or distributing in print or electronic forms without written permission of IGI Global Scientific Publishing is prohibited.

modern supply chain strategies. Using Artificial Intelligence in SSCM adds social risks. For firms seeking to remain competitive, adopting SSCM practices is not only beneficial but increasingly essential.

INTRODUCTION

The globalization of supply chains means that more variables influence their performance. Although the economic and operational aspects are fundamental, their analysis and management cannot be limited to these aspects alone. The social and environmental environment are aspects that focal companies must consider to stay competitive (Bari et al., 2022). Focal companies lead the supply chain, provide direct contact with customers, and design the products or services offered to the market (Seuring & Müller, 2008).

Caring for the environment is an obligation of focal companies in their sphere of influence. Increasing consumption patterns have led to exponential industrialization and large-scale monoculture agriculture, affecting natural ecosystems (Intergovernmental Panel on Climate Change, 2023). Companies must modify their operations as they seek to comply with increasingly stringent environmental regulations (Sánchez-Flores et al., 2020). Likewise, they must take care of their market due to the change in purchasing habits by consumers, who reward and punish companies with their consumption based on their environmentalist vision (Carter & Rogers, 2008).

This study suggests several inclusive implications within the context of Sustainable Supply Chain Management: Integration, Participation, Equity, Justice, Diversity, Adaptation, and Innovation.

Integration of Diverse Factors. The mention of the "Triple Bottom Line" implies that sustainable supply chain management focuses not only on economic performance but also on social and environmental impacts. This involves multiple dimensions beyond financial outcomes, including social justice and environmental protection.

Participation of All Stakeholders. To be truly inclusive, sustainable management must consider all stakeholders in the supply chain, from suppliers to customers, and not just large companies. This could involve integrating small and medium-sized enterprises, as well as respecting and including local communities and workers.

Equity and Social Justice. Sustainable and inclusive management seeks to address issues of equity and social justice, ensuring that company practices benefit not just the companies themselves but also the communities in which they operate. This may involve improving labor conditions and promoting fair trade practices.

Diversity in Research. Bibliometric analysis shows a growing interest in sustainable management, suggesting a greater inclusion of various perspectives and approaches in research. This can lead to a more comprehensive and diverse understanding of how to implement sustainable practices and what factors need to be considered.

Adaptation to Global Standards. Globalization necessitates compliance with various international norms and standards that promote sustainability. Including these standards in supply chain management ensures that companies align with global expectations, contributing to a more inclusive and sustainable economy.

Innovation and Continuous Improvement. Companies can foster innovation and continuous improvement by adopting an inclusive approach to sustainable management. The inclusion of different perspectives and experiences can lead to new ideas and more effective practices for addressing sustainability challenges.

In summary, the inclusive implications of sustainable supply chain management manifest in integrating diverse factors and stakeholders, promoting social equity, and adapting to global standards, ultimately contributing to greater competitiveness and a positive impact on society and the environment.

Industry 4.0 enables companies to track all links within the supply chain. In this way, it contributes to achieving economic, social, and environmental objectives, which are key components of sustainability. Among the technologies that comprise Industry 4.0 are the Internet of Things, Big Data, Blockchain, and Artificial Intelligence.

Artificial Intelligence (AI) is an emerging technology that leverages information from other technologies to identify patterns and problems and suggests the most optimal solutions for them. However, due to the characteristics of the technologies themselves, they can be exclusive, primarily because of their high implementation costs, the required infrastructure, and the specialized human talent necessary for their effective exploitation.

Companies have a responsibility to the society that their operations affect. Although the economic impact is fundamental, the consistency of business policies and corporate governance through the Triple Bottom Line is a factor in their financial performance (Elkington, 2006; Clément et al., 2022).

The environmental variable is the most sensitive to consumers, affecting their financial performance (Gangi et al., 2020). This variable has led to the transformation in the corporate culture of global companies, adapting it to new market requirements (Petridis et al., 2023).

Previously, companies were considered to cover their social work by creating employment directly and indirectly through the supply chain or engaging in philanthropic practices (Signori et al., 2021). Currently, it is how the company interacts with internal and external stakeholders, seeking to have a positive impact through an ethical and institutional business culture (Dinu & Bunea, 2019).

The organizational culture of focal companies and their interaction with stakeholders influence their Supply Chain (SC). A good company reputation allows it to attract employees, suppliers, and customers (Lis et al., 2020; Zhang et al., 2020). Adequate knowledge of the environment where the different stages of the SC are located allows us to prevent changes that affect the operation.

Sustainable Supply Chain Management (SSCM) is an approach that seeks to analyze SC comprehensively. Due to its relevance, there are growing publications on the subject. In this sense, the objective of the research is to carry out a bibliometric analysis of SSCM.

The document is structured by presenting a review of the evolution of SC towards SSCM and its conceptualization. The following are the key concepts related to Artificial Intelligence, followed by the aspects to be considered for incorporating it. It continues with the methodology used to carry out the bibliometric analysis. Subsequently, the results obtained and their discussion. It concludes with the conclusions and limitations, as well as the future lines of research.

SUPPLY CHAIN

The SC brings together all the information and activities associated with the flow and transformation of goods from the moment they are created or extracted until they reach the final consumer (Seuring & Müller, 2008). It can reveal opportunities to reduce costs quickly because of the potential to produce sustainable savings (Roberts, 2003).

Orientation towards global markets and increased performance-based competition, in combination with technology and the economic environment, contribute to market uncertainty (Mentzer et al., 2001). As a result, companies and their SCs require greater flexibility and adaptation to maintain and increase their competitiveness (Valenzo-Jiménez & González-Samaniego, 2021).

The analysis of SC at one origin only contemplated the logistics of resources. Recognized as a strategic activity of the company, it contemplates the relationships of all actors along the chain. It seeks to integrate and improve processes to increase or maintain competitiveness and was conceptualized as Supply Chain Management (Seuring & Müller, 2008).

Supply Chain Management (SCM) can be addressed in its operational terms, involving the flow of materials, products, and information throughout the SC (Stadtler, 2014). It can also be analyzed as a management process implicit in the company's philosophy (Tyndall et al., 1998). Initially, SCM only focused on the efficient and detailed production and delivery system from the raw material stage to the end consumer. The environmental changes within the SC have grown significantly, which entails new challenges for companies (Seitz & Wells, 2006).

Sustainability is defined as meeting people's current needs without compromising the future needs of future generations (Brundtland, 1987). Companies are sometimes unable to understand the meaning of sustainability and its challenges in their operations, so they fail to implement practices to implement it (Seuring & Müller, 2008). By incorporating sustainability into the core functions of a commercial company's SCM, it will achieve a good position in the market and in the global context (Khodakarami et al., 2015).

SUSTAINABLE SUPPLY CHAIN MANAGEMENT

By incorporating sustainability into SCM, Sustainable Supply Chain Management (SSCM) can be conceptualized as the flow of materials, economic resources, and information among SC members, considering their social, financial, and environmental aspects (Seuring & Müller, 2008). Integrating economic, social, and ecological responsibilities into SCM makes it sustainable (Carter & Rogers, 2008). They are the Triple Bottom Line (TBL) (Rogers & Hudson, 2011).

SSCM requires establishing values and high ethics throughout the organization, aligning the corporate strategy, focusing on sustainable development, and covering and protecting the network against environmental risks (Teuteberg & Wittstruck, 2010). It also involves managing raw materials, supplier services, and customer service, improving the social conditions of workers, and caring for the environment (Seitz & Wells, 2006).

Sustainability can lead to cost increases due to process changes; however, the proper development and execution of the SSCM cycle can reduce costs and increase profits (Nidumolu et al., 2009). However, globalized markets are highly competitive, which puts pressure on costs and the ability to supply trending products (Christopher, et al., 2004). Therefore, a high degree of responsiveness is required, combined with a certain level of efficiency that is met by adopting strategies in SSCM, such as just-in-time sourcing (Bruce et al., 2004). Explicitly integrating TBL allows the company to increase its competitiveness (Roy et al., 2018).

Raw material transformation processes are one of the principal sources of environmental damage (Panigrahi et al., 2019). Executing the processes and functions of the SSCM in a manner that preserves the ecological environment as intact and unharmed as possible is crucial. This can be achieved by implementing green procurement strategies and utilizing eco-friendly technologies. The environmental aspect of TBL encompasses objectives, plans, tools, and techniques aimed at fostering greater environmental responsibility and promoting green and pollution-free technologies (Klassen, 2001).

Since the SSCM deals with and manages the integration of TBL, it analyzes, in the same way, the management strategies to adapt to sudden changes, risks, and opportunities in the market, as well as to influence and control its environment to achieve a competitive advantage by distinguishing itself from its competitors (Beske, 2012; Khodakarami et al., 2015).

Rapid changes in customer demand patterns, growing competition, and pressures from governments and other stakeholders have encouraged most companies to adopt SSCM practices (Gopal & Thakkar, 2016). It is a factor in medium- and long-term business decision-making (Motevali Haghighi et al., 2016).

ARTIFICIAL INTELLIGENCE

Industry 4.0 is a concept that involves the convergence of emerging technologies in business processes and supply chains (Yadav et al., 2024). It enables synergies among these technologies, visualizing them as an integrated technological ecosystem and generating resilience in supply chains (Usman, 2024). Industry 4.0 refers to the integration of technologies that enable the automation and digitalization of processes (Samuels & Pelser, 2025).

One of the fundamental characteristics of the Fourth Industrial Revolution is the digitalization and automation of various processes within economic sectors (Kunkel et al., 2022). Industry 4.0 changes existing paradigms, transforming the labor market. Thus, Industry 4.0 contributes to the sustainability of supply chains, enabling more effective and sustainable collaboration and meeting the changing requirements of demand and government regulations (Cataldo et al., 2022).

Within this set of technological processes, the use of Big Data and its analysis, Blockchain, the Internet of Things (IoT), and AI can be considered. AI is a novel concept that can be considered for using and applying information derived from other technologies (Yadav et al., 2024). Thus, AI can now be regarded as the focal technology in Industry 4.0 (Kunkel et al., 2022). AI can be defined as the application of science to enable computers to develop characteristics of intelligence, such as recognizing problems, developing solutions for them, and applying these solutions to resolve them (Liu & Lin, 2021). It recognizes business patterns, identifies various scenarios, and enables the management of risks inherent in supply chains (Ebinger & Omondi, 2020).

A focal point for its use and implementation is the standardization of internal capabilities among users and suppliers throughout the supply chain. Thus, if one link in the supply chain fails to develop the necessary material and human technological capabilities, the entire supply chain can be affected. In this sense, AI is a fundamental technology for achieving objectives in SSCM (Samuels & Pelser, 2025).

Big Data can be considered the primary input for AI, serving as the enabling technology for it (Kunkel et al., 2022). In this way, using information from Big Data, AI identifies patterns—whether of behavior, knowledge, or information—to provide responses that optimize decision-making (Ebinger & Omondi, 2020). In this way, it is a recurrent combination of the concepts (Usman, 2024). The complexity that global supply chains can present, with all their inherent risks, is a field of application for AI. Analyzing the vast amount of information from various links, often in real-time, can contribute to achieving company objectives (Pawlicka & Bal, 2022).

Just as AI leverages the analysis of information from big data, the IoT is the source of the data that big data collects. Through the internet and data from sensors on physical objects, it can control these objects (Bag et al., 2018). This collection is conducted in real-time. It facilitates the development of large infrastructures that collect and unify data from supply chain processes (Ebinger & Omondi, 2020).

The constant flow of materials, financial resources, and information throughout the supply chain can become chaotic. The real-time collection of this data and its near-immediate analysis enable the supply chain to become sustainable (Rejeb et al., 2023). The management of smart warehouses, which utilize sensors to generate real-time information, enables more efficient inventory management, as well as the optimization of energy use and reduction of waste (Yadav et al., 2024). The IoT enables the integration of supply chain components (Liu & Lin, 2021).

Blockchain is a technology that provides security, transparency, and traceability in the supply chain, increasing stakeholder confidence (Rejeb et al., 2023). In this way, when industries integrate Blockchain with big data and AI, they can improve the efficiency of their supply chains by securely digitalizing the links (Usman, 2024). Thus, it enables tracking from raw material to the final consumer, which in turn facilitates verification of compliance with the various certifications necessary for supply chain sustainability (Ebinger & Omondi, 2020). The governance of SSCM is a fundamental aspect that this technology contributes to.

IS ARTIFICIAL INTELLIGENCE AN INCLUSIVE TECHNOLOGY?

Technological advancements offer significant opportunities for SSCM, enhancing management efficiency and achieving higher levels of productivity. However, they also present considerable risks of exclusion for particular sectors of the industry.

Due to the inherent characteristics of AI and other related technologies, their implementation entails substantial initial investment costs, primarily in internal infrastructure and training (Yadav et al., 2024). Large enterprises are typically the ones with access to the necessary financial resources, thereby marginalizing companies with less capital, particularly micro, small, and medium-sized enterprises (SMEs) (Rejeb et al., 2023). Thus, the lack of financing constitutes a significant vulnerability for firms, especially smaller ones (Cataldo et al., 2022).

The position of power within supply chains allows the focal firm to impose its technological standards on the other members. Consequently, smaller suppliers must often bear unforeseen costs to meet technological requirements without being able to fully leverage their benefits (Kunkel et al., 2022). Thus, focal firms may opt to discourage independent innovation among other chain members to maintain power within the network. In the agri-food sector, agricultural producers can be perceived as the most vulnerable actors in the supply chain (Fracarolli Nunes et al., 2020). Smaller companies, lacking the capacity for independent development, require external support to avoid exclusion (Kannan, 2018).

Firms located in emerging economies face greater obstacles to implementing AI and its associated technologies, which are sometimes too advanced for the local environment and not aligned with the country's culture (Kunkel et al., 2022). While this is not the direct responsibility of the firms, they must nevertheless seek to address the resulting challenges (Ebinger & Omondi, 2020). Public infrastructure is a crucial factor in corporate competitiveness (Rejeb et al., 2023). Examples of these deficiencies include the lack of reliable and renewable energy sources, insufficient fiber optic coverage, and an unstable or slow internet connection (Usman, 2024). Those deficiencies suggest a lack of governmental support for the successful implementation of these initiatives.

Weak regulatory frameworks are another characteristic that prevents firms from engaging in long-term planning due to the resulting uncertainty, leading them to opt out of new digital ecosystems (Liu & Lin, 2021). The country's culture itself is identified as an obstacle to inclusion, where local customs and practices are not aligned with consumer expectations, particularly concerning human and labor rights (Kannan, 2018). Firms that fail to meet the standards defined by focal firms will be unable to operate within the supply chain.

Given the nature of Industry 4.0, characterized by constant advancements in knowledge and its application, there is a risk of obsolescence for the human talent required for its implementation and exploitation (Rejeb et al., 2023). The scarcity of qualified personnel with the necessary capabilities to leverage new technologies poses a significant barrier, particularly for firms with less mature technological capabilities within their supply chains (Liu & Lin, 2021). In this context, a significant threat arises for personnel who are unable to assimilate new knowledge, particularly affecting older, more experienced workers. This situation may prompt a significant departure of employees, which could result in the loss of valuable tacit knowledge and contribute to a social crisis related to rising unemployment. (Usman, 2024).

The automation of processes, as supply chains become more efficient, can lead to job losses among less-skilled workers (Bag et al., 2018). Thus, the phenomenon is particularly palpable in less developed countries. The absorptive capacity of a firm allows it to internalize knowledge and subsequently transform the organization to capitalize on new opportunities.

Corporate culture can itself be an exclusionary factor, particularly in firms with a management style averse to change, which can affect the entire chain, precluding them from the inherent benefits of Industry 4.0 (Yadav et al., 2024). Thus, this exclusion can be identified as directly inherent to the firm, as it prefers to step aside rather than implement new supply chain management methods (Liu & Lin, 2021). In the long term, this stance can lead to the firm's demise (Bag et al., 2018).

Digital maturity is a crucial exclusionary aspect, as focal firms prefer to collaborate with enterprises of a similar degree of maturity or those with the potential to achieve it in the short term (Kunkel et al., 2022). Technologically immature firms will be unable to access the benefits resulting from the application of AI and participation in Industry 4.0. This observation highlights the absence of standardization that has emerged from the swift deployment of various technologies (De Brito, 2024). Integration with the company's existing systems is a critical factor.

METHODOLOGY

To achieve the research objective, a bibliometric analysis (BA) was conducted on sustainable supply chain management research. A BA quantifies and analyzes output in an area of science using quantitative techniques (Kraus et al., 2022). The information was analyzed using the Biblioshiny program. A predominant factor of a BA is that other researchers can replicate the methodology. In this sense, an adaptation of the method proposed by Tranfield et al. (2003) was made (Figure 1).

The Web of Science (WoS) and Elsevier Scopus (Scopus) databases were searched due to the quality of the documents they contain (Espinoza-Torres & Segarra-Oña, 2022). The period to be analyzed spanned from 2007, the year the SSCM was first conceptualized, to 2023. The keyword used was "Sustainable Supply Chain Management". The search was conducted using the title, abstract, and keywords. To ensure a comprehensive retrieval of all pertinent studies, no further limitations were placed on the search keywords. This approach was adopted to facilitate a thorough review of the existing literature on SSCM and to determine the prominence of this topic within prevailing research trends. The document type was restricted to articles, review articles, book chapters, and early access. The publication language was not limited, as most publications were written in English, but there were also publications in Spanish and Portuguese. The search was implemented in June 2023.

One thousand one hundred eighty documents were found in Scopus and 941 in WoS, giving 2,121 publications. As a next step, the databases were joined into the BibDesk program. Three hundred ninety-four documents that did not present the complete information to be analyzed or had syntax errors, as well as 485 duplicates, were thrown out, leaving 1,242 documents to be analyzed.

The search term in WoS was: "sustainable supply and chain management" (Topic) and 2007, 2008, 2009, 2010, 2011, 2017, 2016, 2015 or 2014, 2013 or 2012 or 2023 or 2022, 2021 or 2020 or 2019 or 2018 (Publication Years) and Article or Review Article or Early Access or Book Chapters (Document Types) and Management or Green Sustainable Science Technology or Environmental Sciences or Environmental Studies or Operations Research Management Science or Engineering Environmental or Business or Engineering Manufacturing or Economics or Agricultural Economics Policy or Business Finance or Ecology or Food Science Technology (Web of Science Categories). In Scopus, the search term was defined as follows: TITLE-ABS-KEY ("sustainable supply chain management") AND (LIMIT-TO (DOCTYPE, "ar") OR LIMIT-TO (DOCTYPE, "ch") OR LIMIT-TO (DOCTYPE, "re")) AND (LIMIT-TO (SUBJAREA, "BUSI") OR LIMIT-TO (SUBJAREA, "ENVI") OR LIMIT-TO (SUBJAREA, "ECON") OR LIMIT-TO (SUBJAREA, "SOCI")).

Figure 1. Research protocol.

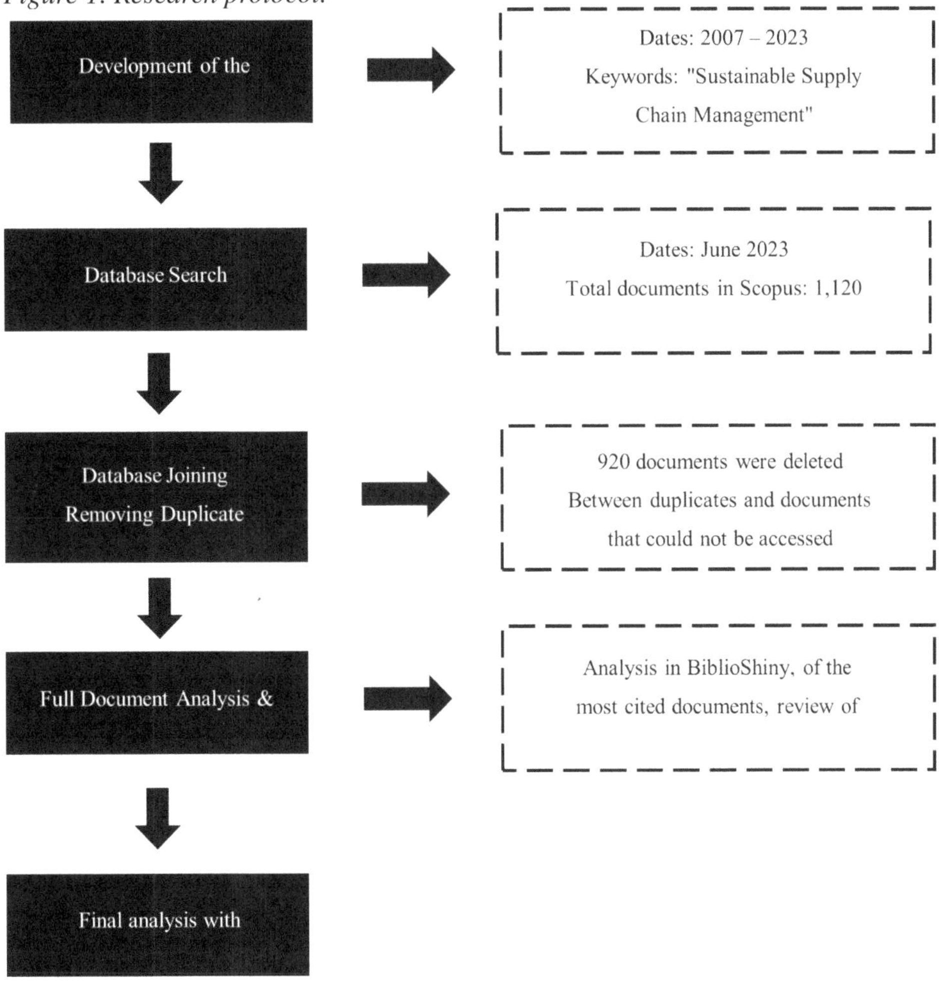

Source: Own elaboration

RESULTS

When analyzing the 1,242 documents, it was found that 98.7% had complete references. Although the databases used are among the most prestigious for the quality of the papers they house, this factor affects the analysis, albeit slightly. Since the conceptualization of the SSCM in 2007, there has been a steady increase in the annual production of documents (Figure 2). A decline was observed during the COVID-19 pandemic. The production has grown from 2 publications in 2007 to a maximum of 179 publications in 2022. During the year 2023, at the date of the study, 47 documents have been published.

Figure 2. Annual production of documents.

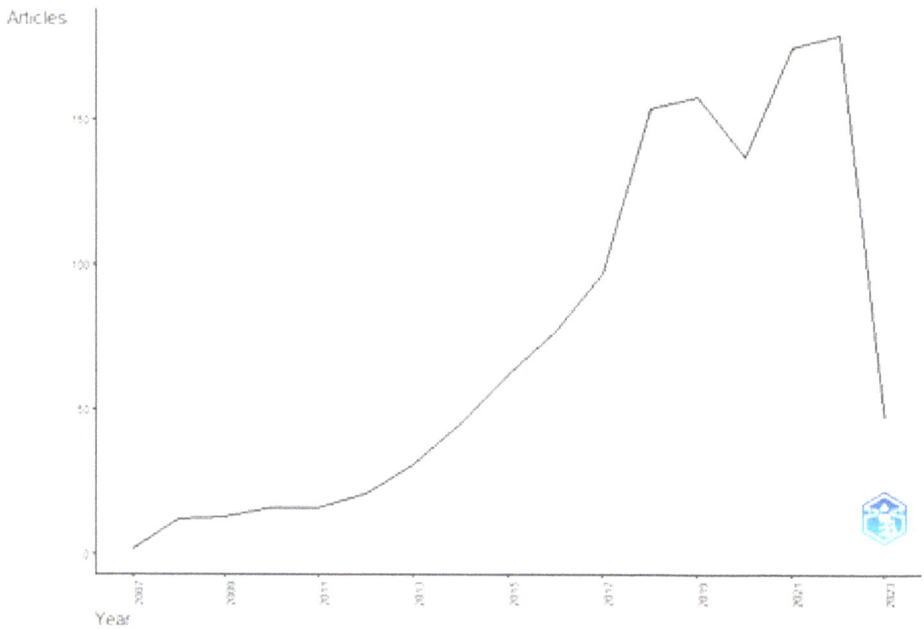

Upon examining the correlation among the top ten publishing nations, their preferred journals, and the prevalent keywords utilized, it becomes evident that China is the foremost contributor in the field of SSCM (Figure 3). This assertion is grounded in the reality that it is a primary center for much of the world's manufacturing production. Following suit are the United Kingdom, Germany, and the United States. Noteworthy is the preference of Chinese researchers for the journal Sustainability, which holds the second highest position in terms of publication volume. The Journal of Cleaner Production is where most research results on SSCM are published. Among the ten keywords, it was found that they are directly related to the concepts of the SSCM and its variants. TBL, Social Sustainability, and Corporate Social Responsibility stand out. It should be noted that the emerging countries of India, Brazil, and Iran appear in this analysis, a sign of the importance given to this branch of science in their respective countries.

Figure 3. Country of publication, journal, and keywords.

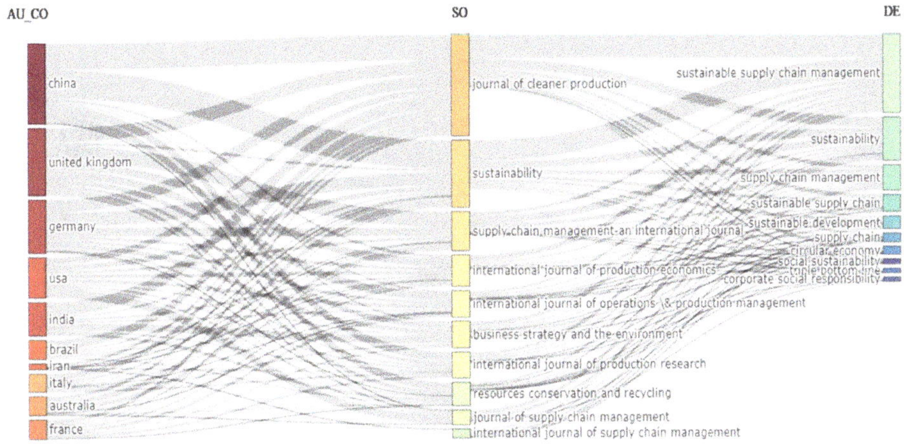

According to the number of documents published, the most relevant source is the Journal of Cleaner Production, with 126 (Figure 4). The second magazine is Sustainability, with 109. The thematic orientation of these journals toward sustainability and sustainable production highlights the importance of embracing a sustainable paradigm within the framework of SC. Three journals directly focused on SC are the Supply Chain Management International Journal, Journal of Supply Chain Management, and International Journal of Supply Chain Management, which appear as the third, eighth, and tenth in relevance according to the number of documents published. The journal Sustainability is the leading venue for publications related to AI and SSCM, with 10 articles published during the analyzed period. It is followed by Resources, Conservation, and Recycling, with six publications, and the Journal of Cleaner Production, with five.

Figure 4. Most relevant sources are based on the number of documents published.

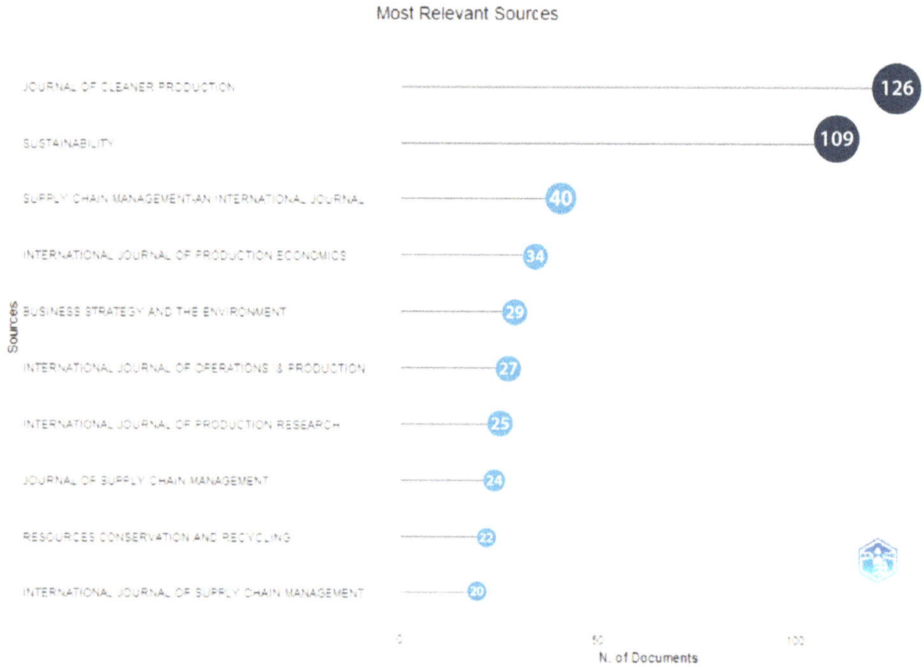

Analyzing sources according to the H-index measures the number of citations received by a journal's publications (Table 1). By ranking them this way, the Journal of Cleaner Production ranks first with an H index of 61, clearly separated from the rest. However, the International Journal of Cleaner Production is the second with an H-index of 26. The Supply Chain Management and International Journal is in third place with an H-index of 25. The journals are established in countries with advanced economies, with four journals in the United Kingdom, three in the United States of America, two in the Netherlands, and one in Switzerland.

Table 1. Most relevant sources are based on the number of documents published and the country of publication.

Journal	Country	Documents	H-index
Journal of Cleaner Production	United States of America	126	61
International Journal of Production Economics	Netherlands	34	26
Supply Chain Management and International Journal	United Kingdom	40	25

continued on following page

Table 1. Continued

Journal	Country	Documents	H-indcx
Sustainability	Switzerland	109	22
International Journal of Production Research	United Kingdom	25	19
Resources Conservation and Recycling	Netherlands	22	19
International Journal of Operations & Production Management	United Kingdom	27	18
Business Strategy and the Environment	United States of America	29	17
Journal of Supply Chain Management	United States of America	24	15
International Journal of Physical Distribution & Logistics Management	United Kingdom	19	13

To identify the ten most influential authors in the SSCM, they were ordered according to the total number of citations (Figure 5). The most influential author is Seuring, S., with a total of 7,403. The number of citations in his works is more than double that of the author Mueller, M., who has a total of 3,272. It is important to note that these authors have published papers together. The following authors to appear are Sarkis, J. with 3,245, Carter, CR. with 2.843, Pagell, M. with 2.345, Wu, Z. with 2.179, Govindan, K., with 2.056, Rogers, DS. with 1,847, Searcy, C. with 1,840, and in tenth place Beske, P. with 1,643. By analyzing the WoS and Scopus databases together, the influence of the authors is found more precisely.

Figure 5. Most relevant authors, according to total citations

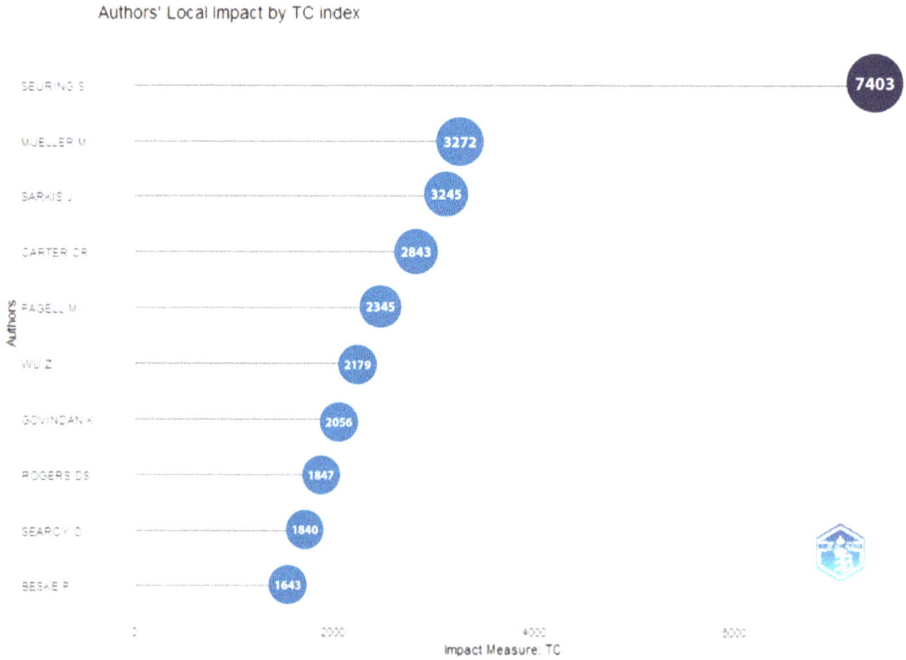

Analyzing the ten most cited documents in the databases investigated, it was found that the publications of Seuring and Müller (2008) and Carter and Rogers (2008) are the most cited, with 3,119 and 1,847 citations, respectively (Table 2). The two documents were published in 2008, so they can be considered the origin of the conceptualization of the SSCM as such. Seuring and Müller's research was conducted through a literature review, while Carter & Rogers' publication was theoretical. Despite its more recent publication, the study by Saberi, Kouhizadeh, Sarkis, and Shen (2019) ranks third, with 1,121 citations.

Table 2. Most relevant documents, according to the total number of citations

Authors	Document Name	Journal	Year	Total Citations
Seuring, S., & Müller, M.	From a literature review to a conceptual framework for sustainable supply chain management.	Journal of Cleaner Production	2008	3,119
Carter, C. R., & Rogers, D. S.	A framework of sustainable supply chain management: moving toward new theory.	International Journal of Physical Distribution & Logistics Management	2008	1,847
Saberi, S., Kouhizadeh, M., Sarkis, J., & Shen, L.	Blockchain technology and its relationships to sustainable supply chain management.	International Journal of Production Research	2019	1,121
Pagell, M., & Wu, Z.	Building a more complete theory of sustainable supply chain management using case studies of 10 exemplars.	Journal of Supply Chain Management	2009	943
Carter, C. R., & Liane Easton, P.	Sustainable supply chain management: evolution and future directions.	International Journal of Physical Distribution & Logistics Management	2011	836
Ahi, P., & Searcy, C.	A comparative literature analysis of definitions for green and sustainable supply chain management.	Journal of Cleaner Production	2013	731
Brandenburg, M., Govindan, K., Sarkis, J., & Seuring, S.	Quantitative models for sustainable supply chain management: Developments and directions.	European Journal of Operational Research	2014	706
Hassini, E., Surti, C., & Searcy, C.	A literature review and a case study of sustainable supply chains with a focus on metrics	International Journal of Production Economics	2012	659
Genovese, A., Acquaye, A. A., Figueroa, A., & Koh, S. L.	Sustainable supply chain management and the transition towards a circular economy: Evidence and some applications.	Omega	2017	625
Seuring, S.	A review of modeling approaches for sustainable supply chain management	Decision Support Systems	2013	625

Examining the ten universities that have produced the most documents on the SSCM, the University of Kassel in Germany is in first position, with 54 publications (Table 3). Two universities in Iran appear in second and third position: Islamic Azad University with 41 documents and Tehran University in third with 14 papers. These two universities are the only ones that appear on this list, and they are located in countries with late development. China has two universities, as well as the United Kingdom. Five universities are in Europe, four are in Asia, and only one is in America; the Toronto Metropolitan University is in Canada.

An analysis of the publications reveals that the University of Johannesburg in South Africa is the most prolific institution in AI-related topics (Industry 4.0, Big Data, Blockchain, and Internet of Things) with seven publications. It is followed by Luleå University of Technology in Sweden with four and the Indian Institute of Technology Delhi in India with three.

Table 3. Most relevant universities are listed according to the number of articles published and the country of location.

University	Country	Documents
University of Kassel	Germany	54
Islamic Azad University	Iran	41
University of Tehran	Iran	14
Hong Kong Polytechnic University	China	13
Delft University of Technology	Netherlands	11
China University of Science and Technology	China	11
University of Sheffield	United Kingdom	11
Cardiff University	United Kingdom	10
University of Southern Denmark	Denmark	10
Toronto Metropolitan University	Canada	9

Collaboration between authors is a fundamental factor in the development of science. In this sense, an analysis was carried out on the collaboration between authors according to the country where they are settled (Figure 6). The United States of America is the country that collaborates the most, with the most relevant node, collaborating mainly with countries located in Europe. The second node of collaboration is in China, which is seen to collaborate extensively with Asian and European countries. Nodes are shown in England, Australia, and India. Brazil is a Latin American country with a developing node of collaboration, in keeping with its position as the leading economy in Latin America.

Based on the corresponding author's country of origin, India leads the field of research in AI and their area with 15 publications. Other significant contributing countries include the United Kingdom wiht nine, South Africa with seven, the USA with five, and Sweden with four. Notably, Latin America is the only region with no representation from corresponding authors in the analyzed literature.

Figure 6. Countries that collaborate the most.

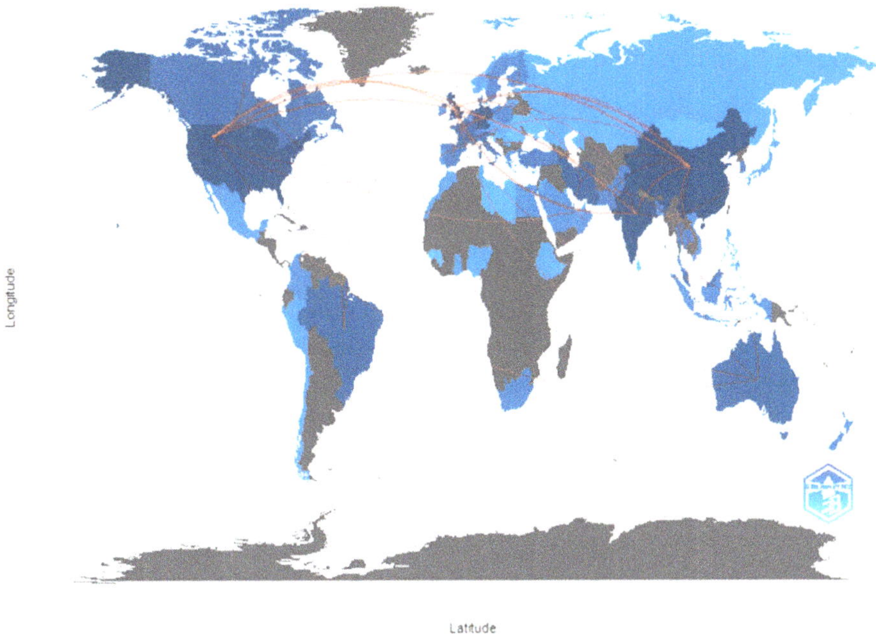

A depuration of keywords was carried out to analyze the co-occurrence of keywords. In the first instance, words that appeared in the singular or plural, such as Supply Chain and Supply Chains, were unified. Next, the acronyms and keywords, such as Sustainable Supply Chain Management or SSCM, are linked. This allowed for increased assertiveness regarding the analysis and influence of a given keyword. Keywords that did not involve a particular area of the SSCM were then filtered based on how the study was conducted. The words literature review, systematic literature review, case study, content analysis, debate, data envelopment analysis, game theory, and conceptual framework were eliminated from the list obtained.

The words with the highest attendance are Sustainable Supply Chain Management with 544 mentions, Sustainability with 308 mentions, Supply Chain Management with 234, Sustainable Supply Chain with 146, Sustainable Development with 112, followed by Supply Chain with 99, Circular Economy with 40, Triple Button Line with 37, Corporate Social Responsibility with 34, and Social Sustainability with 31 (Figure 7).

Upon reviewing the articles, it was found that three of them contained the keyword Artificial Intelligence in their topics. This finding suggests that AI was likely a nascent concept at the time the research was conducted. In contrast, other related terms were more established. It was found that 57 articles contained keywords indirectly related to artificial intelligence, as contemplated by other authors. Of these, 28 were related to the keyword Blockchain, 16 to Industry 4.0, nine to Big Data, and two to the Internet of Things. As a result, Blockchain is the only keyword that appears in the word cloud (Figure 7).

Figure 7. Keyword cloud.

DISCUSSION

SSCM has become increasingly important in the industry and academia (Taylor & Vachon, 2018). Caring for the environment and its effects on the supply chain is a factor that focal companies must integrate into their strategy (Saha et al., 2020). There is a need to integrate SCM into sustainability in the search for the company to be sustainable over time (Oguntegbe et al., 2023). In this sense, it is a factor in maintaining competitiveness.

The capabilities developed by the firm allow it to modify its supply chains and remain competitive in an ever-changing environment (Eikelenboom & de Jong, 2019). A deep understanding of the environment in which it operates allows the SSCM to take advantage of the opportunities implied by a constantly changing market, developing its capacity for collaboration and allowing it to be flexible and adaptable (Luthra & Mangla, 2018).

Understanding Sustainable Development has prompted a redefinition of business values and policies, transforming the comprehension of business operations (Yu & Xu, 2022). His has instigated the evolution of new management approaches that incorporate decisions' social and environmental impacts into economic assessments.

Companies, their suppliers, customers, and business and social stakeholders such as governments, consumers, activists, environmentalists, or employees demand that companies maintain a high ethical standard. These demands pressure companies to provide economic benefits and address environmental and social concerns within the framework of TBL, promoting Corporate Social Responsibility (Meixell & Luoma, 2015). Both concepts are implicit within the SSCM.

Although SC has become globalized in all areas of the economy, the sector of industry where SSCM research is largely focused is the food industry. Regulations seeking to eliminate the likelihood of contamination, hazard analysis, and critical control points in the food industry have led to improving and adapting industry processes (Shekarian et al., 2022).

The integration of AI and adjacent technologies, such as IoT, Big Data, and Blockchain, into SSCM within the Industry 4.0 paradigm promises to deliver unprecedented optimization in its management (Kunkel et al., 2022). Enhanced efficiency, traceability, and transparency within supply chain operations are poised to facilitate the achievement of environmental and economic objectives (Ebinger & Omondi, 2020). However, the implementation of these technologies presents a paradox concerning the social dimension of sustainability. The uncritical implementation of these technologies risks creating new forms of social exclusion. The TBL framework defines sustainability as the equilibrium between economic, environmental, and social pillars (Sánchez-Flores et al., 2020).

Social exclusion can manifest at multiple levels. Primarily, the adoption of Industry 4.0 demands substantial capital investment, thereby creating a digital divide that marginalizes firms with limited financial resources (Kunkel et al., 2022). This issue is particularly acute for SMEs (Rejeb et al., 2023) and for producers in emerging economies or the primary sector, such as the agri-food industry (Fracarolli Nunes et al., 2020). This barrier restricts their participation in increasingly technologized global supply chains. Likewise, automation driven by AI and IoT risks displacing workers with traditional skill sets (Yadav et al., 2024). Mitigating this requires accompanying technological implementation with robust retraining and upskilling programs (Bag et al., 2018). Furthermore, the design of AI algorithms can perpetuate or even amplify existing disparities, negatively impacting vulnerable communities in areas such as hiring and resource allocation (Kunkel et al., 2022).

To mitigate these risks, the transition to an AI-prominent SSCM must proactively integrate principles of social inclusion (Kannan, 2018). To achieve this, it necessitates designing algorithms with a deliberate focus on the diversity of supply chain actors. Without such considerations, the risk of marginalizing vulnerable groups will intensify, thereby undermining the social pillar of SSCM.

The provided text highlights the growing importance of SSCM in industry and academia, emphasizing its role in integrating environmental and social considerations into business strategies. To relate this to the risk of social exclusion, we can explore several vital points: Integration of Sustainability and Risk of Social Exclusion, Capabilities and Inclusiveness,

Integration of Sustainability and Risk of Social Exclusion. The emphasis on integrating SSCM into business strategies reflects the need for companies to adopt practices that align with sustainability over time (Oguntegbe et al., 2023). However, if not implemented inclusively, these sustainability practices could inadvertently exacerbate social exclusion. For example, prioritizing environmental sustainability without considering the social impact might lead to practices disadvantaging certain groups, such as low-income workers or marginalized communities.

Capabilities and Inclusiveness. The capabilities developed by firms to remain competitive (Eikelenboom & de Jong, 2019) can contribute to social exclusion if they focus solely on economic and environmental aspects while neglecting social dimensions. For instance, adapting supply chains to be more flexible and competitive might involve automating jobs or outsourcing to lower-cost regions, potentially leaving behind workers who need more skills to transition to new roles or areas.

Understanding of Sustainable Development and Social Impact. The redefinition of business values and policies due to understanding Sustainable Development (Yu & Xu, 2022) includes integrating social and environmental impacts into economic assessments. This broader perspective should mitigate social exclusion risks by ensuring that business practices support equitable treatment of all stakeholders. However, if businesses only superficially address social impacts or fail to engage with affected communities, there remains a risk that social exclusion issues may persist or worsen.

Ethical Standards and Social Responsibility. As companies face pressures to uphold high moral standards and address environmental and social concerns (Meixell & Luoma, 2015), the risk of social exclusion can be mitigated through comprehensive Corporate Social Responsibility (CSR) initiatives. By actively engaging with social stakeholders and addressing their needs, companies can reduce the risk of excluding vulnerable groups. This includes ensuring fair labor practices, promoting diversity and inclusion, and considering the social implications of their supply chain decisions.

Regulations and Industry Practices. In industries like food production, where SSCM research is prevalent, regulations aimed at improving industry processes (Shekarian et al., 2022) may also impact social exclusion. For example, stricter rules on food safety can lead to improved industry standards but may also affect small-scale or informal producers. Ensuring that such regulations do not disproportionately burden smaller or marginalized producers is crucial to prevent social exclusion within the industry.

While SSCM aims to integrate sustainability into business practices, companies must address the risk of social exclusion by ensuring that their sustainability strategies are inclusive and consider the impacts on all stakeholders. This involves balancing environmental and economic goals with a solid commitment to social equity and inclusiveness.

CONCLUSIONS

The objective of the chapter was to carry out a bibliometric analysis of the SSCM study. One thousand two hundred and forty-two documents published in the Web of Science and Scopus databases were analyzed. The results indicate that for the SC to be sustainable over time, it must integrate social and environmental aspects into the economic factor. This will allow you to be competitive.

Changes in the company's environment involve incorporating new variables that affect its performance. The TBL consists of adding to the company's strategy the care of the environment and a business ethic that respects the rights of its workers and the geographical environment of its influence.

The integration of AI and Industry 4.0 technologies into SSCM presents a complex and multifaceted nature. The benefits of its implementation offer unprecedented potential to strengthen the environmental and economic pillars of TBL. Direct advantages such as resource optimization, enhanced traceability, and operational transparency drive more efficient and ecologically responsible management. However, negative aspects emerge within the social dimension, where the uncritical implementation of these technologies carries significant risks. The widening digital divide, workforce displacement, and asymmetries in resource allocation can generate new forms of exclusion, marginalizing the most vulnerable actors in the supply chain and contradicting the foundational principles of sustainability.

Therefore, a fundamental challenge for the future of SSCM lies not in whether to adopt these technologies, but in how to do so in an ethical and equitable manner. Innovation must extend beyond mere technical efficiency. Only through an approach that consciously integrates the human dimension into the digital transformation can SSCM achieve genuine and robust sustainability, ensuring that technological advancements benefit all SC stakeholders rather than just a fraction

Sustainability means that the company remains competitive. Consumers transform their purchasing decisions, favoring companies they consider to have high ethical values. In the same way, countries create rules based on global changes, such as the 2030 Agenda for Sustainable Development. Companies' globalization means that they must comply with different standards throughout the supply chain. Correct implementation of the SSCM allows us to identify the threats and opportunities in its framework of action, creating strategies that maintain and increase the firm's competitiveness.

A future line of research could involve analyzing empirical research across various areas of industry. Focal companies can leverage these findings to ensure a more robust implementation of the SSCM. Another future line of inquiry is to conduct specific analyses on the influence of AI on SSCM. The value of this approach is amplified when implemented in conjunction with related technologies.

ACKNOWLEDGMENT

We appreciate the support granted by Secihti and the Institute of Science, Technology, and Innovation of the state of Michoacán through the Postdoctoral Stays program.

REFERENCES

Bag, S., Telukdarie, A., Pretorius, J. H. C., & Gupta, S. (2018). Industry 4.0 and supply chain sustainability: framework and future research directions. In *Benchmarking* (Vol. 28, Issue 5, pp. 1410–1450). Emerald Group Holdings Ltd. https://doi.org/DOI: 10.1108/BIJ-03-2018-0056

Bari, N., Chimhundu, R., & Chan, K. C. (2022). Dynamic Capabilities to Achieve Corporate Sustainability: A Roadmap to Sustained Competitive Advantage. *Sustainability (Basel)*, *14*(3), 1531. Advance online publication. DOI: 10.3390/su14031531

Beske, P. (2012). Dynamic capabilities and sustainable supply chain management. *International Journal of Physical Distribution & Logistics Management*, *42*(4), 372–387. DOI: 10.1108/09600031211231344

Bruce, M., Daly, L., & Towers, N. (2004). Lean or agile: A solution for supply chain management in the textiles and clothing industry? *International Journal of Operations & Production Management*, *24*(1–2), 151–170. DOI: 10.1108/01443570410514867

Brundtland, G. H. (1987). *World Commission on Environmental and Development: Our Common Future*. World Commission for Environment and Development.

Carter, C. R., & Rogers, D. S. (2008). A framework of sustainable supply chain management: Moving toward new theory. *International Journal of Physical Distribution & Logistics Management*, *38*(5), 360–387. DOI: 10.1108/09600030810882816

Cataldo, I., Banaitis, A., Samadhiya, A., Banaitienė, N., Kumar, A., & Luthra, S. (2022). Sustainable supply chain management in construction: An exploratory review for future research. *Journal of Civil Engineering and Management*, *28*(7), 536–553. DOI: 10.3846/jcem.2022.17202

Christopher, M., Lowson, R., & Peck, H. (2004). Creating agile supply chains in the fashion industry. *International Journal of Retail & Distribution Management*, *32*(8), 367–376. DOI: 10.1108/09590550410546188

Clément, A., Robinot, É., & Trespeuch, L. (2022). Improving ESG Scores with Sustainability Concepts. *Sustainability (Basel), 14*(20), 13154. DOI: 10.3390/su142013154

De Brito, A. P. (2024). Blockchain and Sustainable Forest Supply Chain Management A Literature Review. In *Blockchain as a Technology for Environmental Sustainability* (pp. 108–132). CRC Press., DOI: 10.1201/9781003260905-7

Dinu, V., & Bunea, M. (2019). The corporate social responsibility of the Romanian banking system. *E+M. Ekonomie a Management, 22*(4), 119–133. DOI: 10.15240/tul/001/2019-4-008

Ebinger, F., & Omondi, B. (2020). Leveraging digital approaches for transparency in sustainable supply chains: A conceptual paper. *Sustainability (Basel), 12*(15), 6129. Advance online publication. DOI: 10.3390/su12156129

Eikelenboom, M., & de Jong, G. (2019). The impact of dynamic capabilities on the sustainability performance of SMEs. *Journal of Cleaner Production, 235*(235), 1360–1370. DOI: 10.1016/j.jclepro.2019.07.013

Elkington, J. (2006). Governance for sustainability. *Corporate Governance, 14*(6), 522–529. DOI: 10.1111/j.1467-8683.2006.00527.x

Espinoza-Torres, D., & Segarra-Oña, M. (2022). Disentangling the relationship between prior knowledge and entrepreneurial orientation: A bibliometric study. *Tec Empresarial, 16*(2), 1–17. DOI: 10.18845/te.v16i2.6167

Fracarolli Nunes, M., Lee Park, C., & Paiva, E. L. (2020). Can we have it all? Sustainability trade-offs and cross-insurance mechanisms in supply chains. *International Journal of Operations & Production Management, 40*(9), 1339–1366. DOI: 10.1108/IJOPM-12-2019-0802

Gangi, F., Daniele, L. M., & Varrone, N. (2020). How do corporate environmental policy and corporate reputation affect risk-adjusted financial performance? *Business Strategy and the Environment, 29*(5), 1975–1991. DOI: 10.1002/bse.2482

Gopal, P. R. C., & Thakkar, J. (2016). Sustainable supply chain practices: An empirical investigation on the Indian automobile industry. *Production Planning and Control, 27*(1), 49–64. DOI: 10.1080/09537287.2015.1060368

Intergovernmental Panel on Climate Change (IPCC). (2023). *Climate Change 2021 – The Physical Science Basis: Working Group I Contribution to the Sixth Assessment Report of the Intergovernmental Panel on Climate Change*. Cambridge University Press., DOI: 10.1017/9781009157896

Kannan, D. (2018). Role of multiple stakeholders and the critical success factor theory for the sustainable supplier selection process. *International Journal of Production Economics*, *195*, 391–418. DOI: 10.1016/j.ijpe.2017.02.020

Khodakarami, M., Shabani, A., Farzipoor Saen, R., & Azadi, M. (2015). Developing distinctive two-stage data envelopment analysis models: An application in evaluating the sustainability of supply chain management. *Measurement*, *70*, 62–74. DOI: 10.1016/j.measurement.2015.03.024

Klassen, R. D. (2001). Plant-level environmental management orientation: The influence of management views and plant characteristics. *Production and Operations Management*, *10*(3), 257–275. DOI: 10.1111/j.1937-5956.2001.tb00374.x

Kraus, S., Breier, M., Lim, W. M., Dabić, M., Kumar, S., Kanbach, D., Mukherjee, D., Corvello, V., Piñeiro-Chousa, J., Liguori, E., Palacios-Marqués, D., Schiavone, F., Ferraris, A., Fernandes, C., & Ferreira, J. J. (2022). Literature reviews as independent studies: Guidelines for academic practice. *Review of Managerial Science*, *16*(8), 2577–2595. DOI: 10.1007/s11846-022-00588-8

Kunkel, S., Matthess, M., Xue, B., & Beier, G. (2022). Industry 4.0 in sustainable supply chain collaboration: Insights from an interview study with international buying firms and Chinese suppliers in the electronics industry. *Resources, Conservation and Recycling*, *182*, 106274. Advance online publication. DOI: 10.1016/j.resconrec.2022.106274

Lis, A., Sudolska, A., & Tomanek, M. (2020). Mapping Research on Sustainable Supply-Chain Management. *Sustainability (Basel)*, *12*(10), 3987. DOI: 10.3390/su12103987

Liu, K. S., & Lin, M. H. (2021). Performance assessment on the application of artificial intelligence to sustainable supply chain management in the construction material industry. *Sustainability (Basel)*, *13*(22), 12767. Advance online publication. DOI: 10.3390/su132212767

Luthra, S., & Mangla, S. K. (2018). When strategies matter: Adoption of sustainable supply chain management practices in an emerging economy's context. *Resources, Conservation and Recycling*, *138*, 194–206. DOI: 10.1016/j.resconrec.2018.07.005

Meixell, M. J., & Luoma, P. (2015). Stakeholder pressure in sustainable supply chain management: A systematic review. *International Journal of Physical Distribution & Logistics Management*, *45*(1/2), 69–89. DOI: 10.1108/IJPDLM-05-2013-0155

Mentzer, J. T., Dewitt, W., Keebler, J. S., Min, S., Nix, N. W., Smith, C. D., & Zacharia, Z. G. (2001). Defining supply chain management. *Journal of Business Logistics*, *22*(2), 1–25. DOI: 10.1002/j.2158-1592.2001.tb00001.x

Motevali Haghighi, S., Torabi, S. A., & Ghasemi, R. (2016). An integrated approach for performance evaluation in sustainable supply chain networks (with a case study). *Journal of Cleaner Production*, *137*, 579–597. DOI: 10.1016/j.jclepro.2016.07.119

Nidumolu, R., Prahalad, C. K., & Rangaswami, M. R. (2009). Why Sustainability Is Now the Key Driver of Innovation. In *Harvard Business Review*.

Oguntegbe, K. F., Di Paola, N., & Vona, R. (2023). Communicating responsible management and the role of blockchain technology: Social media analytics for the luxury fashion supply chain. *The TQM Journal*, *35*(2), 446–469. DOI: 10.1108/TQM-10-2021-0296

Panigrahi, S. S., Bahinipati, B., & Jain, V. (2019). Sustainable supply chain management: A literature review and implications for future research. In *Management of Environmental Quality: An International Journal* (Vol. 30, Issue 5, pp. 1001–1049). Emerald Group Holdings Ltd. https://doi.org/DOI: 10.1108/MEQ-01-2018-0003

Pawlicka, K., & Bal, M. (2022). Sustainable Supply Chain Finances implementation model and Artificial Intelligence for innovative omnichannel logistics. *Management*, *26*(1), 19–35. DOI: 10.2478/manment-2019-0082

Petridis, K., Kiosses, N., Tampakoudis, I., & Ben-Abdelaziz, F. (2023). Measuring the efficiency of mutual funds: Does ESG controversies score affect the mutual fund performance during the COVID-19 pandemic? *Operations Research*, *23*(3), 54. Advance online publication. DOI: 10.1007/s12351-023-00795-5

Rejeb, A., Rejeb, K., Simske, S., & Keogh, J. G. (2023). Exploring Blockchain Research in Supply Chain Management: A Latent Dirichlet Allocation-Driven Systematic Review. In *Information (Switzerland)*. Vol. 14, Issue 10. DOI: 10.3390/info14100557

Roberts, J. S. (2003). The Buzz About Supply Chain. In *Inside Supply Management®* (Vol. 14, Issue 7).

Rogers, K., & Hudson, B. (2011). The Triple Bottom Line: The Synergies of Transformative Perceptions and Practices for Sustainability. *OD Practitioner*, *4*(43), 3–9. https://www.researchgate.net/publication/283710434

Roy, V., Schoenherr, T., & Charan, P. (2018). The thematic landscape of literature in sustainable supply chain management (SSCM): A review of the principal facets in SSCM development. In *International Journal of Operations and Production Management* (Vol. 38, Issue 4, pp. 1091–1124). Emerald Group Holdings Ltd. https://doi.org/DOI: 10.1108/IJOPM-05-2017-0260

Saberi, S., Kouhizadeh, M., Sarkis, J., & Shen, L. (2019). Blockchain technology and its relationships to sustainable supply chain management. *International Journal of Production Research*, *57*(7), 2117–2135. DOI: 10.1080/00207543.2018.1533261

Saha, R., Shashi, , Cerchione, R., Singh, R., & Dahiya, R. (2020). Effect of ethical leadership and corporate social responsibility on firm performance: A systematic review. *Corporate Social Responsibility and Environmental Management*, *27*(2), 409–429. DOI: 10.1002/csr.1824

Samuels, A. B., & Pelser, A. M. (2025). Transitioning from Industry 4.0 to 5.0: Sustainable supply chain management and talent management insights. *SA Journal of Human Resource Management*, *23*. Advance online publication. DOI: 10.4102/sajhrm.v23i0.2874

Sánchez-Flores, R. B., Cruz-Sotelo, S. E., Ojeda-Benitez, S., & Ramírez-Barreto, M. (2020). Sustainable Supply Chain Management—A Literature Review on Emerging Economies. *Sustainability (Basel)*, *12*(17), 6972. DOI: 10.3390/su12176972

Seitz, M. A., & Wells, P. E. (2006). Challenging the implementation of corporate sustainability: The case of automotive engine remanufacturing. *Business Process Management Journal*, *12*(6), 822–836. DOI: 10.1108/14637150610710954

Seuring, S., & Müller, M. (2008). From a literature review to a conceptual framework for sustainable supply chain management. *Journal of Cleaner Production*, *16*(15), 1699–1710. DOI: 10.1016/j.jclepro.2008.04.020

Shekarian, E., Ijadi, B., Zare, A., & Majava, J. (2022). Sustainable Supply Chain Management: A Comprehensive Systematic Review of Industrial Practices. In *Sustainability (Switzerland)* (Vol. 14, Issue 13). https://doi.org/DOI: 10.3390/su14137892

Signori, S., San-José, L., Retolaza, J. L., & Rusconi, G. (2021). Stakeholder value creation: Comparing ESG and value-added in European companies. *Sustainability (Basel)*, *13*(3), 1–16. DOI: 10.3390/su13031392

Stadtler, H. (2014). Supply Chain Management: An Overview. In Stadtler, H., & Kilger, C. (Eds.), *Supply chain management and advanced planning* (pp. 3–28). Springer., DOI: 10.1007/978-3-642-55309-7_1

Taylor, K. M., & Vachon, S. (2018). Empirical research on sustainable supply chains: IJPR's contribution and research avenues. In *International Journal of Production Research* (Vol. 56, Issues 1–2, pp. 950–959). Taylor and Francis Ltd. https://doi.org/DOI: 10.1080/00207543.2017.1402139

Teuteberg, F., & Wittstruck, D. (2010). A systematic review of sustainable supply chain management. *In Multikonferenz Wirtschaftsinformatik*, 203.

Tranfield, D., Denyer, D., & Smart, P. (2003). Towards a Methodology for Developing Evidence-Informed Management Knowledge using Systematic Review. *British Journal of Management*, *14*(3), 207–222. DOI: 10.1111/1467-8551.00375

Tyndall, Gene, Christopher Gopal, Wolfgang Partsch, & John Kamauff. (1998). *Supercharging Supply Chains: New Ways to Increase Value Through Global Operational Excellence*. John Wiley & Sons.

Usman, S. (2024). The Impact of COVID-19 on Industry 4.0 Adoption: An Emerging Economy Perspective. *Operations and Supply Chain Management*, *17*(2), 284–298. DOI: 10.31387/oscm0570428

Valenzo-Jiménez, M. A., & Gonzaléz-Samaniego, A. (2021). Capacidad de adaptación y competitividad en microempresas de abarrotes en Cuitzeo, México. *Mercados y Negocios*, *22*(43), 49–76. DOI: 10.32870/myn.v0i43.7629

Yadav, A., Garg, R. K., & Sachdeva, A. (2024). Artificial intelligence applications for information management in sustainable supply chain management: A systematic review and future research agenda. *International Journal of Information Management Data Insights*, *4*(2), 100292. Advance online publication. DOI: 10.1016/j.jjimei.2024.100292

Yu, Y., & Xu, Q. (2022). Influencing Factors of Enterprise R&D Investment: Post-Subsidy, Sustainability, and Heterogeneity. *Sustainability (Basel)*, *14*(10), 5759. Advance online publication. DOI: 10.3390/su14105759

Zhang, Q., Cao, M., Zhang, F., Liu, J., & Li, X. (2020). Effects of corporate social responsibility on customer satisfaction and organizational attractiveness: A signaling perspective. *Business Ethics (Oxford, England)*, *29*(1), 20–34. DOI: 10.1111/beer.12243

Compilation of References

Abramovich, N., & Vasiliu, A. (2023). Sustainability as fairness: A Rawlsian framework linking intergenerational equity and the sustainable development goals (SDGs) with business practices. *Sustainable Development (Bradford)*, *31*(3), 1328–1342. DOI: 10.1002/sd.2451

Adamson, M., Kelan, E., Lewis, P., Śliwa, M., & Rumens, N. (2021). Introduction: Critically interrogating inclusion in organizations. *Organization*, *28*(2), 211–227. DOI: 10.1177/1350508420973307

Aitken, R., Watkins, L., Williams, J., & Kean, A. (2020). The positive role of labeling on consumers' perceived behavioral control and intention to purchase organic food. *Journal of Cleaner Production*, *255*, 120334. DOI: 10.1016/j.jclepro.2020.120334

Allal-Chérif, O., & Makhlouf, M. (2015). Using serious games to manage knowledge: The SECI model perspective. *Journal of Business Research*, *69*(5), 1539–1543. DOI: 10.1016/j.jbusres.2015.10.013

Allam, M., Bazok, R., Bordewick-Dell, U., Czarniecka-Skubina, E., Kazimierczak, R., Laikoja, K., Luik, A., Fuka, M. M., Muleo, R., Peetsmann, E., Petroselli, V., Roasto, M., Średnicka-Tober, D., Veith, M., Mancinelli, R., & Trafialek, J. (2023). Assistance needed for increasing knowledge of HACCP food safety principles for the organic sector in selected EU countries. *Sustainability (Basel)*, *15*(8), 6605. DOI: 10.3390/su15086605

Allegretti, G., & Herzberg, C. (2004). *Participatory budgets in Europe. Between efficiency and growing local democracy*. Transnational Institute. TNI Briefing Series.

Altieri, M. A., & Toledo, V. M. (2011). The agroecological revolution in Latin America: Rescuing nature, ensuring food sovereignty and empowering peasants. *The Journal of Peasant Studies*, *38*(3), 587–612. DOI: 10.1080/03066150.2011.582947

Alvarado, T. E. G. (2006). *Desarrollo endógeno articulado con la red de cooperación empresarial internacional: el caso de México* (Doctoral dissertation, Universidad Complutense de Madrid).

Alvarado, T. E. (2021). The Al-Invest Contribution to the Resilience of the Chemical Company: Development Cooperation. *Journal of International Cooperation and Development, 4*(2), 1. DOI: 10.36941/jicd-2021-0009

Alvarado, T. E. G. (2003). Al-Invest y los intereses comerciales proteccionistas de la Unión Europea hacia Argentina, Brasil y México. *Contaduría y Administración*, (210), 47–70.

Alvarado, T. E. G. (2012). Internacionalización de empresas y desarrollo económico en zonas pobres. *Universidad & Empresa, 14*(23), 45–69.

Amador, J., Melo Gouveia, C., & Pimenta, A. C. (2023). COVID-19, lockdowns and international trade: Evidence from firm-level data. *Empirical Economics, 65*(5), 2427–2466. DOI: 10.1007/s00181-023-02421-x PMID: 37361946

Amézquita Zegarra, R. (2021). Certificaciones complementarias a global GAP: GRASP y BRCGS en el Perú. https://hdl.handle.net/20.500.12996/4901

Andrews, L., & Bucher, H. (2022). Automating discrimination: AI hiring practices and gender inequality. *Cardozo Law Review, 44*, 145.

Antunes, H., & Pinheiro, P. G. (2019). Linking knowledge management, organizational learning, and memory. *Journal Of Innovation & Knowledge, 5*(2), 140–149. DOI: 10.1016/j.jik.2019.04.002

Aoudia, M., Marji, K., & AlQahsi, D. A. (2015). Assessment of Higher Education Quality by Using Cohort of First-year in University. *Procedia: Social and Behavioral Sciences, 191*, 330–335. DOI: 10.1016/j.sbspro.2015.04.310

Araújo, I. F. D., Perobelli, F. S., & Faria, W. R. (2021). Regional and global patterns of participation in value chains: Evidence from Brazil. *Inter Economics, 165*, 154–171. DOI: 10.1016/j.inteco.2020.12.009

Arnstein, S. R. (1969). A Ladder of Citizen Participation. *Journal of the American Institute of Planners, 35*(4), 216–224. DOI: 10.1080/01944366908977225

Ashforth, B. E., & Fried, Y. (1988). The mindlessness of organizational behaviors. *Human Relations, 41*(4), 305–329. DOI: 10.1177/001872678804100403

Aslam, H., Waseem, M., Muneeb, D., Ali, Z., Roubaud, D., & Grebinevych, O. (2025). Customer integration in the supply chain: The role of market orientation and supply chain strategy in the age of digital revolution. *Annals of Operations Research, 348*(3), 2145–2169. DOI: 10.1007/s10479-023-05191-y PMID: 36846244

ASML. (2023). *2023 Annual Report.* ASML.

Athanasopoulou, A., de Reuver, M., Nikou, S., & Bouwman, H. (2019). What technology enabled services impact business models in the automotive industry? An exploratory study. *Futures, 109*, 73–83. DOI: 10.1016/j.futures.2019.04.001

Atmanspacher, H., & Rickles, D. (2022). *Dual-Aspect Monism and the Deep Structure of Meaning*. Routledge., DOI: 10.4324/9781003270584

Augier, M., & Teece, D. J. (2009). Dynamic Capabilities and the Role of Managers in Business Strategy and Economic Performance. *Organization Science, 20*(2), 410–421. DOI: 10.1287/orsc.1090.0424

Auken, I. (2020, November 11). Welcome to 2030: I own nothing, have no privacy, and life has never been better. Forbes. https://www.forbes.com/sites/worldeconomicforum/2016/11/10/shopping-i-cant-really-remember-what-that-is-or-welcome-to-2030-i-own-nothing-have-no-privacy-and-life-has-never-been-better/

Ayaz, A., Dedebayraktar, D., Inan-Eroglu, E., Besler, H. T., & Buyuktuncer, Z. (2021). How does nutrition education contribute to the consumers' use and attitudes towards food labels? *Nutrition & Food Science, 51*(3), 517–528. DOI: 10.1108/NFS-05-2020-0174

Aydın, E., & Turan, M. (2023). An AI-based shortlisting model for sustainability of human resource management. *Sustainability (Basel), 15*(3), 2737. DOI: 10.3390/su15032737

Aylmer, J. (2024, October 14). Carmakers locking basic features behind paid subscription services. Straight Arrow News. https://san.com/cc/carmakers-locking-basic-features-behind-paid-subscription-services/

Bag, S., Telukdarie, A., Pretorius, J. H. C., & Gupta, S. (2018). Industry 4.0 and supply chain sustainability: framework and future research directions. In *Benchmarking* (Vol. 28, Issue 5, pp. 1410–1450). Emerald Group Holdings Ltd. https://doi.org/DOI: 10.1108/BIJ-03-2018-0056

Baiocchi, G., Ganuza, E. (2014). Participatory Budgeting as if Emancipation Mattered. 29-50. .DOI: 10.1177/0032329213512978

Baker, R. S., & Hawn, A. (2022). Algorithmic bias in education. *International Journal of Artificial Intelligence in Education*, •••, 1–41.

Ban, O. I., Hatos, R., Bugnar, N., Sasu, D., Popa, A. L., & Fora, A. (2024). Evaluation of the Quality of Higher Education Services by Revised IPA in the Perspective of Digitization. *Sustainability (Basel)*, *16*(7), 3017. DOI: 10.3390/su16073017

Barari, M., Ferm, C. L. E., Quach, S., Thaichon, P., & Ngo, L. (2024). The dark side of artificial intelligence in marketing: Meta-analytics review. *Marketing Intelligence & Planning*, *42*(7), 1234–1256. DOI: 10.1108/MIP-09-2023-0494

Bari, N., Chimhundu, R., & Chan, K. C. (2022). Dynamic Capabilities to Achieve Corporate Sustainability: A Roadmap to Sustained Competitive Advantage. *Sustainability (Basel)*, *14*(3), 1531. Advance online publication. DOI: 10.3390/su14031531

Barney, J. B. (1995). Looking inside for a competitive advantage. *The Academy of Management Perspectives*, *9*(4), 49–61. DOI: 10.5465/ame.1995.9512032192

Barocas, S., Hardt, M., & Narayanan, A. (2023). *Fairness and machine learning: Limitations and opportunities*. MIT press.

Bartal, D. (2022). The elusive nature of peace education. In Salomon, G., & Nevo, B. (Eds.), *Peace education: The concept, principles, and practices around the world* (pp. 27–36). Lawrence Erlbaum Associates Publishers.

BCG. (2014). *Transformation, the imperative to change*. BCG. Link: https://www.bcg.com/publications/2014/people-organization-transformation-imperative-change

BCG. (2023, September 2). Rewriting the Rules of Software-Defined Vehicles. BCG Global. https://www.bcg.com/publications/2023/rewriting-rules-of-software-defined-vehicles

Beaver, H. D. (2024, January 2). Automakers' Added Subscription Fees Raise Legal Questions. Kiplinger. https://www.kiplinger.com/personal-finance/automakers-added-subscription-fees-raise-legal-questions

Bejarano Carbo, M. P. (2021). Machine learning applications in the United States criminal justice system: A critical content analysis of the COMPAS recidivism risk assessment.

Belanche, D., Belk, R. W., Casaló, L. V., & Flavián, C. (2024). The dark side of artificial intelligence in services. *Service Industries Journal*, *44*(3–4), 149–172. DOI: 10.1080/02642069.2024.2305451

Bender, E. M., Gebru, T., McMillan-Major, A., & Shmitchell, S. (2021). On the dangers of stochastic parrots: can language models be too big? *FAccT '21: Proceedings of the 2021 ACM Conference on Fairness, Accountability, and Transparency*, 610–623. DOI: 10.1145/3442188.3445922

Bendermacher, G. W. G., Egbrink, M. G. A. O., Wolfhagen, H. A. P., Leppink, J., & Dolmans, D. H. J. M. (2017). Reinforcing pillars for quality culture development: A path analytic model. *Studies in Higher Education*, *44*(4), 643–662. DOI: 10.1080/03075079.2017.1393060

Bennett, E. A., & Grabs, J. (2024). How can sustainable business models distribute value more equitably in global value chains? Introducing "value chain profit sharing" as an emerging alternative to fair trade, direct trade, or solidarity trade. *Business Ethics, the Environment & Responsibility*. Advance online publication. DOI: 10.1111/beer.12666

Benoit, S., Colliard, J.-E., Hurlin, C., & Perignon, C. (2015). Where the Risks Lie: A Survey on Systemic Risk. SSRN *Electronic Journal*. DOI: 10.2139/ssrn.2577961

Berlenbach (2024). *Die Jagd auf Kupfer: Bergbau-Aktien vs. Rohstoff-ETC*. Podcast. Link. https://www.wiwo.de/podcast/lebenmitaktien/podcast-leben-mit-aktien-die-jagd-auf-kupfer-bergbau-aktien-vs-rohstoff-etc/29777844.html

Berry, C., Acharya, N., & Crowter, L. (2024). The light at the end of the tunnel? A systematic review of higher education student experiences of hope. *PLoS One*, *19*(6), e0304596. DOI: 10.1371/journal.pone.0304596 PMID: 38885226

Beske, P. (2012). Dynamic capabilities and sustainable supply chain management. *International Journal of Physical Distribution & Logistics Management*, *42*(4), 372–387. DOI: 10.1108/09600031211231344

Beverelli, C., Stolzenburg, V., Koopman, R. B., & Neumueller, S. (2019). Domestic value chains as stepping stones to global value chain integration. *World Economy*, *42*(5), 1467–1494. DOI: 10.1111/twec.12779

Bevilacqua, D. (2020). Global Food Safety Regulation and the Interplay between Global Standards and WTO Law: How to Close the Legitimacy Gap? In *The Legitimacy of Standardisation as a Regulatory Technique* (pp. 243-265). Edward Elgar Publishing. DOI: https://doi.org/DOI: 10.4337/9781789902952.00018

Bhasin, H. (2023). *Machine Learning for Beginners: Build and deploy Machine Learning systems using Python*. BPB Publications.

Bierenkoven, C. (2023, September 27). BMW's Heated Seat Subscription Is Dead; Others Live On. Edmunds. https://www.edmunds.com/car-news/bmw-relents-on-heated-seat-subscription.html

Bigman, Y. E., Wilson, D., Arnestad, M. N., Waytz, A., & Gray, K. (2023). Algorithmic discrimination causes less moral outrage than human discrimination. *Journal of Experimental Psychology. General, 152*(1), 4–27. DOI: 10.1037/xge0001250 PMID: 35758989

Blackwell, A. F. (2024). *Moral Codes: Designing Alternatives to AI.* MIT Press. DOI: 10.7551/mitpress/14872.001.0001

Blesh, J., Mehrabi, Z., Wittman, H., Kerr, R. B., James, D., Madsen, S., Smith, O. M., Snapp, S., Stratton, A. E., & Bakar, R. (2023). Against the odds: Neservesnd institutional pathways enabling agricult,uthereby diversification. *One Earth, 6*(5), 479–491. DOI: 10.1016/j.oneear.2023.03.004

Boehm, O. (2022). *Radikaler Universalismus: Jenseits von Identität| Ausgezeichnet mit dem Leipziger Buchpreis zur Europäischen Verständigung 2024.* Ullstein Buchverlage.

Bolwig, S., Ponte, S., Du Toit, A., Riisgaard, L., & Halberg, N. (2010). Integrating Poverty and Environmental Concerns into Value-Chain Analysis: A Conceptual Framework. *Development Policy Review, 28*(2), 173–194. DOI: 10.1111/j.1467-7679.2010.00480.x

Bomba, M. Y., & Susol, N. Y. (2020). Main requirements for food safety management systems under international standards: BRC, IFS, FSSC 22000, ISO 22000, Global GAP, SQF. *Scientific Messenger of LNU of Veterinary Medicine and Biotechnologies. Series. Food Technology, 22*(93), 18–25. DOI: 10.32718/nvlvet-f9304

Bose, S. K., & Chatterjee, J. (2008). CHALLENGES FACED BY THE INDIAN TINPLATE PACKAGING INDUSTRY. *Analysis*, •••, 13.

Boss, M. (1974). Economic theory of democracy: An empirical test. *Public Choice, 19*(1), 111–115. DOI: 10.1007/BF01718551

Bozkurt, A. (2024). Cocreation, authorship, ownership, academic ethics and integrity in a time of generative AI. *Open Praxis, 16*(1), GenAI. https://doi-org.wdg.biblio.udg.mx:8443/10.55982/openpraxis.16.1.654

Bracic, A. (2020). *Breaking the exclusion cycle: How to promote cooperation between majority and minority ethnic groups.* Oxford University Press. DOI: 10.1093/oso/9780190050672.001.0001

Brandenburger, A. M., & Stuart, H. W.Jr. (1996). V alue-based B usiness S trategy. *Journal of Economics & Management Strategy*, *5*(1), 5–24. DOI: 10.1111/j.1430-9134.1996.00005.x

Brayne, S. (2021). *Predict and surveil: Data, discretion, and the future of policing*. Oxford University Press.

Bremmer, I., & Suleyman, M. (2023). The AI power paradox: Can states learn to govern artificial intelligence-before it's too late? *Foreign Affairs*, *102*, 26.

Brockie, T., Clark, T. C., Best, O., Power, T., Bourque Bearskin, L., Kurtz, D. L., Lowe, J., & Wilson, D. (2023). Indigenous social exclusion to inclusion: Case studies on Indigenous nursing leadership in four high income countries. *Journal of Clinical Nursing*, *32*(3-4), 610–624. DOI: 10.1111/jocn.15801 PMID: 33942940

Brooks, C., Kovanović, V., & Nguyen, Q. (2023). Predictive modeling of student success. In *Handbook of artificial intelligence in education* (pp. 350–369). Edward Elgar Publishing. DOI: 10.4337/9781800375413.00027

Broussard, M. (2023). *More than a glitch: Confronting race, gender, and ability bias in tech*. MIT Press. DOI: 10.7551/mitpress/14234.001.0001

Browne, K., Banerjea, N., McGlynn, N., Bakshi, L., Beethi, S., & Biswas, R. (2021). The limits of legislative change: Moving beyond inclusion/exclusion to create 'a life worth living'. Environment and Planning C. *Politics and Space*, *39*(1), 30–52.

Bruce, M., Daly, L., & Towers, N. (2004). Lean or agile: A solution for supply chain management in the textiles and clothing industry? *International Journal of Operations & Production Management*, *24*(1–2), 151–170. DOI: 10.1108/01443570410514867

Brundtland, G. H. (1987). *World Commission on Environmental and Development: Our Common Future*. World Commission for Environment and Development.

Bryer, A. (2020). Making Organizations More Inclusive: The Work of Belonging. *Organization Studies*, *41*(5), 641–660. DOI: 10.1177/0170840618814576

Bulathwela, S., Pérez-Ortiz, M., Holloway, C., Cukurova, M., & Shawe-Taylor, J. (2024). Artificial intelligence alone will not democratise education: On educational inequality, techno-solutionism and inclusive tools. *Sustainability (Basel)*, *16*(2), 781. DOI: 10.3390/su16020781

Buolamwini, J. (2024). *Unmasking AI: My mission to protect what is human in a world of machines*. Random House.

Bush, S. R., Oosterveer, P., Bailey, M., & Mol, A. P. J. (2015). Sustainability governance of chains and networks: A review and future outlook. *Journal of Cleaner Production, 107*, 8–19. DOI: 10.1016/j.jclepro.2014.10.019

Business Dictionary. (2024). *Transformational Leadership*. Business Dictionary. Link. http://www.businessdictionary.com/definition/transformational-leadership.html

Butollo, F. (2021). Digitalization and the geographies of production: Towards reshoring or global fragmentation? *Competition & Change, 25*(2), 259–278. DOI: 10.1177/1024529420918160

Buttol, V. (2023). Ethical implications of Artificial Intelligence: the relationship between algorithms and kindness.

Cabanelas, P., Parkhurst, G., Thomopoulos, N., & Lampón, J. F. (2023). A dynamic capability evaluation of emerging business models for new mobility. *Research in Transportation Business & Management, 100964*, 100964. Advance online publication. DOI: 10.1016/j.rtbm.2023.100964

Cambridge Dictionary. (2024). *Inclusion*. Cambridge Dictionary.

Cameron, D. (2025, April 28). Car Subscription Features Raise Your Risk of Government Surveillance, Police Records Show. Wired. https://www.wired.com/story/police-records-car-subscription-features-surveillance/

Canter, E. (2025, March 27). NCIL Welcomes Waymo to Washington, DC; Advocates for Inclusive Innovation in Autonomous Transportation. National Council on Independent Living. https://ncil.org/news/announcements/waymo-dc/

Carmines, E., & Zeller, R. (1979). *Reliability and Validity Assessment*. DOI: 10.4135/9781412985642

Carr, M., Chen, M. A., & Tate, J. (2000). Globalization and Home-Based Workers. *Feminist Economics, 6*(3), 123–142. DOI: 10.1080/135457000750020164

Carter, C. R., & Rogers, D. S. (2008). A framework of sustainable supply chain management: Moving toward new theory. *International Journal of Physical Distribution & Logistics Management, 38*(5), 360–387. DOI: 10.1108/09600030810882816

Casey, D. (2007). Private Food Safety and Quality Standards and the WTO. Social Science Research Network. https://kar.kent.ac.uk/31704/

Castagnoli, R., Büchi, G., Coeurderoy, R., & Cugno, M. (2022). Evolution of industry 4.0 and international business: A systematic literature review and a research agenda. *European Management Journal, 40*(4), 572–589. DOI: 10.1016/j.emj.2021.09.002

Cataldo, I., Banaitis, A., Samadhiya, A., Banaitienė, N., Kumar, A., & Luthra, S. (2022). Sustainable supply chain management in construction: An exploratory review for future research. *Journal of Civil Engineering and Management, 28*(7), 536–553. DOI: 10.3846/jcem.2022.17202

Ceurstemont, S. (2025). Controlling AI's growing energy needs. *Communications of the ACM, 68*(3), 15–17. DOI: 10.1145/3703788

Chadwick, A. (2009). Web 2.0: New Challenges for the Study of E-Democracy in an Era of Informational Exuberance. A Journal of Law and Policy for the Information Society, pp. 9-41. .DOI: 10.7551/mitpress/9006.003.0005

Chaka, C. (2022). Digital marginalization, data marginalization, and algorithmic exclusions: A critical southern decolonial approach to datafication, algorithms, and digital citizenship from the Souths. Journal of e-Learning and Knowledge Society, 18(3), 83-95.

Chalupová, M., Rojík, S., Kotoučková, H., & Kauerová, L. (2020). Food labels (quality, origin, and sustainability): The experience of Czech producers. *Sustainability (Basel), 13*(1), 318. DOI: 10.3390/su13010318

Chan, C. K. Y., & Hu, W. (2023). Students' voices on generative AI: Perceptions, benefits, and challenges in higher education. *International Journal of Educational Technology in Higher Education, 20*(1), 43. https://doi-org.wdg.biblio.udg.mx:8443/10.1186/s41239-023-00411-8. DOI: 10.1186/s41239-023-00411-8

Chang, H., & Andreoni, A. (2020). Industrial Policy in the 21st Century. *Development and Change, 51*(2), 324–351. DOI: 10.1111/dech.12570

Chankseliani, M., & McCowan, T. (2020). Higher education and the Sustainable Development Goals. *Higher Education, 81*(1), 1–8. DOI: 10.1007/s10734-020-00652-w PMID: 33173242

Charalabidis, Y. (2022). Artificial intelligence (AI). In *The Palgrave Encyclopedia of Interest Groups, Lobbying and Public Affairs* (pp. 43–50). Springer International Publishing. DOI: 10.1007/978-3-030-44556-0_129

Chee, F. Y. (2025, March 5). EU plans law to give car services groups access to vehicle data. Reuters. https://www.reuters.com/business/autos-transportation/eu-plans-law-give-car-services-groups-access-vehicle-data-2025-03-04/?utm_source=chatgpt.com

Chen, J., Weng, G. K., Cho, R. L., & Wei, H. (2024). Knowledge dissemination trajectory of bim in construction engineering applications. *Journal of Civil Engineering and Management, 30*(4), 343–353. DOI: 10.3846/jcem.2024.21353

Chen, W. L., & Wang, C.-J. (2012). Study of the Construction of Assessment System on Regional Innovation Capacity in Knowledge Management. *Procedia Engineering*, *29*, 1830–1834. DOI: 10.1016/j.proeng.2012.01.221

Chen, Y., Pan, X., Liu, P., & Vanhaverbeke, W. (2024). How does digital transformation empower knowledge creation? Evidence from Chinese manufacturing enterprises. *Journal Of Innovation & Knowledge*, *9*(2), 100481. DOI: 10.1016/j.jik.2024.100481

Chen, Z. (2023). Artificial intelligence-virtual trainer: Innovative didactics aimed at personalized training needs. *Journal of the Knowledge Economy*, *14*(2), 2007–2025. DOI: 10.1007/s13132-022-00985-0 PMID: 40479149

Chiu, T. K. F. (2023). The impact of Generative AI (GenAI) on practices, policies and research direction in education: A case of ChatGPT and Midjourney. *Interactive Learning Environments*, *32*(10), 6187–6203. DOI: 10.1080/10494820.2023.2253861

Chkanikova, O., & Sroufe, R. (2021). Third-party sustainability certifications in food retailing: Certification design from a sustainable supply chain management perspective. *Journal of Cleaner Production*, *282*, 124344. DOI: 10.1016/j.jclepro.2020.124344

Chopra, A., Patel, H., Rajput, D. S., & Bansal, N. (2024). Empowering Inclusive Education: Leveraging AI-ML and Innovative Tech Stacks to Support Students with Learning Disabilities in Higher Education. In *Applied Assistive Technologies and Informatics for Students with Disabilities* (pp. 255–275). Springer Nature Singapore. DOI: 10.1007/978-981-97-0914-4_15

Chor, D., Manova, K., & Yu, Z. (2021). Growing like China: Firm performance and global production line position. *Journal of International Economics*, *130*, 103445. DOI: 10.1016/j.jinteco.2021.103445

Cho, S. (2008). Post-racialism. *Iowa Law Review*, *94*, 1589.

Christopher, M., Lowson, R., & Peck, H. (2004). Creating agile supply chains in the fashion industry. *International Journal of Retail & Distribution Management*, *32*(8), 367–376. DOI: 10.1108/09590550410546188

CIPD. (2019). *Building Inclusive Workplaces: Assessing the Evidence. Research report*, September. CIPD. Link: https://www.cipd.co.uk/Images/building-inclusive-workplaces-report-sept-2019_tcm18-64154.pdf accessed 18-05-2024.

Ciravegna, L., & Michailova, S. (2022). Why the world economy needs, but will not get, more globalization in the post-COVID-19 decade. *Journal of International Business Studies*, *53*(1), 172–186. DOI: 10.1057/s41267-021-00467-6 PMID: 34511653

Claborn, K. (2024). *Exploring the Spread, Use, and Impact of Buzzwords on Decision Making in Conservation: A Mixed Methods Approach.* Arizona State University.

Clapp, J., Moseley, W. G., Burlingame, B., & Termine, P. (2022). The case for a six-dimensional food security framework. *Food Policy, 106*, 102164. DOI: 10.1016/j.foodpol.2021.102164

Claydon, L. S. (2015). Rigour in quantitative research. *Nursing Standard, 29*(47), 43–48. DOI: 10.7748/ns.29.47.43.e8820 PMID: 26198528

Clément, A., Robinot, É., & Trespeuch, L. (2022). Improving ESG Scores with Sustainability Concepts. *Sustainability (Basel), 14*(20), 13154. DOI: 10.3390/su142013154

Coccia, M. (2010). Democratization is the driving force for technological and economic change. *Technological Forecasting and Social Change, 77*(2), 248–264. DOI: 10.1016/j.techfore.2009.06.007

Codex Alimentarius Commission (CAC). (2023). *Codex texts and standards.* https://www.fao.org/fao-who-codexalimentarius

Coeckelbergh, M. (2024). *Why AI Undermines Democracy and What To Do about It.* Polity Press.

Coglianese, C., & Lai, A. (2021). Algorithm vs. algorithm. *Duke Law Journal, 71*, 1281.

Combs, G. M., Milosevic, I., & Bilimoria, D. (2019). Introduction to the Special Topic Forum: Critical Discourse: Envisioning the Place and Future of Diversity and Inclusion in Organizations. *Journal of Leadership & Organizational Studies, 26*(3), 277–286. DOI: 10.1177/1548051819857739

Comşa, I. S., Molnar, A., Tal, I., Bergamin, P., Muntean, G. M., Muntean, C. H., & Trestian, R. (2021). A machine learning resource allocation solution to improve video quality in remote education. *IEEE Transactions on Broadcasting, 67*(3), 664–684. DOI: 10.1109/TBC.2021.3068872

Conteduca, F. P., Giglioli, S., Giordano, C., Mancini, M., & Panon, L. (2025). Trade fragmentation unveiled: Five facts on the reconfiguration of global, US and EU trade. *Economia e Politica Industriale.* Advance online publication. DOI: 10.1007/s40812-024-00337-w

Contractor, F. J. (2022). The world economy will need even more globalization in the post-pandemic 2021 decade. *Journal of International Business Studies, 53*(1), 156–171. DOI: 10.1057/s41267-020-00394-y PMID: 33551513

Contractor, F. J., Kumar, V., Kundu, S. K., & Pedersen, T. (2010). Reconceptualizing the Firm in a World of Outsourcing and Offshoring: The Organizational and Geographical Relocation of High-Value Company Functions. *Journal of Management Studies, 47*(8), 1417–1433. DOI: 10.1111/j.1467-6486.2010.00945.x

Cook, D., & Patel, N. (2023). Dollar invoicing, global value chains, and the business cycle dynamics of international trade. *Journal of International Economics, 145*, 103839. DOI: 10.1016/j.jinteco.2023.103839

Cooke, B., & Kothari, U. (2001). *Participation: The New Tyranny*. Zed Books.

Coots, M., Linn, K. A., Goel, S., Navathe, A. S., & Parikh, R. B. (2025). Racial bias in clinical and population health algorithms: A critical review of current debates. *Annual Review of Public Health, 46*(1), 46. DOI: 10.1146/annurev-publhealth-071823-112058 PMID: 39626231

Cordero, J., Torres-Zambrano, J., & Cordero-Castillo, A. (2024). Integration of Generative Artificial Intelligence in Higher Education: Best Practices. *Education Sciences, 15*(1), 32. DOI: 10.3390/educsci15010032

Córdoba, J. (2007). Developing Inclusion and Critical Reflection in Information Systems Planning. *Organization, 14*(6), 909–927. DOI: 10.1177/1350508407082266

Cornwall, A. (2008). Unpacking 'Participation': Models, meanings, and practices. *Community Development Journal: An International Forum, 43*(3), 269–283. DOI: 10.1093/cdj/bsn010

Cottrill, K., Lopez, P. D., & Hoffman, C. C. (2014). How authentic leadership and inclusion benefit organizations. *Equality, Diversity and Inclusion*. Advance online publication. DOI: 10.1108/EDI-05-2012-0041

Coveri, A., Cozza, C., Nascia, L., & Zanfei, A. (2020). Supply chain contagion and the role of industrial policy. *Economia e Politica Industriale, 47*(3), 467–482. DOI: 10.1007/s40812-020-00167-6

Crawford, K. (2021). *The atlas of AI: Power, politics, and the planetary costs of artificial intelligence*. Yale University Press.

Cremin, H., & Bevington, T. (2017). *Positive Peace in Schools: Tackling Conflict and Creating a Culture of Peace in the Classroom*. Routledge., DOI: 10.4324/9781315304236

Cruz, C. A., & Matos, F. (2023). ESG Maturity: A software framework for the challenges of ESG data in investment. *Sustainability (Basel), 15*(3), 2610. DOI: 10.3390/su15032610

Csaszar, F. A., Ketkar, H., & Kim, H. (2024). Artificial Intelligence and Strategic Decision-Making: Evidence from Entrepreneurs and Investors. *Strategy Science*, *9*(4), 322–345. Advance online publication. DOI: 10.1287/stsc.2024.0190

Cuconato, M. (2023). Participation and Social Innovation as a Compass towards Integration: The Rationale behind the INTE-great Project. *Societies (Basel, Switzerland)*, *13*(6), 145. DOI: 10.3390/soc13060145

Dahl, R. (1998). *On Democracy*. Yale University Press.

Dai, M., Maitra, M., & Yu, M. (2016). Unexceptional exporter performance in China? The role of processing trade. *Journal of Development Economics*, *121*, 177–189. DOI: 10.1016/j.jdeveco.2016.03.007

Davies, D. (2025). *The Unaccountability Machine: Why Big Systems Make Terrible Decisions—and How the World Lost Its Mind*. University of Chicago Press.

Davies, S., Seitamaa-Hakkarainen, P., & Hakkarainen, K. (2024). Knowledge creation through maker practices and the role of teacher and peer support in collaborative invention projects. *International Journal of Computer-Supported Collaborative Learning*, *19*(3), 283–310. DOI: 10.1007/s11412-024-09427-2

Davis, K. F., Downs, S., & Gephart, J. A. (2021). Towards food supply chain resilience to environmental shocks. *Nature Food*, *2*(1), 54–65. DOI: 10.1038/s43016-020-00196-3 PMID: 37117650

Day, G. S. (2011). Closing the Marketing Capabilities Gap. *Journal of Marketing*, *75*(4), 183–195. DOI: 10.1509/jmkg.75.4.183

De Brito, A. P. (2024). Blockchain and Sustainable Forest Supply Chain Management A Literature Review. In *Blockchain as a Technology for Environmental Sustainability* (pp. 108–132). CRC Press., DOI: 10.1201/9781003260905-7

Deguchi, A., Hirai, C., Matsuoka, H., Nakano, T., Oshima, K., Tai, M., & Tani, S. (2020). *What is Society 5.0?* En Society., DOI: 10.1007/978-981-15-2989-4_1

Del Giudice, M., Scuotto, V., & Papa, A. (2023). Knowledge Management and AI in Society 5.0. https://doi.org/DOI: 10.4324/9781003258056

DeMatthews, D. (2021). Undoing systems of exclusion: Exploring inclusive leadership and systems thinking in two inclusive elementary schools. *Journal of Educational Administration*, *59*(1), 5–21. DOI: 10.1108/JEA-02-2020-0044

Demchig, B. (2015). Knowledge Management Capability Level Assessment of the Higher Education Institutions: Case Study from Mongolia. *Procedia: Social and Behavioral Sciences*, *174*, 3633–3640. DOI: 10.1016/j.sbspro.2015.01.1082

DeStefano, T., & Timmis, J. (2024). Robots and export quality. *Journal of Development Economics*, *168*, 103248. DOI: 10.1016/j.jdeveco.2023.103248

Dhal, S. B., & Kar, D. (2024). Transforming Agricultural Productivity with AI-Driven Forecasting: Innovations in Food Security and Supply Chain Optimization. *Forecasting*, *6*(4), 925–951. DOI: 10.3390/forecast6040046

Diekman, C., Ryan, C. D., & Oliver, T. L. (2023). Misinformation and disinformation in food science and nutrition: Impact on practice. *The Journal of Nutrition*, *153*(1), 3–9. DOI: 10.1016/j.tjnut.2022.10.001 PMID: 36913465

Dinu, V., & Bunea, M. (2019). The corporate social responsibility of the Romanian banking system. *E+M. Ekonomie a Management*, *22*(4), 119–133. DOI: 10.15240/tul/001/2019-4-008

Doğan, M., Celik, A., & Arslan, H. (2025). AI In Higher Education: Risks and Opportunities From the Academician Perspective. *European Journal of Education*, *60*(1), e12863. DOI: 10.1111/ejed.12863

Dogru, T., Line, N., Hanks, L., Acikgoz, F., Abbott, J., Bakir, S., Berbekova, A., Bilgihan, A., Iskender, A., Kizildag, M., Lee, M., Lee, W., McGinley, S., Mody, M., Onder, I., Ozdemir, O., & Suess, C. (2023). The implications of generative artificial intelligence in academic research and higher education in tourism and hospitality. *Tourism Economics*, *0*(0), 13548166231204065. https://doi-org.wdg.biblio.udg.mx:8443/10.1177/13548166231204065

Dolan, C., & Humphrey, J. (2004). Changing Governance Patterns in the Trade in Fresh Vegetables between Africa and the United Kingdom. *Environment and Planning A. Environment & Planning A*, *36*(3), 491–509. DOI: 10.1068/a35281

Donate, M. J., & Canales, J. I. (2012). A new approach to the concept of knowledge strategy. *Journal of Knowledge Management*, *16*(1), 22–44. DOI: 10.1108/13673271211198927

Doron, G., Genway, S., Roberts, M., & Jasti, S. (2024). Generative AI: Driving productivity and scientific breakthroughs in pharmaceutical R&D. *Drug Discovery Today*, *104272*. Advance online publication. DOI: 10.1016/j.drudis.2024.104272 PMID: 39675517

Dos Santos, R. B., Torrisi, N. M., & Pantoni, R. P. (2021). Third party certification of agri-food supply chain using smart contracts and blockchain tokens. *Sensors (Basel)*, *21*(16), 5307. DOI: 10.3390/s21165307 PMID: 34450749

Draws, T., Szlávik, Z., Timmermans, B., Tintarev, N., Varshney, K. R., & Hind, M. (2021). *Disparate Impact Diminishes Consumer Trust Even for Advantaged Users* (Vol. 12684)., DOI: 10.1007/978-3-030-79460-6_11

Driscoll, P. J., Parnell, G. S., & Henderson, D. L. (Eds.). (2022). *Decision making in systems engineering and management*. John Wiley & Sons.

Dufour, M., Elias-Pinsonnault, S., & Tremblay-Pepin, S. (2025). An international interface: Democratic planning in a global context. *Competition & Change*, *29*(1), 83–100. DOI: 10.1177/10245294231212681

Ebinger, F., & Omondi, B. (2020). Leveraging digital approaches for transparency in sustainable supply chains: A conceptual paper. *Sustainability (Basel)*, *12*(15), 6129. Advance online publication. DOI: 10.3390/su12156129

Egbert, S., & Mann, M. (2021). Discrimination in predictive policing: The (dangerous) myth of impartiality and the need for STS analysis. In *Automating crime prevention, surveillance, and military operations* (pp. 25–46). Springer International Publishing. DOI: 10.1007/978-3-030-73276-9_2

Egede, E. A. (2013). International and National Marketing Channel Decisions For Emerging Markets. *Developing Country Studies*, *3*(10), 149.

Eikelenboom, M., & de Jong, G. (2019). The impact of dynamic capabilities on the sustainability performance of SMEs. *Journal of Cleaner Production*, *235*(235), 1360–1370. DOI: 10.1016/j.jclepro.2019.07.013

Eisenhardt, K. M., & Martin, J. A. (2000). Dynamic Capabilities: What Are They? *Strategic Management Journal*, *21*(10/11), 1105–1121. DOI: 10.1002/1097-0266(200010/11)21:10/11<1105::AID-SMJ133>3.0.CO;2-E

Elkadi, L. (2021). Student Engagement with Specialised Videos in Higher Education (Doctoral dissertation, University of East Anglia).

Elkington, J. (2006). Governance for sustainability. *Corporate Governance*, *14*(6), 522–529. DOI: 10.1111/j.1467-8683.2006.00527.x

Emma, L. (2024). *The Ethical Implications of Artificial Intelligence: A Deep Dive into Bias*. Fairness, and Transparency.

Emmert-Aronson, B. O., Moore, M. T., & Brown, T. A. (2014). Differential Item Functioning of the Symptoms of Major Depression by Race and Ethnicity: An Item Response Theory Analysis. *Journal of Psychopathology and Behavioral Assessment*, *36*(3), 424–431. DOI: 10.1007/s10862-014-9407-4

ESG (2024). *What is Materiality in ESG? - ESG | The Report*. Link: esgthereport.com

Espinoza-Torres, D., & Segarra-Oña, M. (2022). Disentangling the relationship between prior knowledge and entrepreneurial orientation: A bibliometric study. *Tec Empresarial*, *16*(2), 1–17. DOI: 10.18845/te.v16i2.6167

Faber, M., Kilic, K., Kozliakov, G., & Marin, D. (2025). Global value chains in a world of uncertainty and automation. *Journal of International Economics*, *155*, 104079. DOI: 10.1016/j.jinteco.2025.104079

Falk, M. (2021). Artificial stupidity. *Interdisciplinary Science Reviews*, *46*(1-2), 36–52. DOI: 10.1080/03080188.2020.1840219

FAO. (2021). *The state of food security and nutrition in the world 2021*. Food and Agriculture Organization of the United Nations., DOI: 10.4060/cb4474en

Ferdman, B. M. (2017). Paradoxes of Inclusion: Understanding and Managing the Tensions of Diversity and Multiculturalism. *The Journal of Applied Behavioral Science*, *53*(2), 235–263. DOI: 10.1177/0021886317702608

Ferdman, F. M., & Deane, B. R. (2014). *Diversity at Work: The Practice of Inclusion*. Jossey-Bass., DOI: 10.1002/9781118764282.ch1

Ferigotti, C. M. S., da Cunha, S. K., & dos Santos, J. S. (2020). Dynamic capabilities and business model in the transition to sustainability: The case of Bosch/Curitiba-Brazil. *International Business, Trade and Institutional Sustainability*, 81-95. https://doi.org/DOI: 10.1007/978-3-030-26759-9_5

Fernandes, A. M., Kee, H. L., & Winkler, D. (2022). Determinants of Global Value Chain Participation: Cross-Country Evidence. *The World Bank Economic Review*, *36*(2), 329–360. DOI: 10.1093/wber/lhab017

Fernández, I. A. (2023). Innovation and international business: A systematic literature review. *Heliyon*, *9*(1), e12956. DOI: 10.1016/j.heliyon.2023.e12956 PMID: 36704276

Feroz, A. K., Khan, G. F., & Sponder, M. (2024). *Digital analytics for marketing*. Routledge.

Fialho, I., Cid, M., & Coppi, M. (2023). Pedagogical Assessment in Higher Education: The Importance of Training. *Education Sciences*, *13*(12), 1248. DOI: 10.3390/educsci13121248

Fincham, F. D., & Linfield, K. J. (1997). A new look at marital quality: Can spouses feel positive and negative about their marriage? *Austin. Journal of Family Psychology*, *11*(4), 489–502. DOI: 10.1037/0893-3200.11.4.489-502

Fishkin, J. (2011). *When the People Speak: Deliberative Democracy and Public Consultation*. Academic., DOI: 10.1093/acprof:osobl/9780199604432.001.0001

Floridi, L. (2023). AI as Agency Without Intelligence: On ChatGPT, Large Language Models, and Other Generative Models. *Philosophy & Technology*, *36*(1), 15. Advance online publication. DOI: 10.1007/s13347-023-00621-y

Fracarolli Nunes, M., Lee Park, C., & Paiva, E. L. (2020). Can we have it all? Sustainability trade-offs and cross-insurance mechanisms in supply chains. *International Journal of Operations & Production Management*, *40*(9), 1339–1366. DOI: 10.1108/IJOPM-12-2019-0802

Freund, C., Mattoo, A., Mulabdic, A., & Ruta, M. (2024). Is US trade policy reshaping global supply chains? *Journal of International Economics*, *152*, 104011. DOI: 10.1016/j.jinteco.2024.104011

Frey, C. B., & Osborne, M. (2013). The Future of employment: How susceptible are jobs to computerisation? https://www.oxfordmartin.ox.ac.uk/publications/the-future-of-employment

Fui-Hoon Nah, F., Zheng, R., Cai, J., Siau, K., & Chen, L. (2023). Generative AI and ChatGPT: Applications, challenges, and AI-human collaboration. *Journal of Information Technology Case and Application Research*, *25*(3), 277–304. https://doi-org.wdg.biblio.udg.mx:8443/10.1080/15228053.2023.2233814. DOI: 10.1080/15228053.2023.2233814

Fukuta, Y., Murata, K., & Orito, Y. (2020). Perceived Risk and Desired Protection: Towards A Comprehensive Understanding of Data Sensitivity. In Societal Challenges in the Smart Society (pp. 573-586). Universidad de La Rioja.

Fung, A. (2006). Varieties of Participation in Complex Governance. *Public Administration Review*, *66*(s1), 66–75. DOI: 10.1111/j.1540-6210.2006.00667.x

Galdames, I. S. (2024). Modelos de gestión del conocimiento en educación superior. *European Journal of Education and Psychology*, •••, 1–23. DOI: 10.32457/ejep.v16i2.2437

Galesic, M., Barkoczi, D., Berdahl, A. M., Biro, D., Carbone, G., Giannoccaro, I., Goldstone, R. L., Gonzalez, C., Kandler, A., Kao, A. B., Kendal, R., Kline, M., Lee, E., Massari, G. F., Mesoudi, A., Olsson, H., Pescetelli, N., Sloman, S. J., Smaldino, P. E., & Stein, D. L. (2023). Beyond collective intelligence: Collective adaptation. *Journal of the Royal Society, Interface*, *20*(200), 20220736. DOI: 10.1098/rsif.2022.0736 PMID: 36946092

Galtung, J. (1996). *Peace by peaceful means: Peace and conflict, development and civilization. International Peace Research Institute Oslo*. Sage Publications. DOI: 10.4135/9781446221631

Gangi, F., Daniele, L. M., & Varrone, N. (2020). How do corporate environmental policy and corporate reputation affect risk-adjusted financial performance? *Business Strategy and the Environment*, *29*(5), 1975–1991. DOI: 10.1002/bse.2482

García-Espín, P. (2023). Class Inequalities and Participatory Democracy: Assessing the Impact of Social Inclusion Tools in Citizens' Assemblies. *Political Studies Review*, *22*(3), 585–607. DOI: 10.1177/14789299231179081

Gartner, D. R., Maples, C., Nash, M., & Howard-Bobiwash, H. (2023). Misracialization of Indigenous people in population health and mortality studies: A scoping review to establish promising practices. *Epidemiologic Reviews*, *45*(1), 63–81. DOI: 10.1093/epirev/mxad001 PMID: 37022309

Gastil, J., & Levine, P. (2005). *The Deliberative Democracy Handbook: Strategies for Effective Civic Engagement in the Twenty-First Century*. Jossey-Bass.

Gaventa, J. (2009). Finding the Spaces for Change: A Power Analysis. *IDS Bulletin*, *37*(6), 23–33. DOI: 10.1111/j.1759-5436.2006.tb00320.x

Gebreyohans, G., Croasdell, D., & Meshesha, M. (2022). A Systematic Literature Review on Digital Knowledge Sharing in Higher Education. *Proceedings Of The . . . Annual Hawaii International Conference On System Sciences/Proceedings Of The Annual Hawaii International Conference On System Sciences*. https://doi.org/ DOI: 10.24251/HICSS.2022.668

Geffner, C. J. (2023). *Building a new leadership ladder: Transforming male-dominated organizations to support women on the rise*. Mit Press. DOI: 10.7551/mitpress/14386.001.0001

Geiger, R. S., Cope, D., Ip, J., Lotosh, M., Shah, A., Weng, J., & Tang, R. (2021). " Garbage In, Garbage Out" Revisited: What Do Machine Learning Application Papers Report About Human-Labeled Training Data? arXiv preprint arXiv:2107.02278.

George, G., Lakhani, K. R., & Puranam, P. (2020). What has changed? The impact of Covid pandemic on the technology and innovation management research agenda. *Journal of Management Studies*, *57*(8), 1754–1758. DOI: 10.1111/joms.12634

Gerardi, A. (2023). Global Food Safety Initiative (GFSI): underpinning the safety of the global food chain, facilitating regulatory compliance, trade, and consumer trust. In *Present Knowledge in Food Safety* (pp. 1089-1098). Academic Press.

Gereffi, G. (2001). Beyond the Producer-driven/Buyer-driven Dichotomy *The Evolution of Global Value Chains in the Internet Era. IDS Bulletin*, *32*(3), 30–40. DOI: 10.1111/j.1759-5436.2001.mp32003004.x

Gereffi, G. (2014). Global value chains in a post-Washington Consensus world. *Review of International Political Economy, 21*(1), 9–37. DOI: 10.1080/09692290.2012.756414

Gereffi, G. (n.d.). GLOBAL VALUE CHAIN ANALYSIS. *PRiMER: Peer-Reviewed Reports in Medical Education Research.*

Gereffi, G., Humphrey, J., Kaplinsky, R., & Sturgeon, T. J. (2001). Introduction: Globalisation, Value Chains and Development. *IDS Bulletin, 32*(3), 1–8. DOI: 10.1111/j.1759-5436.2001.mp32003001.x

Gereffi, G., Humphrey, J., & Sturgeon, T. (2005). The governance of global value chains. *Review of International Political Economy, 12*(1), 78–104. DOI: 10.1080/09692290500049805

Gereffi, G., & Lee, J. (2012). Why the World Suddenly Cares About Global Supply Chains. *The Journal of Supply Chain Management, 48*(3), 24–32. DOI: 10.1111/j.1745-493X.2012.03271.x

Gereffi, G., & Lee, J. (2016). Economic and Social Upgrading in Global Value Chains and Industrial Clusters: Why Governance Matters. *Journal of Business Ethics, 133*(1), 25–38. DOI: 10.1007/s10551-014-2373-7

Gereffi, G., Pananond, P., & Pedersen, T. (2022). Resilience Decoded: The Role of Firms, Global Value Chains, and the State in COVID-19 Medical Supplies. *California Management Review, 64*(2), 46–70. DOI: 10.1177/00081256211069420

Ghobakhloo, M., Fathi, M., Iranmanesh, M., Vilkas, M., Grybauskas, A., & Amran, A. (2024). Generative artificial intelligence in manufacturing: Opportunities for actualizing Industry 5.0 sustainability goals. *Journal of Manufacturing Technology Management, 35*(9), 94–121. DOI: 10.1108/JMTM-12-2023-0530

Ghosh, S. K., Hughes, M., Hodgkinson, I. R., & Hughes, P. (2022). Digital transformation of industrial businesses: A dynamic capability approach. *Technovation, 113*, 102414. DOI: 10.1016/j.technovation.2021.102414

Gibbon, P., Bair, J., & Ponte, S. (2008). Governing global value chains: An introduction. *Economy and Society, 37*(3), 315–338. DOI: 10.1080/03085140802172656

Gigerenzer, G. (2022). *How to stay smart in a smart world: Why human intelligence still beats algorithms.* MIT Press.

Gligor, D. M., Davis-Sramek, B., Tan, A., Vitale, A., Russo, I., Golgeci, I., & Wan, X. (2022). Utilizing blockchain technology for supply chain transparency: A resource orchestration perspective. *Journal of Business Logistics, 43*(1), 140–159. DOI: 10.1111/jbl.12287

Glimcher, P. W. (2022). Efficiently irrational: Deciphering the riddle of human choice. *Trends in Cognitive Sciences*, *26*(8), 669–687. DOI: 10.1016/j.tics.2022.04.007 PMID: 35643845

Godwin Olaoye, J. O., Flypaper, D., Oluwaseyi, J., & Brightwood, S. (2024). Ai-driven adaptive learning systems: enhancing student engagement.

Gogoll, J., Zuber, N., Kacianka, S., Greger, T., Pretschner, A., & Nida-Rümelin, J. (2021). Ethics in the software development process: From codes of conduct to ethical deliberation. *Philosophy & Technology*, *34*(4), 1085–1108. DOI: 10.1007/s13347-021-00451-w

Golgeci, I., Makhmadshoev, D., & Demirbag, M. (2021). Global value chains and the environmental sustainability of emerging market firms: A systematic review of literature and research agenda. *International Business Review*, *30*(5), 101857. DOI: 10.1016/j.ibusrev.2021.101857

Gonzalez-Nucamendi, A., Noguez, J., Neri, L., Robledo-Rella, V., & García-Castelán, R. M. G. (2023, October). Predictive analytics study to determine undergraduate students at risk of dropout. [). Frontiers Media SA.]. *Frontiers in Education*, *8*, 1244686. DOI: 10.3389/feduc.2023.1244686

González, T. E., & Martín, M. A. (2018). Redes de cooperación empresaria internacionales en el sector ambiental y cooperación triangular. *Revista Universidad y Empresa*, *20*(35), 51–77. DOI: 10.12804/revistas.urosario.edu.co/empresa/a.5307

González-Torres, T., Rodríguez-Sánchez, J.-L., Montero-Navarro, A., & Gallego-Losada, R. (2020). Visualizing Research on Industrial Clusters and Global Value Chains: A Bibliometric Analysis. *Frontiers in Psychology*, *11*, 1754. DOI: 10.3389/fpsyg.2020.01754 PMID: 32793074

Gopal, P. R. C., & Thakkar, J. (2016). Sustainable supply chain practices: An empirical investigation on the Indian automobile industry. *Production Planning and Control*, *27*(1), 49–64. DOI: 10.1080/09537287.2015.1060368

GRI & UN. (2018). *Integrating the SDGs into Corporate Reporting: A Practical Guide*. GRI & UNGC. Link: https://sdgs.un.org/sites/default/files/2021-07/GRI%20-%20Integrating%20SDGs%20in%20Global%20Reporting.pdf

Griffin, T. A., Green, B. P., & Welie, J. V. (2024). The ethical agency of AI developers. *AI and Ethics*, *4*(2), 179–188. DOI: 10.1007/s43681-022-00256-3

Gschwendtner, C., Sinsel, S. R., & Stephan, A. (2021). Vehicle-to-X (V2X) implementation: An overview of predominate trial configurations and technical, social and regulatory challenges. *Renewable & Sustainable Energy Reviews*, *145*, 110977. DOI: 10.1016/j.rser.2021.110977

Gürhan-Canli, Z., Sarial-Abi, G., & Hayran, C. (2018). Consumers and Brands across the Globe: Research Synthesis and New Directions. *Journal of International Marketing*, *26*(1), 96–117. DOI: 10.1509/jim.17.0063

Guzman, J. H. E., Zuluaga-Ortiz, R. A., Garizabal-Donado, L. E., Mora-Garcia, Y. A., Sandoval-Karam, M., Molina-Guerrero, C. J., & Delahoz-Dominguez, E. J. (2023). Determining elements used to measure knowledge management in higher education institutions' research divisions. *Procedia Computer Science*, *224*, 538–543. DOI: 10.1016/j.procs.2023.09.078

Hamid, S. T., & Kuo, R. (2022). (Forthcoming). Towards Collective Safety: Transformative Methodologies. First Monday. *Special Issue on Online Harm and Abuse*.

Harding, X. (2023, August 7). Facial Recognition Bias: Why Racism Appears In Face Detection Tech. Mozilla Foundation. https://www.mozillafoundation.org/en/blog/facial-recognition-bias/

Harris, I. (2009). History of Peace Education.

Hart, P. F., & Rodgers, W. (2023). Competition, competitiveness, and competitive advantage in higher education institutions: A systematic literature review. *Studies in Higher Education*, *49*(11), 2153–2177. DOI: 10.1080/03075079.2023.2293926

Hayakawa, K., & Mukunoki, H. (2021). Impacts of COVID -19 on Global Value Chains. *The Developing Economies*, *59*(2), 154–177. DOI: 10.1111/deve.12275 PMID: 33821021

Hegre, H., Ellingsen, T., Gates, S., & Gleditsch, N. (2001). Toward a Democratic Civil Peace? Democracy, Political Change, and Civil War, 1816-1992. *The American Political Science Review*, *95*(1), 33–48. https://www.jstor.org/stable/3117627. DOI: 10.1017/S0003055401000119

Helfat, C. E., Finkelstein, S., Mitchell, W., Peteraf, M., Singh, H., Teece, D., & Winter, S. G. (2007). *Dynamic Capabilities: Understanding Strategic Change in Organizations*. John Wiley & Sons.

Helfat, C. E., & Raubitschek, R. S. (2018). Dynamic and integrative capabilities for profiting from innovation in digital platform-based ecosystems. *Research Policy*, *47*(8), 1391–1399. DOI: 10.1016/j.respol.2018.01.019

He, Y., Liu, Y., & Pu, Q. (2024). Is ESG a 'Scam'? Correlation Between ESG and Corporate Performance. *Highlights in Business. Economics and Management, 24*, 1485–1493.

Higgins, J., & Green, S. (2008). *Definition of qualitative research.* Cochrane Handbook for Systematic Review of Interventions. handbook.cochrane.org/v5.0.0

Hinrix, F., Sanghera, J. K., Pak, T., Pankaj, V., Palepu, U. S., Turner-Rahman, S., . . . Beyer, J. L. (2024). AI Applications for Small & Medium Sized Enterprises. https://static1.squarespace.com/static/66708a0c236025663ebcd96f/t/680f8af480ae1a52c5ed58a1/1745849082806/AI+Applications+EN+cover.pdf

Holah, J. (2023). Principles of hygienic practice in food processing and manufacturing. In *Food Safety Management* (pp. 587–613). Academic Press., DOI: 10.1016/B978-0-12-820013-1.00029-2

Holstein, K., & Doroudi, S. (2021). Equity and artificial intelligence in education: will" aied" amplify or alleviate inequities in education? *arXiv preprint arXiv:2104.12920.*

Hongfu, N., Daocheng, Z., & Siyi, P. (2024). A new method for measuring industrial chain risk exposure: A regional perspective in China. *Journal of Economic Surveys, 38*(5), 1760–1794. DOI: 10.1111/joes.12626

Hoover, S., & Lee, L. (2015). Democratization and Disintermediation: Disruptive Technologies and the Future of Making Things. *Research Technology Management, 58*(6), 31–37. DOI: 10.5437/08956308X5806069

Horner, R. (2017). Beyond facilitator? State roles in global value chains and global production networks. *Geography Compass, 11*(2), e12307. DOI: 10.1111/gec3.12307

Horvath, L. (2001). Collaboration: The key to value creation in supply chain management. *Supply Chain Management, 6*(5), 205–207. DOI: 10.1108/EUM0000000006039

Howard-Grenville, J. (2021). ESG impact is hard to measure-but it is not impossible. *Harvard Business Review.* https://doi.org/DOI: 10.17863/CAM.64207

Hu, A. (2024). Developing an ai-based psychometric system for assessing learning difficulties and adaptive system to overcome: A qualitative and conceptual framework. arXiv preprint arXiv:2403.06284.

Huang, S., Wang, B., Li, X., Zheng, P., Mourtzis, D., & Wang, L. (2022). Industry 5.0 and Society 5.0—Comparison, complementation and co-evolution. *Journal of Manufacturing Systems, 64*, 424–428. DOI: 10.1016/j.jmsy.2022.07.010

Hu, L., Zheng, Y., Woods, T. A., Kusunose, Y., & Buck, S. (2023). The market for private food safety certifications: Conceptual framework, review, and future research directions. *Applied Economic Perspectives and Policy*, *45*(1), 197–220. DOI: 10.1002/aepp.13226

Hull, G. (2023). Dirty data labeled dirt cheap: Epistemic injustice in machine learning systems. *Ethics and Information Technology*, *25*(3), 38. DOI: 10.1007/s10676-023-09712-y

Humphrey, J., & Schmitz, H. (2002). How does insertion in global value chains affect upgrading in industrial clusters? *Regional Studies*, *36*(9), 1017–1027. DOI: 10.1080/0034340022000022198

IEPC. (2021). Results of the Local Electoral Process. Obtained from https://www2.iepcjalisco.org.mx/tablero-electoral-2021/?page_id=1307

Ikram, M., Sroufe, R., Rehman, E., Shah, S. Z. A., & Mahmoudi, A. (2020). Do quality, environmental, and social (QES) certifications improve international trade? A comparative grey relation analysis of developing vs. developed countries. *Physica A*, *545*, 123486. DOI: 10.1016/j.physa.2019.123486

INEGI. (July 24, 2024). National Urban Public Security Survey (ENSU). Obtained from https://www.inegi.org.mx/contenidos/programas/ensu/doc/ensu2024_junio_presentacion_ejecutiva.pdf

Intergovernmental Panel on Climate Change (IPCC). (2023). *Climate Change 2021 – The Physical Science Basis: Working Group I Contribution to the Sixth Assessment Report of the Intergovernmental Panel on Climate Change*. Cambridge University Press., DOI: 10.1017/9781009157896

International Electrotechnical Commission (IEC). (2022). *Smart agriculture standards and tools*. https://www.iec.ch

International Organization for Standardization (ISO). (2021). *ISO 22000: Food safety management systems*. https://www.iso.org/iso-22000-food-safety-management.html

Investopedia (2024). (ESG) Investing. What Is ESG Investing? *Investopedia*.

Ireland, R. D., & Webb, J. W. (2007). A multi-theoretic perspective on trust and power in strategic supply chains. *Journal of Operations Management*, *25*(2), 482–497. DOI: 10.1016/j.jom.2006.05.004

Jangam, B. P., & Rath, B. N. (2021). Do global value chains enhance or slog economic growth? *Applied Economics*, *53*(36), 4148–4165. DOI: 10.1080/00036846.2021.1897076

Janssens, M., & Zanoni, P. (2014). Alternative Diversity Management: Organizational practices fostering Ethnic Equality at Work. *Scandinavian Journal of Management, 30*(3), 317–331. DOI: 10.1016/j.scaman.2013.12.006

Jereb, E., & Urh, M. (2024). The Use of Artificial Intelligence among Students in Higher Education. *Organizacija, 57*(4), 333–345. DOI: 10.2478/orga-2024-0024

Jiménez-Jiménez, D., & Sanz-Valle, R. (2010). Innovation, organizational learning, and performance. *Journal of Business Research, 64*(4), 408–417. DOI: 10.1016/j.jbusres.2010.09.010

Jones, C. E. (2024). The Language of Medical Racism: Strategies for Anti-Oppressive Scientific Writing and Communication (Doctoral dissertation, Northeastern University).

Jones, C. (2021). Western centric research methods?: Exposing international practices. *Journal of ASEAN Studies, 9*(1), 87–100. DOI: 10.21512/jas.v9i1.7380

Jones-Jang, S. M., & Park, Y. J. (2023). How do people react to AI failure? Automation bias, algorithmic aversion, and perceived controllability. *Journal of Computer-Mediated Communication, 28*(1), zmac029. DOI: 10.1093/jcmc/zmac029

Jüttner, U., Christopher, M., & Baker, S. (2007). Demand chain management-integrating marketing and supply chain management. *Industrial Marketing Management, 36*(3), 377–392. DOI: 10.1016/j.indmarman.2005.10.003

Kaiser, B. (2019). *Targeted: My Inside Story of Cambridge Analytica and How Trump, Brexit and Facebook Broke Democracy*. HarperCollins.

Kannan, D. (2018). Role of multiple stakeholders and the critical success factor theory for the sustainable supplier selection process. *International Journal of Production Economics, 195*, 391–418. DOI: 10.1016/j.ijpe.2017.02.020

Kano, L., Tsang, E. W. K., & Yeung, H. W. (2020). Global value chains: A review of the multi-disciplinary literature. *Journal of International Business Studies, 51*(4), 577–622. DOI: 10.1057/s41267-020-00304-2

Kant, I. (1870). *Grundlegung zur metaphysik der sitten*. L. Heimann.

Kao, A. B., Banerjee, S. C., Francisco, F. A., & Berdahl, A. M. (2024). Timing decisions as the next frontier for collective intelligence. *Trends in Ecology & Evolution, 39*(10), 904–912. DOI: 10.1016/j.tree.2024.06.003 PMID: 38964933

Kaplinsky, R., & Kraemer-Mbula, E. (2022). Innovation and uneven development: The challenge for low-and middle-income economies. *Research Policy, 51*(2), 104394. DOI: 10.1016/j.respol.2021.104394

Kassens-Noor, E., Siegel, J., & Decaminada, T. (2021). Choosing Ethics Over Morals: A Possible Determinant to Embracing Artificial Intelligence in Future Urban Mobility. *Frontiers In Sustainable Cities*, *3*, 723475. Advance online publication. DOI: 10.3389/frsc.2021.723475

Katta, S. (2025, March 11). The EU Data Act: A catalyst for change. Smartcar. https://smartcar.com/blog/eu-data-act

Kayyali, M. (2025a). The Future of AI in Education: Predictions and Emerging Trends. Next-Generation AI Methodologies in Education, 367-406.

Kayyali, M. (2025b). Ethical Implications of Generative AI in Education: Privacy, Bias, and Integrity. In Transformative AI Practices for Personalized Learning Strategies (pp. 185-218). IGI Global Scientific Publishing.

Kayyali, M. (2025c). AI in Higher Education: Revolutionizing Curriculum and Administration. In AI Adoption and Diffusion in Education (pp. 31-62). IGI Global Scientific Publishing.

Kayyali, M. (2025d). Harnessing AI for Digital Entrepreneurship: Strategies and Best Practices. In Improving Entrepreneurial Processes Through Advanced AI (pp. 1-20). IGI Global.

Kayyali, M. (2024). Future possibilities and challenges of AI in education. In *Transforming education with generative AI: Prompt engineering and synthetic content creation* (pp. 118–137). IGI Global Scientific Publishing. DOI: 10.4018/979-8-3693-1351-0.ch006

Kazekula, H. (2014). *A global value chain perspective to understanding and unpacking the development trajectory of the horticultural industry in Zambia: The case of small-scale farmers based in Lusaka*. https://www.academia.edu/90102473/A_global_value_chain_perspective_to_understanding_and_unpacking_the_development_trajectory_of_the_horticultural_industry_in_Zambia_the_case_of_small_scale_farmers_based_in_Lusaka

Keles, S. (2023). Navigating in the moral landscape: Analysing bias and discrimination in AI through philosophical inquiry. *AI and Ethics*, •••, 1–11.

Kenney, M., Serhan, H., & Trystram, G. (2020). Digitization and platforms in agriculture: Organizations, power asymmetry, and collective action solutions. *Power Asymmetry, and Collective Action Solutions (June 20, 2020).*

Kerlinger, F., & Lee, H. (2002). *Investigación del comportamiento, métodos de investigación en ciencias sociales.*

Keskar, A. (2019). Exploring business models for software-defined vehicles: Subscription-based paradigms and their impact on automotive innovation and consumer adoption. *World Journal of Research and Review, 1*(2), 61–77. DOI: 10.30574/wjarr.2019.1.2.0004

Ketchen, D. J.Jr, & Hult, G. T. M. (2007). Bridging organization theory and supply chain management: The case of best value supply chains. *Journal of Operations Management, 25*(2), 573–580. DOI: 10.1016/j.jom.2006.05.010

Kettinger, W. J., Ryoo, S. Y., & Marchand, D. A. (2021). We're engaged! Following the path to a successful information management capability. *The Journal of Strategic Information Systems, 30*(3), 101681. DOI: 10.1016/j.jsis.2021.101681

Khan, M., Serafeim, G., & Yoon, A. (2016). Corporate sustainability: First evidence on materiality. *The Accounting Review, 91*(6), 1697–1724. DOI: 10.2308/accr-51383

Khatri, B. B., & Karki, P. D. (2023). Artificial Intelligence (AI) in Higher Education: Growing Academic Integrity and Ethical Concerns. *Nepalese Journal Of Development and Rural Studies, 20*(01), 1–7. DOI: 10.3126/njdrs.v20i01.64134

Khoa, B. T., & Huynh, T. T. (2023). The effectiveness of knowledge management systems in motivation and satisfaction in higher education Institutions: Data from Vietnam. *Data in Brief, 49*, 109454. DOI: 10.1016/j.dib.2023.109454 PMID: 37577732

Khodakarami, M., Shabani, A., Farzipoor Saen, R., & Azadi, M. (2015). Developing distinctive two-stage data envelopment analysis models: An application in evaluating the sustainability of supply chain management. *Measurement, 70*, 62–74. DOI: 10.1016/j.measurement.2015.03.024

Khorana, S., Escaith, H., Ali, S., Kumari, S., & Do, Q. (2022). The changing contours of global value chains post-COVID: Evidence from the Commonwealth. *Journal of Business Research, 153*, 75–86. DOI: 10.1016/j.jbusres.2022.07.044 PMID: 35996441

Kılıç, S. (2016). Cronbach's alpha reliability coefficient. *Journal of Mood Disorders, 6*(1), 47–48. DOI: 10.5455/jmood.20160307122823

Klassen, R. D. (2001). Plant-level environmental management orientation: The influence of management views and plant characteristics. *Production and Operations Management, 10*(3), 257–275. DOI: 10.1111/j.1937-5956.2001.tb00374.x

Klewitz, J., & Hansen, E. G. (2014). Sustainability-oriented innovation of SMEs: A systematic review. *Journal of Cleaner Production, 65*, 57–75. DOI: 10.1016/j.jclepro.2013.07.017

Knight, G. (2000). Entrepreneurship and Marketing Strategy: The SME under Globalization. *Journal of International Marketing*, *8*(2), 12–32. DOI: 10.1509/jimk.8.2.12.19620

Knight, G. A. (2001). Entrepreneurship and strategy in the international SME. *Journal of International Management*, *7*(3), 155–171. DOI: 10.1016/S1075-4253(01)00042-4

Knorr, D., & Augustin, M. A. (2021). Food processing needs, advantages and misconceptions. *Trends in Food Science & Technology*, *108*, 103–110. DOI: 10.1016/j.tifs.2020.11.026

Koberg, E., & Longoni, A. (2019). A systematic review of sustainable supply chain management in global supply chains. *Journal of Cleaner Production*, *207*, 1084–1098. DOI: 10.1016/j.jclepro.2018.10.033

Koshiyama, A., Kazim, E., Treleaven, P., Rai, P., Szpruch, L., Pavey, G., Ahamat, G., Leutner, F., Goebel, R., Knight, A., Adams, J., Hitrova, C., Barnett, J., Nachev, P., Barber, D., Chamorro-Premuzic, T., Klemmer, K., Gregorovic, M., Khan, S., & Chatterjee, S. (2024). Towards algorithm auditing: Managing legal, ethical and technological risks of AI, ML and associated algorithms. *Royal Society Open Science*, *11*(5), 230859. DOI: 10.1098/rsos.230859 PMID: 39076787

Koster, A., Lang, N., Collie, B., Xie, A., & Hagenmaier, M. (2023). Software-Defined Vehicles Will Create a More Than $650 Billion Value Potential for the Auto Industry by 2030. https://www.bcg.com/press/7september2023-software-defined-vehicles-create-650-billion-value-potential

Kovacs, I., & Keresztes, E. R. (2022). Perceived consumer effectiveness and willingness to pay for credence product attributes of sustainable foods. *Sustainability (Basel)*, *14*(7), 4338. DOI: 10.3390/su14074338

Kraus, S., Breier, M., Lim, W. M., Dabić, M., Kumar, S., Kanbach, D., Mukherjee, D., Corvello, V., Piñeiro-Chousa, J., Liguori, E., Palacios-Marqués, D., Schiavone, F., Ferraris, A., Fernandes, C., & Ferreira, J. J. (2022). Literature reviews as independent studies: Guidelines for academic practice. *Review of Managerial Science*, *16*(8), 2577–2595. DOI: 10.1007/s11846-022-00588-8

Krooi, M., Whittingham, J., & Beausaert, S. (2024). Introducing the 3P conceptual model of internal quality assurance in higher education: A systematic literature review. *Studies in Educational Evaluation*, *82*, 101360. DOI: 10.1016/j.stueduc.2024.101360

Kudesia, R. S. (2019). Mindfulness as metacognitive practice. *Academy of Management Review*, *44*(2), 405–423. DOI: 10.5465/amr.2015.0333

Kumar, D., Menon, M. K., Balasubramani, N., Sadalaxmi, A., & Banerjee, M. (2023). Certification of Organic Agriculture and Trade Issues. In *Transforming Organic Agri-Produce into Processed Food Products* (pp. 113-151). Apple Academic Press. eBook ISBN9781003329770 DOI: 10.1201/9781003329770-7

Kunkel, S., Matthess, M., Xue, B., & Beier, G. (2022). Industry 4.0 in sustainable supply chain collaboration: Insights from an interview study with international buying firms and Chinese suppliers in the electronics industry. *Resources, Conservation and Recycling*, *182*, 106274. Advance online publication. DOI: 10.1016/j.resconrec.2022.106274

Kusa, R., Suder, M., & Duda, J. (2024). Role of entrepreneurial orientation, information management, and knowledge management in improving firm performance. *International Journal of Information Management*, *78*, 102802. DOI: 10.1016/j.ijinfomgt.2024.102802

Kyriakidou, O. (2025). Algorithms and global diversity management. In *Research Handbook on Global Diversity Management* (pp. 148–163). Edward Elgar Publishing. DOI: 10.4337/9781035311170.00018

Laal, M. (2011). Knowledge management in higher education. *Procedia Computer Science*, *3*, 544–549. DOI: 10.1016/j.procs.2010.12.090

Labayen, M., Vea, R., Flórez, J., Aginako, N., & Sierra, B. (2021). Online student authentication and proctoring system based on multimodal biometrics technology. *IEEE Access : Practical Innovations, Open Solutions*, *9*, 72398–72411. DOI: 10.1109/ACCESS.2021.3079375

Lambert, R., & Frenz, M. (2021). The economic impact for manufacturing sites operating to BRCGS certification. Downloaded from: https://eprints.bbk.ac.uk/id/eprint/46546/

Lampón, J. F., Carballo-Cruz, F., & Velando-Rodríguez, M. (2024a). The irruption of autonomous and connected vehicle technologies and the repositioning of the periphery in the European automotive industry. *Kybernetes*. Advance online publication. DOI: 10.1108/K-02-2024-0447

Lampón, J. F., & Muñoz-Dueñas, P. (2023). Are sustainable mobility firms reshaping the traditional relationships in the automotive industry value Chain? *Journal of Cleaner Production*, *413*, 137522. DOI: 10.1016/j.jclepro.2023.137522

Lampón, J. F., Pérez-Moure, H., Carballo-Cruz, F., & Velando-Rodríguez, M. E. (2024b). New mobility technologies and regional status in the automotive industry value chain: The case of Spain and Portugal. *Technology in Society*, *78*, 102624. DOI: 10.1016/j.techsoc.2024.102624

Lane, H., & Dyshel, M. (2025). *Natural language processing in action*. Simon and Schuster.

Lang, B., & Conroy, D. M. (2022). When food governance matters to consumer food choice: Consumer perception of and preference for food quality certifications. *Appetite*, *168*, 105688. DOI: 10.1016/j.appet.2021.105688 PMID: 34509543

Larson, J., Mattu, S., Kirchner, L., & Angwin, J. (2016). How we analyzed the COMPAS recidivism algorithm. ProPublica, 23 May. https://www.propublica.org/article/how-we-analyzed-the-compas-recidivism-algorithm

Lau, J. (2024). *Partner, HLB Australia, Melbourne, The Importance of being an ESG-Centric business for long-term success*. HLB.

Lavassani, K. M., & Movahedi, B. (2021). Firm-Level Analysis of Global Supply Chain Network: Role of Centrality on Firm's Performance. *International Journal of Global Business and Competitiveness*, *16*(2), 86–103. DOI: 10.1007/s42943-021-00026-8

Lederach, J. P. (1997). *Building Peace: Sustainable Reconciliation in Divided Societies*. United States Institute of Peace Press.

Lee, J., & Gereffi, G. (2015). Global value chains, rising power firms and economic and social upgrading. *Critical Perspectives on International Business*, *11*(3/4), 319–339. DOI: 10.1108/cpoib-03-2014-0018

Leng, J., Zhu, X., Huang, Z., Li, X., Zheng, P., Zhou, X., Mourtzis, D., Wang, B., Qi, Q., Shao, H., Wan, J., Chen, X., Wang, L., & Liu, Q. (2024). Unlocking the power of industrial artificial intelligence towards Industry 5.0: Insights, pathways, and challenges. *Journal of Manufacturing Systems*, *73*, 349–363. DOI: 10.1016/j.jmsy.2024.02.010

Leonard-Barton, D. (1992). Core capabilities and core rigidities: A paradox in managing new product development. *Strategic Management Journal*, *13*(S1), 111–125. DOI: 10.1002/smj.4250131009

Lettieri, M. (2025). Embracing Empathy: How AI Technologies Enhance the Pedagogy of Kindness in Education. In Redefining Education With Pandemic Pedagogies (pp. 167-186). IGI Global.

Levin, T. (2022, November 22). Car companies want to make billions by charging monthly fees for features like heated seats, but buyers won't pay up. Business Insider. https://www.businessinsider.com/car-feature-subscriptions-add-ons-bmw-ford-toyota-gm-2022-2

Lijphart, A. (1997). Unequal Participation: Democracy's Unresolved Dilemma. *The American Political Science Review*, *14*(1), 1–14. Advance online publication. DOI: 10.2307/2952255

Li, M., Yin, D., Qiu, H., & Bai, B. (2021). A systematic review of AI technology-based service encounters: Implications for hospitality and tourism operations. *International Journal of Hospitality Management*, *95*, 102930. DOI: 10.1016/j.ijhm.2021.102930

Lin, Y., Mistree, F., Allen, K. J., Tsui, K., & Chen, P. C. V. (2004). A Sequential Exploratory Experimental Design Method: Development of Appropriate Empirical Models in Design. *International Design Engineering Technical Conferences in Computers and Information in Engineering Conference, DETC2004-57527*, 1021-1035. https://doi.org/DOI: 10.1115/DETC2004-57527

Lirio, P., Lee, M. D., Williams, M. L., Haugen, L. K., & Kossek, E. E. (2008). The Inclusion Challenge with Reduced Load Professionals: The Role of The Manager. *Human Resource Management*, *47*(3), 443–461. DOI: 10.1002/hrm.20226

Lis, A., Sudolska, A., & Tomanek, M. (2020). Mapping Research on Sustainable Supply-Chain Management. *Sustainability (Basel)*, *12*(10), 3987. DOI: 10.3390/su12103987

Liu, J. (2024). Dilemma of ESG Development: Investors' Perspectives. Advances in Economics. *Management and Political Sciences*, *74*(1), 209–215. DOI: 10.54254/2754-1169/74/20241546

Liu, K. S., & Lin, M. H. (2021). Performance assessment on the application of artificial intelligence to sustainable supply chain management in the construction material industry. *Sustainability (Basel)*, *13*(22), 12767. Advance online publication. DOI: 10.3390/su132212767

Liu, P., Lai, Y., & Liu, D. (2024). Artificial intelligence research in organizations: A bibliometric approach. *Cogent Business & Management*, *11*(1), 2408439. Advance online publication. DOI: 10.1080/23311975.2024.2408439

Liu, Y., Guo, M., Han, Z., Gavurova, B., Bresciani, S., & Wang, T. (2023). Effects of digital orientation on organizational resilience: A dynamic capabilities perspective. *Journal of Manufacturing Technology Management, 35*(2), 268–290. DOI: 10.1108/JMTM-06-2023-0224

Liu, Z., Zhang, W., & Zhao, F. (2022). Impact, Challenges and Prospect of Software-Defined Vehicles. *Automotive Innovation, 5*(2), 180–194. DOI: 10.1007/s42154-022-00179-z

Lloyd, P. (2022). Ethical imagination and design. In *About Designing* (pp. 85–99). CRC Press.

London, T., & Hart, S. L. (2004). Reinventing strategies for emerging markets: Beyond the transnational model. *Journal of International Business Studies, 35*(5), 350–370. DOI: 10.1057/palgrave.jibs.8400099

Loureiro, A. (2018). There is a fourth industrial revolution: The digital revolution. *Worldwide Hospitality and Tourism Themes, 10*(6), 740–744. DOI: 10.1108/WHATT-07-2018-0044

Lowitt, K., Hickey, G. M., Ganpat, W., & Phillip, L. (2015). Linking Communities of Practice with Value Chain Development in Smallholder Farming Systems. *World Development, 74*, 363–373. DOI: 10.1016/j.worlddev.2015.05.014

Ludke, R. (2020). Competitive, Integrated Employment: A Driver of Long-Term Value Creation. The Harkin Institute for Public Policy & Citizen Engagement. https://harkininstitute.drake.edu/wp-content/uploads/sites/103/2022/06/Harkin-Disability_Inclusion_and_Long_Term_Value_Creation-design_Final-6.6.22.pdf

Lugo-Morin, D. R. (2024). Artificial Intelligence on Food Vulnerability: Future Implications within a Framework of Opportunities and Challenges. *Societies (Basel, Switzerland), 14*(7), 106. DOI: 10.3390/soc14070106

Luo, Y., Kumar, N., & Yazdanmehr, A. (2024). Ai Nudging and Decision Quality: Evidence from Randomized Experiments in Online Recommendation Setting. Available at *SSRN* 4967812. DOI: 10.2139/ssrn.4967812

Luthra, S., & Mangla, S. K. (2018). When strategies matter: Adoption of sustainable supply chain management practices in an emerging economy's context. *Resources, Conservation and Recycling, 138*, 194–206. DOI: 10.1016/j.resconrec.2018.07.005

Macgilchrist, F. (2023). Design justice and educational technology: Designing in the fissures. In *World Yearbook of Education 2024* (pp. 294–310). Routledge.

Machamer, P., Darden, L., & Craver, C. F. (2000). Thinking about mechanisms. *Philosophy of Science*, *67*(1), 1–25. DOI: 10.1086/392759

Machin, J. E., Mirabito, A. M., Azzari, C. N., Crosby, E., & Adkins, N. R. (2024). Disadvantaged Consumers, Market Access, and Consumer Well-Being. In *Fostering Consumer Well-Being: Theory, Evidence, and Policy* (pp. 69–90). Springer Nature Switzerland. DOI: 10.1007/978-3-031-59144-0_5

Maghsudi, S., Lan, A., Xu, J., & van Der Schaar, M. (2021). Personalized education in the artificial intelligence era: What to expect next. *IEEE Signal Processing Magazine*, *38*(3), 37–50. DOI: 10.1109/MSP.2021.3055032

Ma, H., Qian, C., Li, L., Qu, X., & Ran, B. (2025). Risk quantification based Adaptive Cruise control and its application in approaching behavior at signalized intersections. *Accident; Analysis and Prevention*, *212*, 107939. DOI: 10.1016/j.aap.2025.107939 PMID: 39879919

Malhotra, D. (2015). Social paradigms of the digital marketing- an Indian perspective of Social Media Marketing. *MPRA Paper*, Article 66405. https://ideas.repec.org//p/pra/mprapa/66405.html

Mancini, M., Montalbano, P., Nenci, S., & Vurchio, D. (2024). Positioning in Global Value Chains: World Map and Indicators, a New Dataset Available for GVC Analyses. *The World Bank Economic Review*, *38*(4), 669–690. DOI: 10.1093/wber/lhae005

Mangion, A. (2024). Making good on migration: Exploring narratives of aspiration and imagined futures with students from migrant backgrounds (Doctoral dissertation, Australian Catholic University).

Manning, L., Brewer, S., Craigon, P. J., Frey, J., Gutierrez, A., Jacobs, N., Kanza, S., Munday, S., Sacks, J., & Pearson, S. (2022). Artificial intelligence and ethics within the food sector: Developing a common language for technology adoption across the supply chain. *Trends in Food Science & Technology*, *125*, 33–42. DOI: 10.1016/j.tifs.2022.04.025

Mannuru, N. R., Shahriar, S., Teel, Z. A., Wang, T., Lund, B. D., Tijani, S., Pohboon, C. O., Agbaji, D., Alhassan, J., Galley, J., Kousari, R., Ogbadu-Oladapo, L., Saurav, S. K., Srivastava, A., Tummuru, S. P., Uppala, S., & Vaidya, P. (2023). Artificial intelligence in developing countries: The impact of generative artificial intelligence (AI) technologies for development. *Information Development*, *0*(0), 02666669231200628. Advance online publication. DOI: 10.1177/02666669231200628

Manova, K., & Yu, Z. (2016). How firms export: Processing vs. ordinary trade with financial frictions. *Journal of International Economics*, *100*, 120–137. DOI: 10.1016/j.jinteco.2016.02.005

Maphalala, M. C., & Ajani, O. A. (2025). Leveraging artificial intelligence as a learning tool in higher education. *Interdisciplinary Journal Of Education Research*, *7*(1), a01. DOI: 10.38140/ijer-2025.vol7.1.01

Marcato, M. B. (2023). Regional Dynamics in Global Production Sharing: Evidence from "Factory South America.". *European Journal of Development Research*, *35*(5), 1173–1196. DOI: 10.1057/s41287-022-00572-8 PMID: 36573215

Marchant, G. E., & Gutierrez, C. I. (2022). Soft law 2.0: An agile and effective governance approach for artificial intelligence. *Minnesota Journal of Law, Science & Technology*, *24*, 375.

Marinovic, A. (2025). Universities and the digital divide: The capabilities approach from a Latin American perspective. In Torres Jarrín, M. (Ed.), *The University in the Digital Age* (pp. 201–220). Peter Lang.

Mariotti, S. (2022). A warning from the Russian–Ukrainian war: Avoiding a future that rhymes with the past. *Economia e Politica Industriale*, *49*(4), 761–782. DOI: 10.1007/s40812-022-00219-z

Mars, M. M. (2011). Chapter 9: An Innovative Vision for Economic Development in Higher Education: An Essay on Balancing Community Growth and Global Competitiveness. In *Advances in the study of entrepreneurship, innovation, and economic growth* (pp. 219–233). https://doi.org/DOI: 10.1108/S1048-4736(2011)0000022012

Martínez-Martínez, O. A., Gil-Vasquez, K., & Romero-González, M. B. (2023). Food insecurity and levels of marginalization: Food accessibility, consumption and concern in Mexico. *International Journal for Equity in Health*, *22*(1), 178. DOI: 10.1186/s12939-023-01977-5 PMID: 37667336

Masoumik, S. M., Abdul-Rashid, S. H., & Olugu, E. U. (2014). Gaining Competitive Advantage through Strategic Green Supply Chain Management: From a Literature Review towards a Conceptual Model. *International Journal of Supply Chain Management*, *3*(3), 3. Advance online publication. DOI: 10.59160/ijscm.v3i3.964

Mattsson, V. (2022). Thesis: Governing Data in a Worker Cooperative. *Management*, *49*, 424-438. https://urn.fi/URN:NBN:fi:aalto-202302051941

Mauti, J. M., & Ayieko, D. S. (2025). Ethical Implications of Artificial Intelligence in University Education. *East African Journal of Education Studies*, *8*(1), 159–167. DOI: 10.37284/eajes.8.1.2583

Mayer, A., Zimmermann, J., Hoyer, J., Salzer, S., Wiltink, J., Leibing, E., & Leichsenring, F. (2019). Interindividual Differences in Treatment Effects Based on Structural Equation Models with Latent Variables: An EffectLiteR Tutorial. *Structural Equation Modeling*, *27*(5), 798–816. DOI: 10.1080/10705511.2019.1671196

McCarthy, J. (2022). Artificial intelligence, logic, and formalising common sense. Machine Learning and the City: Applications in Architecture and Urban Design, 69-90.

McDaniel, A. (2023). *How Do At-Risk and Non-At-Risk School District Business Leaders Approach and Perceive Planning for Capital Projects?* Hofstra University.

McDonald, R. P. (1985). *Factor Analysis and Related Methods*. Erlbaum.

McKinsey & Company. (2020). *Diversity wins: How inclusion matters*. McKinsey & Company. Link. https://www.mckinsey.com/business-functions/people-and-organizational-performance/our-insights/diversity-wins-how-inclusion-matters

McKinsey & Company. (2023). Automotive software electronics market 2030. https://www.mckinsey.com/industries/automotive-and-assembly/our-insights/mapping-the-automotive-software-and-electronics-landscape-through-2030

Media, S. A. E. (2023, October 10). The Chaos of Automotive Data Privacy. https://www.mobilityengineeringtech.com/component/content/article/49351-sae-ma-07256

Meijer, G. W., Detzel, P., Grunert, K. G., Robert, M. C., & Stancu, V. (2021). Towards effective labelling of foods. An international perspective on safety and nutrition. *Trends in Food Science & Technology*, *118*, 45–56. DOI: 10.1016/j.tifs.2021.09.003

Meixell, M. J., & Luoma, P. (2015). Stakeholder pressure in sustainable supply chain management: A systematic review. *International Journal of Physical Distribution & Logistics Management*, *45*(1/2), 69–89. DOI: 10.1108/IJPDLM-05-2013-0155

Mendoza Pachas, C. J., & Pumasunco Silva, L. E. (2021). Conocimiento de los enfoques de gestión de calidad beneficiosos para alcanzar los estándares de certificación relevantes dentro del mercado estadounidense en el contexto agroexportador del Perú. http://hdl.handle.net/20.500.12404/19266

Meng, B., Peters, G. P., Wang, Z., & Li, M. (2018). Tracing CO2 emissions in global value chains. *Energy Economics*, *73*, 24–42. DOI: 10.1016/j.eneco.2018.05.013

Mentzer, J. T., Dewitt, W., Keebler, J. S., Min, S., Nix, N. W., Smith, C. D., & Zacharia, Z. G. (2001). Defining supply chain management. *Journal of Business Logistics*, *22*(2), 1–25. DOI: 10.1002/j.2158-1592.2001.tb00001.x

Meyer, C. B. (2001). A Case in Case Study Methodology. *Field Methods*, *13*(4), 329–352. DOI: 10.1177/1525822X0101300402

Michels, A., De Graaf, L. (2010). Examining Citizen Participation: Local Participatory Policy Making and Democracy. Local Government Study, 477-491, http:// .DOI: 10.1080/03003930.2010.494101

Mikalef, P., Conboy, K., & Krogstie, J. (2021). Artificial intelligence as an enabler of B2B marketing: A dynamic capabilities micro-foundations approach. *Industrial Marketing Management*, *98*, 80–92. DOI: 10.1016/j.indmarman.2021.08.003

Mikalef, P., Conboy, K., Lundström, J. E., & Popovič, A. (2022). Thinking responsibly about responsible AI and 'the dark side' of AI. *European Journal of Information Systems*, *31*(3), 257–268. DOI: 10.1080/0960085X.2022.2026621

Milberg, W. (2008). Shifting sources and uses of profits: Sustaining US financialization with global value chains. *Economy and Society*, *37*(3), 420–451. DOI: 10.1080/03085140802172706

Miri, P., Stankovski, V., Kochovski, P., & Klun, M. (2023). Technological Solutions for Transparent Monitoring, Citizen Engagement, and Achieving the Sustainable Development Goals. https://www.researchgate.net/publication/372860663_Technological_Solutions_for_Transparent_Monitoring_Citizen_Engagement_and_Achieving_the_Sustainable_Development_Goals

Mithun, P., Kumar, R. D., & Dikshit, S. (2024, April). IntelliCampus: AI-Powered College Portal with Auto-Scheduler and News Sharing. In *2024 International Conference on Knowledge Engineering and Communication Systems (ICKECS)* (Vol. 1, pp. 1-11). IEEE. DOI: 10.1109/ICKECS61492.2024.10616672

Mogalakwe, M. (2006). The use of documentary research methods in social research. *African Sociological Review, 10(*1), 221–230. https://www.jstor.org/stable/afrisocirevi.10.1.221

Mol, A. P. J. (2015). Transparency and value chain sustainability. *Journal of Cleaner Production*, *107*, 154–161. DOI: 10.1016/j.jclepro.2013.11.012

Mook, A., & Overdevest, C. (2021). What drives market construction for fair trade, organic, and GlobalGAP certification in the global citrus value chain? Evidence at the importer level in the Netherlands and the United States. *Business Strategy and the Environment*, *30*(7), 2996–3008. DOI: 10.1002/bse.2784

Moore, K. R., Williams, D. R., & Baird, D. D. (2021). Disparities by skin color among young African-American women. *Journal of Racial and Ethnic Health Disparities*, *8*(4), 1002–1011. DOI: 10.1007/s40615-020-00856-x PMID: 32888171

Moore, S. B., & Manring, S. L. (2009). Strategy development in small and medium sized enterprises for sustainability and increased value creation. *Journal of Cleaner Production, 17*(2), 276–282. DOI: 10.1016/j.jclepro.2008.06.004

Moor, J. H. (1985). What is computer ethics? *Metaphilosophy, 16*(4), 266–275. DOI: 10.1111/j.1467-9973.1985.tb00173.x

Mor Barak, M. E. (2011). *Managing Diversity: Toward a Globally Inclusive Workplace*. SAGE.

Mor Barak, M. E. (2015). Inclusion is the key to diversity management, but what is inclusion? *Human Service Organizations, Management, Leadership & Governance, 39*(2), 83–88. DOI: 10.1080/23303131.2015.1035599

Mora, C. O., Ortíz, K. H., & Silva, R. (2024). Fortalecimiento de la transparencia en México: Responsabilidad social y participación ciudadana como impulsores de democracia y eficiencia gubernamental. *Revista Venezolana de Gerencia, 29*(106), 581–592. DOI: 10.52080/rvgluz.29.106.8

Morgan, E. H., Hawkes, C., Dangour, A. D., & Lock, K. (2018). Analyzing food value chains for nutrition goals. *Journal of Hunger & Environmental Nutrition, 14*(4), 4. Advance online publication. DOI: 10.1080/19320248.2018.1434106

Motevali Haghighi, S., Torabi, S. A., & Ghasemi, R. (2016). An integrated approach for performance evaluation in sustainable supply chain networks (with a case study). *Journal of Cleaner Production, 137*, 579–597. DOI: 10.1016/j.jclepro.2016.07.119

Moura, I. (2022, November 7). Addressing Disability and Ableist Bias in Autonomous Vehicles: Ensuring Safety, Equity and Accessibility in Detection, Collision Algorithms and Data Collection. Disability Rights Education & Defense Fund. https://dredf.org/addressing-disability-and-ableist-bias-in-autonomous-vehicles-ensuring-safety-equity-and-accessibility-in-detection-collision-algorithms-and-data-collection/

Moussir, C.-E. (2025). Morocco's Economic Prospects: A Dynamic ARDL Simulation on Global Value Chain Integration. *ECONOMICS, 13*(1), 179–196. DOI: 10.2478/eoik-2025-0009

Moya, B. A., Eaton, S. E., Pethrick, H., Hayden, K. A., Brennan, R., Wiens, J., McDermott, B., & Lesage, J. (2023). Academic integrity and artificial intelligence in higher education contexts: A rapid scoping review protocol. *Canadian Perspectives on Academic Integrity, 5*(2), 59–75. https://doi-org.wdg.biblio.udg.mx:8443/10.11575/cpai.75990

Muca, E., Cavallini, D., Odore, R., Baratta, M., Bergero, D., & Valle, E. (2022). Are Veterinary Students Using Technologies and Online Learning Resources for Didactic Training? A Mini-Meta Analysis. *Education Sciences, 12*(8), 573. DOI: 10.3390/educsci12080573

Mudambi, R. (2008). Location, control and innovation in knowledge-intensive industries. *Journal of Economic Geography, 8*(5), 699–725. DOI: 10.1093/jeg/lbn024

Mulgan, G. (2006). The Process of Social Innovation. *Innovations: Technology, Governance, Globalization, 1*(2), 145–162. DOI: 10.1162/itgg.2006.1.2.145

Muller, M., & Strohmayer, A. (2022, April). Forgetting practices in the data sciences. In *Proceedings of the 2022 CHI Conference on Human Factors in Computing Systems* (pp. 1-19).

Murata, K., & Orito, Y. (2020). Rethinking the concept of the right to information privacy: a Japanese perspective. In Routledge eBooks (pp. 215-227). https://doi.org/ DOI: 10.4324/9781003075011-16

Murata, K. (2022). Post-truth: Organisational social responsibility in an AI-driven society. In Bounfour, A. (Ed.), *Platforms and Artificial Intelligence: The Next Generation of Competences* (pp. 269–281). Springer., DOI: 10.1007/978-3-030-90192-9_13

Murray, R., Caulier-Grice, J., & Mulgan, G. (2010). *The Open Book of Social Innovation*. Nesta.

Murtaza, A. A., Saher, A., Zafar, M. H., Moosavi, S. K. R., Aftab, M. F., & Sanfilippo, F. (2024). Paradigm Shift for Predictive Maintenance and Condition Monitoring from Industry 4.0 to Industry 5.0: A Systematic Review, Challenges and Case Study. *Results in Engineering, 102935*, 102935. Advance online publication. DOI: 10.1016/j.rineng.2024.102935

Naidoo, V. (2006). International education. *Journal of Research in International Education, 5*(3), 323–345. DOI: 10.1177/1475240906069455

Nansai, K., Kondo, Y., Giurco, D., Sussman, D., Nakajima, K., Kagawa, S., Takayanagi, W., Shigetomi, Y., & Tohno, S. (2019). Nexus between economy-wide metal inputs and the deterioration of sustainable development goals. *Resources, Conservation and Recycling, 149*, 12–19. DOI: 10.1016/j.resconrec.2019.05.017

Navaratne, A., & Anthony, J. O. M. (2023). Methods of Incorporating Sustainability Contexts in Marketing and the Expected Response–A Fuzzy Approach. SocArXiv, Article kec8w_v1. https://ideas.repec.org//p/osf/socarx/kec8w_v1.html DOI: 10.31235/osf.io/kec8w

Nguyen, A., Ngo, H. N., Hong, Y., Dang, B., & Nguyen, B. P. T. (2023). Ethical principles for artificial intelligence in education. *Education and Information Technologies*, *28*(4), 4221–4241. DOI: 10.1007/s10639-022-11316-w PMID: 36254344

Nguyen, C. T. (2018). Echo chambers and epistemic bubbles. *Episteme (Edinburgh)*, *17*(2), 141–161. DOI: 10.1017/epi.2018.32

NHTSA. (2015). Critical Reasons for Crashes Investigated in the National Motor Vehicle Crash Causation Survey (DOT HS 812 115; TRAFFIC SAFETY FACTS). https://crashstats.nhtsa.dot.gov/Api/Public/ViewPublication/812115

Nicholls, A., & Murdock, A. (2012). *Social Innovation: Blurring Boundaries to Reconfigure Markets*. Palgrave Macmillan. DOI: 10.1057/9780230367098

Nickel, J. (2021). Trade-offs in Design: A Theory Building Qualitative Study on the Role of Problem Formulation and Framing in Resolving Trade-offs in Design (Master's thesis, University of Waterloo).

Nidumolu, R., Prahalad, C. K., & Rangaswami, M. R. (2009). Why Sustainability Is Now the Key Driver of Innovation. In *Harvard Business Review*.

Nie, Y. Y., Liang, A. R. D., & Wang, E. C. (2022). Third-party certification labels for organic food: Consumers' purchase choice and willingness-to-pay. *British Food Journal*, *124*(11), 3993–4008. DOI: 10.1108/BFJ-07-2021-0777

Nikou, S., De Reuver, M., & Mahboob Kanafi, M. (2022). Workplace literacy skills—How information and digital literacy affect adoption of digital technology. *The Journal of Documentation*, *78*(7), 371–391. DOI: 10.1108/JD-12-2021-0241

Nishii, L. H. (2013). The benefits of climate for inclusion for gender-diverse groups. *Academy of Management Journal*, *56*(6), 1754–1774. DOI: 10.5465/amj.2009.0823

Nissenbaum, H. (1996). Accountability in a computerized society. *Science and Engineering Ethics*, *2*(1), 25–42. DOI: 10.1007/BF02639315

Niu, M., Wang, Z., Zhang, Y., & Mao, Y. (2025). The chasing dragon: To what extent and how does China catch up with USA under global value chains? *Applied Economics*, *57*(8), 839–852. DOI: 10.1080/00036846.2024.2309460

Niu, W., Xu, Z., Liu, B., & Liu, C. (2023). INTERNATIONALIZATION OF THE CONSTRUCTION INDUSTRY IN THE GLOBAL VALUE CHAIN. *Technological and Economic Development of Economy*, *29*(4), 1336–1352. DOI: 10.3846/tede.2023.19426

Nonaka, I. (1994). A Dynamic Theory of Organizational Knowledge Creation. *Organization Science*, *5*(1), 14–37. DOI: 10.1287/orsc.5.1.14

Noon, M., & Ogbonna, E. (2021). Controlling management to deliver diversity and inclusion: Prospects and limits. *Human Resource Management Journal, 31*(3), 619–638. DOI: 10.1111/1748-8583.12332

Nurhas, I., Aditya, B. R., Geisler, S., & Pawlowski, J. (2020). Why Does Cultural Diversity Foster Technology-enabled Intergenerational Collaboration? DOI: 10.48550/ARXIV.2001.07630

Nurse, K. (2016). Study on Alternative and Innovative Funding Mechanisms for ACP Cultural Industries. *Final Executive Summary. European Union and the ACP Secretariat, December.*

O'riordan, T. (2014). *Environmental science for environmental management.* Routledge. DOI: 10.4324/9781315839592

Oates, C., Alevizou, P., & McDonald, S. (2016). Challenges for Marketers in Sustainable Production and Consumption. *Sustainability (Basel), 8*(1), 75. DOI: 10.3390/su8010075

Odumeru, J. A., & Ogbonna, I. G. (2013). Transformational vs. transactional leadership theories: Evidence in literature. *International Review of Management and Business Research, 2*(2), 355.

OECD. (2024). Public Innovation for Social Inclusion in Ibero-America. OECD. https://www.oecd.org/en/publications/public-innovation-for-social-inclusion-in-ibero-america_97d84618-en.html

Oguntegbe, K. F., Di Paola, N., & Vona, R. (2023). Communicating responsible management and the role of blockchain technology: Social media analytics for the luxury fashion supply chain. *The TQM Journal, 35*(2), 446–469. DOI: 10.1108/TQM-10-2021-0296

Okuda, T., & Shoda, S. (2018). AI-based Chatbot Service for Financial Industry. *Fujitsu Scientific and Technical Journal, 54*(2), 4–8.

Ordóñez, S. (2024). Global Production Networks and Dynamic Cores in the World's Main Nodes: The Technological-Productive Transition of the Automotive Industry. *World Review of Political Economy, 15*(1), 46–81. DOI: 10.13169/worlrevipoliecon.15.1.0046

Orito, Y., Fukuta, Y., & Murata, K. (2014). *I Will Continue to Use This Nonetheless: Social Media Survive Users' Privacy Concerns.* International Journal Of Virtual Worlds And Human Computer Interaction., DOI: 10.11159/vwhci.2014.010

Ortakand, B. R. (2024). Monitor and Predict Student Engagement and Retention Using Learning Management System (LMS). In Teaching and Learning in the Digital Era: Issues and Studies (pp. 259-277).

Pacheco, J. N., Turro, A., & Urbano, D. (2025). Open social innovation: A systematic literature review and future research agenda. *Technological Forecasting and Social Change*, *V-216*, 124160. Advance online publication. DOI: 10.1016/j.techfore.2025.124160

Palma, M. (2021). Artificial intelligence enhances the sex industry. Predict, 27 February. https://medium.com/predict/artificial-intelligence-enhances-the-sex-industry-7294cf80dd16

Pande, C. B., Srivastava, A., Moharir, K. N., Radwan, N., Mohd Sidek, L., Alshehri, F., Pal, S. C., Tolche, A. D., & Zhran, M. (2024). Characterizing land use/land cover change dynamics by an enhanced random forest machine learning model: A Google Earth Engine implementation. *Environmental Sciences Europe*, *36*(1), 84. DOI: 10.1186/s12302-024-00901-0

Panigrahi, S. S., Bahinipati, B., & Jain, V. (2019). Sustainable supply chain management: A literature review and implications for future research. In *Management of Environmental Quality: An International Journal* (Vol. 30, Issue 5, pp. 1001–1049). Emerald Group Holdings Ltd. https://doi.org/DOI: 10.1108/MEQ-01-2018-0003

Pariser, E. (2011). *The Filter Bubble: What the Internet Is Hiding from You*. Penguin Press.

Pasquali, G., Godfrey, S., & Nadvi, K. (2021). Understanding regional value chains through the interaction of public and private governance: Insights from Southern Africa's apparel sector. *Journal of International Business Policy*, *4*(3), 368–389. DOI: 10.1057/s42214-020-00071-9

Pateman, C. (1970). *Participation and Democratic Theory*. Cambridge University Press., DOI: 10.1017/CBO9780511720444

Patterson, K. A. (2025). Predictive Policing Technology: Community Perceptions of ShotSpotter in West Denver (Master's thesis, University of Colorado Colorado Springs).

Pawlicka, K., & Bal, M. (2022). Sustainable Supply Chain Finances implementation model and Artificial Intelligence for innovative omnichannel logistics. *Management*, *26*(1), 19–35. DOI: 10.2478/manment-2019-0082

Peixoto, T., Fox, J. (2016). When Does ICT-Enabled Citizen Voice Lead to Government Responsiveness? Opening Governance, 21-32. .DOI: 10.19088/1968-2016.104

Pérez-Moure, H., Lampón, J. F., & Cabanelas, P. (2024b). Collective Intelligence Approach for New Mobility. In Advances in business information systems and analytics book series, 149-174. https://doi.org/DOI: 10.4018/979-8-3693-7272-2.ch006

Pérez-Moure, H. (2025). The new dimension of mobility companies: Dynamic capabilities, sustainability, and digitalization. *Suma de Negocios*, *16*(34), 10–20. DOI: 10.14349/sumneg/2025.V16.N34.A2

Pérez-Moure, H., Lampón, J. F., Velando-Rodriguez, M., & Rodríguez-Comesaña, L. (2023). Revolutionizing the road: How sustainable, autonomous, and connected vehicles are changing digital mobility business models. *European Research on Management and Business Economics*, *29*(3), 100230. DOI: 10.1016/j.iedeen.2023.100230

Pérez-Moure, H., Ochoa-Urrego, L. C., & Arbelaez-Giraldo, M. (2024). Mobility business models toward a digital tomorrow: Challenges for automotive manufacturers. *Futures*, *156*, 103309. DOI: 10.1016/j.futures.2023.103309

Periáñez, Á., Fernández Del Río, A., Nazarov, I., Jané, E., Hassan, M., Rastogi, A., & Tang, D. (2024). The digital transformation in health: How AI can improve the performance of health systems. *Health Systems and Reform*, *10*(2), 2387138. DOI: 10.1080/23288604.2024.2387138 PMID: 39437247

Petridis, K., Kiosses, N., Tampakoudis, I., & Ben-Abdelaziz, F. (2023). Measuring the efficiency of mutual funds: Does ESG controversies score affect the mutual fund performance during the COVID-19 pandemic? *Operations Research*, *23*(3), 54. Advance online publication. DOI: 10.1007/s12351-023-00795-5

Phills, J., Deiglmeier, K., & Miller, D. (2008). Rediscovering Social Innovation. Stanford Social Innovation Review, 34–43. DOI: 10.48558/GBJY-GJ47

Pietrobelli, C., & Rabellotti, R. (2011). Global Value Chains Meet Innovation Systems: Are There Learning Opportunities for Developing Countries? *World Development*, *39*(7), 1261–1269. DOI: 10.1016/j.worlddev.2010.05.013

Pilcher, J. M. (2023). *Food in world history*. Routledge. DOI: 10.4324/9781003332039

Pless, N. M., & Maak, T. (2004). Building an Inclusive Diversity Culture: Principles, Processes and Practice. *Journal of Business Ethics*, *4*(2), 129–147. DOI: 10.1007/s10551-004-9465-8

Podsiadlowski, A., & Hofbauer, A. (2014). Envisioning 'inclusive organization'. *Equality, Diversity and Inclusion*, *33*(3), 214–219. DOI: 10.1108/EDI-01-2014-0008

Poirier, L. (2021). Reading datasets: Strategies for interpreting the politics of data signification. *Big Data & Society*, *8*(2), 20539517211029322. DOI: 10.1177/20539517211029322

Pomfret, R. (2021). 'Regionalism' and the global trade system. *World Economy*, *44*(9), 2496–2514. DOI: 10.1111/twec.13155

Ponte, S., & Gibbon, P. (2005). Quality standards, conventions and the governance of global value chains. *Economy and Society*, *34*(1), 1–31. DOI: 10.1080/0308514042000329315

Portaankorva, L. (2024). Values-Based Model to Foster Inclusive Organizational Culture.

Poszler, F., & Lange, B. (2024). The impact of intelligent decision-support systems on humans' ethical decision-making: A systematic literature review and an integrated framework. *Technological Forecasting and Social Change*, *204*, 123403. DOI: 10.1016/j.techfore.2024.123403

Potts, M., & Nelson, R. (2008). Understanding the effect of stigmatization on food consumer knowledge, perception and behaviour in Northern Ireland. *International Journal of Consumer Studies*, *32*(4), 366–373. DOI: 10.1111/j.1470-6431.2008.00676.x

Povich, E. S. (2018a, November 27). Late Payment? A 'Kill Switch' Can Strand You and Your Car. Stateline. https://stateline.org/2018/11/27/late-payment-a-kill-switch-can-strand-you-and-your-car/

Povich, E. S. (2018b, December 2). States Look at "Kill Switches" Used to Disable Cars With Late Payments. Route Fifty. https://www.route-fifty.com/management/2018/12/kill-switch-payments/153205/

Pruksachatkun, Y., McAteer, M., & Majumdar, S. (2023). *Practicing trustworthy machine learning*. O'Reilly Media, Inc.

Prylipko, T. M., Kostash, V. B., Fedoriv, V. M., Lishchuk, S. H., & Tkachuk, V. P. (2021). Control and identification of food products under EC regulations and standards. *International Journal of Agricultural Extension*, *9*(5), 83–91. DOI: 10.33687/ijae.009.00.3964

Pushaw, R. J.Jr, & Silver, C. (2022). The Unconstitutional Assertion of Inherent Powers in Multidistrict Litigations. *BYU L. Rev.*, *48*, 1869.

Putnam, R. D. (2000). *Bowling alone: The collapse and revival of American community*. Touchstone Books/Simon & Schuster., DOI: 10.1145/358916.361990

PwC. (2024, October 3). What is an SDV (Software Defined Vehicle)? Defining SDVs beyond just vehicles. PwC. https://www.pwc.com/jp/en/knowledge/column/definition-of-sdv.html

Quero, M. (2010). Confiabilidad y coeficiente de Alfa de Cronbach. *Telos*, *12*(2), 248–252.

Qutieshat, A. (2025). *Artificial Intelligence in Higher Education: A Contemporary Examination of Illich's Theories*. Springer Nature. DOI: 10.1007/978-981-97-9989-3

Radu, E., Dima, A., Dobrota, E. M., Badea, A. M., Madsen, D. Ø., Dobrin, C., & Stanciu, S. (2023). Global trends and research hotspots on HACCP and modern quality management systems in the food industry. *Heliyon*, *9*(7), e18232. Advance online publication. DOI: 10.1016/j.heliyon.2023.e18232 PMID: 37539220

Rafanelli, L. M. (2022). Justice, injustice, and artificial intelligence: Lessons from political theory and philosophy. *Big Data & Society*, *9*(1), 20539517221080676. DOI: 10.1177/20539517221080676

Rahiman, H. U., & Kodikal, R. (2023). Revolutionizing education: Artificial intelligence empowered learning in higher education. *Cogent Education*, *11*(1), 2293431. Advance online publication. DOI: 10.1080/2331186X.2023.2293431

Rahmani, E., Zandi, S., & Kiani, F. (2024). AI in Public Administration: Legal Implications for Automated Government Decision-Making. *Legal Studies in Digital Age*, *3*(1), 35–43.

Raman, P. (2022). *The Role of Integrative Analytics in Knowledge Building: Supporting Practices of Care* (Order No. 29397271). Available from ProQuest One Academic. (2743512512). http://wdg.biblio.udg.mx:2048/login?url=https://www.proquest.com/dissertations-theses/role-integrative-analytics-knowledge-building/docview/2743512512/se-2

Rampa, F., Lammers, E., Linnemann, A., Schoustra, S., & de Winter, D. (2020). *Pathways to improved food and nutrition security of the poor: The promise of African indigenous foods and technologies*. NWO WOTRO.

Randhawa, K., Wilden, R., & Hohberger, J. (2016). A Bibliometric Review of Open Innovation: Setting a Research Agenda. *Journal of Product Innovation Management*, *33*(6), 750–772. DOI: 10.1111/jpim.12312

Rane, N., Choudhary, S., & Rane, J. (2023). Education 4.0 and 5.0: Integrating artificial intelligence (AI) for personalized and adaptive learning.

Rao, S. (2014). The Last Mile: Gateway to rural empowerment in India. *Field Actions Science Reports. The journal of field actions, Special Issue 12*, Article Special Issue 12. https://journals.openedition.org/factsreports/3711

Reckinger, R. (2022). Values-based territorial food networks: Qualifying sustainable and ethical transitions of alternative food networks. *Regions & Cohesion : the Journal of the Consortium for Comparative Research on Regional Integration and Social Cohesion*, *12*(3), 78–109. DOI: 10.3167/reco.2022.120305

Rejeb, A., Rejeb, K., Simske, S., & Keogh, J. G. (2023). Exploring Blockchain Research in Supply Chain Management: A Latent Dirichlet Allocation-Driven Systematic Review. In *Information (Switzerland)*. Vol. 14, Issue 10. DOI: 10.3390/info14100557

Rejmaniak, R. (2021). Bias in artificial intelligence systems. *Białostockie Studia Prawnicze*, *3*(26), 25–42. DOI: 10.15290/bsp.2021.26.03.02

Rennstam, J., & Sullivan, K. R. (2018). Peripheral inclusion through informal silencing and voice—A study of LGB officers in the Swedish police. *Gender, Work and Organization*, *25*(2), 177–194. DOI: 10.1111/gwao.12194

Ridoutt, B., Bogard, J. R., Dizyee, K., Lim-Camacho, L., & Kumar, S. (2019). Value Chains and Diet Quality: A Review of Impact Pathways and Intervention Strategies. *Agriculture*, *9*(9), 185. DOI: 10.3390/agriculture9090185

Rigo, D. (2021). Global value chains and technology transfer: New evidence from developing countries. *Review of World Economics*, *157*(2), 271–294. DOI: 10.1007/s10290-020-00398-8

Rinelli, L. (2022). Voice segmentation for early identification of neurodegenerative diseases (Doctoral dissertation, Politecnico di Torino).

Rísquez Ramos, M., & Ruiz-Gálvez, M. E. (2024). The transformation of the automotive industry toward electrification and its impact on global value chains: Inter-plant competition, employment, and supply chains. *European Research on Management and Business Economics*, *30*(1), 100242. DOI: 10.1016/j.iedeen.2024.100242

Robbins, S. P., & Coulter, M. (2007). *Principles of management. Translated by Seyyed Mohammad Arabi and Mohammed Ali Hamid Rafiee and Behrouz Asrari Ershad* (4th ed.). Office of Cultural Studies.

Roberson, Q. M. (2006). Disentangling the Meanings of Diversity and Inclusion in Organizations. *Group & Organization Management*, *31*(2), 212–236. DOI: 10.1177/1059601104273064

Roberts, J. S. (2003). The Buzz About Supply Chain. In *Inside Supply Management®* (Vol. 14, Issue 7).

Robin, D. P., & Reidenbach, R. E. (1987). Social Responsibility, Ethics, and Marketing Strategy: Closing the Gap between Concept and Application. *Journal of Marketing*, *51*(1), 44–58. DOI: 10.1177/002224298705100104

Roblek, V., Meško, M., Pušavec, F., & Likar, B. (2021). The role and meaning of the digital transformation as a disruptive innovation on small and medium manufacturing enterprises. *Frontiers in Psychology*, *12*, 592528. DOI: 10.3389/fpsyg.2021.592528 PMID: 34177680

Rodríguez, J. J. (2023, March 7). Survey: 69% Of Americans Don't Want Subscription-Based Options In Their Cars. Jalopnik. https://www.jalopnik.com/car-buyers-dont-want-subscription-based-options-survey-1850194708/

Rodríguez, M., & Mendivelso, F. (2018). Diseño de investigación de Corte Transversal. *Revista Médica Sanitas*, *21*(3), 141–146. DOI: 10.26852/01234250.20

Rogers, K., & Hudson, B. (2011). The Triple Bottom Line: The Synergies of Transformative Perceptions and Practices for Sustainability. *OD Practitioner*, *4*(43), 3–9. https://www.researchgate.net/publication/283710434

Rouse, W. B. (2024). *From Human-Centered Design to Human-Centered Society: Creatively Balancing Business Innovation and Societal Exploitation*. CRC Press.

Roy, V., Schoenherr, T., & Charan, P. (2018). The thematic landscape of literature in sustainable supply chain management (SSCM): A review of the principal facets in SSCM development. In *International Journal of Operations and Production Management* (Vol. 38, Issue 4, pp. 1091–1124). Emerald Group Holdings Ltd. https://doi.org/DOI: 10.1108/IJOPM-05-2017-0260

Rupprecht, C. D., Fujiyoshi, L., McGreevy, S. R., & Tayasu, I. (2020). Trust me? Consumer trust in expert information on food product labels. *Food and Chemical Toxicology*, *137*, 111170. DOI: 10.1016/j.fct.2020.111170 PMID: 32014536

Ryzheva, N., Nefodov, D., Romanyuk, S., Marynchenko, H., & Kudla, M. (2024). Artificial Intelligence in higher education: Opportunities and challenges. *Revista Amazonia Investiga*, *13*(73), 284–296. DOI: 10.34069/AI/2024.73.01.24

Sabbaghan, S., & Eaton, S. E. (2025). Navigating the Ethical Frontier: Graduate Students' Experiences with Generative AI-Mediated Scholarship. *International Journal of Artificial Intelligence in Education*. Advance online publication. DOI: 10.1007/s40593-024-00454-6

Saberi, S., Kouhizadeh, M., Sarkis, J., & Shen, L. (2019). Blockchain technology and its relationships to sustainable supply chain management. *International Journal of Production Research, 57*(7), 2117–2135. DOI: 10.1080/00207543.2018.1533261

Saha, R., Shashi, , Cerchione, R., Singh, R., & Dahiya, R. (2020). Effect of ethical leadership and corporate social responsibility on firm performance: A systematic review. *Corporate Social Responsibility and Environmental Management, 27*(2), 409–429. DOI: 10.1002/csr.1824

Şahin, O., Van der Toorn, J., Jansen, W. S., Boezeman, E. J., & Ellemers, N. (2019). Looking beyond our similarities: How perceived (in) visible dissimilarity relates to feelings of inclusion at work. *Frontiers in Psychology, 10*, 575. DOI: 10.3389/fpsyg.2019.00575 PMID: 30971969

Salvato, C. (2021). Dynamic Capabilities and Routine Dynamics. In Feldman, M. S., Pentland, B. T., D'Adderio, L., Dittrich, K., Rerup, C., & Seidl, D. (Eds.), *Cambridge Handbook of Routine Dynamics* (1st ed., pp. 460–480). Cambridge University Press., DOI: 10.1017/9781108993340.039

Samuels, A. B., & Pelser, A. M. (2025). Transitioning from Industry 4.0 to 5.0: Sustainable supply chain management and talent management insights. *SA Journal of Human Resource Management, 23*. Advance online publication. DOI: 10.4102/sajhrm.v23i0.2874

Sánchez-Flores, R. B., Cruz-Sotelo, S. E., Ojeda-Benitez, S., & Ramírez-Barreto, M. (2020). Sustainable Supply Chain Management—A Literature Review on Emerging Economies. *Sustainability (Basel), 12*(17), 6972. DOI: 10.3390/su12176972

Santati, P., Sulastri, Perizade, B., & Widiyanti, M. (2024). Intellectual capital for higher Education competitiveness. *KnE Social Sciences*. https://doi.org/DOI: 10.18502/kss.v9i14.16120

Santos, E., Carvalho, M., & Martins, S. (2024). Sustainable Enablers of Knowledge Management Strategies in a Higher Education Institution. *Sustainability (Basel), 16*(12), 5078. DOI: 10.3390/su16125078

Santos, N. J. C., & Laczniak, G. R. (2009). Marketing to the Poor: An Integrative Justice Model for Engaging Impoverished Market Segments. *Journal of Public Policy & Marketing, 28*(1), 3–15. DOI: 10.1509/jppm.28.1.3

Sartori, L., & Theodorou, A. (2022). A sociotechnical perspective for the future of AI: Narratives, inequalities, and human control. *Ethics and Information Technology, 24*(1), 4. DOI: 10.1007/s10676-022-09624-3

Sauga, M. (2024). *Europa muss mehr Kapitalismus wagen. Kolumne - DER SPIEGEL*. Spiegel Magazin.

Saul, J., & Kurlander, C. P. (2022). ESG: Right Thesis, Wrong Data. *J. Financ. Transform*, 56, 79-84.

Sawhney, N. (2022). Contestations in urban mobility: Rights, risks, and responsibilities for Urban AI. *AI & Society*, *38*(3), 1083–1098. DOI: 10.1007/s00146-022-01502-2

Scaini, L. (2018). The Way How Anthropological Culture Shapes Consumes: An Exploratory Comparative Study. *European Scientific Journal*. Advance online publication. DOI: 10.19044/esj.2018.c3p6

Schleifer, P., & Sun, Y. (2020). Reviewing the impact of sustainability certification on food security in developing countries. *Global Food Security*, *24*, 100337. DOI: 10.1016/j.gfs.2019.100337

Scott, K. L., Zagenczyk, T. J., Schippers, M., Purvis, R. L., & Cruz, K. S. (2014). Co-worker exclusion and employee outcomes: An investigation of the moderating roles of perceived organizational and social support. *Journal of Management Studies*, *51*(8), 1235–1256. DOI: 10.1111/joms.12099

Seitz, M. A., & Wells, P. E. (2006). Challenging the implementation of corporate sustainability: The case of automotive engine remanufacturing. *Business Process Management Journal*, *12*(6), 822–836. DOI: 10.1108/14637150610710954

Sengupta, A. (2014). Brand Analyses of Global Brands Versus Local Brand in Indian Apparel Consumer Market. *Theses and Dissertations--Retailing and Tourism Management*. https://uknowledge.uky.edu/mat_etds/6

Serdült, U., & Welp, Y. (2012). Direct Democracy Upside Down. Taiwan journal of democracy, 69-92. DOI: 10.5167/UZH-98412

Seuring, S., & Müller, M. (2008). From a literature review to a conceptual framework for sustainable supply chain management. *Journal of Cleaner Production*, *16*(15), 1699–1710. DOI: 10.1016/j.jclepro.2008.04.020

Sharma, S. K. (2014). Drawing Modelling Canvas For The International Positioning Of Indian Beverage Products. *Industrial Engineering Letters*, *4*(7), 30.

Shekarian, E., Ijadi, B., Zare, A., & Majava, J. (2022). Sustainable Supply Chain Management: A Comprehensive Systematic Review of Industrial Practices. In *Sustainability (Switzerland)* (Vol. 14, Issue 13). https://doi.org/DOI: 10.3390/su14137892

Shekhar, N., & Valeri, M. (2023). Trends in knowledge management research in small businesses. *European Business Review*, *35*(5), 573–599. DOI: 10.1108/EBR-10-2022-0200

Sherbin, L., & Rashid, R. (2017). Diversity doesn't stick without inclusion. *Harvard Business Review*, *1*, 1–5.

Shore, L. M., Cleveland, J. N., & Sanchez, D. (2018). Inclusive Workplaces: A Review and Model. *Human Resource Management Review*, *28*(2), 176–189. DOI: 10.1016/j.hrmr.2017.07.003

Shore, L. M., Randel, A. E., Chung, B. G., Dean, M. A., Holcombe Ehrhart, K., & Singh, G. (2011). Inclusion and Diversity in Work Groups: A Review and Model for Future Research. *Journal of Management*, *37*(4), 1262–1289. DOI: 10.1177/0149206310385943

Shuhaimi, A. A. M., Ab Karim, M. S., Fatimah, S., Mohamad, U. F. U. Z. A., & Arshad, M. M. (2022). A review on Halal and Kosher regulations, certifications, and industrial practices. *International Journal of Academic Research in Business & Social Sciences*, *12*(2), 182–192. DOI: 10.6007/IJARBSS/v12-i2/12175

Signori, S., San-José, L., Retolaza, J. L., & Rusconi, G. (2021). Stakeholder value creation: Comparing ESG and value-added in European companies. *Sustainability (Basel)*, *13*(3), 1–16. DOI: 10.3390/su13031392

Silva, J. (1998). Valores / Lo que vale: ¿Dónde están los Valores, *Periódico Reforma*. 17-May-1998.

Sinkovics, N., Sinkovics, R. R., Hoque, S. F., & Czaban, L. (2015). A reconceptualisation of social value creation as social constraint alleviation. *Critical Perspectives on International Business*, *11*(3/4), 340–363. DOI: 10.1108/cpoib-06-2014-0036

Sinnreich, A., & Gilbert, J. (2024). *The secret life of data: Navigating hype and uncertainty in the age of algorithmic surveillance*. MIT Press. DOI: 10.7551/mitpress/14040.001.0001

Sjödin, D., Parida, V., & Kohtamäki, M. (2023). Artificial intelligence enabling circular business model innovation in digital servitization: Conceptualizing dynamic capabilities, AI capacities, business models and effects. *Technological Forecasting and Social Change*, *197*, 122903. DOI: 10.1016/j.techfore.2023.122903

Solebello, N., Tschirhart, M., & Leiter, J. (2016). The paradox of inclusion and exclusion in membership associations. *Human Relations*, *69*(2), 439–460. DOI: 10.1177/0018726715590166

Sorbo, A., Pucci, E., Nobili, C., Taglieri, I., Passeri, D., & Zoani, C. (2022). Food safety assessment: Overview of metrological issues and regulatory aspects in the European Union. *Separations*, *9*(2), 53. DOI: 10.3390/separations9020053

Spicer, T. (2023). *Man-Made: How the bias of the past is being built into the future*. Simon and Schuster.

St. Petersburg State University. Nefedov, K. S., Panibratov, A. Yu., & St. Petersburg State University. (2017). Global value chain analysis: Main dimensions and further research agenda. *Vestnik of Saint Petersburg University. Management, 16*(3), 364–397. DOI: 10.21638/11701/spbu08.2017.302

Stabell, C. B., & Fjeldstad, Ø. D. (1998). Configuring value for competitive advantage: On chains, shops, and networks. *Strategic Management Journal*, *19*(5), 413–437. DOI: 10.1002/(SICI)1097-0266(199805)19:5<413::AID-SMJ946>3.0.CO;2-C

Stadtler, H. (2014). Supply Chain Management: An Overview. In Stadtler, H., & Kilger, C. (Eds.), *Supply chain management and advanced planning* (pp. 3–28). Springer., DOI: 10.1007/978-3-642-55309-7__1

Stahl, B. C. (2025). Locating the Ethics of ChatGPT—Ethical Issues as Affordances in AI Ecosystems. *Information (Basel)*, *16*(2), 104. DOI: 10.3390/info16020104

Stahl, B. C., & Eke, D. (2024). The ethics of ChatGPT – Exploring the ethical issues of an emerging technology. *International Journal of Information Management*, *74*, 102700. DOI: 10.1016/j.ijinfomgt.2023.102700

Stanciu, M., Popescu, A., Antonie, I., Sava, C., & Nistoreanu, B. G. (2022). Good practices on reducing food waste throughout the food supply chain. *Amfiteatru Economic*, *24*(60), 566. DOI: 10.24818/EA/2022/60/566

Stankosky, M. A. (2005). Advances in Knowledge Management: University Research Toward an Academic Discipline. In *Elsevier eBooks* (pp. 1-14). https://doi.org/DOI: 10.1016/B978-0-7506-7878-0.50005-3

Starobin, S. M. (2021). Credibility beyond compliance: Uncertified smallholders in sustainable food systems. *Ecological Economics*, *180*, 106767. DOI: 10.1016/j.ecolecon.2020.106767

Statt, N. (2020, February 7). Tesla remotely disables Autopilot on used Model S after it was sold. The Verge. https://www.theverge.com/2020/2/6/21127243/tesla-model-s-autopilot-disabled-remotely-used-car-update

Steggemann, M. (2023). Collective Intelligence synergizing into Collective Resilience. Mercados y negocios, 24(49), 65-82.

Steggemann, M. (2015) *Complementariedad entre universalismo y particularismo en la empresa filial de la trasnacional alemana ubicada en México.* Universidad La Salle, https://doi.org/DOI: 10.13140/RG.2.1.3687.8564

Steggemann, M. (2023). Collective Intelligence synergizing into Collective Resilience. *Mercados y Negocios, 24*(49), 65–82. DOI: 10.32870/myn.vi49.7700

Steggemann, M. (2025). Managing AI in the Workplace to Enhance Collective Intelligence and Resilience. In *Navigating Collective Intelligence for Sustainable Futures* (pp. 33–64). IGI Global Scientific Publishing.

Stein, C. M., Morris, N. J., & Nock, N. L. (2011). Structural equation modeling. In *Methods in molecular biology* (pp. 495-512). https://doi.org/DOI: 10.1007/978-1-61779-555-8_27

Stein, A. J., & Santini, F. (2022). The sustainability of "local" food: A review for policy-makers. *Review of Agricultural, Food and Environmental Studies, 103*(1), 77–89. DOI: 10.1007/s41130-021-00148-w PMID: 38624674

Stenseke, J. (2024). On the computational complexity of ethics: Moral tractability for minds and machines. *Artificial Intelligence Review, 57*(4), 105. DOI: 10.1007/s10462-024-10732-3

Strantz, A. (2025). Coding Ethically as a Writer and Designer. In *The Routledge Handbook of Ethics in Technical and Professional Communication* (pp. 221–229). Routledge. DOI: 10.4324/9781003434375-26

Subramaniam, L., Jalaludin, F. W., Hen, K. W., & Yap, C. S. (2023). The second and third levels of digital divide among Malaysian university students during the Covid-19 pandemic. *Telkomnika, 21*(6), 1326. DOI: 10.12928/telkomnika.v21i6.25258

Sullivan, Y., & Wamba, F. S. (2024). Artificial intelligence and adaptive response to market changes: A strategy to enhance firm performance and innovation. *Journal of Business Research, 174*, 114500. DOI: 10.1016/j.jbusres.2024.114500

Sum, N., & Jessop, B. (2012). Competitiveness, the Knowledge-Based Economy and Higher Education. *Journal of the Knowledge Economy, 4*(1), 24–44. DOI: 10.1007/s13132-012-0121-8

Sun, Q., Sridhar, N., & O'Brien, M. (2009, April). *Consumer Perception Of Product Stimuli: An Investigation into Indian Consumer Psychology and its Implications for New Product Development, Process and Strategy.* D2B2: the 2nd Tsinghua International Design Management Symposium, Tsinghua University, Beijing, China. https://eprints.hud.ac.uk/id/eprint/5273/, https://www.hud.ac.uk/news/

Swain, R. B. (2018). A Critical Analysis of the Sustainable Development Goals. In Leal Filho, W. (Ed.), *Handbook of Sustainability Science and Research*. World Sustainability Series. Springer., DOI: 10.1007/978-3-319-63007-6_20

Szalavetz, A. (2024). In-house software development for software-defined vehicles: Major changes ahead in automotive value chains? *International Journal of Automotive Technology and Management*, *24*(5), 22–39. DOI: 10.1504/IJATM.2024.142127

Taeihagh, A. (2025). Governance of Generative AI. *Policy and Society*, *44*(1), 1–22. Advance online publication. DOI: 10.1093/polsoc/puaf001

Tahir, G. A. (2024). Ethical Challenges in Computer Vision: Ensuring Privacy and Mitigating Bias in Publicly Available Datasets. arXiv preprint arXiv:2409.10533.

Talmage, C., & Knopf, R. C. (2017). Rethinking Diversity, Inclusion, and Inclusiveness: The Quest to Better Understand Indicators of Community Enrichment and Well-Being. In Kraeger, P., Cloutier, S., & Talmage, C. (Eds.), *New Dimensions in Community Well-Being. Community Quality-of-Life and Well-Being*. Springer., DOI: 10.1007/978-3-319-55408-2_2

Taneja, A., Nair, G., Joshi, M., Sharma, S., Sharma, S., Jambrak, A. R., Roselló-Soto, E., Barba, F. J., Castagnini, J. M., Leksawasdi, N., & Phimolsiripol, Y. (2023). Artificial Intelligence: Implications for the Agri-Food Sector. *Agronomy (Basel)*, *13*(5), 1397. DOI: 10.3390/agronomy13051397

Tarasenko, O., Lysenko, S., Tarlopov, I., Pidkaminnyi, I., & Verhun, M. (2024). Analysis of the competitiveness of higher education institutions in Ukraine in the context of recovery and development after the war. *Multidisciplinary Science Journal, 6,* 2024ss0210. https://doi.org/DOI: 10.31893/multiscience.2024ss0210

Tarrow, S. (2005). *The New Transnational Activism*. Cambridge University Press. DOI: 10.1017/CBO9780511791055

Tavakol, M., & Dennick, R. (2011). Making sense of Cronbach's alpha. *International Journal of Medical Education*, *2*, 53–55. DOI: 10.5116/ijme.4dfb.8dfd PMID: 28029643

Taylor, K. M., & Vachon, S. (2018). Empirical research on sustainable supply chains: IJPR's contribution and research avenues. In *International Journal of Production Research* (Vol. 56, Issues 1–2, pp. 950–959). Taylor and Francis Ltd. https://doi.org/DOI: 10.1080/00207543.2017.1402139

Taylor, J. (2023). *Digital tools, rhetoric, and meaning-making: A critical exploration of addressing the digital divide and accessibility to improve our digital landscape*. Iowa State University.

Teece, D. (2014). A dynamic capabilities-based entrepreneurial theory of the multinational enterprise. *Journal of International Business Studies*, *45*(1), 8–37. DOI: 10.1057/jibs.2013.54

Teece, D. (2020). Hand in glove: Open innovation and the dynamic capabilities framework. *Strategic Management Review*, *1*(2), 233–253. DOI: 10.1561/111.00000010

Teece, D. J. (2007). Explicating dynamic capabilities: The nature and microfoundations of (sustainable) enterprise performance. *Strategic Management Journal*, *28*(13), 1319–1350. DOI: 10.1002/smj.640

Teece, D. J. (2018). Tesla and the Reshaping of the Auto Industry. *Management and Organization Review*, *14*(3), 501–512. DOI: 10.1017/mor.2018.33

Teece, D. J., & Linden, G. (2017). Business models, value capture, and the digital enterprise. *J Org Design*, *6*(1), 8. DOI: 10.1186/s41469-017-0018-x

Teece, D. J., Pisano, G., & Shuen, A. (1997). Dynamic capabilities and strategic management. *Strategic Management Journal*, *18*(7), 509–533. DOI: 10.1002/(SICI)1097-0266(199708)18:7<509::AID-SMJ882>3.0.CO;2-Z

Teuteberg, F., & Wittstruck, D. (2010). A systematic review of sustainable supply chain management. *In Multikonferenz Wirtschaftsinformatik*, 203.

The Dallas Morning News. (2025, February 25). Americans Don't Trust Self-Driving Cars Says AAA Survey. CPA Practice Advisor. https://www.cpapracticeadvisor.com/2025/02/25/americans-dont-trust-self-driving-cars-says-aaa-survey/156524/

The Last Mile: Gateway to rural empowerment in India. (n.d.). Retrieved May 18, 2025, from https://journals.openedition.org/factsreports/3711

Thijssen, L., Van Tubergen, F., Coenders, M., Hellpap, R., & Jak, S. (2022). Discrimination of black and muslim minority groups in western societies: Evidence from a meta-analysis of field experiments. *The International Migration Review*, *56*(3), 843–880. DOI: 10.1177/01979183211045044

Thiyagalingam, J., Shankar, M., Fox, G., & Hey, T. (2022). Scientific machine learning benchmarks. *Nature Reviews. Physics*, *4*(6), 413–420. DOI: 10.1038/s42254-022-00441-7

Thomas, J. J. (2022). Biases and Obstacles to Critical Thinking. In Developing Cross-Cultural Competence for Leaders (pp. 79-98). Routledge. DOI: 10.4324/9781003213352-7

Timmer, M. P., Los, B., Stehrer, R., & De Vries, G. J. (2013). Fragmentation, incomes and jobs: An analysis of European competitiveness. *Economic Policy*, *28*(76), 613–661. DOI: 10.1111/1468-0327.12018

Todic, J., Cook, S. C., Spitzer-Shohat, S., Williams, J. S.Jr, Battle, B. A., Jackson, J., & Chin, M. H. (2022). Critical theory, culture change, and achieving health equity in health care settings. *Academic Medicine*, *97*(7), 977–988. DOI: 10.1097/ACM.0000000000004680 PMID: 35353723

Trager, R. F., & Luca, L. M. (2022). Killer robots are here—And we need to regulate them. *Foreign Policy*, *11*(May). https://foreignpolicy.com/2022/05/11/killer-robots-lethal-autonomous-weapons-systems-ukraine-libya-regulation/

Tranfield, D., Denyer, D., & Smart, P. (2003). Towards a Methodology for Developing Evidence-Informed Management Knowledge using Systematic Review. *British Journal of Management*, *14*(3), 207–222. DOI: 10.1111/1467-8551.00375

Trivedi, P.University of Luckno. (2015). Department of Business Administration, & Trivedi, P. (2015). A conceptual model for driving green purchase among indian consumers. *Journal of Marketing and Consumer Behaviour in Emerging Markets*, *2015*(2), 49–59. DOI: 10.7172/2449-6634.jmcbem.2015.2.4

Tyler, M. (2019). Reassembling difference? Rethinking inclusion through/as embodied ethics. *Human Relations*, *72*(1), 48–68. DOI: 10.1177/0018726718764264

Tyndall, Gene, Christopher Gopal, Wolfgang Partsch, & John Kamauff. (1998). *Supercharging Supply Chains: New Ways to Increase Value Through Global Operational Excellence*. John Wiley & Sons.

UN. (1948). *Universal Declaration of Human Rights*. United Nations.

UN. (2015). *Sustainable development goals: 17 goals to transform our world*. United Nations.

UN. (2015). *Transforming our world: the 2030 Agenda for Sustainable Development*. United Nations.

UN. (2020). *UN Comprehensive Response to COVID-19: Saving Lives, Protecting Societies, Recovering Better*. United Nations.

UNESCO. (1999). *Declaration and Program of Action on a Culture of Peace*. UNESCO.

Usman, S. (2024). The Impact of COVID-19 on Industry 4.0 Adoption: An Emerging Economy Perspective. *Operations and Supply Chain Management*, *17*(2), 284–298. DOI: 10.31387/oscm0570428

Utouh, H. M. L., & Kitole, F. A. (2024). Forecasting effects of foreign direct investment on industrialization towards realization of the Tanzania development vision 2025. *Cogent Economics & Finance*, *12*(1), 2376947. DOI: 10.1080/23322039.2024.2376947

Valenzo-Jiménez, M. A., & Gonzaléz-Samaniego, A. (2021). Capacidad de adaptación y competitividad en microempresas de abarrotes en Cuitzeo, México. *Mercados y Negocios*, *22*(43), 49–76. DOI: 10.32870/myn.v0i43.7629

Vallabhaneni, A. S., Perla, A., Regalla, R. R., & Kumari, N. (2024). The Power of Personalization: AI-Driven Recommendations. In Minds Unveiled (pp. 111-127). Productivity Press.

Vallet-Bellmunt, T., Martínez-Fernández, M. T., & Capó-Vicedo, J. (2011). Supply chain management: A multidisciplinary content analysis of vertical relations between companies, 1997–2006. *Industrial Marketing Management*, *40*(8), 1347–1367. DOI: 10.1016/j.indmarman.2011.03.002

Vdovic, H., Babic, J., & Podobnik, V. (2019). Automotive Software in Connected and Autonomous Electric Vehicles: A Review. *IEEE Access : Practical Innovations, Open Solutions*, *7*, 166365–166379. DOI: 10.1109/ACCESS.2019.2953568

Venet, A. S. (2023). *Equity-centered trauma-informed education*. Routledge. DOI: 10.4324/9781032677989

Vermeulen, S., Woodhill, A. J., Proctor, F., & Delnoye, R. (2008). *Chain-wide learning for inclusive agrifood market development: A guide to multi-stakeholder processes for linking small-scale producers to modern markets*. International Institute for Environment and Development. https://research.wur.nl/en/publications/chain-wide-learning-for-inclusive-agrifood-market-development-a-g

Vincent, J. (2022, July 12). BMW starts selling heated seat subscriptions for $18 a month. The Verge. https://www.theverge.com/2022/7/12/23204950/bmw-subscriptions-microtransactions-heated-seats-feature

Volti, R., & Croissant, J. (2024). *Society and technological change*. Waveland Press.

Von Delft, S., Kortmann, S., Gelhard, C., & Pisani, N. (2019). Leveraging global sources of knowledge for business model innovation. *Long Range Planning*, *52*(5), 101848. DOI: 10.1016/j.lrp.2018.08.003

Voss, A. (2024). The Future We're Building: How Today's Innovations Will Shape Tomorrow's World. eBookIt. com.

Voss, E., Cushing, S. T., Ockey, G. J., & Yan, X. (2023). The use of assistive technologies including generative AI by test takers in language assessment: A debate of theory and practice. *Language Assessment Quarterly, 20*(4–5), 520–532. https://doi-org.wdg.biblio.udg.mx:8443/10.1080/15434303.2023.2288256. DOI: 10.1080/15434303.2023.2288256

Vu, M. C., & Burton, N. (2024). Beyond the Inclusion-Exclusion Binary: Right Mindfulness and Its Implications for Perceived Inclusion and Exclusion in the Workplace. *Journal of Business Ethics, 191*(1), 147–165. DOI: 10.1007/s10551-023-05457-2

Vyhmeister, E., Castane, G., Östberg, P. O., & Thevenin, S. (2023). A responsible AI framework: Pipeline contextualisation. *AI and Ethics, 3*(1), 175–197. DOI: 10.1007/s43681-022-00154-8

Walach, H. (2003). *Generalisierte Quantentheorie (Weak Quantum Theory): Eine theoretische Basis zum Verständnis transpersonaler Phänomene. Auf dem Weg zu einer Psychologie des Bewusstseins.* Bibliotheks-und Informationssystem der Universität Oldenburg, 13-46.

Wales, W. J., Covin, J. G., Schüler, J., & Baum, M. (2023). Entrepreneurial orientation as a theory of new value creation. *The Journal of Technology Transfer, 48*(5), 1752–1772. DOI: 10.1007/s10961-023-10021-1

Wampler, B. (2012). Participatory Budgeting: Core Principles and Key Impacts. Journal of Deliberative Democracy, doi https://doi.org/.DOI: 10.16997/jdd.138

Wang, A., Morgenstern, J., & Dickerson, J. P. (2025). Large language models that replace human participants can harmfully misportray and flatten identity groups. *Nature Machine Intelligence, 7*(3), 1–12. DOI: 10.1038/s42256-025-00986-z

Wang, S., Wang, X., & Chen, S. (2022). Global value chains and carbon emission reduction in developing countries: Does industrial upgrading matter? *Environmental Impact Assessment Review, 97*, 106895. DOI: 10.1016/j.eiar.2022.106895

Wang, Y. (2021). When artificial intelligence meets educational leaders' data-informed decision-making: A cautionary tale. *Studies in Educational Evaluation, 69*, 100872. DOI: 10.1016/j.stueduc.2020.100872

Warrilow, S. (2012). Transformational leadership theory- The 4 key components in leading change & managing change. *Harvard Business Review, 2*(3), 101–104.

Warshawsky, D. N. (2024). *Food Waste, Food Insecurity, and the Globalization of Food Banks.* University of Iowa Press.

Watermeyer, R., Phipps, L., Lanclos, D., & Knight, C. (2023). Generative AI and the Automating of Academia. *Postdigital Science And Education*, *6*(2), 446–466. DOI: 10.1007/s42438-023-00440-6

WB. (2017). *Who cares wins: connecting financial markets to a changing world.* World Bank Group.

Wehr, H. M. (2007). Codex Alimentarius: What It Is and Why It Is Important. In *Microbial Food Contamination* (pp. 517-546). CRC Press.

Weinberg, L. (2024). *Smart University: Student Surveillance in the Digital Age.* JHU Press. DOI: 10.56021/9781421450018

Welz, C., Ikonen, E., & Kristiansen, A. (2023). Learning through Listening and Responding: Probing the Potential and Limits of Dialogue in Local and Online Environments. *Religions*, *14*(2), 241. DOI: 10.3390/rel14020241

Westley, F., Zimmerman, B., & Patton, M. (2006). *Getting to Maybe: How the World is Changed.* Random House Canada.

WHO. (2018). *Understanding the Codex Alimentarius.* Food & Agriculture Org.

Wiggins, C., & Jones, M. L. (2023). *How data happened: A history from the age of reason to the age of algorithms.* WW Norton & Company.

Williams, D. P. (2022). Belief, Values, Bias, and Agency: Development of and Entanglement with "Artificial Intelligence" (Doctoral dissertation, Virginia Polytechnic Institute and State University).

Witt, M. A. (2019). De-globalization: Theories, predictions, and opportunities for international business research. *Journal of International Business Studies*, *50*(7), 1053–1077. DOI: 10.1057/s41267-019-00219-7

Xiao, G., Samian, N., Faizal, M. F. M., As'ad, M. A. Z. M., Fadzil, M. F. M., Abdullah, A., & Hermadi, I. (2024). A Framework for Blockchain and Internet of Things Integration in Improving Food Security in the Food Supply Chain. *Journal of Advanced Research in Applied Sciences and Engineering Technology*, *34*(1), 24–37. DOI: 10.37934/araset.34.1.2437

Xiao, H., Meng, B., Ye, J., & Li, S. (2020). Are global value chains truly global? *Economic Systems Research*, *32*(4), 540–564. DOI: 10.1080/09535314.2020.1783643

Xu, X., Lu, Y., Vogel-Heuser, B., & Wang, L. (2021). Industry 4.0 and Industry 5.0—Inception, conception and perception. *Journal of Manufacturing Systems*, *61*, 530–535. DOI: 10.1016/j.jmsy.2021.10.006

Yadav, A., Garg, R. K., & Sachdeva, A. (2024). Artificial intelligence applications for information management in sustainable supply chain management: A systematic review and future research agenda. *International Journal of Information Management Data Insights*, *4*(2), 100292. Advance online publication. DOI: 10.1016/j.jjimei.2024.100292

Yadav, D., Dutta, G., & Kumar, S. (2021). Food safety standards adoption and its impact on firms' export performance: A systematic literature review. *Journal of Cleaner Production*, *329*, 129708. DOI: 10.1016/j.jclepro.2021.129708

Yalamati, S. (2024). The Contribution of Artificial Intelligence to Foster Sustainable Food Systems in Agriculture. In *Artificial Intelligence and Machine Learning for Sustainable Development* (pp. 236–248). CRC Press., DOI: 10.1201/9781003497189-18

Yang, Z., Fang, G., & Sun, W. (2025). Embodied carbon emissions and their transfer pathways in global aluminum trade: The value chain perspective. *Journal of Cleaner Production*, *494*, 145057. DOI: 10.1016/j.jclepro.2025.145057

Yin, Y., Jia, N., & Wakslak, C. J. (2024). AI can help people feel heard, but an AI label diminishes this impact. *Proceedings of the National Academy of Sciences of the United States of America*, *121*(14), e2319112121. DOI: 10.1073/pnas.2319112121 PMID: 38551835

Younas, A., & Zeng, Y. (2024). A Philosophical Inquiry into AI-Inclusive Epistemology. Available at *SSRN* 4902415.

Yucer, S., Tektas, F., Al Moubayed, N., & Breckon, T. (2024). Racial bias within face recognition: A survey. *ACM Computing Surveys*, *57*(4), 1–39. DOI: 10.1145/3705295

Yunus, M. (2007). *Creating a World Without Poverty: Social Business and the Future of Capitalism*. Public Affairs.

Yu, P. K. (2021). Beyond transparency and accountability: Three additional features algorithm designers should build into intelligent platforms. *NEULR*, *13*, 263.

Yu, Y., & Xu, Q. (2022). Influencing Factors of Enterprise R&D Investment: Post-Subsidy, Sustainability, and Heterogeneity. *Sustainability (Basel)*, *14*(10), 5759. Advance online publication. DOI: 10.3390/su14105759

Zallio, M., & Clarkson, P. J. (2021). Inclusion, diversity, equity and accessibility in the built environment: A study of architectural design practice. *Building and Environment*, *206*, 108352. DOI: 10.1016/j.buildenv.2021.108352

Zaninović, P. A., & Bugarčić, F. Ž. (2023). THE EFFECTS OF INTERNATIONAL LOGISTICS IN GLOBAL VALUE CHAIN TRADE. *Journal of Business Economics and Management*, *24*(5), 841–856. DOI: 10.3846/jbem.2023.20443

Zepf, V., Reller, A., Rennie, C., Ashfield, M., & Simmons, J. (2014). *Materials critical to the energy industry. An introduction.* 2nd edition. BP.

Zhang, M. (2015). Google Photos tags two African-Americans as gorillas through facial recognition software. *Forbes*, *1*(July). https://www.forbes.com/sites/mzhang/2015/07/01/google-photos-tags-two-african-americans-as-gorillas-through-facial-recognition-software/

Zhang, Q., Cao, M., Zhang, F., Liu, J., & Li, X. (2020). Effects of corporate social responsibility on customer satisfaction and organizational attractiveness: A signaling perspective. *Business Ethics (Oxford, England)*, *29*(1), 20–34. DOI: 10.1111/beer.12243

Zhang, Y., & Kamargianni, M. (2022). A review on the factors influencing the adoption of new mobility technologies and services: Autonomous vehicle, drone, micromobility and mobility as a service. *Transport Reviews*, *43*(3), 407–429. DOI: 10.1080/01441647.2022.2119297

Zhang, Z., Zhu, K., & Hewings, G. J. D. (2017). A multi-regional input–output analysis of the pollution haven hypothesis from the perspective of global production fragmentation. *Energy Economics*, *64*, 13–23. DOI: 10.1016/j.eneco.2017.03.007

Zhao, F., Song, H., Liu, Z., Zhao, F., Song, H., & Liu, Z. (2022, January 31). Identification and Analysis of Key Technical Elements and Prospects for Software-Defined Vehicles. SAE 2021 Intelligent and Connected Vehicles Symposium Part II. https://doi.org/DOI: 10.4271/2022-01-7002

Zhou, M., Abhishek, V., Derdenger, T., Kim, J., & Srinivasan, K. (2024). Bias in Generative AI. arXiv (Cornell University). https://doi.org//arxiv.2403.02726DOI: 10.48550

Zhu, Y. (2024). The Impact of Algorithmic Control and Algorithmic Management in Online Labor Platforms (Doctoral dissertation, University of Arkansas).

Zhu, Z., Puliga, M., Cerina, F., Chessa, A., & Riccaboni, M. (2014). *Global Value Trees*. DOI: 10.48550/ARXIV.1410.4694

Zou, S., & Cavusgil, S. T. (2002). The GMS: A Broad Conceptualization of Global Marketing Strategy and Its Effect on Firm Performance. *Journal of Marketing*, *66*(4), 40–56. DOI: 10.1509/jmkg.66.4.40.18519

Zutshi, A., Creed, A., Bhattacharya, A., Sohal, A., & Bavik, A. (2023). Mandated media innovation impacts on knowledge dissemination in workplace training. *Knowledge Management Research and Practice*, •••, 1–17. DOI: 10.1080/14778238.2023.2209745

About the Contributors

Tania Elena González has technical studies in Computer Science (1990), Bachelor's degree in Business Administration (1994), and a master's degree in Finance (2003), the three degrees awarded by UNAM. She obtained a doctorate from the Complutense University of Madrid in the Doctorate of International Economics and Development with an Outstanding Cum Laude; at this same university, she maintained the distinction of Honorary Collaborator for more than ten years. His academic and research career spans 32 years. He has been part of the faculty of the University of Vigo, Complutense University of Madrid, UNAM, Banking and Commercial School, La Salle University, and the College of Civil Engineers, in addition to the University of Guadalajara, teaching classes, conferences, and supervising thesis under research projects. He has collaborated on international projects linked to the business and productive sector, from which his publications and work in the classroom are derived. He is currently a member of the National System of Researchers, has the desirable PRODEP profile, is a Member of the consolidated Academic Body UDG-CA-484 "Strategies, Competitiveness, Knowledge Management and Sustainability" and president of the Academy of Applied Marketing, University of Guadalajara, Mexico.

Jesús F. Lampón Industrial Engineer and PhD in Business Administration is professor of Business Organization at the University of Vigo. He has been a lead researcher in more than fifty research projects with different institutions and firms. His research has been published in more than 40 journals such as the International Journal of Production Research, Journal of Business Research, Production Planning & Control, Papers in Regional Science, Regional Studies or Journal of Manufacturing Technology Management. He was Manager of the Programme to Promote Business Research and Innovation in the Economy and Industry Council of the Galicia Government (Spain). He is Editor of the European Research on Management and Business Economics and SAGE Open, and member of the Editorial Board of

Kybernetes, International Journal of Automotive Technology and Management, and Regional Science Policy & Practice.

***

Almeirim Isabel Acosta Bahena is a researcher at the Universidad de Guadalajara and a doctoral candidate in the Ph.D. program Innovation and Sustainability in Business. Her academic trajectory integrates the disciplines of nutrition, marketing, and food service management, with a specific focus on sustainability, consumer behavior, and certification systems within the agri-food sector. She holds a bachelor's degree in Nutrition, which provided a scientific foundation in food science, health, and dietetics. Motivated by an interest in understanding market dynamics and strategic communication, she pursued a Master's in Marketing Management. This dual academic formation enables a comprehensive and interdisciplinary approach to research questions related to food systems, combining technical knowledge with behavioral and market-oriented analysis. Her professional and academic experience centers on food service management, particularly in the areas of food certifications and consumer behavior. She has developed expertise in the analysis and implementation of certification schemes—such as organic, fair trade, and sustainability labels—and their influence on consumer decision-making processes. Her work seeks to elucidate how certification mechanisms function not only as tools for market differentiation but also as instruments for promoting transparency, trust, and sustainability. Currently, her doctoral research examines the role of collective intelligence in shaping green consumer behavior. This investigation explores how participatory knowledge, collaborative networks, and digital platforms contribute to the formation of sustainable consumption patterns. Her work aims to generate insights into the mechanisms through which collective knowledge and social influence can foster environmentally responsible choices, with implications for policy, business strategy, and consumer education. At the Universidad de Guadalajara, Almeirim participates in interdisciplinary research projects that intersect sustainability studies, innovation management, and consumer research. Her academic contributions aim to support the development of inclusive and sustainable food systems through evidence-based frameworks and critical analysis. Almeirim Isabel Acosta Bahena's scholarly agenda is grounded in the commitment to advancing interdisciplinary knowledge that informs both academic debate and practical implementation. Her research interests contribute to a growing body of work that addresses urgent global challenges related to environmental sustainability, food security, and ethical consumption.

Luis Bellon-Alvarez Professor-Researcher recognized by Mexico's National Research System (SNI), currently teaching in Marketing with a research focus on Organizational Growth

Nihar Suresh Dahake is currently serving as an Assistant Professor in the Department of MBA at G H Raisoni College of Engineering, Nagpur. He holds a B.Com, M.Com, and MBA from Rashtrasant Tukdoji Maharaj Nagpur University and earned his Ph.D. from Sant Gadge Baba Amravati University, Amravati. In addition to his academic qualifications, Dr. Dahake has successfully qualified the State Eligibility Test (SET) in both Commerce and Management, demonstrating his strong foundation in these disciplines. With a rich academic background, he brings 14 years of teaching experience and 8 years of dedicated research experience to his role. Throughout his career, he has consistently contributed to academic excellence and research development. Dr. Dahake's areas of expertise include Financial Accounting, Consumer Behavior, Marketing Management, and Financial Management. His multidisciplinary knowledge allows him to effectively engage with a wide range of topics in business and management studies. Passionate about both teaching and research, he strives to inspire students while also contributing meaningfully to the academic community through his scholarly work. His professional journey reflects a deep commitment to education, research, and the advancement of management studies in higher education institutions.

Parihar Suresh Dahake is an accomplished academician and researcher with over 15 years of experience in teaching and research in the fields of Commerce and Management. Currently serving as an Assistant Professor at the School of Management, Ramdeobaba University, Nagpur, he holds a diverse educational background, including B.Tech (Applied Electronics), MBA (Marketing & Financial Management), M.Com, PGDIBO, M.A. (Psychology), and a Ph.D. in Business Management. His doctoral work focused on the impact of marketing strategies of DTH services on consumer behavior in Nagpur. Dr. Dahake's research interests span Business Analytics, Consumer Behavior, Predictive Analytics, and Marketing Communication. A recognized Ph.D. supervisor, he guides multiple doctoral candidates under the faculty of Commerce. He has published extensively in peer-reviewed, Scopus, and ABDC-indexed journals and authored books on Marketing Management and Consumer Behavior. He also holds a patent in wage sheet automation and actively contributes as a reviewer for prestigious journals. A recipient of multiple accolades, including the Young Researcher and Research Excellence Awards, Dr. Dahake is also a sought-after speaker and trainer. His commitment to academic excellence and innovative pedagogy has made significant contributions to management education, research, and institutional development in Central India.

Haomin Fu is a doctoral student in Department of Automotive Science at Kyushu University, Japan. Her research explores the evolving electric vehicle ecosystem, with a focus on the downstream value chain, resource integration, and digital transformation in the Chinese automotive industry.

Yasunori Fukuta is a professor of Marketing Research at the School of Commerce, Meiji University, Tokyo, Japan. He was a visiting scholar at Cardiff Business School, Cardiff University, UK, and has served as a member of the board of directors of both the Japan Management Diagnosis Association and the Japan Society for Information and Management. His research interests include statistical modeling of market dynamics, the influence of social practices on the value co-creation process, and ethics in marketing research and data collection through IoT.

Arcadio González-Samaniego received a PhD in Sciences from the Instituto de Investigaciones Económicas y Empresariales of the Universidad Michoacana de San Nicolás de Hidalgo, Mexico. He has a master's degree in administration from the same university. He is currently doing a postdoctoral stay financed by Mexico's Secretary of Science, Humanities, Technology, and Innovation. She has been a speaker at several international conferences. He belongs to the National System of Researchers of Mexico. He is an Honorary State Researcher of Michoacán and a member of the Michoacán Science Outreach Register. He researches and writes on issues of sustainability, competitiveness, SMEs, and development.

César Mora-Pérez PhD in Fiscal Studies with a focus on Public Finance from the University of Guadalajara. He is a Professor-Researcher in the Department of Administration at the University Center for Administration (CUCEA) of the University of Guadalajara (UdeG). He is a member of the National System of Researchers (SNII) of the National Council for Humanities, Sciences and Technologies (CONAHCYT), level C. He is also the Founder and President of the College of Administrators of Jalisco (CONLA Jalisco). He has experience in the public and social sectors. His research interests include Public Finance, Audit and Fiscal Sustainability, Innovation and Government Efficiency. He is also a member of groups focused on transparency and public management.

Kiyoshi Murata is Director of the Centre for Business Information Ethics and Professor of MIS at the School of Commerce, Meiji University, Tokyo, Japan. He has studied information ethics since 1997 following his career of research on economics, operational research, business administration and management information systems, and established the Centre for Business Information Ethics in April 2006, which is the only research institute to study information ethics in Japan. Kiyoshi has been an international research associate at the Centre for Computing and Social

Responsibility, De Montfort University, Leicester, UK since 2005 and an advisor of the Computer Ethics Society based in Hong Kong since 2012, and was a president of the Japan Society for Information and Management from AY 2016 to 2019. He has published his papers in scholarly journals including Journal of Information, Communication and Ethics in Society; Journal of the Association for Information Systems; AI and Society; International Review of Information Ethics; and Journal of Business Ethics.

Jorge Pelayo Maciel is a full-time professor and researcher at the University of Guadalajara's Center for Economic and Administrative Sciences (CUCEA), where he is affiliated with the Department of Marketing and International Business. He holds a Ph.D. in Economic-Administrative Sciences from the University of Guadalajara, is a Level I member of Mexico's National System of Researchers (SNII), and maintains an active PRODEP profile. He has a distinguished academic and research career focused on business competitiveness, dynamic capabilities, corporate governance, knowledge management, and international business. He is a member of the academic research group "Strategies, Competitiveness, Knowledge Management, and Sustainability" (UDG-CA-484), where he collaborates on inter-institutional and multidisciplinary projects aimed at strengthening small and medium-sized enterprises (SMEs) in Mexico. Dr. Pelayo Maciel has authored over 40 scholarly publications, including peer-reviewed articles, book chapters, and collective works. His academic contributions have significantly advanced the understanding of key factors influencing organizational competitiveness, particularly in the context of digital transformation and the knowledge economy. His most recent research focuses on organizational innovation, Industry 4.0, human capital, and corporate sustainability. He is also actively engaged in the training of high-level professionals, serving as advisor and committee member for undergraduate, master's, and doctoral theses, as well as an evaluator of academic projects. Dr. Pelayo Maciel's commitment to academic excellence and regional development has made him a recognized authority in the fields of business management and internationalization in Mexico.

Hugo Pérez Moure Cum laude Doctor in Economic Analysis and Business Strategy from the University of Vigo, with two master's degrees: one in East Asian Studies from the Autonomous University of Madrid and another in International Trade from the University of Vigo. Despite his young age, he has collaborated on numerous European projects across a wide range of business-related fields, such as entrepreneurship and mobility. He also has several publications in high-impact JCR and Scopus journals, including Technology in Society, European Research on Management and Business Economics, Futures, Industrial Marketing Management, and Suma de Negocios y Dirección y Organización. Additionally, he is part of various international research networks, such as AEDEM, RIICO, and GERPISA. Through these networks and his participation in conferences, some of his research has received awards, including the ESIC Award for Knowledge Transfer to Business and Society.

Wasswa Shafik (Member, IEEE) received a Bachelor of Science degree in information technology from Ndejje University, Uganda, a Master of Engineering degree in Information Technology (Computer and Communication Networks) from Yazd University, Iran, and a PhD in Computer Science with the School of Digital Science, Universiti Brunei Darussalam, Brunei Darussalam. He is also the Founder and Research Director of the Dig Connectivity Research Laboratory (DCRLab) after serving as a Research Associate at the Network Interconnectivity Research Laboratory at Yazd University. Prior to this, he worked as a Community Data Analyst at Population Services International (PSI-Uganda), a Community Data Officer at the Programme for Accessible Health Communication (PACE-Uganda), a Research Assistant at the Socio-Economic Data Centre (SEDC-Uganda), Uganda, an Assistant Data Officer at TechnoServe, Kampala, Uganda, and Asmaah Charity Organization as Cheif Executive Officer. He has hundreds of publications with renowned publishers. His research interests include Artificial Intelligence, Neural Networks, Computer Vision, Smart Agriculture, Digital Health, and Green Computing.

Michael Steggemann has extensive experience in project management and business administration, having worked internationally with companies from Germany, the United States, Canada, and Mexico. His career has provided him with deep understanding of cross-cultural business dynamics and strategic project leadership. He began his professional journey with an apprenticeship as a dairy technician, then graduated in Food & Dairy Engineering from the University of Applied Sciences in Hannover, Germany, in 1980. He later completed Master's degrees in Administration, Finance, and Marketing at the Escuela Bancaria y Comercial in Mexico City (2007–2012) and obtained his Ph.D. in Business Administration from Universidad La Salle, Mexico City, in 2016. His current research interests include collective intelligence, resilience, coordination, cooperation, and collaboration when using artificial intelligence.

Mariana Toussaint is a Fishery Officer working in the Food and Agriculture Organization of the United Nations (FAO) headquarters in Rome (Italy) since 2016. She is part of the FAO GLOBEFISH Team, GLOBEFISH is a multidonor funded project that promotes and provides up-to-date information on trade, trends and markets of fisheries and aquaculture products. Her thematic areas of work include fisheries policy development and management, issues related to international trade and market access, international fisheries trade agreements and market-based instruments, sustainability, social responsibility, decent work and gender. Mariana has a Ph.D. in Social Sustainability, cum laude, a master's degree in International Trade, and a bachelor's degree in Trade. All her studies have been carried out at the University of Vigo (Spain). In 2020, the EAE Business School awarded Mariana received the award for the Best Research in Ethics and Responsibility.

Jesus Vaca PhD in Fiscal Studies with a focus on Public Finance from the University of Guadalajara. He is a professor in the Department of Administration at the University Center for Administration (CUCEA) of the University of Guadalajara (UdeG). He is a candidate for National Research by the National System of Researchers (SNII) of the National Council for Humanities, Sciences and Technologies (CONAHCYT). He is also the founder and treasurer of the College of Administrators of Jalisco (CONLA Jalisco). He has experience in both the public and private sectors. His research interests include public finance, inequality, and economic growth.

Gustavo Vaca Medina PhD in Fiscal Studies with a focus on Public Finance from the University of Guadalajara. He is a professor in the Department of Administration at the University Center for Administration (CUCEA) of the University of Guadalajara (UdeG). He is a member of the National System of Researchers (SNII) of the National Council for Humanities, Sciences and Technologies (CONAHCYT), level C. He is also the founder and vice president of the College of Administrators of Jalisco (CONLA Jalisco). He has experience in both the public and private sectors. His research interests focus on Public Finance.

Marco Alberto Valenzo-Jiménez holds a Ph.D. in International Business from the Institute for Economic and Business Research at the Universidad Michoacana de San Nicolás de Hidalgo (UMSNH), Mexico, where he also obtained a Master's degree in International Business. Since 2013, he has served as a Full Research Professor at UMSNH, affiliated with the School of Accounting and Administrative Sciences. He currently holds the position of Head of the Graduate Studies Division within the same school. Dr. Valenzo-Jiménez has been an invited speaker at numerous international academic conferences. He is a Level 1 member of the National System of Researchers (Sistema Nacional de Investigadores, SNI) of Mexico, has been recognized as an Honorary State Researcher of Michoacán, and is listed in the Michoacán State Register of Science Disseminators. His research interests encompass supply chains, sustainability, competitiveness, and value chains, contributing to both scholarly knowledge and practical advancements in these fields.

Cinthya Zaragoza Ortiz is a doctoral candidate in Administration from the Instituto de Investigaciones Económicas y Empresariales of the Universidad Michoacana de San Nicolás de Hidalgo, Mexico., where she investigates sustainability, competitiveness, and SSCM. She holds dual master's degrees in Business Creation and Innovation from the University of Extremadura, Spain and Management and Marketing from the Universidad Popular Autónoma del Estado de Puebla, Mexico.

Index

A

B

C

D

E

R

S

T

V

W

www.ingramcontent.com/pod-product-compliance
Lightning Source LLC
LaVergne TN
LVHW080907300926
849162LV00003B/588